The Economic Thought of Sir James Steuart

James Steuart published *An Inquiry into the Principles of Political Œconomy* in 1767, the first systematic treatise on economics, nine years before Adam Smith's *Wealth of Nations*. Traditional historiography has tended to disregard and even deny Steuart's oeuvre, categorizing him as the last, outdated advocate of mercantilist policies in Britain.

A clear portrait of a modernizing and enlightened Steuart emerges from this book, opening up an alternative approach to many key developments in economic theory. This book brings together a diverse international team of experts to overturn the "advocate of mercantilism" myth and explore different interpretations of Steuart's work within the context of the writings of other contemporary authors. A diverse range of specialists – historians, economists, political scientist, and sociologists – reflecting the diversity of James Steuart's work explore various aspects of the life, works, and influence of James Steuart, including his links to other authors who conceive – as Steuart did – the economic system of "natural liberty" as an artificial creation. The portrait of a demarginalized, modernizing, and enlightened Steuart emerges clearly in this book.

This book is not reduced to old authors whose ideas would be at the Museum of Dead Ideas; it has a very contemporary resonance. The subjects and the way Steuart tackles them could have a big influence on future authors who recognized some advantages of an alternative approach to many key developments in economic theory. This will also be of interest to scholars of history of economic thought, intellectual history, and 18th century history.

José M. Menudo is Professor of History of Economic Analysis at Pablo de Olavide University, Spain.

Routledge Studies in the History of Economics

Schumpeter's Capitalism, Socialism and Democracy
A Twenty-First-Century Agenda
Edited by Leonardo Burlamaqui and Rainer Kattel

Divine Providence in Early Modern Economic Thought
Joost Hengstmengel

Macroeconomics without the Errors of Keynes
The Quantity Theory of Money, Saving, and Policy
James C.W. Ahiakpor

The Political Economy of the Han Dynasty and Its Legacy
Edited by Cheng Lin, Terry Peach and Wang Fang

A History of Utilitarian Ethics
Samuel Hollander

The Economic Thought of Michael Polanyi
Gábor Biró

Ideas in the History of Economic Development
The Case of Peripheral Countries
Edited by Estrella Trincado, Andrés Lazzarini and Denis Melnik

Ordoliberalism and European Economic Policy
Between Realpolitik and Economic Utopia
Edited by Malte Dold and Tim Krieger

The Economic Thought of Sir James Steuart
First Economist of the Scottish Enlightenment
Edited by José M. Menudo

For more information about this series, please visit www.routledge.com/series/SE0341

The Economic Thought of Sir James Steuart

First Economist of the Scottish Enlightenment

Edited by José M. Menudo

Routledge
Taylor & Francis Group
LONDON AND NEW YORK

First published 2020
by Routledge
2 Park Square, Milton Park, Abingdon, Oxon OX14 4RN

and by Routledge
52 Vanderbilt Avenue, New York, NY 10017

Routledge is an imprint of the Taylor & Francis Group, an informa business

First issued in paperback 2021

British Library Cataloguing-in-Publication Data
A catalogue record for this book is available from the British Library

Library of Congress Cataloging-in-Publication Data
A catalog record for this book has been requested

ISBN: 978-1-138-33596-7 (hbk)
ISBN: 978-1-03-208718-4 (pbk)
ISBN: 978-0-429-44342-8 (ebk)

Typeset in Times New Roman
by Apex CoVantage, LLC

To Martina, Antonio, and Paqui

Contents

Contributors

Nesrine Bentemessek is Research Fellow at the IRG-Institut de Recherche en Gestion, France.

Christopher J. Berry is Professor Emeritus at the University of Glasgow.

Gilles Campagnolo is Research Fellow at the Centre national de la recherche scientifique, France.

Cecilia Carnino is Research Fellow at the Università de Turin, Italy.

Jean Cartelier is Professor Emeritus at the Université de Paris X, France.

Francis Clavé is Associate Professor at the Université Paris II, France.

Mauricio C. Coutinho is Professor at the State University of Campinas, Brazil.

Ghislain Deleplace is Professor Emeritus at the University Paris VIII, France.

Yutaka Furuya is Associate Professor at the Tohoku University, Japan.

Rebeca Gomez Betancourt is Professor at Université Lyon 2, France.

José M. Menudo is Associate Professor at Pablo de Olavide University, Spain.

Matari Pierre Manigat is Research Fellow at the Universidad Autónoma de la Ciudad de México, Mexico.

Eyüp Özveren is Professor at the Middle East Technical University, Turkey.

Simona Pisanelli is Associate Professor at the Università del Salento, Italy.

Aida Ramos is Associate Professor at the University of Dallas, United States of America.

Alexander Tobon is Associate Professor at the Universidad de Antioquia, Colombia.

Shigeki Tomo is Research Fellow at the Kyoto Sangyo University, Japan.

Ramón Tortajada is Emeritus Professor at the Université Grenoble-Alpes, France.

Foreword

The Second International Conference on the work of Sir James Steuart,[1] *Sir James Steuart and the economy without invisible hands*, organized by the Professor José M. Menudo, was held in Sevilla, Spain, on October 26 and 27, 2017 – *i.e.*, 250 years after the publication of his major work.[2] The First International Conference was held in France at the Museum of the French Revolution at the Château de Vizille on September 14, 15, and 16 1995.

To my knowledge, no conference or workshop on the work of one of the two great Scottish economists of the 18th century (the other being Adam Smith) was held in the United Kingdom. It may not be a paradox. On the one hand, if we take into consideration his biography, as highlighted by the long introduction of Andrew Skinner,[3] with the *Grand Tour* from 1735 to 1740 that had to be made by every young gentleman and his exile from 1745 to 1763, Steuart spent more than a third of his life on the continent. On the other hand, if its influence in England was negligible, it was not the same for the economists of the continent, especially the Germans, before the influence of Smith takes precedence,[4] not to mention that the translation into French (1789–90) attributed to Étienne-François de Sénovert was not without influence during the establishment of Assignats in the first phase of the French Revolution (Albertone 1999).

The First International Conference, *James Steuart in 1995*, was published in 1999 at Routledge under the title *The Economics of James Steuart*.

The challenge of this first Conference was to put on the agenda a 'forgotten' or 'neglected' economic thought. The main cause of this 'forgetfulness', it seems to us, was the dominance of the liberal problematics which, with Adam Smith, swept over the work of economists and often led to Steuart's work being put in the tote box all called 'mercantilists'. Marx made of Steuart's book the 'scientific' expression of mercantilism, and Pibram placed Steuart among the 'last champions of mercantilism'.[5] Also, it is necessary to specify the origin of this term. The name 'mercantile' was a creation of the Physiocrats, particularly by the Marquis de Mirabeau; it was taken up and extended by Adam Smith, but in a different way. The first focused on the origin of the net product, the second on the monetary dimension. In a marginal note, incidentally, Mirabeau pointed out that the origin of the net product could not be found in the 'mercantile' activity (1763: 329). Adam Smith, in *Wealth of Nations*, devoted eight chapters out of nine of Book IV, 'Of the System of Political

Economy', to show that the wealth of the nation could not be reduced to the amount of money or gold and silver held as suggested by the 'Mercantil System'. While Mirabeau did not cite any author, Smith referred to many of the earlier authors, beginning with Locke and Mun, but he did not mention Steuart in any way.

The aim of the Vizille International Conference was to show that there was an awakening of interest in Steuart's economic work.

The International Conference of Seville, *Sir James Steuart: A Society without Invisible Hands*, was not reduced to a conference of old authors whose ideas would be at the Museum of Dead Ideas; it has a very contemporary resonance: what about today the 'invisible hand'?

The Smithian metaphor of the 'invisible hand'[6] is ultimately only the affirmation of faith in the virtues of economic liberalism or, as it was called then, in the virtues of *laissez-faire et laisser aller*. This faith occupies a major place in most contemporary economic theories, even far removed from the Smithian problematic. Perhaps it is enough to recall the title of the book of Bruna Ingrao and Giorgio Israel, *The Invisible Hand?* According to these authors the challenge of the large part of economic theories is to show that economic relations left to themselves lead to equilibrium or oscillate around the point of equilibrium.[7]

Faith in this 'invisible hand' does not limit its effects to the 'purest' economic theory – the most remote, it seems, of the actual economic policies of the various governments and institutions. It serves as a fulcrum for most contemporary market liberalization measures, whether financial or non-financial. Authorities should allow adjustments to be made on their own, since markets left to themselves would be 'efficient'. The global financial crisis of the years 2005–2008, its depth as well as its magnitude are the fruits of it.

Another approach to economic relations, apart from any 'invisible hand', has become a necessity. Research in the history of economic thought thus joins the questions about the economic practices of today. The foundations of an alternative approach seem to us to be found in Sir James Steuart's work, which must be subjected to thorough criticism. It is not a question of resuming analyses as they are but of *changing the point of departure*. Steuart's approach differs from the *Wealth of Nations* in three respects: First, political authorities are not excluded *a priori* from the economic game; their intervention is required for the normal functioning of domestic markets and international trade; second, economic reasoning can not exclude the monetary dimension *a priori*, it is no longer a matter of reasoning first in real terms to reintroduce money; finally, the economic objective is not so much wealth in itself as the maintenance of domestic full employment.

May this conference contribute to the renewal of economic theories that ultimately form the basis of economic policy recommendations.

Notes

1 Sir James Denham Steuart of Coltness and Goodtrees (3rd Baronet) belonged to the hereditary aristocracy for two generations. His grandfather, James Steuart (1635–1713), did not receive the Baronet title until 1695 (Skinner 1999a: 3). According to Marx, the

awareness of this status would have had significant consequences on his approach to economic relations, in particular that would have led Sir James Steuart to place himself on the historical terrain neglected by other economists. Although the quote from Marx is a bit long, let's go back to it: 'To the eighteenth-century prophets – who carry on their shoulders all Smith and all Ricardo – he [the individual] appears as an ideal whose existence they have placed in the past. For them, it was not a historical achievement, but the starting point of the story. It is because, according to their idea of human nature, the individual is in conformity with nature as a being born from nature and not as a fruit of history. This illusion has hitherto been peculiar to every new epoch. Steuart, who in many ways opposes the eighteenth century, and as *an aristocrat*, [the stress belongs to me – RT] stands more on the historical ground, knew how to avoid this naive error'(Marx 1857: 236).

2 Sir James Steuart stayed in Sevilla in the spring of 1737, during his *Grand Tour* (Skinner 1999b: 139–150).

3 Professor Andrew Skinner played a crucial role in the renewal of the studies of these two great authors in political economy: Adam Smith and Sir James Steuart, one was for the Union of Scotland with England and the other for the restoration of an independent kingdom of Scotland. The work of Andrew Skinner is often referred to as the 1976 edition of Smith's *Economic Works*. However, as Donald Winch in his tribute did not fail to recall: 'Andrew's first love as a student of Scottish economic thinking, however, was not Smith but the rival whom Smith supplanted, partly by the unfair device of failing to mention Sir James Steuart's *Inquiry into the Principles of Political Economics* in the work that displaced it. Andrew began publishing on Steuart before he was appointed to a post at Glasgow, but it was there that he was commissioned by the Scottish Economic Society to publish the *Inquiry* for a series of articles on Scottish economic classics' (2012: 482). Is it necessary, also, to recall that Professor Skinner also played an important role in holding the First International Conference in Vizille.

4 '*An Inquiry into the Principles of Political Economy*, accordingly was never much of a success in England even before it was completely overshadowed by the *Wealth of Nations*. But it received rather more than its due from some of the Germans' (Schumpeter 1967: 176).

5 In the first chapter of *Theories on the surplus value*, Marx presented the work of Steuart saying: 'All in all, Sir James Steuart did not come out of this narrow concept [that which gives rise to profit only from 'exchange'], on the contrary, it must be considered as its scientific propagator'. He thus concludes the chapter saying, 'In this respect [Marx referred to the analysis of *profit upon alienation*] Steuart is therefore the rational expression of the monetary system and the mercantile system' (Marx 1974: 27, 30). Pibram (1986: 86) did not make him a 'naïve mercantilist' but a mercantilist anyway: 'Unlike almost all the mercantilists who had preceded him, Steuart strove to transform political economy into a comprehensive study of life in society, and to tell an imaginary statesman everything you need to know about the policy to be followed to ensure the well-being of the country'.

6 However it should be noted that Adam Smith's economic liberalism was more complex and not so absolute as his successors understood (Viner 1927).

7 'Just as an "invisible hand" places in equilibrium a pendulum oscillating around its center or sees to it that a liquid flowing between connecting chambers finds its own level, Adam Smith's invisible hand "is a poetic expression of the most fundamental of economic balance relations, the equalization of rates of return, as enforced by the tendency of factors to move from low to high returns"' (Arrow & Hahn cited by Ingrao & Israel 1990: ix).

Bibliography

Albertone, M. (1999), The Difficult Reception of James Steuart at the End of the Eighteenth Century in France, in R. Tortajada (ed.), *The Economics of James Steuart*, London: Routledge: 41–56.

Ingrao, B. & Israel, G. (1990), *The Invisible Hand: Economic Equilibrium in the History of Science*, Cambridge, MA & London: MIT Press.

Marx, K. (1857), *Introduction générale à la critique de l'économie politique in Œuvres*, vol. 1, Paris: Gallimard, 1965: 231–266.

———. (1861–1863), *Théories sur la plus-value*, vol. 1, Paris: Éditions Sociales, 1974.

Mirabeau, H.G. comte de. (1763), *Philosophie rurale*, Amsterdam: n.p.

Pibram, K. (1983), *Les Fondements de la pensée économique*, Paris: Economica, 1986.

Schumpeter, J.A. (1954), *History of Economic Analysis*, London: Allen & Unwin, 1967.

Skinner, A.S. (1999a), Sir James Steuart and the Jacobite Connection, in R. Tortajada (ed.), *The Economics of James Steuart*, London: Routledge: 1–23.

———. (1999b), Steuart: Aspects of Economic *Policy*, in R. Tortajada (ed.), *The Economics of James Steuart*, London: Routledge: 139–150.

Smith, A. (1776), *An Inquiry into the Nature and Causes of the Wealth of Nations*, Oxford: Oxford University Press, 1976.

Viner, J. (1927), Adam Smith and Laissez-Faire, *Journal of Political Economy*, 35(2): 198–232.

Winch, D. (2012), Andrew Skinner, 1935–2011, *The European Journal of History of Economic Thought*, 19(3): 481–484.

Ramón Tortajada
Université Grenoble-Alpes

Preface

Sir James Steuart published *An Inquiry into the Principles of Political Œconomy* in 1767, the first systematic treatise on economics as a science, nine years before Adam Smith's *Wealth of Nations*. Traditional historiography has tended to disregard and even deny Steuart's oeuvre, banishing his contribution to the last, outdated advocate of mercantilist policies in Britain. This book overturns the myth of the 'advocate of mercantilism' and proposes different approaches to the analysis of Steuart's oeuvre within the context of the writings of other 18th-century authors. A diverse range of specialists reflecting the diversity of James Steuart's work—historians, economists, political scientist, and sociologists – explore various aspects of the life, works, and influence of James Steuart, including his links to other authors who conceive – as Steuart did – the economic system of 'natural liberty' as an artificial creation. The portrait of a demarginalized, modernizing, and enlightened Steuart emerges clearly from this book; in so doing, it opens up an alternative approach to many key developments in economic theory.

Through detailed analysis, the essays on Steuart collected in this volume investigate the authors opposed to Adam Smith's apologetic invisible hand, the anti-quantity theories of money, fiat money and payment systems, the transmission and reception of James Steuart's works around the world, and Steuart's role of the statesman within the new institutions that allow the exchange economy. In order to organize these contributions, this book is divided into three parts. However, the high academic quality of the chapters invites readers to forget about this necessary organization of the content. Thus, the role of the statesman is also going to be analyzed in chapters dedicated to money, monetary policy is dealt with in great detail in chapters dedicated to mercantilism, and so on.

James Steuart argues that the interest of individuals must be identified with the general interest, and that it is the *art of politics* – the job of the legislator – to bring about an *artificial identification of interests*. Sir James Steuart belongs to authors who conceive the economic system of 'natural liberty' as an artificial creation. Through detailed analysis, the first part of this book investigates Steuart's vision of society. In Chapter One, Christopher J. Berry studies the idea of the 'public' or 'common' good utilized by Steuart. The usage of this term in his *Principles* is directly linked to his key idea of a 'statesman', and Berry has accordingly decided to investigate that notion. To set the scene, Berry outlines three versions – i.e., 'objective', 'agonistic', and mutually beneficial by-product – of how the idea of a public good has been understood. Steuart's will be the fourth. In each case the relation between the public and the private is pivotal. In Chapter Two, Matari Pierre Manigat examines the sociogenesis of the state in Steuart's *Principles*. More precisely, she highlights the social foundations of the state, the nature of its fiscal regime, the relationship of different social classes to this system, and the functions of the state in the reproduction of the conditions of labour that foster capitalist development. The sociogenesis of the state in Steuart's *Principles* involves specific economic fundamentals: the generalized circulation of commodities and money. The dynamics of these phenomena involve a change in the balance of power between classes as well as a new form of public power, where the state is separated from society and set above classes. In Chapter Three, Simona Pisanelli clarifies Steuart's position in the 18th century debate on slavery within commercial society, with special reference to the dynamics of production in the 'commercial society', technical progress, and the increase in national wealth. British intellectuals – like their French counterparts – participated in the debate on the pros and cons of abolishing slavery in the second half of the 18th century. This debate has many different aspects (ethical, juridical, and economic) and was carried out in the context of attitudes and projects designed to favour the transformation of society in a capitalist direction. James Steuart, too, deals with the phenomenon of slavery. In Chapter Four, Aida Ramos studies the formation of Steuart's *spirit of the people*. This concept and its uses can thus be read as both a manifestation of the pervasiveness of the emphasis on the local and culture in Scottish intellectual life and the latest iteration of the importance of custom. Steuart's *spirit of the people* is thus explored as an application of an old theory to the new science of political economy. The last chapter of this first section compares the idea of political economy in James Steuart and Adam Smith (Chapter Five). The aim of Francis Clavé is to give a better understanding about how Steuart and Smith connect three fields: economics, politics, and science. Albeit Steuart technically defines political economy as covering the external field to domestic (family) economy, his *Principles* affirms the pre-eminence of politics over economy. The statesman has to increase the wealth of the country and define the general interest. On the contrary, Smith thinks the growth of wealth fundamentally lies with economic agents, whereby statesmen or legislators just have to establish the right framework. In Clavé's chapter, political economy tends to depart from economics and become the scientific study of the links between jurisprudence, politics, and economics through the notion of *Systems of Political Economy*.

Money, credit, and prices in Steuart's economic thought provide the content of the second part. Initially in Chapter Six, Jean Cartelier explains Steuart's position on the implementation of John Law's system in France at the time of the *Régence*. Steuart devotes 12 chapters of his *Principles* to the 'system' John Law has implemented in France. More precisely, the purpose of the chapter is to elucidate whether Steuart's sympathetic attitude to the 'system' may be attributed to a pragmatic appreciation of what Law was trying to do and to a quest for a better management of such an innovation, on the one hand, or to a common theory of money and credit and beyond that to a common vision of what economics is about, on the other. Both views make sense, but the latter opens more promising developments. In Chapter Seven, Ghislain Deleplace deals with David Ricardo's view of the monetary theory contained in Steuart's *Principles*. Ricardo's judgment on Steuart reveals that the position of both authors towards monetary orthodoxy can thus be evaluated through their positions towards the quantity theory of money and the price-specie flow mechanism. Chapters Eight and Nine analyze Steuart's theory of credit. Nesrine Bentemessek and Rebeca Gomez Betancour insist in Chapter Eight that Steuart's analysis of public debt is very heterodox and will have a big influence to future authors, which recognized some advantages of the public debt for the macroeconomic system. Among other reasons explained by the authors, Steuart was original because he developed the functioning of the primary and secondary public debt market and due to the importance devoted to the management of the public debt. In Chapter Nine, Shigeki Tomo clarifies, from our modern macroeconomic viewpoint, the naïveté of Sir James Steuart's theory of money and credit. Since the establishment of the Consols, an abbreviated name for the Consolidated Threes, took place in the mid-18th century in England, Sir James Steuart confronted, before publishing his inquiry, the same economic institutions as John Maynard Keynes eventually would. Nevertheless, Steuart left in his masterpiece almost nothing concerning the ideas or philosophy that led to the liquidity preference theory. The following proposes a reason for this omission, from the vantage of Steuart's statesman philosophy and from an observation concerning the complicated sinking fund measures of the time. The last chapter of this section is dedicated to price determination in the economic theory of James Steuart (Chapter Ten). Alexander Tobon suggests formalizing some ideas related to prices in the work of Sir James Steuart, adopting the modern classical perspective of production prices. To achieve this objective, Tobon starts with the standard formalization in the perspective developed by Von Neumann, Leontief, and Sraffa, which allows determining an equilibrium price vector in order to show the compatibility of manufacturers' production decisions. The reconstruction of the theory of prices in Steuart's work leads us to discuss the formation of the social surplus and to emphasize that merchants concentrate the most important economic information for the performance of economy as a whole.

The third part of this book dealt with the influence of Steuart's economic thought and the influence on Steuart's economic ideas. In Chapter Eleven, Yutaka Furuya shows how Steuart learned from Davenant and how decisive an impact Davenant's arguments on public revenues and war finance had on his thought. Steuart, when reading Davenant's arguments on the topic, was able to shape a clear understanding of how credit drastically developed in Britain since Davenant's time. In Chapter Twelve, Mauricio C. Coutinho makes a review of the senses (context, ideas involved) in which some eminent commenters have considered Steuart a mercantilist. This implies a revision of Steuart's comments on balance of trade and balance of payments, exchange rate, rate of coinage, debasement, and the state of the metallic circulating media. Steuart's approaches to all these topics are subordinated to his general understanding of money, including the consequences of the 'realization' of money of account in coins. The purpose of this chapter is to take Steuart's supposed mercantilist leanings as a means to illuminate some angles of his monetary theory. Next, Eyüp Özveren reconsiders the idea of Smith's work as outperforming Steuart's. Chapter Thirteen will dwell on the identification of the different mixes of the 'old' and the 'new' that characterize Steuart's and Smith's two texts and to what extent either text offers a point of departure for a new economic science. Özveren has noted that to show Steuart in a new light, the Smithian vice – i.e., the idolized automatism associated with market equilibrium – was essential. Without its rise and fall, a linear cumulative development from Steuart to current heterodox economics could have been highly unlikely. Gilles Campagnolo shall discuss the Hegelian interest in economic themes and Hegel's reading of Steuart and Chamley's positions (Chapter Fourteen). The author explores Hegel's steps to see how his encounter with the science of political economy was thereafter dependent on his reading of works by so-called 'late mercantilist' Sir James Steuart and so-called 'classics' anchored in Smith's views, as well as earlier German 'Cameralists'. This whole pivotal moment displays how to come to grips with the issue of modernity in material life as it appears then, interestingly depicted in this key relationship. Finally, Cecilia Carnino investigates the first circulation in Italy of Steuart's *Principles*, through the thinking of Giovanni Tamassia (Chapter Fifteen). This chapter intends to reconstruct the transnational cultural channels – Italian, British, and French – through which Tamassia discovered the book and the subsequent success of Steuart's work in the Napoleonic Italy.

To sum up, the subjects and the ways Steuart tackles them have constantly been a source of inspiration for economists from the 19th century until now. However, his reputation of being a complex author seems to make it difficult for those interested in Steuart to go in depth into his ideas. By taking an interdisciplinary approach, by means of a diverse range of methods, it will be possible to grasp Steuart's ideas and to understand his influence.

José M. Menudo
Universidad Pablo de Olavide

Acknowledgements

This book grew out of a conference held in Seville on October 26–27, 2017, to commemorate the 250th anniversary of the publication of *An Inquiry into the Principles of Political Œconomy* (1767). Most of the chapters of this book have been discussed as part of this scientific conference. I would like to thank the researchers who have sat through these lectures and made comments that have improved the manuscript. My greatest debt to those institutions that sponsored and supported this conference: Colegio de Economistas de Sevilla, the European Society for the History of Economic Thought, TRIANGLE (Université Lyon 2), the Universidad Internacional Menéndez y Pelayo, and the Universidad Pablo de Olavide. I owe a special thanks to Bertram Schefold, Christopher Berry, Eyüp Özveren, Yutaka Furuya, Rebeca Gomez Betancourt, and Ramón Tortajada for outstanding research assistance, to Natalie Tomlinson for editorial suggestions, and Gilles Campagnolo, Simona Pisanelli, and Alexander Tobon for suggestions on individual chapters.

Note on citation practice

Throughout this book, all citations to James Steuart's *An Inquiry into the Principles of Political Economy* are to *The Works, Political, Metaphysical, and Chronological, of the Late Sir James Steuart of Coltness, Bart. Now first collected by Gen. Sir James Steuart, Bart., his son.*, 6 vols., Cadell and Davies, London, 1805. References to this edition are inserted in the text by volume number and page.

Part I

A society without invisible hands

1 James Steuart on the public good[1]

Christopher J. Berry

The idea of the 'public' or 'common' good is a long-standing theme in the history of Western thought, and it is one utilized by Steuart. My aim here is to explore this utilization and assess what significance it has in his thought. To set the scene, I outline three versions of how the idea of a public good has been understood. Steuart's will be the fourth. In each case the relation between the public and the private is pivotal.

Three versions

The first version I label the 'objective'. It is characteristic of 'classical' thought and its paradigm exemplar is Aristotle. In Book 1 of *The Politics*, Aristotle distinguishes the economic sphere of the household (*oikos*) from the 'political' sphere within the polis as a whole. This distinction, in line with Aristotle's teleological philosophy, was determined by their respective functions or ends. The purpose of the household was the procurement and maintenance of what was necessary for everyday life – food, clothing, shelter. Essentially (that is, this is its definitive nature) the household was concerned with the instrumental business of mere living. The purpose of the polis is the realization of the 'good life' (*eu zen*) (Aristotle 1944: 1252b31). This comprises not instrumental activity but what is intrinsically worthwhile. It is in the polis where citizens or free men deliberate on what is for the common good (Aristotle 1944: 1279a23).

There is a clear hierarchy here. Instrumental actions are subordinate to the end to which they are the means. With respect to the household/polis distinction, the former is the realm of particularity, and its 'good' is correspondingly specific; the latter is the realm of generality and its corresponding good is what is common or public. This established a moralized context for both 'politics' and 'economics'. This moralization rested on a conception of a worthwhile human (male) life. The public good as a teleological realization, *kata phusin*, was what benefited the objectively true interests of all. More pointedly, this public good is debased if a human life is spent slavishly pursuing private ends. Within this conception there lay a criterion to identify a source of disorder or corruption, when, that is, private interests subvert the public good. In sum, the public good was the objective end or *telos* of properly human action and was normatively superior to the pursuit of private interests.

The second version I label the 'agonistic'. Here the exemplar is Machiavelli, as manifest in his *Discorsi sopra la prime deca di Tito Livio* (1532). In contrast to the Aristotelian version, Machiavelli does not set up a privileged normative view of the public good as an end to which all virtuous men should subscribe and who, in failing to subscribe, manifest a lack of freedom. Instead, for Machiavelli, liberty is valuable as a means by which individuals can realize their own goals whatever they may be – for some power, for others security or glory, and so on. This is an instrumental view. Liberty can only be attained in a free republic, but for that to happen the correct *ordini* (or institutions) have to be in place. The Roman republic provided a key precedent. There the common or public good was the offspring of the differing private interests of the nobility (*i grandi*) and the people (*il populo*) (Machiavelli 1988: Bk I Ch.5).

These interests more than differ they conflict (hence my label 'agonistic'). The nobles wish to dominate, the people do not want to be dominated. In early Rome these opposed interests were embodied in different assemblies but for any law to be passed the consent of both assemblies was required. This institutional mechanism was, Machiavelli says, the *prima causa* of their liberty because it turned individual or private interests into a concern for the *commune bene* or public good (Machiavelli 1988: I, 4). However, like his classical forebearers, Machiavelli is ever fearful that this structure will be corrupted and the channelled private interests will break their institutional bonds, a fate that befell the Republic when, in the words of Livy, 'riches brought in avarice and luxury' to universal ruin (Livius 1925: I, §12). Thus the longstanding antipathy was set up between luxury/commerce/wealth and the common good.

This is not Steuart's view, nor is it that of my third version, the public good as a mutually beneficial by-product. Smith is the exemplar here. The first impression is that Smith seems similar to Machiavelli. Both seem to say that the common good is the unintentional consequence of private interests. This similarity is, however, misleading. Smith does not present an agonistic picture. For him, mutual advantage is the key. This is a far more reliable interactive base than the uneasy instability in Machiavelli's version, and, it follows, the common good is thereby more reliably achieved.

The central Smithian version of the public good has both a positive and negative dimension. At the heart of the positive view is Smith's notion of 'natural liberty'. According to this 'system' (as he calls it), 'every man, as long as he does not violate the laws of justice is left perfectly free to pursue his own interest his own way'. Smith immediately follows this definition with his threefold identification of the tasks of government; protection from external foes, maintenance of public works and 'an exact administration of justice'. This leads into the negative view. Government polices any such violations of justice but is 'completely discharged from a duty . . . of superintending the industry of private people and of directing it towards the employments most suitable to the interest of society' (Smith 1982a: IV.ix.51/687). Any such superintendence is not only ineffectual in its deliberate attempt to direct industry in the name of the public good, but it is also dangerous to trust public authority with that task (Smith 1982a: V.ii.9–10/456).

Smith's prime target here is the policy of the mercantilists, including by implication elements in Steuart.[2] As is well known, Smith predicts that in the *Wealth of Nations*, 'every false principle in it [Steuart's book] will meet a clear and distinct confutation' (Smith 1987: 132/164). The outcome of the mercantilist endeavour to force trade into a particular channel is less beneficial than if the trade had been left to find its own course (Smith 1982a: IV.v.a.3,24/506, 516). It is also contrary to the principle of impartiality by favouring some industries over others. Moreover, this mercantilist aim is delusional because such forced steering is 'a performance of which no human wisdom or knowledge could ever be sufficient' (Smith 1982a: IV.ix.51/687). All these are issues where Steuart's stance is different.

Before turning to Steuart's version of the public good, an argument implicit in Smith's version needs briefly explicating. It is a fundamental Smithian axiom that commercial transactions rely on the fact that, as with the beef, bread, and beer produced by the butcher, the baker, and the brewer, each is acting out of their self-interest. These self-interested exercises of private liberty produce universal opulence. This is an undeniable good. In Smith, there is no Aristotelian, Livian, Machiavellian, or even perhaps at times Steuart-ian principled opposition to opulence/luxury.[3] Since this good is an unintended consequence of private commercial activity, then invoking a conception of the public good that requires some more overtly political or deliberate superintendence is superfluous.

I will return on occasion to Smith, but now I turn to Steuart's version of the public good.

Steuart's version of the public good

I start with two quotations which will serve as the thread to help guide my argument through the self-styled labyrinth of the *Principles* (I, 21). The quotations both come from the brief introduction to Book II and both feature his central notion of a 'statesman'.[4] The first reads: 'the principle of self-interest . . . is the mainspring and only motive which a statesman should make use of to engage a free people to concur in the plans which he lays down for their government' (I, 218). The second appearing a few paragraphs later announces that 'it is the combination of every private interest which forms the public good, and of this the public, that is the statesman only, can be the judge' (I, 221).

Two basic claims are here being made. First, individuals are self-interested. This Steuart proclaims is 'a general key' and 'the ruling principle' of his argument; as he explicitly states in the same chapter, in the actions of individuals any idea of the public good is 'superfluous' (I, 220). More strongly, he later affirms that the common or public good is a union of every private interest, and it is the statesman's task to achieve that unification (II, 212). Thus the Smithian argument that the public good is product of private interactions is not sufficient. Nor is the public good the expression of some transcendent principle. Hence contrary to commentators like S.R. Sen or Robert Urquhart, this is a clear rejection of the Aristotelian objective view;[5] there is no *telos* on which all rational men converge. For Aristotle the ruling principle (*archē*) of human action is subscription to the dictates of *logos* or right reason.

Steuart does not claim that humans are solely self-interested but states for his purposes it is the universal spring of human actions (I, 219).[6] This is the sum total of what he says in *Principles* and his other declaration, in his *Considerations on the Interest of the County of Lanark*, that in political life private interest is the 'great spring of all actions' is equally unelaborated (V, 309). The reasonable conclusion is that in Steuart, self-interest has the status of a scientific axiom or 'theoretical and methodological' assumption (Kobayashi 1995: 77). The second claim made in these quotations is that self-interest should not determine the statesman's conduct, rather, to quote from the same part of the text, the 'public spirit . . . ought to be all-powerful in the statesman' (I, 218) so that 'self-interest when considered in regard to him is public spirit' (*ibid.*). The statesman, as the second of my two opening quotations reveals, embodies the 'public'.

I now interrogate these claims. In doing so, in addition to reference back to the three other versions, I will make some other illustrative comparisons. This interrogation will address three questions. One, how are the public and private good related or what is the relation between the statesman and the governed? Two, how do the actions of the statesman, as the embodiment of the public interest interact with the private self-interest of the governed or, more precisely, what is the role of the public spirit? Third, what does the statesman do that will bring about the public good? Throughout my enquiry I will try to elicit Steuart's assumptions as he goes about answering these questions that I have posed.

The statesman and the people

Steuart never articulates the relation between the statesman and those he governs. He does, like Hume, Smith, and other compatriots, rule out a contractual basis. He openly states that the 'rights of kings' are not founded 'upon the supposition of tacit contracts between them and their people' (I, 320). To clarify, this is not the same as what Steuart terms the 'general tacit contract' of 'reciprocal obligations' that constitute in a free society the social bond and which it is the statesman's responsibility to maintain (I, 109 cf. I, 138). The statesman has to combine private and divergent interests to form the 'common weal' or to 'cement his society' (II, 181; II, 191). Following Hume's critique, Steuart's statesman does not have this responsibility because he is contractually obliged. Rather, again like Hume and the others, he makes the claim that the foundation of government is to be 'sought for in history' (I, 320).

True to his intent of articulating 'principles', Steuart gives no details.[7] However, just before this statement he had declared that 'modern liberty' meant liberation from feudal ties, where the lower classes depended upon their superiors for their subsistence. This liberation had been brought about by the 'introduction of industry'. Steuart's story is to all intents and purposes identical to Smith's in Book III of the *Wealth of Nations* and is prefigured in outline in Hume's (1985) *Political*

Discourses of 1752. All three talk of this change from feudal to commercial as a 'revolution', and all three characterize this as introducing modern liberty (I, 201, I, 314–315; Smith 1982a: III.iv.16/422, III.iii.5/400; Hume 1894: II, 602–603). The agreed essence of this modern liberty is the rule of law. In a nice turn of phrase, Steuart declares liberty to be precarious when it rested on 'the ambulatory will of any man or set of men', where, that is, the laws were liable to changed 'through favour or prejudice to particular persons or particular classes' (I, 314–315). In contrast, where people are 'governed by general laws', which can only be changed 'in a regular and uniform way', and there they are 'free' (*ibid.*).

This commitment constrains the statesman. He must act in a regular way and the particular political or constitutional form that the function of the statesmen assumes is not critically important. This view is consistent with Steuart's insistence that he is dealing with 'general principles' and putting forward a 'scientific' or deductive account of political economy and not with a 'collection of institutions' (I, xi). Nonetheless the question remains as to the relation between the statesman dedicated to the public good and the private goods pursued by the governed. The relation is identified as a form of subordination (I, 316) and, as a form of 'political' dependence, it is authorized by it being proportional to the degree of dependency (I, 317). Since the statesman will, by definition, act with due proportion, then the subordination will be just. From which it follows that all that is asked of subjects, as they follow 'the dictates' of their private interests, is 'strict obedience to the laws' (II, 212).[8] Since, ex hypothesi, the statesman's laws are 'good', then this obedience is in the interest of everyone (I, 223). This is the nearest Steuart comes to answering the question of why the self-interested subjects should recognize the statesman's authority. But it does not explain the basis of this recognition. I will, though, return to Steuart's position on authority when discussing his account of duty as part of the answer to my third question. But I now turn to the second question.

Public spirit and self-interest

Steuart declares 'governing' to comprise 'protecting, cherishing and supporting as well as punishing, restraining and exacting' but this to be done 'according to the spirit' of a people (I, 82). My focus in this section is on this notion of 'spirit'. Steuart announces at the beginning of *Principles* that his 'real object' is to 'influence the spirit of the people' through the mechanism of the statesman (I xviii). And in the book itself he states that the statesman's 'chief object' is to 'model the spirit of his people' in such a way that they will be disposed to concur with his plan (III, 148; I, 202) or, more strongly, so that they will 'relish' necessary change (I, 16). The 'great art' of political economy, he says, is twofold; to adapt its operation to the 'spirit, manners and habits and customs of the people' and then 'to model these circumstances' so as to introduce new and useful institutions (I, 3). Or, again, as put a couple of paragraphs later, the business of the statesman is 'to model the minds of his subjects so as to induce them from the allurements of private interest to concur in the execution of his plan' (I, 4).

This notion of modelling is clearly important, but what does Steuart mean by it? No clear-cut answer is supplied, but what is certain is that it is a powerful force, since the axiomatic self-interest can, it now seems from that last quotation, be mitigated. The best guess is that the potency possessed by modelling assumes some sort of forming or shaping or moulding (all available 18th-century usages) capacity on behalf of the statesman. The object of this shaping is not merely to construct in the manner of Machiavelli appropriate institutions but to cultivate an underlying 'spirit'.

The obvious reference point here is Baron Montesquieu, who Steuart openly acknowledges to be an author for whom he has the 'highest esteem' (II, 43; I, 160; cf. Omori 2003: 108). In Chapter 4 of Book 19 of his *De l'Esprit des Lois* (1748), Montesquieu (1961) famously outlines *un esprit général* that comprises climate, religion, laws, mores, and manners. Although Montesquieu does in the following chapter mention a legislator, he refers explicitly to him '*à suivre l'esprit de la nation*'. But, unlike Steuart, Montesquieu is not concerned with modelling the spirit of self-interested subjects. How does the statesman get these self-interested subjects to concur with his plan? Here a brief comparison with Jean-Jacques Rousseau might throw some light. In the final chapter of Part II of *Du Contrat Social* (published 1762), Rousseau itemizes a classification of laws, the most important of which is that which preserves the spirit of the people (Rousseau acknowledges Montesquieu). This *esprit* is located not in legislation but in the hearts of the citizens, in their manners, customs, and opinion (Rousseau 1962: 272). Steuart, for his part, says that the spirit of a people is 'formed upon a set of received opinions', and once confirmed by 'long and constant habit' this 'forms the basis of all laws' (I, 10). In Rousseau, the effect of this 'law' is to substitute habit for authority, and this is where Rousseau's Legislator '*s'occupe en secret*' (Rousseau 1962: 272). Purely coincidentally, since I am not claiming any direct link, Rousseau uses some of the same terms as Steuart. His Legislator is the '*mécanicien*' who invents the 'machine' and who lays down '*le modèle*' to be followed (Rousseau 1962: 260).

I want, however, to pick out another coincidental similarity. Rousseau refers to the move from habit to authority as occurring insensibly (*insensiblement*) (Rousseau 1962: 272). Steuart uses the same term. For example, 'it is the business of the statesman to work upon the spirit of his people so as to model their taste for expence by insensible degrees' (I, 247, cf. I 295, I,348, I,384). In all these examples insensibility signifies the work of time (II, 122). The 'spirit' of a people is equally chronic; it is the result of 'long and constant habit' (I, 10), and it cannot be cultivated over night (as it were).[9] I want to make two comments on this usage, one incidental and the other more central.

Adam Smith, too, frequently employs the term 'insensibly', especially in the context of social change and the development of language (e.g., Smith 1982a: III. iv.10/418; Smith 1983: 1/204). In the *Wealth of Nations* this is a gradual process and is marked by a change in 'property and manners'. This is a shift in 'habits'. All the thinkers of the Scottish Enlightenment recognize the significance and role of habits. Both Hume and Smith, for example, use it to explain the authority possessed by rulers (Hume 1985: 468; Smith 1982b: 322).[10] This is consistent with Steuart, but there is a difference.

In Smith's case, the revolution that brought in the public good in the form of regular government and the rule of law was the outcome of the mutually self-interested actions of landlords and merchants without either having the 'least intention to serve the public' (Smith 1982a: III.iv.17/422). No modelling is implicated. But in Steuart's account social change is the product of modelling, and this in spite of the fact that, like Smith, he affirms that the 'spirit of a people' changes but by 'slow degrees' (I, 14; I, 9). This is the more central issue in his use of 'insensibility'. How does deliberate or purposeful modelling comport with the insensible or imperceptible character of social change?

The implicit mode of modelling here is education. It is, Steuart says, 'hardly a possibility' that changing the 'manners of a people' can be achieved other than by 'proper attention to the education of the youth' (I, 383). Unlike many of his French contemporaries, such as Claude Helvétius, and later English writers like Robert Owen of New Lanark, Steuart provides no account of the role, scope, and efficacy of education. The reasonable assumption is that the requisite 'proper attention' is paid by the statesman as a modeller.

That granted, this now reinforces the issue of the relation between modelling and the insensibility of change. To be consistent, Steuart's position seems to be that the self-interested actions of the governed have, from their education, been preformed by their 'spirit', which itself has been engineered by the statesman. This we could say is, in Rousseau's sense, 'secret'. Rousseau thought the Legislator could *pour ainsi dire* transform human behaviour (Rousseau 1962: 261). Steuart envisages no such transformation. To correct the manners of the people the statesman has to engage a 'motive of self-interest' (I, 354). How is that 'correction' achieved? All that Steuart, with his frequent talk of habit and gradualism, can consistently countenance is that 'interests' privately followed are so constituted that they do concur with the statesman's plans. This concurrence is contrived; the 'inclinations' of the subjects must be 'bent' so that 'by degrees' they attain the desired end (I, 200). Moreover, Steuart says explicitly that what 'appears' to be the 'direct object of private interest to every individual' has, thanks to the statesman's modelling, advanced 'the common good' (I, 357; I, 16).[11] Steuart's public good may not be the result of a Smithian invisible hand, but its realization (at least in part) is the product of the insensible handiwork of the statesman as modeller.

This insensibility leaves uncertain how transparent or (conversely) how secret the statesman's actions are. He does say at one point, though not without ambiguity, that the motives of statesmen 'lie very deep' (III, 161). This question also bears on Steuart's notion of a 'general tacit contract' that the statesman has to maintain. It would be consistent with his argument if Steuart judged that the contractees were unaware of, or insensible to, this purposefully modelled maintenance.

But modelling the spirit is not the only lever at the statesman's disposal in effecting the public good. This leads to the third question: What constitutes the public good that the statesman's plans seek to implement and what other levers or tools does he employ to achieve it?

Achieving the public good

A frequent metaphor employed by Steuart to depict the actions of the statesman is dealing with 'vibrations' in the economy. Sometimes these too are insensible but at other times they are perceptible (I, 267). The latter clearly are not susceptible to the long-term fix that deals with the 'spirit' of the people and discussed in the last section. Vibrations are deviations from the basic default situation of the balance where, with regard to trade, exchange is for an 'equivalent fit for supplying every want' (I, 223). In a 'free society' there is the 'circulation of a real equivalent for everything transferred and for every service performed' (I, 399)

If 'equivalence' is taken in a broad sense then there is a long list of measures that the statesman takes to ensure or preserve it. Given this extensiveness I will merely supply a few examples. In relatively representative passages on the promotion of infant trade, the following policies are included and the statesman can or should pursue: encouraging manufacture by extending consumption, keeping an eye on profits allowing them to rise in order to promote dexterity and emulation in invention and improvement, relieving the industrious of work if demand falls short, and procuring regardless of expense the ablest masters in every branch of industry to ensure success (I, 402). Among other measures, and seemingly consistent with his notion of freedom, the statesman can 'collect the children of the wretched into workhouses and breed them for employment (in trades where hands are needed)' (I, 379). In addition there are a number of more ostensibly 'moral' measures. Sobriety should be supported (I, 393), vice suppressed (II, 68), and 'in small states' sumptuary laws can be enacted (II, 18; II, 245) – a species of legislation that Smith thought the 'the highest impertinence and presumption' in its aim of watching over the economy of private people. (Smith 1982a: II.iii.36/346). Steuart does say, however, that his statesman is not concerned with 'trivial maters' and affirms that his plans are 'absolutely inconsistent with every arbitrary or irregular measure' (I, 426).

Prominent among the tools that the statesman has at his disposal are fiscal and monetary measures. These can be presumed to work because they will incentivize or deter self-interested actors. In addition, there is threat of punishment that again can be presumed, to rely on self-interest (it is human nature to avoid pain), and to produce compliance (I, 221). While coercive powers are explicitly not in his remit, Steuart does identify other tools. As we have already noted, using the formative power of education is one. He can also 'cajole and intrigue' (I, 278) and because it is human nature to love imitation, he, along with his 'favourites and servants', can set an example (II, 180; II, 172; I, 372). This latter case fits with his key objective of achieving a concurrence between his disinterested proposals for the public good and the self-interestedness of the governed, since this concurrence is explicitly said to be the effect of his 'influence'. The greater the extent of this influence then the easier the concurrence is to achieve (I, 425). Here, again, the notion of the statesman as a 'modeller' who moulds the manners and spirit of a people is invoked (III, 147–148).

But in the use of the levers at his disposal what does Steuart presume about the statesman being able successfully to employ them? What, in other words, does he presume about the public good being successfully instituted?

The statesman is a deliberately idealized or artificial figure (at one point Steuart openly contrasts this figure with a ruler who is 'defective' and is therefore excluded from his analysis [III, 460]). What are the attributes of this figure? He is 'impartially just' (I, 200) and virtuous (IV, 219). And since he alone pursues the common good, two things follow. One, the public good and virtue are closely linked and, two, the people, as self-interested, do not, contrary to Aristotle or Machiavelli, exhibit virtue (*aretē* and *virtù* respectively). Much more could be said about this, but since Stuart himself does not elaborate I will not here pursue it.

There are, however, many references to the statesman doing his 'duty' (e.g., II, 112; IV, 219; IV, 237). Unlike Aristotle and Smith, but like Machiavelli, Steuart is no moral philosopher. The closest he comes to expressing a moral principle is when in the preface (and he repeats the phrase later verbatim) he lays down as a 'general maxim' that the characteristic of a 'good action' is the 'conformity between the motive and duty of the agent' (I, xvi; II, 213). This hardly advances matters. The statesman's duty can perhaps be best understood as the responsibility of office – in the way that judges, for example, are obliged (duty-bound) to uphold the law. In some support of that interpretation, Steuart does say the statesman needs the confidence of the people (IV, 149). This could reasonably (as well as etymologically) be read to mean they trust him; a conviction sustained by their faith that he is not motivated by private interest (III, 460). Steuart is in line with the mainstream contemporary view that it is a mistake, indeed irreligious, to reduce of morality to self-interest. There is an echo of this in his short dissertation on obedience to the laws of God (appended perhaps to his critique of baron D'Holbach's *Système de la Nature* [1770]). There he says children with pleasure obey their parents out of the conviction that this obedience is for their good. Similarly soldiers with pleasure obey a commander in whom they have confidence. Steuart then generalizes to say that, analogous to obedience to God, the foundation of all obedience is the belief that the command is just when the motive of the legislator is hidden (VI, 85). Here, perhaps, lies the underlying principle or basis of Steuart's notion of authority. The statesman possesses authority because the governed have the confidence that he is doing his duty. But it also raises again the question of secrecy and transparency. This attribution of authority to the statesman, alongside the trust they have in him, is the insensible outcome of successful modelling.

As further attributes, the statesman is capable and intelligent (III, 460), and to be effective he requires 'exact knowledge' (I, 106; II, 73). The sort of knowledge Smith believed to be delusional when it comes to superintending the economy. But exact knowledge is not the same as omniscience (the statesman has no 'supernatural gift' [IV, 140]). Stuart is clear that events can elude his statesman's plans and thus presumably his foresight (II, 3; IV, 140). Nonetheless there is the critical assumption that the statesman knows best. The statesman can assess broader, long-term public consequences that would be beyond the narrow perspective of individuals (cf., IV, 117). Hence a worker who is directed from one job to another would not necessarily know that that shift is in his best interest. Neither is Steuart's figure omnipotent. As we have already noted, he has to conform to the law. He also has to comply with custom (III, 226), even if he has engineered it, and he can lack the power to overcome opposition, as from the 'monied interest' for example (III, 178). In the end, of course, Steuart has to presume his statesman is powerful and wise enough to implement policies for the public good.

Conclusion

By way of a conclusion I want to return to the three versions of the 'public good' that I outlined at the start of this exploration. Steuart's notion of the public or general good is not some Aristotelian objective end because for Steuart what is in practice the public good is circumstantial. That practical task is the responsibility of the statesman. The statesman's default modus operandi is modelling, not coercion. The effect of this modelling is to induce the confident belief or trust in the people that his actions are for their benefit (cf., IV, 148 cf., Urquhart [1996: 399]). This trust will be present, albeit unreflectively or insensibly, even in the 'wretched' parents of those children who are placed in workhouses.

Steuart is fundamentally committed to the principle that the public good has to be a goal. It cannot be a Machiavellian by-product of conflicting private interests. He is explicit in his *Considerations* (on Lanark) that the separate interests of the landowners and the merchants leads to animosity, which causes them to overlook the common interest (V, 309). For Steuart, there truly is a contextually dependent common interest, and it is his conviction that its realization should inform public policy deliberately and intentionally. It is the same conviction that underlies Steuart's argument that a Smithian reliance on mutual self-interested interactions is an insufficient mechanism to realize the public good. That realization cannot be left to Smith's invisible hand. Rather, there is a need, as he puts it, for an 'artful' and 'helping hand' (I, 308; I, 312).

Notes

1 I am grateful to Jose Menudo for the invitation to present (a version of) this chapter in Sevilla.

2 According to Screpanti and Zamagni (1993: 53), the *Principles* is the 'last defence of mercantilist thought'. A more nuance view is offered by Hirschman (1977: 82) while Sen (1957: 152) interprets him as 'no mercantilist in the *conventional* sense' (p. 152 Sen's emphasis). For further observations see Coutinho in this volume.

3 See Ramos (2011) for a discussion of Steuart on luxury.

4 The statesman is explicitly a supposition and is defined by its role as 'the head of government, systematically conducting every part of it' rather than any particular constitutional form (I, 161).

5 Pace Sen (1957: 25, 180) and Urquhart (1996: 403 cf Urquhart 1999).

6 At the opening of Bk 1, Ch. 1, Steuart declares that is universally the case that, in addition to self-interest humans act 'from the principles of 'expediency, duty or passion' (I, 7) and later clarifies that the 'supposition' of private interested action applies to 'what regards the public' (II, 212), that is, presumably in family and personal relations the supposition does not necessarily apply. Urquhart correctly points out the importance of the constancy and predictability of self-interest (1996: 381). This association is a commonplace.

7 It is not clear what (if anything) the use of *Principles* in his title signifies. The term had become commonplace probably thanks to its employment in two texts – Descartes's *Principia Philosophiae* (1644) and Newton's *Principia Mathematica* (1686).

8 In some tension to his basic positon he also says in his Recapitulation of Book II that this obedience is their 'only public spirited sentiment' [II, 212]).
9 This is underlined when Steuart says a 'monied interest *of a long standing*, may . . . have influence enough to produce a change a change upon the spirit and manners of a people' (IV, 118 my emphasis)
10 For the link between time, custom, and authority in Hume see Berry (2018).
11 This is perhaps the nearest textual basis for Kobayashi's (1998: lxxxvii) otherwise bald declaration that the statesman has 'to uphold the "public spirit' in the sea of people with self-love'.

Bibliography

Aristotle. (1944), *The Politics*, London: Loeb Library.

Berry, C. (2018), Hume and the Customary Causes of Industry, Knowledge and Humanity, reprinted in C. Berry, *Essays on Hume, Smith and the Scottish Enlightenment*, Edinburgh: Edinburgh University Press: 184–207.

Hirschman, A. (1977), *The Passions and the Interests*, Princeton, NJ: Princeton University Press.

Hume, D. (1894), *History of England*, 3 vols., London: George Routledge.

———. (1985), *Essays: Moral, Political and Literary*, Indianapolis: Liberty Press.

Kobayashi, N. (1995), On the Method of Sir James Steuart, *Principles of Political Economy, Keizai-Ronso*, 63: 61–83.

———. (1998), The First System of Political Economy, in A. Skinner, N. Kobayshi & H. Mizuta (eds.), *An Inquiry into the Principles of Political Oeconomy: Being an Essay on the Science of the Domestic Policy in Free Nations Principles*, London: Pickering & Chatto: lxix–xcix.

Livius, Titus. (1925), *Ab Urbe Condita*, London: Loeb Library.

Machiavelli, N. (1988), Discorsi sopra la Prima Deca di Tito Livio, in *Tutte le Opere*, Firenze: Newton.

Montesquieu, C. (1961), *De l'Espirit des Lois*, Paris: Garnier.

Omori, I. (2003), The 'Scottish Triangle' in the Shaping of Political Economy: David Hume, Sir James Steuart and Adam Smith, in T. Sakamoto & H. Tanka (eds.), *The Rise of Political Economy in the Scottish Enlightenment*, London: Routledge: 103–118.

Ramos, A. (2011), Luxury, Crisis and Consumption: Sir James Steuart and the Eighteenth Century Luxury Debate, *History of Economics Review*, 53: 55–72.

Rousseau, J.-J. (1962), *Du Contrat Social*, Paris: Garnier.

Screpanti, E. & Zamagni, S. (1993), *An Outline of the History of Economic Thought*, Oxford: Clarendon Press.

Sen, S. (1957), *The Economics of Sir James Steuart*, London: Bell.

Smith, A. (1982a), *Inquiry into the Nature and Causes of the Wealth of Nations*, Indianapolis: Liberty Press.

———. (1982b), *Lectures on Jurisprudence*, Indianapolis: Liberty Press.

———. (1983), Considerations on the First Formation of Language, in J. Bryce (ed.), *Lectures on Rhetoric and Belles-Lettres*, Indianapolis: Liberty Press: 201–226.

———. (1987), *Correspondence of Adam Smith*, Indianapolis: Liberty Press.

Urquhart, R. (1996), The Trade Wind, the Statesman and the System of Commerce: Sir James Steuart's Vision of Political Economy, *European Journal of the History of Economic Thought*, 3: 403–404.

———. (1999), Steuart's Method: Aristotelian Political Economy, in R. Tortajada (ed.), *The Economics of James Steuart*, London: Routledge: 121–136.

2 The sociogenesis of the modern state in Sir James Steuart's *Principles of Political Economy*

Matari Pierre Manigat

Introduction

This chapter examines the sociogenesis of the state in the *Inquiry into the Principles of Political Economy* of James Steuart. More precisely, it highlights the foundations of the state, the nature of its fiscal regime, the relationship of different social classes to this system, and the functions of the state in the reproduction of the conditions of labour that foster capitalist development. The question of the role of the state is found in diffuse form throughout the five books that make up Steuart's *Principles* and is also treated, directly or indirectly, in most commentaries on the Scottish author's work.

The analysis of the role and nature of the state in Steuart's work can be divided into two general approaches.[1] The first emphasizes the pioneering attempt to set down the principles of political economy, in systematic form, at the dawn of the Industrial Revolution and the classical school of economics. This is the perspective of a majority of studies of the reception and trajectory of Steuart's work, beginning with its divergences and then its eclipse by the work of Adam Smith (Didot 1789; Cunningham 1891; Rae 1895; Sen 1957; Chamley 1962; Meek 1967; Skinner 1966, 1981; Lutfalla 1981; Hudson 1992; Diatkine & Rosier 1998; Albertone 1999; Omori 2005; Ramos & Mirowski 2011; Coutinho & Suprinyak 2017; Tiran 2017). An analogous approach examines Steuart's sources and influences, with emphasis on his relationship with Montesquieu (Skinner 1981; Hirschman 1977; Groenewegen 1999). The question of the state in Steuart highlights the differences between two of the founding traditions of contemporary economic thought: British classical liberalism and the German historical school. Whereas the former focuses on the differences between Steuart and Smith, the latter points to the similarities between Steuart's neo-mercantilism and the industrializing interventionism of List (Kobayashi 1967; Faure-Soulet 1970: 164; Skinner 1999b: 148), in spite of the differences in their historicism (Kobayashi 1999: 117). Finally, Dockès shows how Steuart served as a secret source of inspiration for Thünen (Dockès 1969).

The second general approach projects Steuart's thinking in *Principles* onto the problems of the present. In this view, Steuart appears to be a kind of putative father of Keynesianism *avant la lettre* (Sen 1957; Chamley 1962; Denis 1999; McColloch 2011; Gnos 2005), an advance critic of the public choice school (Khalil 1987), or a distant precursor to the questioning of the role of the state in the development of the prerequisites to industrialization (Perelman 2000). These perspectives show the reach but also the ambivalence of the 'rediscovery' of Steuart in the second half of the 20th century. If the twilight of liberalism in the 1930s favoured the rereading of a relatively forgotten author, the political context of his 'rediscovery' brings with it the risk of anachronistic readings, as Meek (1967) warned. Meek's warning is all the more relevant if *Principles* stands out in the history of economic thought precisely for its author's sense of history.

Steuart's historical approach has been compared with analogous perspectives, especially with Montesquieu's Four Stages Theory of Society, a common denominator among most of the Scottish Enlightenment thinkers (Meek 1976; Hirschman 1977; Menudo 2018). But the differences in the application of that theory, especially those between Smith and Steuart (Hutchison 1988) are less differences in conjectural hypotheses (Kobayashi 1999: 109) than a contrast in the way they focus on their object of study. Marx was the first to show how Steuart analyzed the origin of economic relations, rather than considering them as *a priori*, natural points of departure – as in the description of individuals with a natural inclination to mercantile exchange in Smith's *Wealth of Nations* and Ricardo's *Principles* (Marx 1857: 17–18). More fundamentally, in examining the historical formation of these relations, Steuart's work describes the mechanisms of primitive accumulation, that is, the separation of the direct producers from the objective conditions of production (Marx 1905: 352; Kobayashi 1967; Perelman 1983). This primitive accumulation, which goes hand in hand with the transition from feudalism to capitalism, underlies and determines Steuart's thinking about the sociogenesis of the modern state.

This chapter will consider the sociogenesis of the modern state, highlighting the nature and role of state power in bringing about capitalist relations of labour; it is a contribution to the study of the origins of theories of the bourgeois state as well as the role of political power in the formation of mercantile and capitalist relations.

The chapter is organized as follows: First, it introduces the problem, based on what Steuart called 'the spirit of the people' who plays, along with the class relations, the role of genetic principles of the forms of the State. Second, it examines how Steuart proceeds on this basis to show how the dissolution of feudal relationships, accompanied by the development of a mercantile economy, disrupted the foundations of state power and gave it an impersonal form, separate from and above society. Third, this process, as we will see, takes hold with the establishment of a system of centralized tax collection and specific class relations in taxation. Fourth, we will consider the role of the state in the establishment and reproduction of the conditions of wage labour. The final section offers some conclusions, highlighting Steuart's anticipation of some of the basic elements of modern theories of the state.

The "spirit of the people" and class relations as foundations of state forms

According to Steuart, the 'spirit of the people' is made up of 'opinions' about morals, government, and manners (I, 11). While the first is accessible through the study of religion and the second through the political history of a community, the third is the most difficult; it is the basis of relations of cultural otherness between different communities and gives the spirit of the people its 'ethnic and national' connotation (Kobayashi 1999: 109). The definition of the spirit of the people is not without its ambiguities; if opinion about the government is one of its three constitutive elements, it is also true that this spirit defines the 'plan of government'. What is certain is that regardless of the concrete characteristics of the spirit of the people, any consideration of the 'political economy' of a nation is based on the nature of that spirit (Urquhart 1999: 126).

Steuart's thoughts on the relationship between the spirit of the people and the form of the state are simultaneously genetic and normative. From the genetic perspective, the form of the state reflects and condenses the spirit of the people. 'If governments be taken in general', he notes, 'we shall find them analogous to the spirit of the people' (I, 13). A number of commentators have compared Steuart's position with the relationship between the spirit of the people and political forms found in Montesquieu's *Considerations on the Causes of the Greatness of the Romans and their Decline* and Hegel's *Lectures on the Philosophy of History* (Cunningham 1891; Chamley 1963; Caboret 1999; Ege 1999; McColloch 2011; Waszek 2009; Wokler 1997). But beyond the question of origins (Montesquieu) or of giving birth to a philosophy of history (Hegel), Steuart's link anticipates a central aspect of the relationship described by Alexis de Tocqueville between the society ('*état social*'), the 'spirit of liberty', and the modern state (Tocqueville 1835: 99–114). The ideological differences between Tocqueville, the liberal, and Steuart, the late mercantilist, obscure useful connections to be made between these two observers, who both considered the peak of bourgeois society from an aristocratic class position. Both expressed their thoughts in contexts immediately following the great political revolutions of their time: The English and Dutch Revolutions in the case of Steuart, and the American and French Revolutions for Tocqueville. And above all, for each the '*état social*' shapes existing political forms and, in the case of Steuart, involves the relationships of civil society (I, 13).

The spirit of a people is not a permanent given. Its evolution is endogenous but slow[2] and is seen first from a generational point of view. Steuart points to the differences and potential antagonisms between the 'active generations' of a society – those aged 20–30 and those older than 50. Second, there are differences within the classes that make up society. In effect, Steuart distinguishes the differences in values and ethics among different social classes: for example, the value of 'glory' for the feudal nobility, or the 'love of money' for the 'proprietors of funds'. This modifications in the spirit of the people from a class point of view acquires its importance for the statesman at the moment of judging and mediating social antagonisms.

That said, the modern era has been characterized by a 'universal' modification of the economic underpinning of political relationships and states. In the wake of the great discoveries, the circulation of commodities and money has established the basis of modern states. This metamorphosis corresponds to the transition from a feudal state form to one appropriate to a 'free' or commercial economy. The transition does not erase the differences between spirits of the people; these remain, but their implications from now on move within the mercantile relationships that contain them. The sociogenesis of the modern state in Steuart goes hand in hand with the broadening of mercantile exchange, as well as with the 'artificial institutions' that act as an incentive to the beginnings of a market (Perelman 2000: 153; Menudo 2018). The difference between these state forms, and the content of the transition, lies in the elimination of the 'chain of subordination' that characterizes the feudal form of government:

> The great alteration in the affairs of Europe within these three centuries, by the discovery of America and the Indies, the springing up of industry and learning, the introduction of trade and the luxurious arts, the establishment of public credit, and a general system of taxation, have entirely altered the plan of government every where. From feudal and military, it is become free and commercial. I oppose freedom in government to the feudal system, to mark only that there is not found now that chain of subordination among the subjects, which made the essential part of the feudal form. The head there had little power, and the lower classes of the people little liberty. Now every industrious man, who lives with oeconomy, is free and independent under most forms of government. Formerly, the power of the barons swallowed up the independency of all inferior classes. I oppose commercial to military; because the military governments now are made to subsist from the consequences and effects of commerce only, that is, from the revenue of the state, proceeding from taxes. Formerly, everything was brought about by numbers; now, numbers of men cannot be kept together without money.
>
> (I, 13–14)

The elimination of the 'chain of subordination' corresponds to the separation between political function and social class, which implies a disruption in class relations. The development of a monetary economy operates above all to break up the political power of the landowners and at the same time as a force that pauperizes the 'attendants of the nobility' (I, 68). This separation has an effect on judicial and executive powers as well as in administration. It becomes obvious in the reorganization of institutions in charge of the means of physical violence with the formation of paid armies. The use of paid soldiers objectively translates into a change in the financial foundations of the state and subjectively expresses the gradual replacement of the love of glory with the love of money. The separation reveals a new objectification of political power, which appears as impersonal public power, situated above social classes and disconnected from them. Steuart compares this power to a 'machine' (I, 331), a metaphor for the separation between civil society and the modern state whose use enters the history of political ideas in the 17th century (Althusser 1979: 452). More than a moderation of absolute despotism, as in Montesquieu (Hirschman 1977: 81–86), it is the mechanism of mercantile and industrial economic life, which demands a similar separation in the organization of modern political power:

> When once a state begins to subsist by the consequences of industry, there is less danger to be apprehended from the power of the sovereign. The mechanism of his administration becomes more complex, and . . . he finds himself so bound up by the laws of his political oeconomy, that every transgression of them runs him into new difficulties.
>
> (I, 330–331)

The public and impersonal character of the modern state does not derive from an abstract social contract between rulers and ruled. 'The rights of Kings are to be sought for in history; and not founded upon the supposition of tacit contracts between them and their people, inferred from the principles of an imaginary law of nature, which makes all mankind equal' (I, 320). The public and impersonal character of political power stems from the transformations of the relations between the classes of the owners and those of the producers following the establishment of commerce and industry.

> I deduce the origin of the great subordination under the feudal government, from the necessary dependence of the lower classes for their subsistence. They consumed the produce of the land, as the price of their subordination, not as the reward of their industry in making it produce. I deduce modern liberty from the independence of the same classes, by the introduction of industry, and circulation of an adequate equivalent for every service. If this doctrine be applied in order to resolve the famous question so much debated, concerning the origin of supreme authority, so far as it is a question of the law of nature, I do not find the decision so very difficult: All authority is in proportion to dependence, and must vary according to circumstances.
>
> (I, 319)[3]

Now, from a normative point of view, Steuart's composite sketch of the statesman obeys the two major properties that derive from these considerations: The correspondence between the action of the statesman with the spirit of the people and the impersonal character of the political power. He recommends, first, that the administrators' decisions be guided by the characteristics of the spirit of the people (Omori 2005). To inspire agreement with a change in governance, the statesman and the administrator should introduce 'innovations' that correspond to these characteristics as well as their 'degree of maturity'. Steuart's pragmatic reformism throughout his *Principles* derives above all from the slowness of change in the spirit of the people.

> The great art of governing is to divest oneself of prejudices and attachments to particular opinions, particular classes, and above all to particular persons;

> to consult the spirit of the people, to give way to it in appearance, and in so doing to give it a turn capable of inspiring those sentiments which may induce them to relish the change, which an alteration of circumstances has rendered necessary.
>
> (I, 16)

The statesman must likewise be impartial, incorruptible, and situated above the interests of individuals and social groups. Steuart frequently uses the figure of Lycurgus to illustrate his ideal statesman. The Spartan legislator embodies the ideal values of a head of state not only subjectively (incorruptible character, magnanimity, etc.) but also in knowing how to establish and modify the manners of the spirit of the people based on the most 'profound' of revolutions: Education (Book II, Chapter 14).

This apologia for Lycurgus does not in any way imply an espousal of the principle of equality of social condition; on the contrary, the state and its administrators work to reproduce the class structure.[4] Modern class relations are organized around a tripartite structure (landlords, manufacturers, workers); a conception of which Steuart is the precursor with other 18th-century economists like Millar or, later, Smith (Perkin 1969: 23).

Nor does Steuart identify the statesman's form of government with a particular political regime – monarchy or republic – although the latter would seem more suited to the flourishing of trade (II, 242–244; Skinner 1999b: 144–145).[5] He does, however, give the sense that the interests of the 'middle classes' or bourgeoisie[6] will have a decisive influence on the administration of this state.

What is true is that the modern state was based on a new financial modality based on systems of taxation and public credit. Both systems emerged during the 'financial revolution' in the wake of the Glorious Revolution (Hill 1969: 144–151), the decisive moment of the 'political constitution' of the English bourgeoisie (Marx 1847: 196), and the catalyst for the sociogenesis of the form of the state Steuart examines (I, 29).

The system of taxation and public credit in the sociogenesis of the modern state

For Steuart, merchant division of labour does not obey a tendency inherent to human nature, as Smith would claim (1776: 25) but is the result of a historical process bringing together different 'artificial institutions', dominated by the merchant class (Menudo 2018). The development of a monetary economy laid the foundation of the modern state, which emerged alongside a centralized system of tax collection:

> For as long as the earth nourishes directly those who are upon her surface, as long as she delivers her fruits into the very hand of him who consumes them, there is no alienation, no occasion for money, consequently no possibility of establishing an extensive taxation, as shall in its place be fully explained.

> From this principle is, I imagine, to be deduced the reason, why we find taxation so little known under the feudal form of government.
>
> (I, 65)

We have already seen how the circulation of commodities acts as a catalyst for the dissociation of members of the feudal nobility from their former public role, becoming a stimulus to the formation of an impersonal political power. It does so, first, because it attacks natural forms of surplus consumption at their root. The dynamics of trade and industrial development undermine landowners' traditional ways of consuming the fruits of their vassals' surplus labour. Increasingly, the personal services of their subjects are transformed into money rents, which promotes the renting to farmers of lands 'formerly consumed in [their] fruits' (I, Charter 10; Kobayashi 1999: 111–112). Second, the intensification in the circulation of commodities opens the way to the centralized collection of taxes in money. The sovereign is freed from the mediation of multiple centres in the feudal structure. This overlap in the development of a monetary economy, fiscal monopolization, and the formation of political power is distinct from civil society and is at the heart of classical theories of modern state formation, from historical materialism to Elias via the 'rational state' of Weber (Marx & Engels 1846; Bauer 1905: 189–194; Weber 1923; Pashukanis 1924; Elias 1939).

Cities, the focal points of development in manufacturing, trade, and luxury consumption, were the original crucibles for the modern taxation system and thus for the new state power in Western Europe. 'In short', Steuart writes, 'the only dawning of public liberty to be met with during the feudal government, was in the cities; no wonder then if they increased' (I, 66–67). The very notion of taxation is, for Steuart, a modern one, or one previously found almost exclusively in cities. The revitalization of cities beginning in the 15th century, together with the spread of the mercantile economy and the great discoveries, accelerated the transformation of the traditional forms of consumption. Along with the transformation of the vassals' services into money rent, the migration to cities of a growing number of nobility increased the circulation of money and reinforced the centralized political power of the courts established in the capital cities. It is here that we see the organic relationships between the formation of absolute monarchies and the rise of the merchant bourgeoisie (Marx 1867: 709; Anderson 1974).

> The courts of princes then became magnificent; the feudal lords insensibly began to frequent them with more assiduity than formerly. The splendor of the prince soon eclipsed those rays which shone around them upon their own lands. They now no more appeared to one another as objects of jealousy, but of emulation. They became acquainted, began to relish a court life, and every one proposed to have a house in the capital. A change of habitation made a change of circumstances, both as to city and country. As to the city; so far as inhabitants were increased, by the addition of the great lords, and of those who

> followed their example, so far demand increased for every sort of provision and labour; and this quickly drew more inhabitants together.
>
> (I, 67)

Steuart addresses the question of taxation both from a sociological and an economic perspective. In the first, conscious of the reluctance to pay taxes in general,[7] he considers the interests and spirit that predominate in each social class with respect to each type of tax. Along with their material interests, the spirit, and more precisely the values of different social classes, explains their particular hostility to certain taxes.

> The great abuse of governors in the application of taxes contributes not a little to entertain and augment this repugnancy in the governed: but besides abuse, there is often too little management used to prepare the spirits of the people for such innovations; for we see them upon many occasions submitting with cheerfulness to very heavy impositions, provided they be well-timed, and consistent with their manners and disposition. A French gentleman, who cannot bear the thought of being put upon a level with a peasant in paying a land-tax, pays contentedly, in time of war, a general tax upon all his effects, under a different name. To pay for your head is terrible in one country; to pay for light appears as terrible in another.
>
> (I, 17)

From an economic perspective, Steuart addresses the effect of taxes on the dynamics of the economic system, making a distinction between 'income', which should be taxed, and 'funds', which should not. Given that taxes are always assessed on expenses, the administrative difficulty is in how to characterize different expenses in order not to tax funds. Steuart classifies existing taxes into three broad categories: 'proportional' taxes, assessed on consumption, 'cumulative' taxes, applied to property, and 'personal' taxes, on services. The most fundamental are the proportional taxes, which depend on the expansion of the circulation of commodities and money. For this reason, from the point of view of class relations, these taxes allow the 'industrious' (among whom the proprietors of funds make up the manufacturing bourgeoisie) to exploit those classes that only consume, that is, the feudal landowners.

> Under the pure monarchy, the prince seems jealous, as it were, of growing wealth, and therefore imposes taxes upon people who are growing richer. Under the limited government they are calculated chiefly to affect those who from rich are growing poorer. Thus the monarch imposes a tax upon industry, where everyone is rated in proportion to the gain he is supposed to make by his profession. The poll-tax and *taille* are likewise proportioned to the supposed opulence of everyone liable to them. . . . In limited governments, impositions are more generally laid upon consumption. They encourage industry and leave the full profits of it to make up a stock for the industrious persons.
>
> (II, 24)

Marx would salute Steuart for highlighting this 'primitive goal of the tax on consumption' (Marx 1847: 196). This advantage of 'proportional' taxes is so important that landowners succeed in opposing taxation of their rents, to the extent that they maintain considerable political power.

This analysis of the formation of the system of taxation is connected with the birth of the system of public credit (Tiran 2014), that is, the confidence of creditors in the capacity of the state to pay its debts. This system was also a product of the transformation in the form of the state following the Glorious Revolution (Book IV, Chapter 3). For Steuart, the confidence of creditors is not based on abstract patriotic sentiment. It makes specific political demands, like parliamentary control of the treasury, as well as the existence of the financial apparatus of the state: The state institutions, headed by a treasury, that borrow and administer public debt according to so-called *principe d'unversalité budgétaire* (i.e., without committing a particular tax to the repayment of a loan) and that collects taxes directly, without intermediaries that act as 'parasites' on the state. The financial apparatus of the state also includes private banking institutions invested with public attributes, like the Bank of England and the Bank of Amsterdam. Based on this idea, and following Davenant (1701; Stettner 1945), Steuart pronounces himself in favour of a system of public credit based on 'short-term loans'.[8] Good administration of public credit is essential to the reproduction of the payment system (Piteau 2002) and more generally to the liquidity of the credit system as a whole (Bentemessek 2012). However, the development of the credit system itself carries the possibility of an increase in public debt and thus of taxes, which alters the balance of power in favour of the 'monied interest':[9]

> The more the national debts increase, by the monied interest realizing into this branch of solid property the funds, the more the taxes must augment; and consequently, the more the proprietors of the funds themselves must be affected by such taxes, as well as the landlords.
>
> (IV, 124–125)

The modern systems of taxation and public credit reflect a double transformation. First, they translate the rise of an economy based on the circulation of commodities and money into the language of the state. Second, in a sociological sense, they capture the change in the 'balance of wealth' between landowners and proprietors of funds. These are the economic and social foundations of the modern state that show the form of a public and impersonal power. Unlike states based on servitude, the collusion between the modern state and the propertied classes is not direct but indirect. 'Steuart perceived that the government in modern free society had been carried out in the form of indirect control by means of money', writes Omori (2005: 106). Now, however, we will look at how the formation of this state apparatus led to the establishment of a new social order characterized by a type of relation between producers, landowners, and proprietors of funds.

The creation of 'free hands' and state management of labour power

The relations of exploitation underlying the extraction of surplus labour are a consequence of the difficulties of agricultural production, as well as the prevailing property relations; in a formal sense, both slavery and wage labour are methods of extracting this surplus.

> When the earth is not in common to those who live upon her spontaneous fruits, but is appropriated by a few, there either slavery or industry must be introduced among those who consume the surplus of the proprietors; because these will expect either service or work in return for their superfluity. . . . Slavery in former times had the same effect in peopling the world that trade and industry have now. Men were then forced to labour because they were slaves to others; men are now forced to labour because they are slaves to their own wants.
>
> (I, 31)

Steuart considers the different ways of organizing social production, that is, the forms of existence of the labour force, from the perspective of their place in history. If he is in no hurry to condemn the economics of slavery in the name of the greater productivity and efficiency of 'free labour', it is less because he has underestimated the ethical contradictions of the persistence of slavery in the modern era than because he has perceived the civilizing role of direct compulsion in the extraction of surplus labour in preindustrial societies.[10] These are methods that allow for production beyond that which is necessary, leading to the development of new needs, both individual and social, even when they are confined to those who are not slaves or 'inferiors'. 'To make mankind labour beyond their wants, to make one part of a state work to maintain the other gratuitously', Steuart writes, 'could only be brought about by slavery, and slavery was therefore introduced universally' (I, 38).

According to Steuart, dependence is 'the only bond of society'. Slavery, serfdom, and wage labour are different forms of labour determined by relations of subordination that result from differences in the degree of dependence. While dependence for the preservation of life is the foundation of slavery, the dependence for 'the means of procuring subsistence' determines serfdom. Finally, dependence on 'the sale of the product of its industry' founds wage labour. The latter is therefore only possible on the basis of generalization of market relations (II, 239). Steuart thus sketches a certain correspondence between the form of social existence of the labour force, the nature of the relations between owners and producers, and the political form of the state.

More fundamentally, however, the differences in productivity in the agriculture define the capacity to generate a surplus that determines the development of cities as focus sites of trade, industry, and luxury (Book I, Chapter 10). The natural conditions and the labour conditions of production for an agricultural surplus define two types of workers: The 'necessary' and the useless. The latter constitutes a latent agricultural overpopulation, whose exodus to the cities demands a revolution in the agrarian structure according to the prevailing historical circumstances and spirit of the people. And in order to 'cleanse' the useless from the countryside it is necessary to separate the producers from the land, with the introduction of modern private ownership of land, an essential condition of the establishment of capitalism. Here are the fundamental elements of Steuart's analysis of primitive accumulation, as noted by Marx (1867: 708–709) and systematically analyzed by Kobayashi, and especially Perelman, who considers Steuart the 'greatest classical theorist of primitive accumulation' (Perelman 2000: 170). Steuart's analysis constitutes his second great contribution to the development of Marx's thought, next to his theory of money (Gomez Betancourt & Pierre Manigat 2018). But both contributions have been obscured, among other reasons, because of his means of expressing them. 'The abstract categories are in his work still in process of differentiation from their material content', notes Marx, 'and therefore appear to be blurred and ambiguous' (Marx 1859: 297).[11]

The expropriation of the rural population was supported by law and state violence, in a process that privileged the replacement of cultivated fields with enclosed pasture, which Hill describes as the cause and consequence of the disappearance of independent farmers (Hill 1969: 222–224); its echoes are found in the British social literature since at least Thomas More. The extreme methods of the expropriation reached their classic and most brutal form in the so-called 'clearing of estates' in the highlands, with the transformation of communal property into private holdings after the Jacobite rebellions, in which the young Steuart participated (Marx 1867: 719–720; Hill 1969: 182–183; Skinner 1999a). Finally, along the same lines, the transformation of the feudal nobility into modern landowners and the strengthening of the power of the gentry gave form to Steuart's thinking about the agrarian revolution as a step in the development of capitalism (Perelman 1983: 146–147), and as a process that faced objective obstacles (lack of money) as well as subjective ones (the spirit of the feudal class).

This generalization of capitalist landed property also demanded the intervention of state power in developing the labour conditions for urban industry. The creation of 'free hands', a population freed from the farm and thus available to produce non-agricultural goods, combined the separation of the direct producers with their means of subsistence. Steuart classifies the free hands into two distinct and antagonistic categories:

> The first, those to whom this surplus directly belongs, or who, with a revenue in money already acquired, can purchase it. The second, those who purchase it with their daily labour or personal service. Those of the first condition may live where they please; those of the second, must live where they can.
>
> (I, 63)

Steuart's free hands describe the two fundamental social classes of industrial capitalism: the proletariat and the bourgeoisie. After the transformation of the agrarian structures and the destruction of all the forms of subsistence agriculture – the *sine qua non* condition of capitalism consisting of 'the separation between parent earth and her laborious children' – the directing of the 'superfluous mouths' of agriculture towards the city and its industries is the complementary step. The criticism of Steuart arises less from his positive presentation of the mechanisms of primitive accumulation than from the abrupt rhythm of his introductions; the critics are in agreement with his thoughts on the spirit of the people, the support for his ideas of pragmatic reform, and the prudence behind his general maxims of political economy. What is true is that Steuart's critical observations about the 'rhythm' of the process are open to a normative reading of *Principles*, an exercise that Perelman, who begins with Steuart, carries out in order to question certain proposals from contemporary theory of the role of the state in the creation of preindustrial conditions (Perelman 2000: 151–153). Finally, these conditions of agricultural production support Steuart's thinking about demography and the policy it implies. His demographic analysis is based on Hume and criticizes Wallace (Omori 2005), while his analysis of the relationship between the means of subsistence and the ability to reproduce, between *virtus nutritiva* and *virtus generativa*, places him halfway between the 'populationism' of classical continental mercantilism (Vilquin 2001: 97) and Malthusianism.

Beyond Steuart's ambivalence in matters of demography, however, his thinking highlights the historical nature of the problem. He thus approaches the action of the state in the reproduction of its population based on historical differences. First, he disapproves of morganatic marriages: marriage policy ought to favour unions within social classes. If marriage contributes to the reproduction of the existing class structure, it allows for the preservation of the spirit of each class (I, 66). More fundamentally, however, Steuart's historicism allows for an understanding of the laws and demographic policies that correspond to the needs of each historical form of production. For this reason, he calls for the establishment of a systematic census of all social classes:

> There is no governing a state in perfection, and consequently no executing the plan for a right distribution of the inhabitants, without exactly knowing their situation as to numbers, their employment, the gains upon every species of industry, the numbers produced from each class.
>
> (I, 81)

On the one hand, a state based on slavery, for example, seeks to promote marriages among the upper classes, inspired by the example of the *jus trium liberorum* decreed by Augustus to 'correct the prodigal, dissolute life' of wealthy bachelors and slow the declining birth rate and weakening of civic virtue (Vilquin 2001: 19). On the other hand, these societies are involved in the reproduction of slaves and in general of the 'lower classes' by means of the slave trade – as was true both in antiquity and in the African slave trade of Steuart's time.

The problem of reproducing the population has particular difficulties in the case of the direct producers, or 'lower classes'. While the reproduction of slave labour is based on the slave trade, there is a particular problem in the reproduction of the proletarian labour force: a distinction between the reproduction of labour power and its daily preservation:

> This lowest class therefore must be kept up, and . . . by its own multiplication. But where every one lives by his own industry, a competition comes in, and he who works cheapest gains the preference. How can a married man, who has children to maintain, dispute this preference with one who is single? The unmarried therefore force the others to starve; and the basis of the pyramid is contracted.
>
> (I, 93)

This contradiction between reproduction and preservation is the pretext for 'state management of labor power', to use the concept of Brunhoff (1971). This state management contributes to the reproduction of the 'capitalist features in the use of wage labor', beginning with two characteristics that are fundamental: Work discipline and the insecurity of employment.[12] It takes different forms in different historical periods and is supported primarily by elements and institutions of 'different ages'. During the period of primitive accumulation in Western Europe, state intervention took the form of rules that established legal wage rates in the city and the country. In England, legislation limited wages beginning in the 16th century (Marx 1867: 724–730). For Steuart, the regulation of wage rates assures a minimal subsistence 'in the price of labor' but prevents an excessive increase in order to assure the profits of the proprietors of funds. The state also contributes to increasing the discipline of the labour force, by establishing, for example, a system of piece rates instead of an hourly wage (Karayiannis 1994). Likewise, Steuart calls for the state to take charge of workers who are expired (retired) or defective (ill), and for orphans to be placed with the lower classes, in order to increase the number of hands and weaken their bargaining power in the labour market (I, 68). The final goal is to maintain a number of free hands that is proportional to the rest of the economy.

Conclusions

This chapter has highlighted the contribution of Steuart to the study of the origins of the modern state, as well as his role in the construction of mercantile and capitalist relations. The sociogenesis of the state in Steuart's *Principles* involves specific economic fundamentals: the generalized circulation of commodities and money. The dynamics of these phenomena involve a change in the balance of power between landowners, 'proprietors of funds', and 'monied interests', as well as a new form of public power, where the state is separated from society and set above classes. This modification in the balance of power within the ruling class accompanies a deeper change in the relations between owners and producers. However, Steuart does not limit himself to describing the economic conditions of the formation of this state. The sociogenesis of the state involves a specific sociocultural environment, what he calls the 'spirit of the people', an ambiguous notion that contains basic elements of a theory of the nation-state. While the economic foundations and class relations determine the form of the state, the spirit of the people imprints its concrete figure.

The modern state rests on a specific type of financing that is only possible with a monetary economy, centralized tax collection, and political power that is separate from and above social classes. The tax system and the growing influence of merchants and monied interests open the way to a fiscal system centred on consumption taxes, whose dynamics favour a balance of wealth in favour of the proprietors of funds. This fiscal system is complemented by a system of public credit that presupposes a particular organization of public finance, which began with the Glorious Revolution, the watershed moment in the political constitution of the bourgeoisie. Steuart compares the workings of this new impersonal public power to those of a machine, a metaphor that systematically describes the separation between the modern state and civil society.

As the product of a socioeconomic revolution, the new state participates, conversely, in the creation and reproduction of conditions favouring the development of mercantile exchange and capitalist production. Steuart explains the formation of relations of exploitation, from slavery to wage labour, on the basis of the need to generate an agricultural surplus. The 'industrial system', although it is superior to slavery, involves a transformation in the social form of existence of the labour force. This process calls for state intervention in at least three senses. First, the state is needed to expropriate the surplus rural population and convert it into free hands, that is, potential factory owners and urban proletarians. Second, the state guides workers into the cities, the sites of industry and manufacture. Third, it assures the reproduction of the worker population as well as wage levels that meet the demands of capital and the impossibility of worker self-reproduction.

All of these ideas of Steuart make up the precursor to an analysis of state management of labour power under capitalism. Some of the ideas he developed – the concomitance of a monetary economy, fiscal monopolization, and the objectivization of political power apart from society – anticipate fundamental elements of contemporary theories of the state, including historical materialism, the theories of Weber, and especially the monopolization of taxation that lies at the heart of Elias's thinking on the sociogenesis of the state.

Notes

1 This is an analytical distinction for purposes of convenience in presentation. Some of the studies to be discussed include a mixture of the two approaches.

2 Steuart considers the case of an exogenous evolution of the spirit of the people, but he notes the obstacles to this possibility in their manners. Here is where we find his objective condemnation of the relationships of domination between peoples, as well as change imposed by foreigners (I, 12–13). He would contradict this position in practice during the American War, in which he supported keeping the 13 colonies, even though he opposed the use of military force to put down the rebellion (Raynor & Skinner 1994).

3 Machiavelli (1532: 279–280) and Hobbes (1651: 103–106) offer the first systematizations of the two great distinctive properties of the modern state form: A definite articulation between force and consensus as the foundation of the state (represented by the image of Centaur Chiron) and a clear separation between the state and the society (represented by the image of Leviathan). Generally speaking, the separation between the state and civil society constitutes the ground on which the economic and political thoughts are articulated during the period of generalization of mercantile exchange in Western Europe in the 17th and 18th centuries. This can be observed through the desire to found public law (i.e., state law) from private law (i.e., mercantile law) among jusnaturalism theorists (Pashukanis 1924; Strauss 1954).

4 It is just as wrong to consider Steuart as an apologist *avant la lettre* of '"totalitarian economic planning' in the sense given to this concept during the Cold War as do Anderson and Tollisson (1984).

5 However, he did express a certain scepticism about this form. See Kobayashi (1999: 117–118).

6 In England of the 18th and 19th centuries, the notion of the middle classes corresponds to the concept of *bourgeoisie* understood in a sociological sense, that is to say from the following four criteria: Consciousness of a common identity, type of professional activity, level of education, and employment of domestic workers (Hobsbawm 1975: 283–286; Bédarida 1976: 79–80).

7 With the reluctance to pay taxes, another relationship between power and taxation is established in a merchant society. The state has more and more problems to exercise its power because accessing the wealth of citizens is more complicated (I, 277–278).

8 In the French version of the *Principles,* Steuart completes this analysis, contrasting the English situation with the French through a comparison of Davenant's analysis with that of Cardinal Richelieu. He highlights their differences but describes the superiority of English public credit (Book IV, Chapter 4). Some of the elements in this line of thought anticipate the fiscal crisis that would be a major factor in the fall of the *Ancien Régime* (Ardant 1956).

9 By 'monied interest' Steuart refers to 'those only who have money, not realized upon any fund, and who either employ it in the way of trade, in the way of industry, in jobbing in land, in stock, or in any way they please, so as to draw from it an annual income' (II, 447).

10 See Pisanelli in this volume.

11 Steuart distinguishes between labour and industry. Industry presupposes liberty; the motivation behind work is to acquire through exchange an equivalent with which to buy what is necessary, plus a surplus (as recompense for one's diligence). Labour may be forced, but this provides no greater recompense than subsistence.

12 Steuart sees the disastrous effects of the abrupt introduction of machine-tools, with an increase in 'superfluous mouths' worsening the living conditions of the lower classes (I, 178–188).

Bibliography

Albertone, M. (1999), The Difficult Reception of James Steuart at the End of the Eighteenth Century in France, in R. Tortajada (ed.), *The Economics of James Steuart*, London: Routledge: 41–56.

Althusser, L. (1979), Marx dans ses limites, in *Écrits philosophiques et politiques*, vol. 1, Paris: Stock, 1994: 359–524.

Anderson, G.M. & Tollison, R.D. (1984), Sir James Steuart as the Apotheosis of Mercantilism and His Relation to Adam Smith, *Southern Economic Journal*, 51: 456–468.

Anderson, P. (1974), *Lineages of Absolute State*, London: Verso, 2013.

Ardant, G. (1956), *Histoire de l'impôt*, vol. 2, Paris: Fayard.

Bauer, O. (1905), *La question des nationalités et la social-démocratie*, vol. 2, Paris: EDI, 1987.

Bédarida, F. (1976), *La société anglaise du milieu du XIXe siècle à nos jours*, Paris: Seuil, 1990.

Bentemessek, N. (2012), Public Credit and Liquidity in James Steuart's *Principles*, *European Journal of the History of Economic Thought*, 19(4): 501–528.

Brunhoff, S. (1971), *Etat et Capital*, Paris: PUG Maspero.

Caboret, D. (1999), The Market Economy and Social Classes in James Steuart and G. W. F. Hegel, in R. Tortajada (ed.), *The Economics of James Steuart*, London: Routledge: 57–75.

Chamley, P. (1962), Sir James Steuart: inspirateur de la *Théorie Générale* de Lord Keynes, *Revue d'économie politique*, 72: 303–313.

———. (1963), *Économie et philosophie chez Steuart et Hegel*, Paris: Dalloz.

Coutinho, M. & Suprinyak, C.E. (2017), *Steuart, Smith and the System of Commerce: International Trade and Monetary Theory in Late 18th Century British Political Economy*, Working paper 575, CEDEPAL.

Cunningham, W. (1891), The Progress of Economic Doctrine in England in the Eighteenth Century, *Economic Journal*, 1: 72–94.

Davenant, C. (1701), *An Essay upon Ways and Means of Supplying the War*. London: Jacob Tonson.

Denis, H. (1999), Marx's Polemics against Steuart, in R. Tortajada (ed.), *The Economics of James Steuart*, London: Routledge: 76–83.

Diatkine, S. & Rosier, M. (1998), Systèmes bancaires et croissance chez Steuart et Smith, *Economies et Sociétés, série P.E.*, 27: 247–268.

Didot, F.-A. (1789), *Introduction à l'édition française de Recherche des principes de l'économie politique ou essai sur la science de la police intérieure des nations libres*, Paris: Didot l'aîné.

Dockès, P. (1969), *L'espace dans la pensée économique du XVIeme siècle*, Paris: Flammarion.

Ege, R. (1999), The New Interpretation of Steuart by Paul Chamley, in R. Tortajada (ed.), *The Economics of James Steuart*, London: Routledge: 84–101.

Elias, N. (1939), *The Civilizing Process, Vol. II: State Formation and Civilization*, Oxford: Blackwell, 1982.

Faure-Soulet, J.-F. (1970), *De Malthus à Marx. L'histoire aux mains des logiciens*, Paris: Gauthier villars.

Gnos, C. (2005), L'économie d'échange, une fable ? La contribution de James Steuart à la théorie de l'économie monétaire de production, in G. Bensimon (ed.), *Histoire des représentations du marché*, Paris: Michel Houdiard: 214–230.

Gomez Betancourt, R. & Pierre Manigat, M. (2018), James Steuart and the Making of Karl Marx's Monetary Thought, *The European Journal of the History of Economic Thought*, 25(5): 1022–1051.

Groenewegen, P. (1999), Sir James Steuart and Richard Cantillon, in R. Tortajada (ed.), *The Economics of James Steuart*, London: Routledge: 27–40.

Hill, C. (1969), *The Penguin Economic History of Britain, Vol. 2: 1530–1780: Reformation to Industrial Revolution*, London: Penguin.

Hirschman, O. (1977), *The Passions and the Interests: Political Arguments for Capitalism before Its Triumph*, Princeton, NJ: Princeton University Press.

Hobbes of Malmesbury, T. (1651), *Leviathan or the Matter, Forme and Power of a Common-Wealth Ecclesiasticall and Civil*, London: Andrew Crooke.

Hobsbawm, E. (1975), *The Age of capital 1848–1875*, London: Abacus, 1995.

Hudson, M. (1992), *Trade, Development, and Foreign Debt: A History of Theories of Polarisation and Convergence in the International Economy, Vol 1: International Trade*, London: Pluto Press.

Hutchison, T. (1988), *Before Adam Smith – The Emergence of Political Economy, 1662–1776*, Oxford: Basil Blackwell.

Karayiannis, A. (1994), Sir James Steuart on the Managed Market, in D. Reisman (ed.), *Economic Thought and Political Theory*, Dordrecht: Springer: 37–61.

Khalil, E.L. (1987), Sir James Steuart vs. Professor James Buchanan: Critical Notes on Modern Public Choice, *Review of Social Economy*, 45(2): 113–132.

Kobayashi, N. (1967), *James Steuart, Adam Smith and Friedrich List*, Tokyo: Science Council of Japan.

———. (1999), On the method of Sir James Steuart's Principles of Poltical Œconomy, in R. Tortajada (ed.), *The Economics of James Steuart*. London: Routledge, 102–120.

Lutfalla, M. (1981), *Aux origines de la pensée économique*, Paris: Economica.

Machiavelli, N. (1532), *The Prince*, Cambridge: Hackett Publishing, 1976.

Marx, K. (1847), The Poverty of Philosophy, in K. Marx & F. Engels (eds.), *Collected Works*, vol. 6, London: Lawrence & Wishart, 1976.

———. (1857), Introduction to Economic Manuscripts of 1857–58, in K. Marx & F. Engels (eds.), *Collected Works*, vol. 28, London: Lawrence & Wishart. 1986.

———. (1859), Contribution to Critique of Political Economy, in K. Marx & F. Engels (eds.), *Collected Works*, vol. 29, London: Lawrence & Wishart, 1987.

———. (1867), Capital Book I, in K. Marx & F. Engels (eds.), *Collected Works*, vol. 35, London: Lawrence & Wishart, 1996.

———. (1905), Theories of Surplus Value, in K. Marx & F. Engels (eds.), *Collected Works*, vol. 30, London: Lawrence & Wishart, 1988.

Marx, K. & Englels, F. (1846), The German Ideology, in K. Marx & F. Engels (eds.), *Collected Works*, vol. 5, London: Lawrence & Wishart, 1987.

McColloch, W. (2011), *Marx's Appreciation of James Steuart: A Theory of History and Value*, Working Paper Series, Salt Lake City: University of Utah, Department of Economics.

Meek, R.L. (1967), The Rehabilitation of Sir James Steuart, in *Economics and Ideology and Other Essays: Studies in the Development of Economic Thought*, London: Chapman & Hall Ltd: 3–17.

———. (1976), *Social Science and the Ignoble Savage*, New York: Cambridge University Press.

Menudo, J.M. (2018), Sir James Steuart on the Origins of Commercial Nations, *Journal of the History of Economic Thought*, 40(4): 561–578.

Omori, I. (2005), The 'Scottish Triangle' in the Shaping of Political Economy: David Hume, Sir James Steuart, and Adam Smith, in *The Rise of Political Economy in the Scottish Enlightenment*, London: Routledge: 117–132.

Pashukanis, E. (1924), *General Theory of Law and Marxism*, London: Transaction Publishers, 2003.

Perelman, M. (1983), Classical Political Economy and Primitive Accumulation: The Case of Smith and Steuart, *History of Political Economy*, 15(3): 451–494.

———. (2000), *The Invention of Capitalism*, Durham: Duke University Press.

Perkin, H. (1969), *The Origins of Modern English Society*, London: Routledge, 2002.

Piteau, M. (2002), Monnaie de compte et système de paiements chez James Steuart. Quel rôle pour la stabilité bancaire?, *Revue économique*, 53(2): 245–271.

Rae, J. (1895), *Life of Adam Smith*, London: Macmillan.

Ramos, A. & Mirowski, P. (2011), A Universal Scotland of the Mind: Steuart and Smith on the Need for a Political Economy, *Poroi*, 7(1): 3–44.
Raynor, D. & Skinner, A. (1994), Sir James Steuart Nine Letters on the American Conflict, 1775–1778, *The William and Mary Quarterly*, 51(4): 755–776.
Sakamoto, T. & Tanaka, H. (2005), *The Rise of Political Economy in the Scottish Enlightenment*, London: Routledge.
Sen, S.R. (1957), *The Economics of Sir James Steuart*, London: G. Bell & Sons Ltd.
Skinner, A. (1966), Introduction, in J. Steuart, *An Inquiry into the Principles of Political Economy*, Chicago: The University of Chicago Press.
———. (1981), Sir James Steuart: Author of a System, *Scottish Journal of Political Economy*, 28(1): 20–42.
———. (1993), Sir James Steuart: The Market and the State, *History of Economic Ideas*, 1(1): 1–43.
———. (1999a), Sir James Steuart and the Jacobite Connection, in R. Tortajada (ed.), *The Economics of James Steuart*. London: Routledge: 1–23.
———. (1999b), James Steuart: aspects of economic policy, in R. Tortajada (ed.), *The Economics of James Steuart*. London: Routledge: 139–50.
Smith, A. (1776), *An Inquiry into the Nature and Causes of the Wealth of Nations*, Indianapolis: Liberty Fund, 1981.
Stettner, W.F. (1945), Sir James Steuart on the Public Debt, *Quarterly Journal of Economics*, 59(3): 451–476.
Strauss, L. (1954), *Natural Right and History*, Chicago: The University of Chicago Press.
Tiran, A. (2014), Dette publique et fiscalité chez James Steuart, in J.-P. Potier (ed.), *Les marmites de l'histoire. Mélanges en l'honneur de Pierre Dockès*, Paris: Garnier: 41–53.
———. (2017), Steuart 'critique de Smith', Seville: *Conference James Steuart and an Economy without Invisible Hands*.
Tocqueville, A. (de). (1835), *De la démocratie en Amérique*, Paris: Garnier, 1981.
Urquhart, R. (1999), Steuart's Method: Aristotelian Political Economy, in R. Tortajada (ed.), *The Economics of James Steuart*, London: Routledge: 121–136.
Vilquin, É. (2001), Histoire de la pensée démographique jusqu'en 1940, in G. Caseli, J. Vallin & G. Wunsch (eds.), *Démographie: Histoire des idées et politiques de population*, vol. 7, Paris: INED: 11–55.
Waszek, N. (2009), *Appareil critique de G.W.F. Hegel, La philosophie de l'histoire*, Paris: Le livre de Poche.
Weber, M. (1923), *Histoire économique. Esquisse d'une histoire universelle de l'économie et de la société*, Paris: Gallimard, 1991.
Wokler, R. (1997), The French Revolutionary Roots of Political Modernity, *Hegel's Philosophy, or the Enlightenment at Dusk*, 18(1): 71–89.

3 James Steuart

Slavery and commercial society in his *Principles of Political Economy*

Simona Pisanelli

Introduction

When dealing with an author like James Steuart and his *Inquiry into the Principles of Political Economy* (1767), the first impression is that his work has been neglected for a long time, especially if compared with the more well-known *Inquiry into the nature and causes of the wealth of nations* (1776) by Adam Smith.

This impression is widespread, as some scholars point out:

> The *chevalier* Steuart . . . has been rarely quoted, it is true; but he was often copied. Mr. Smith himself, in his very rightly famous work, has combined in the first three books everything our author has said about the same subjects, but without going as deeply into them.
>
> (Chamley 1962: 312)

> Smith is, of course, familiar to nearly everyone; Steuart is less well-known, and often omitted in surveys of the Scottish Enlightenment, but deserves better. By many accounts, including those from the 18th century, it was Steuart who deserved the laurels for the invention of political economy, publishing his *Inquiry into the Principles of Political Economy* in 1767, almost a decade before Smith's *Wealth of Nations*.
>
> (Ramos & Mirowski 2011: 3)

In addition, 'the first work to deal with [the] issues [of political economy] as a separate discipline' was 'not that of Adam Smith' but that published in 1767 by James Steuart (Ramos & Mirowski 2011: 10; Kobayashi 2003: 102).

Apart from whether or not one recognizes that political economy 'as a separate discipline' is a product of the work of Steuart and not of Smith, we cannot ignore the criticisms that economists and historians of economic thought have addressed to the former. According to the severe judgement of Schumpeter – who, however, defines *Principles* as 'the only great system of economics that Great Britain had produced before Smith'[1] (Schumpeter 2003: I, 302) – it was only Steuart's theory of population that had left a clear mark in the history of political economy, whereas the other theories (commerce, industry, money, credit, taxes, etc.) were weak and inconsistent (Schumpeter 2003: I, 214). This judgement was anticipated by the

Italian economist Luigi Cossa, who harshly criticized the 'long-winded treatise' by Steuart, 'in which it is true that there are some good ideas about population, machines, the influence of the market, the changes in agricultural systems, etc., but they are mixed with the strangest mistakes, and weakened by tedious digressions' (Cossa 1892: 256–257).

We have briefly mentioned these opinions not because we want to make a detailed reconstruction of Steuart's success but because also on the subject of slavery, which we will deal with in this chapter, we find his reflections contradictory and ambiguous. In the secondary literature, Steuart's reflections on the issue of slavery are generally considered with reference to his theory of population. This is no surprise because population is the basis for his entire inquiry:

> to him, population is not a mere matter of means and resources necessary for the production of wealth or power; it rather constitutes an end in itself, an objective for society to attain, and is the essential aim of economy as a moral and political science.
>
> (Gislain 2003: 169)[2]

Ragip Ege's work represents an interesting exception because it deals with the topic of slavery independently from the issue of population. As far as the relation between *the Hegelien theme of work* and Steuart's influence on the German philosopher is concerned, Ege maintains: 'according to the mercantilist author, the greatest change in the spirit of modern times was the abolition of slavery'. In a general sense, this is true. Nevertheless, the fact that 'slavery has . . . formed the major obstacle against economic development in history' (Ege 2003: 90)[3] does not imply that, according to Steuart, this is true in every sector of production and in every country.

In order to demonstrate that Steuart's thought about slavery is not so unequivocal and linear, the purposes of this chapter are:

1 To take a fresh look at the relationship between slave labour and demographic dynamics analyzed by Steuart in Book I, Chapter 7 of his *Principles*: 'The Effects of Slavery upon the Multiplication and Employment of Mankind'.
2 To examine Steuart's ideas about slavery in depth, through a reconstruction of the reflections contained in Book II, Chapter 1: 'Of the reciprocal Connections between Trade and Industry'.
3 To detect the outcomes emerging on the specific issue of slavery and its possible abolition, comparing Steuart and the French and Scottish scholars' views involved in this debate.

Ancient and modern society: From slavery of men to slavery of desires

In Book I, Chapter 7 of his *Principles*, 'The Effects of Slavery upon the Multiplication and Employment of Mankind', Steuart attempts to explain how slavery influences the demographic growth and the employment of individuals in a society. His starting point is the difference between the quantity and the kind of men's desires in ancient and modern times.

In the ancient world, a sovereign could say he was satisfied with having a great army and a large population. The needs of a large population were quite limited and could be met almost exclusively through agricultural goods, then considered the main recipient of investments. The manufacturers produced artefacts and luxury goods to be exchanged with food, but this was not considered indispensable, as was demonstrated by the fact that a large number of workers were employed in the most prestigious homes rather than in the handicraft sector (I, 50).

In any case, a part of the population has to work in order to feed the wider population. The institution of slavery had this main purpose: 'if mankind be not forced to labour, they will labour for themselves only; and if they have few wants, there will be little labour' (I, 50). Actually, the institution of slavery was 'a violent method of making mankind labour' with the aim of raising food and population,[4] whatever the level of 'civilization' (I, 119):

> the barbarian peoples who lived by hunting and gathering and were often involved in wars, saved the lives of the prisoners and enslaved them, both guaranteeing their survival and satisfying the needs of the community; the same happened in 'countries where a good police prevailed', where slaves were forced to work in order to feed "both them and the idle freemen".
>
> (I, 51)

Whereas in ancient societies the secondary sector appeared as auxiliary compared with agriculture, in modern society – which Steuart identified with a 'system of trade and industry' – commerce and industry acquired an increasing importance, like the new types of work linked to them. In the past 'men were . . . forced to labour because they were slaves to others', now 'they are . . . forced to labour because they are slaves to their own wants' (I, 52)[5] (see also Sen 1995: 35). The former were slaves in the proper meaning of the term, the latter – formally free – became slaves of their wants as a result of the process of civilization.

Steuart is particularly interested in industrial and commercial activities because he believes that these processes modify the equilibrium of employment and progressively reduce the importance of agriculture. In fact, while it is true that the spontaneous products of the soil provide sufficient food to satisfy the needs of a given quantity of men in a country, it is also true that in order to increase the population and to strengthen a nation it is absolutely necessary to 'add work to the natural activity of the soil'. However, since the number of men used for farming depends on the level of development of a society, Steuart looks for a more advanced analytical view in order to explain the new social organization, though emphasizing the importance of agriculture in every type of society. Such an approach is suggested by a methodological consideration: 'it is sometimes of ill consequence to fix one's attention too much upon any one object, however important' (like that of the central role of agriculture in ancient societies) (I, 32).

From the scientific point of view this restriction could hinder a full comprehension of a new and more complicated social system.

Indeed, the surplus produced in agriculture would have no reason to exist unless it was necessary to feed the population employed in the production of handicrafts (Eagly 1961: 54), nor would artisans produce their goods to meet the needs of farmers, without receiving the food they needed:

> we may lay it down as a principle, that a farmer will not labour to produce a superfluity of grain relatively to his own consumption, unless he finds some want which may be supplied by means of that superfluity; neither will other industrious persons work to supply the wants of the farmer for any other reason than to procure subsistence, which they cannot otherwise so easily obtain.
>
> (I, 36)

Considering the development of the system of production in the society of his times, Steuart expresses concern both for the disproportionate attention to the primary sector and for the consequent neglect of 'luxurious arts'. This was a shared view. For example, David Hume regarded the production of luxury goods as a support and an impetus for agriculture:

> When a nation abounds in manufactures and mechanic arts, the proprietors of land, as well as the farmers, study agriculture as a science, and redouble their industry and attention. The superfluity, which arises from their labour, is not lost; but is exchanged with manufactures for those commodities, which men's luxury now makes them covet.
>
> (Hume 1809: 277)[6]

Since Steuart maintains his real interest is 'to treat of the political economy of *free nations only*', it is necessary to explain the forms of the transition from a society exclusively based on agriculture – and on 'slavery . . . contrary to the advancement of private industry' (I, 315; emphasis added) – to a new kind of society. In the latter, the primary and secondary sector help each other to develop, contributing to the widening of the range of desires ('slavery of desires'). The new social balance arises when 'inhabitants . . . multiply; and, according to their increase, a certain number of the whole, proportional to such superfluity of nourishment produced, . . . apply themselves to industry and to the supplying of other wants' (I, 40). As Steuart stated, this transition from one form of equilibrium to another would not be automatic. It presupposes the action of the statesman,[7] who has the task of facilitating the social conditions in which the 'reciprocal wants' increase and 'bind the society together' (I, 36), adopting 'appropriate political and economic measures' (Ege 2003: 94). As far as individuals are concerned, Steuart does not regard them as 'citizens conscious of belonging to a universal whole which is the State', but only as 'economic agents caught in the whirlpool of diversified needs and specialized work' (*ibidem*).

In such a context, defined by the statesman's intervention, the workers of the secondary sector – called 'free hands' by Steuart – increase: They buy the agricultural surplus with what they earn through the sale of handicrafts, which meets the needs of employees in agriculture and the luxury desires of the lords. 'The spirit of the times' encourages the birth of new needs and desires, producing continuous social changes and pressing the handicraft workers to freely modify their production, adapting it to the 'wants of the society' (I, 40). The term utilized by Steuart, then, has nothing to do with the 'free labour' that the Physiocrats opposed to 'slave labour', mainly employed in agriculture, and it does not suggest an abolitionist view, related to the idea of a major productivity of 'free labour'. As he clearly shows in Book II, Chapter 1 of *Principles*, Steuart analyzes this issue in a very unusual and different manner from that emerging in the debates of his time. Only in one circumstance does he seem to be closer to the other Enlightenment thinkers considered in this chapter. Nevertheless, this isolated reflection does not predominantly characterise his approach and it does not change Steuart's acceptance of slavery in the colonies.

'Industry', 'labour': The 'problem' of slavery in James Steuart

Steuart begins the chapter 'Of the reciprocal Connections between Trade and Industry' by defining the concept of 'industry'. It is 'the application to ingenious labour in a free man, in order to procure, by the means of trade, an equivalent, fit for the supplying of every want' (I, 223). Steuart is not the sole author who defines industry as 'the engine behind the movement of modern society', but unlike 'most scholars of the Enlightenment' (Kobayashi 2003: 110), he expressly distinguishes the terms 'industry' and 'labour'. Labour can be forced and, as a result, carried out by slaves, 'the *labor* still implied servility and unfreedom' (Drescher 2002: 16). By contrast, 'industry' represents a higher stage of production because the agents are acting intentionally: 'industry evoked voluntary work' (obviously this does not mean labour free of charge).

In any society, a choice can be made between two ways of applying labour: In an organization based on slave labour or in an organization based on free labour. Both systems could grant an adequate answer to the social needs and to the growth of the population (Drescher 2002: 38). However, the two forms of labour are incompatible if used in the same sector of production. The use of slaves in the same sectors of production where free workers are employed (handicraft sector) could determine distortions in competitive mechanisms, given the difference between the cost of slave labour and that of wage work. On the other hand, the use of slaves in the agricultural sector allows the labour supply for the others sectors making it more profitable for them to use wage labour there and reducing the 'employers' competition for wage labor' (Holt 1992: 32–33).

According to Steuart, the use of slaves involves lower production costs in comparison with those of wage labour for two reasons. First of all, slaves are more productive because of their loneliness and lack of family responsibilities. Secondly, the slave owners have to supply them with what is strictly necessary to their survival. 'The slaves have all their wants supplied by the master, who may keep them within the limits of sobriety' (I, 225). Conversely, wage workers (because of the needs of their families) require a greater economic commitment, leading to higher production costs. As a result, the slave owners could sell the final goods on the market at lower prices than those produced by free wage workers.

From this reasoning, we can deduce that Steuart does not even take the idea of the abolition of slavery into consideration. Rather, given its economic convenience, he seeks out a means to ensure a balance between the two types of work, without slavery becoming an obstacle to the country's industrial development; 'judicious regulations' should be adopted in order 'to confine slavery, for example, to the country; that is, to set the slaves apart for agriculture, and to exclude them from every other service of work' (I, 226).

This reinforces Steuart's idea that 'slavery and industry . . . are incompatible with one another', unless great restraints are placed on the former (I, 224). Such a restraint seems to be conceived as preservation of slavery only in the colonies, without hindering the advance of invention and industry in the mother country (Groenewegen 2001: 85; Drescher 2002: 38). Steuart definitely denies slaves the 'protection' that 'society guarantees' to European people employed in the secondary sector (Menudo 2013: 10). So, his statement that 'every political subordination should there be general and equal: no person, no class should be under a greater subordination than another' (I, 321) does not include the figure of the slave. That's not all, for 'wherever any notable advantage is found accompanying slavery, it is the duty of a modern statesman to fall upon a method of profiting by it, without wounding the spirit of European liberty' (I, 227).

Such positions are bewildering: Steuart seems to be anything but an Enlightenment theoretician. In the 'Age of Reason', intellectuals identified the persistence of slavery as one of the most important social ills. Slavery was seen as a weakness in the economic and social model and, at the same time, as an obstacle to human progress. Steuart's attitude towards the phenomenon of slavery, however, seems to lead him in the opposite direction, since he considers it a 'constitutive' element of the modern economy and tries to make it compatible with society's new ways of organizing production. Now, while Steuart's analytical position on the economic utility of slavery is not an isolated case (as shown by the harsh debates about its abolition), it is surprising to see the marginal role that he attributes to the ethical and juridical aspect of the issue. This is even more significant if we consider the alleged proximity of Steuart to Montesquieu's *Esprit des Lois*, which – on the contrary – focused on the doubtful juridical legitimacy of slavery and its ethical unacceptability. As we will see, Steuart's category of 'spirit of the people' is in fact not close to the '*esprit des lois*' of Montesquieu.

Productive inefficiency and costs of slavery

It is widely believed that Steuart had acquired a thorough knowledge of the European society of his times. As stated by Marx, he, a 'large landowner in Scotland . . . banished from Great Britain for alleged complicity in the Stuart plot and through long residence and his journeys on the Continent made himself familiar with economic conditions in various countries' (Holland, France, Spain, Italy, Germany and Flanders) (Engels 1974: 242).[8]

Yet Steuart's analysis, with particular reference to the phenomenon of slavery, does not seem to grasp either in amplitude or in depth the typical features of the debates going on in the rest of Europe. He neglects both a detailed analysis of the effects that slavery produces in the production systems in which it is used, and a careful reflection on the juridical and ethical contradictions created by the persistence of slavery in modern society. In fact, as we shall see, the 'Enlightenment theoreticians (Condorcet, Dupont de Nemours, etc.), who sided with the abolitionist cause' were committed to a careful assessment of the relationship between slavery and modern production systems (Pisanelli 2017: 68). Their first aim was to check whether slave labour was compatible with the new ways of production.

On his part, Steuart completely neglects the issue of the general incompatibility between the institution of slavery and the development of the modern systems of production, considering this question only in the limited form that we have mentioned earlier. From his point of view, the problem is not the abolition of slavery but its exclusive use in the primary sector in order to sustain the improvement of industry. Reading the chapters of *Principles* devoted to slavery, one has the impression that Steuart does not have a real awareness of a series of issues widely considered in the contemporary debate:

- The stumbling block of the institution of slavery in the increase of productivity of the modern economy.
- The inadequacy of the distinction between slave labour and free labour on the basis of the types of productive activity.
- The problem of the scarcity of slaves and their rising cost.

As far as the first aspect is concerned, one will recall that Steuart 'showed in some detail how such a society came into being and developed. . . . At first mankind lives on the spontaneous fruits of the soil; then the pressure of population and the desire for improvement lead man to "add his labour *and industry* to the natural activity of the soil" (I, 27; emphasis added)' (Meek 1958: 299–300). Therefore, he seems to be aware of the fact that the progress of society and the growth of population depend on the application of technology also in the agriculture sector. Emphasizing the role of innovations and technological applications based on the development of intellectual talent ('the application to ingenious labour'), 'he drew a distinction between cultivation for subsistence, which was typical of the feudal state, and the application of industry to the soil as found in the modern situation' (Skinner 1981: 24). Nevertheless, the use of slave labour in agriculture does not seem able to promote the innovative processes, which presuppose 'the application to ingenious labor'. Steuart therefore seems to be convinced that agriculture is fundamentally a sector characterized by a low propensity to innovate, where the increase in output can mainly be determined by the cultivation of new land (extensive agriculture).[9]

He starts from the idea that the use of slaves in agriculture could free the workers for other activities and, by lowering the pressure on the labour market, would help to keep the level of wages low. These wage levels would be acceptable to workers because of the low price of agricultural products, as guaranteed by the use of slaves. However, during the contemporary debates on slavery a totally different belief had arisen; it was not the use of slavery in agriculture that would reduce production costs and commodity prices on the market but the greater productivity of wage labour in agriculture. This increase in labour productivity would allow a low wage level, which would enable workers to purchase a greater amount of goods to satisfy their needs. Moreover, low commodity prices would favour international trade and make it possible to enter new markets.

In this regard, it is sufficient to recall what Adam Smith wrote, identifying the inefficiency of production by slaves as one of the 'major reasons . . . for the slow progress of opulence in Europe' (Salter 1996: 243).[10] According to Smith, this is true both for the primary and for the secondary sector. Such 'inefficiency' derives from the fact that slaves were not allowed to give their contribution to a more efficient reorganization of work: 'should a slave propose any improvement' in order to relieve or to shorten the workload,

> his master would be very apt to consider the proposal as the suggestion of laziness, and a desire to save his own labour at the master's expense. The poor slave, instead of reward, would probably meet with much abuse, perhaps with some punishment.
>
> (Smith 1979: II, 684)

French intellectuals committed to the abolition of slavery basically shared this approach. Dupont, introducing substantial changes to the *Réflexions sur la formation et la distribution des richesses* by Turgot, wrote: 'The slaves have no reason to carry out the work they are forced to do with intelligence and care that could ensure their success'. As a result, 'these works produce very little' (Dupont in Turgot 1914: 545). Sharing Dupont's idea, Condorcet added that slave labour costs much more than wage labour. In this regard, he recalls the example of the employment of slaves in the United States, showing that they tended to slow down the intensity of work, once they understood that any effort in the opposite direction would not achieve any improvement in their living conditions. Therefore, slave labour and wage labour were not comparable in terms of productivity (Condorcet 2009: 80).[11]

In other words, slaves lack the motivation that Steuart recognizes for men who freely choose to work: the 'self-love or a desire of ease and happiness, which prompts those who find in themselves any superiority, whether personal or political, to make use of every natural advantage' (I, 28). And also:

> Set a man to labour at so much a day, he will go on at a regular rate, and never seek to improve his method: let him be hired by the piece, he will find a thousand expedients to extend his industry. This is exactly the difference between

> the slave and the free man. From this I account for the difference between the progress of industry in ancient and modern times.
>
> (I, 258)

This awareness does not prevent Steuart from tolerating the persistence of a productive organization based on the criteria of ancient society (the colonies that exploit slaves), if it represents a 'crutch' to the economy of modern European societies.

As far as the second aspect is concerned, in his *Réflexions sur l'abolition de l'esclavage*, Condorcet opposed the idea that some types of economic activity necessarily required the employment of slaves. Even if it were true that Europeans were less resistant to the hot weather of the colonies, in any case it was not justified that the negroes must work in slavery. They could do it as wage workers with positive effects on labour productivity (Condorcet 2009: 76). Another factor to consider was the reduction in the average life expectancy of slaves, worn out by unsustainable work rhythms and ill-treatment. This would mean a further increase in costs as a result of the need to replace them frequently.

Furthermore, Steuart completely neglects the problem of the lack of slaves. According to him, 'the master . . . may . . . recruit [slaves] from abroad, or take care of the children, just as he finds it his advantage. If the latter should prove unprofitable . . . they are prevented from breeding at all'. Steuart does not particularly focus on the issue of rearing the slaves' offspring, saying 'the expences of rearing children [are] supposed to be great' (I, 225), but he expresses his preference for the importation of adult slaves ready to be employed (Drescher 2002: 31).

In the same years, other analysts seemed to be worried about the relative scarcity of slaves and, above all, about the increasing difficulties in importing them from Africa. Think, for instance, of Le Mercier de la Rivière who had denounced the 'scarcity' of Negroes (Le Mercier 1978: 109), believing that 'Africa can no longer deliver slaves' in a quantity sufficient to sustain and extend the Western production systems (Le Mercier 1978: 253–254). Le Mercier concluded (unlike Steuart) that the cost of slaves would certainly rise both because of increased demand and because of higher shipping costs.[12]

A third aspect, concerning the use of slaves only in agriculture, seems to be shared by Le Mercier and Steuart. As we have mentioned, Steuart proposed to confine the use of slave labour to agriculture in the colonies in order not to hinder the advance of innovation and industry in the mother country. Also, the Physiocrat Le Mercier, when he was Intendant of Martinique,[13] proposed a similar solution but started from a different supposition. He was worried about the use of slaves in the secondary sector since this might weaken agriculture, the most important sector for economic and social improvement. In fact, it would mean reducing the capital invested in agriculture. Steuart seems to share only part of this reasoning because of his belief that industry is the distinctive feature of the modern organization of production and that within it agriculture will play an increasingly marginal role. In some ways, this seems to reduce the affinities between Steuart and Physiocracy that some authors emphasize. According to Weulersse, for instance, both Steuart and the Physiocrats attributed a central role to agriculture and emphasized the need to move beyond its traditional organization: 'He had no doubts that his plans required the destruction of traditional agriculture. In this respect, Steuart displayed one of his numerous affinities with the Physiocrats' (Weulersse 1910: 2, 147–148). The removal of the excessive apportionment of lands and the spread of innovations were essential in order to achieve a 'capitalistic' organization of production (Perelman 2000: 148).

Of course, agriculture plays an essential role in Steuart's thought because it determines demographic growth. But, moving his attention to the new type of society and the features of 'industry and [the] commercial system', Steuart attributes to industry a propulsive and progressive role, leaving agriculture with an auxiliary role, serving the development of the secondary and tertiary sectors.

The marginal role of the ethical and juridical aspect in Steuart's analysis of slavery

As mentioned, Steuart completely neglects the ethical and juridical aspect of the issue of slavery, as his comparison between the conditions of slaves and wage workers shows. From this point of view, his attitude is in some ways astonishing. According to him, the status of the slave is preferable to that of the wage worker: Slaves get more advantages from their relationship with the masters than wage workers can do from their relationship with the 'statesman'. This would be true because 'the slaves have all their particular masters, who can take better care of them, than any statesman can take of the industrious freemen; because their liberty is an obstacle to his care' (I, 225). Therefore, Steuart does not deal with the issue of legitimacy of a situation that extends the property right from things to man. In order to grasp Steuart's distance from the debate of his times, it suffices to recall the views of Montesquieu, Condorcet, and Smith.

Condorcet defined slavery as a crime even worse than theft: The slave was deprived of all the material wealth he needed in order to live and that he had produced with his own work. In addition, every right, including the freedom to dispose of his own time and his person, was taken away from him. This injustice was not only tolerated but also explicitly foreseen by legislators. In fact, even though the idea of justice was at a higher level than the exigencies of 'commercial prosperity' and of the increase in 'national wealth', it was systematically subordinated to the priority of economic interests at the expense of men who had the misfortune of not being able to be economically autonomous or of being prisoners of war.

As we know, Smith pointed out the considerable difficulties existing with reference to this specific aspect because the abolition of slavery might appear in contradiction with the property rights recognized by law. As a result, a sovereign intervention aimed at abolishing the right to own slaves (considered part of capital) might be interpreted as an abuse of power against the masters (see *LJ* of

16/02/1763), although the right to own men denies the inviolable right to freedom. In order to resolve this contradiction, Smith placed the right to freedom among the natural rights of man and right to property among the acquired rights (see Smith 1978; Haakonssen 1981; Salter 1996).

Since natural rights are principles of a higher level than acquired rights, Smith recognized that the right to liberty had a higher rank than the right to property. While from a theoretical point of view, the problem seemed to be resolved, the fact of its real abolition remained, given that slavery continued to exist. Its abolition was hindered by several factors.

1 On the one hand, the opposition of the slave owners, who complained about an unacceptable economic loss.
2 On the other, the predisposition of man to exercise his power over other human beings. Among the Scottish Enlightenment thinkers, both Adam Smith and John Millar point out this psychological aspect of human nature, in their main works:

> Slavery therefore has been universal in the beginnings of society, and the love of domination and authority over others will probably make it perpetual.
>
> (Smith 1978: 187)

> The pride of man makes him love to domineer, and nothing mortifies him so much as to be obliged to condescend to persuade his inferiors. Wherever the law allows it, and the nature of the work can afford it, therefore, he will generally prefer the service of slaves to that of freemen.
>
> (Smith 1979: I, 388)

> It is difficult to ascertain the degree of authority which, from the principles of justice and humanity, we are, in any situation, permitted to assume over our fellow-creatures. But the fact admits of no question, that people have commonly been disposed to use their power in such a manner as appears most conducive to their interest, and most agreeable to their predominant passions.
>
> (Millar 1806: 246)

> The possession of power is too agreeable to be easily relinquished.
>
> (Millar 1806: 255)

Furthermore, there are two other noteworthy reasons:

3 The difficulty of overcoming a cultural attitude socially established and accepted. Once again, Millar's words are illustrative:

> This institution [the slavery], however inconsistent with the rights of humanity, however pernicious and contrary to the true interest of the master, has

> generally remained in those countries where it was once established, and has been handed down from one generation to another, during all the successive improvements of society, in knowledge, arts, and manufactures.
>
> (Millar 1806: 256)

4 The difficulty of introducing appropriate laws in order to abolish slavery.

In the work of Steuart, these last two topics appear with reference to the 'spirit of the people', seen as the set of 'manners, government, and morals . . . formed by history': It determines the ethical, political, and economic balance of a nation (Ramos & Mirowski 2011: 15). From his historical perspective, Steuart acquires the idea that each political economy must necessarily be different because 'the variety of forms of government, laws, climate, and manners' tends to diversify 'different countries' and, in each of them, 'the distribution of property, subordination of classes, genius of people' (Ramos & Mirowski 2011: 20). Moreover, he insists on the fact that there is nothing that changes as quickly as the laws of the people (I, 9).

In the literature, the 'spirit of the people' has often been compared to the '*esprit des lois*' by Montesquieu, emphasizing that 'the influence of Montesquieu's thought is evident throughout his work, with respect to both general principles and numerous specific points of analysis' (Hirschman 1977: 81; Cunningham 1891: 84; Kobayashi 2003: 105). After all, this was inevitable, since Montesquieu's approach 'quickly became a hallmark of the Scottish Enlightenment' (Guenther 2011: 453). But, in their reflection on slavery, a radical difference emerges between Montesquieu and Steuart.

Montesquieu recognized the existence of countries and regions (for instance, the American plantations colonized by Europeans), where climate was such as to prevent a spontaneous commitment and a natural application to work,[14] if not solicited by the use of force and the threat of punishments. Nevertheless, he believed that Enlightened societies could not be organized following 'the law of the strongest', but they should adopt laws able to balance relationships among men, strengthening their positive propensities and limiting their vicious attitudes. In the specific case of slavery, the legislator should feel the duty to remove laws that justified the inequalities amongst men as regards climatic or environmental factors. He pointed out that while it is true that the '*esprit des lois*' can produce different political organizations and constitutions in every nation, slavery has to be seen as unacceptable in every constitution. In fact, it is to be understood, without any exception, as the 'sick fruit' of bad laws.[15]

In my opinion, Steuart is doubly mistaken in his approach to Montesquieu's '*esprit des lois*'. First of all, he misunderstands the real intention of the French author about the relation between slavery and climate, when he attacks him:

> If you abstract from . . . natural advantages, all nations are upon an equal footing as to trade. Industry and labour are no properties attached to place, any more than economy and sobriety. This proposition may be called in question, upon the principle of M. de Montesquieu, who deduces the origins of many laws, customs and even religions, from the influence of climate . . . but in my method of treating this subject, I do not suppose that these causes are ever to

> be allowed to produce their natural and immediate effects, when such effects would be followed by a political inconvenience.
>
> (I, 363)

Steuart seems to stumble upon the same error of interpretation of many other authors (both of his and our times) who have not grasped Montesquieu's ironic criticism of those explanations that linked slavery to the peculiar climatic conditions of Africa.[16]

Second, Steuart utilizes a particular interpretation of the broad vision of Montesquieu. His concept of the 'spirit of the people', seen as a justification for the relativity of political and institutional structures, is related more to the Western world than to humankind as a whole, since Steuart generally talks about the 'spirit of the people' with reference to the history of Europe, both in terms of political organizations ('free modern governments', 'spirit of European liberty') and in terms of economic structures ('modern system of trade and industry', 'free, industrious and laborious Europeans') (Kobayashi 2003: 109).

From this point of view, with this Eurocentric vision overlapping his own particular conception of 'space in the economy' (Correia da Silva 2004: 4), one may be able to accept the hypothesis that Steuart had adopted the view of a sharp 'geographic separation between freedom and slavery' (Drescher 2002: 19), 'acknowledging [that] free labor superiority at home did not require advocating it abroad' (Drescher 2002: 16).

In Steuart's work, there is a passage that seems to suggest a different interpretation. He states, 'freedom itself, *imposed* upon a people groaning under the greatest slavery, will not make them happy, unless it is made to undergo certain modifications, relative to their established habits' (I, 13). Nevertheless, he does not develop this statement. He does not specify either that the slaves' 'habits' have been 'established' by their masters (not by themselves), nor that the 'habits' and the 'cultures' of the lands from which the slaves come are determined by the production needs of colonizers.

In *Principles*, there is no trace of a critical assessment of the institution of slavery, nor – of course – of possible abolitionist policies. Essentially, Steuart does not regard slavery as a problem to solve. When he talks about overcoming slavery, hoping to move from the 'feudal system' to the 'freedom in government', he does it – once again – with reference to the events typical of European states, by analyzing situations where the constraints of subordination are already noticeably weakened (I, 13).

His view of the future does not seem to include the emancipation of the slaves, either as a means to recognize a right unjustly denied to the enslaved populations (principles ruled by Reason) or as a result of the spread of Enlightenment in Europe.

Conclusions

With reference to slavery, many of Steuart's contemporary authors used economic explanations in order to support the abolitionist cause, giving them more chance of success with the public (in particular, among the agricultural entrepreneurs). This kind of explanation might also have been more effective in supporting philosophical, ethical, and humanitarian arguments, since the authors were aware that their abolitionist efforts would meet strong resistance in their society. Thus the demonstration was needed that slavery represented a brake on economic growth and a hindrance to the construction of a progressive social order (Pisanelli 2018: 169).

Steuart, too, recognized that this social change would have involved profound cultural and institutional transformations ('spirit of the people'). Nevertheless, he placed more trust in a 'statesman' with 'a particular talent' than in the awareness of the citizens who had to promote the economic and social transformations because of his belief that 'by properly conducting . . . nothing is impossible'. According to Steuart, the statesman was supposed to be able to lead citizens to 'approve . . . the scheme that is the most conducive to their interest and prosperity' (I, 15). However, even this general principle is not used by Steuart in relation to the specific case of slavery and its possible abolition. The reader who looks into his *Principles* in search of a more profound link between Steuart and the other Enlightenment intellectuals on these topics will be disappointed. Such dissatisfaction stems especially from the presence in his work of theoretical insights of a certain interest, which – in the end – are not adequately developed:

1 Steuart announces the inevitable overcoming of slavery in the proper sense of the word ('slavery to misery') and its replacement with 'slavery to desires', determined by the continuous increase in needs ('desire effect') as a result of the growing wealth ('slavery to opulence'). Nevertheless, he does not dwell on the reasons for its persistence in modern society. He merely refers to the 'spirit of the people' and the role of the 'statesman', but he does not make a detailed and convincing analysis on this issue.
2 Steuart's reflections on slavery pay absolutely no attention to its ethical and legal aspects. This should not surprise the reader, since – also in the case of the debate on luxury – Steuart is very clear: 'my subject is too extensive of itself to admit of being confounded with the doctrine either of morals, or of government, however closely these may appear connected with it' (I, 42).[17] This is confirmed by his general opinion about the 'duty' of 'a scientist': He has not 'to make ethical judgements on [a] subject, as such judgements would disallow his propositions as those which "must be assented to universally" (I, xiii)' (see Kobayashi 2003: 106; Menudo 2013: 3). Nevertheless, if one compares his position with the deep analysis of slavery that other authors of his time had put forward, one finds it seriously lacking. As we mentioned, the literature emphasizes the influence of Montesquieu on Steuart's theory of 'the spirit of the people', but this interpretation turns out to be inadequate because of the profound difference between Steuart's view and Montesquieu's '*esprit des lois*'.
3 Finally, Steuart grasps the incompatibility between slavery and the industrial system, but this insight is not adequately explored. On the one hand, by confining slavery to the primary sector, he does not perceive its negative effect on capitalist production processes, as the other Enlightenment thinkers

do instead; on the other hand, he seems to consider agriculture as a sector with a low propensity to innovate.

In my opinion, the third point represents the most serious weakness in Steuart's work. However, other than that, the general impression is that Steuart proceeds, in a confused way, by overlapping two levels of analysis. On a general level he clearly distinguishes the economic and social systems that progressively develop over time, identifying their defining features using a valid theoretical approach (Marx 1859). However, he does not correctly reconstruct the relationships between the various sectors of production and the causes of their endogenous changes. The statesman is often considered a *deus ex machina* used in order to solve problems whose solutions depend on the endogenous dynamics of the economic system. This attitude emerges also with reference to slavery. Steuart perceived that it was a feature of an obsolete economic and social system, correctly analyzing its usefulness for the genesis and development of the modern economy. He was also aware that slavery would be overcome in the industrial and commercial society, but, surprisingly, he hypothesized and supported the persistence of slavery in the agricultural sector in modern society (partially based on the colonial system), neglecting the economic factors widely discussed by his contemporaries. The latter, beyond the juridical and ethical reasons, were pushing for the use of free labour and the definitive elimination of slavery.

Notes

1 Actually, Schumpeter was not very generous with Smith, either. However, this weakness in Steuart contrasts with the good opinion that Marx expressed of him, in his *Critique of Political Economy*, defining him as 'the first Briton who elaborated the general system of bourgeois economics' (Marx 1859: 65). According to Marx, Steuart was 'more firmly on historical ground' (Marx 1859: 267) than the other 18th-century scholars (Meek 1967: 7). For Marx's appreciation of Steuart's approach, see also Sen (1995: 187–188).
2 On this, see also the reference to Strangeland 1966 in Gislain (2003: 169).
3 On the same page, following Chamley's indications, Ege introduces the interesting question of the fundamental role that Christianity is thought to have played in the abolition of slavery, according to Steuart and Hegel. On this occasion we do not have the opportunity to go into the subject in depth. However, it would be sufficient to look at Poivre's commitment to abolishing slavery. The hopes he placed in Christianity were disappointed, since it allowed only the abolition of the slave trade, not of slavery itself (Pisanelli 2018: 143–149).
4 The sole alternative would be charity: Farmers could voluntarily take on the task of producing a surplus in order to feed the unemployed poor (Gislain 2003: 171).
5 International trade involves a general improvement 'of the world . . . by rendering the inhabitants of one country industrious in order to supply the wants of another, without any prejudice to themselves' (I, 157–158; cf. also Skinner 1963: 441–442).
6 On the role of luxuries, during the Enlightenment an intense debate led to several orientations. Voltaire and Montesquieu maintained that luxuries would encourage progress (Pisanelli 2017: 68); Rousseau, absolutely opposed to their spread, was afraid that the over-complex needs determined by the civilization process pushed the individual to become estranged from himself and from his authenticity (Gioia 2016: 48–51). An inquiry into these two aspects could be made with the opportune theoretical mediations

(as Smith did, for example, in his *Theory of Moral Sentiments*, discussing 'Of the corruption of our moral sentiments', 2004: I.iii.3, 72–77).
On Steuart's contributions to the debates about luxury consumption, see Ramos (2011).

7 Generally, 'Steuart uses the term with the meaning of an enlightened or to-be-policy maker interested only in the public good' (Hirschman 1977: 85; note e).

8 As Engels states in the second *Preface* in 1885, Marx wrote Chapter 10 of the section regarding the economy ('From the "Critical History"') (Engels 1974: 7). About Steuart's travels on the continent, see also Kobayashi (2003: 105) and Hirschman (1977: 81).

9 This view was shared – in very different analytical contexts – by thinkers like Malthus (see his *An Essay on the Principle Population*, book I, Chapter 1: "Statement of the subject. Ratios of the increase of population and food", p. 8) and Ricardo (see his *Principles of Political Economy and Taxation,* Chapter 2: 'On Rent', especially p. 227 and Chapter 32: 'Mr. Malthus's Opinions on Rent', especially p. 529).

10 On Smith's reflections about the 'inefficiency' of production by slaves, see Pisanelli (2018: 168–181) and Coutinho (2016).

11 On the distinction between *produit net* and *produit gros* and about the misunderstanding that led slavery to be considered more productive than free labour, see Condorcet (2009: 80).

12 On these aspects, see Pisanelli (2017: 75–78).

13 The king called on Le Mercier to administer the colony of Martinique (1759–1764) and to bring it to an acceptable level of productivity, in order to guarantee a larger financial contribution to the coffers of the crown.

14 On this, see also Hume's attempt to explain the typical inertia of the tropical countries: 'It is probable that one cause of this phenomenon is the warmth and the equality of weather in the torrid zone, which render clothes and houses less requisite for the inhabitants, and thereby remove, in part, that necessity, which is the great spur to industry and invention' (Hume 1809: 284).

15 'Bad laws having made lazy men, they have been reduced to slavery because of their laziness' (Montesquieu 2005: 298). On slavery as the result of bad laws, see also Voltaire (1774: 101), Condorcet (2009: 70–74), Poivre (1768: 134).

16 On such misinterpretations, see Biondi (1979: 138–159). This misguided conception has recently been re-proposed by D. Felice in his *Introduzione a Montesquieu* (2013).

17 On the complete separation between ethics and economics in his analyses, although Steuart was 'a devout Christian', see Sen (1995: 19).

Bibliography

Biondi, C. (1979), *Ces esclaves sont des hommes. Lotta abolizionista e letteratura negrofila nella Francia del Settecento*, Pisa: Editrice Libreria Goliardica.

Chamley, P. (1962), Sir James Steuart: inspirateur de la *Théorie Générale de Lord Keynes, Revue d'économie politique*, 72: 303–313.

Condorcet, J.A.N.-C. (1847–1849), Lettre aux auteurs du Journal de Paris, in *Œuvres de Condorcet*, vol. 1, Paris: Firmin Didot Frères.

———. (2009), *Réflexions sur l'esclavage des nègres*, Paris: Éditions Flammarions.

Correia da Silva, J. (2004), *Space in Economics: A Historical Perspective*, Porto: University of Porto.

Cossa, L. (1892), *Introduzione allo studio dell'economia politica*, Milan: Hoepli.

Coutinho, M. (2016), Silva Lisboa on Free Trade and Slave Labor: The Fate of Liberalism in a Colonial Country, in A. Mendes Cunha & C.E. Suprinyak (eds.), *The Political Economy of Latin American Independence*, London: Routledge: 58–80.

Cunningham, W. (1891), The Progress of Economic Doctrine in England in the Eighteenth Century, *Economic Journal*, 1: 84–86.

Drescher, S. (2002), *The Mighty Experiment: Free Labor versus Slavery in British Emancipation*, Oxford: Oxford University Press.
Dupont De Nemours, P.S. (1914), Réflexions sur la Formation et la Distribution des Richesses, in A.-R.-J. Turgot (ed.), *Œuvres de Turgot et documents le concernant*, vol. 2, Paris: Librairie Félix Alcan.
Eagly, R.V. (1961), Sir James Steuart and the 'Aspiration Effect', *Economica*, 28: 53–61.
Ege, R. (2003), The New Interpretation of Steuart by Paul Chamley, in R. Tortajada (ed.), *The Economics of James Steuart*, London: Routledge: 84–101.
Engels, F. (1974), Anti-Dühring, in K. Marx & F. Engels (eds.), *Opere*, vol. 25, Rome: Editori Riuniti.
Felice, D. (2013), *Introduzione a Montesquieu*, Bologna: CLUEB.
Gioia, V. (2016), Diseguaglianze e sviluppo. Le radici antiche di un problema attuale, in B. Giovanola (ed.), *Etica pubblica, giustizia sociale, diseguaglianze*, Roma: Carocci.
Gislain, J.J. (2003), James Steuart: Economy and Population, in R. Tortajada (ed.), *The Economics of James Steuart*, London: Routledge: 169–185.
Groenewegen, P. (2001), Thomas Carlyle, 'the Dismal Science', and the Contemporary Political Economy of Slavery, *History of Economics Review*, 34: 74–94.
Guenther, M. (2011), A Peculiar Silence: The Scottish Enlightenment, Political Economy, and the Early American Debates over Slavery, *Atlantic Studies*, 8(4): 447–483.
Haakonssen, K. (1981), *The Science of a Legislator*, Cambridge: Cambridge University Press.
Hirschman, A. (1977), *Passions and Interests*, Princeton, NJ: Princeton University Press.
Holt, T. (1992), *The Problem of Freedom: Race, Labor, and Politics in Jamaica and Britain, 1832–1938*, Baltimore: Johns Hopkins University Press.
Hume, D. (1809), Of Commerce, in *Essays and Treatises on Several Subjects in Two Volumes: Essays, Moral, Political, and Literacy*, vol. 1, London: James Clarke for T. Cadell.
Kobayashi, O. (2003), On the Method of Sir James Steuart's *Principles of Political Œconomy*, in R. Tortajada (ed.), *The Economics of James Steuart*, London: Routledge: 102–120.
Le Mercier, P.P. (de La Rivière). (1978), *Mémoire sur la Martinique. 8 Septembre 1762*, in L. P. May (ed.), Paris: Centre National de la Recherche Scientifique.
Marx, K. (1859), A contribution to the *Critique of Political Economy*, Chicago: Charles H. Kerr & Co, 1904.
Meek, R.L. (1958), The Economics of Control Prefigured by Sir James Steuart, *Science and Society*, 22(4): 289–305.
———. (1967), The Rehabilitation of Sir James Steuart, in *Economics and Ideology and Other Essays: Studies in the Development of Economic Thought*, London: Chapman & Hall Ltd: 3–17.
Menudo, J.M. (2013), Sir James Steuart's Theory of Justice, *Économies et sociétés. Série PE*, 49: 1659–1679.
Mill, J.S. (1870), *Principles of Political Economy with Some of Their Applications to Social Philosophy*, vol. 1, New York: D. Appleton and Company.
Millar, J. (1806), *The Origin of the Distinction of Ranks: Or, an Inquiry into the Circumstances Which Give Rise to Influence and Authority, in the Different Members of Society*, Edinburgh: William Blackwood-Longman, Hurst, Rees, & Orme.
Montesquieu, C.L. de Secondat (de). (2005), The Spirit of Laws, in *Œuvres complètes*, vol. 1, New Jersey: The Lawbook Exchange, Ltd.
Perelman, M. (2000), *The Invention of Capitalism: Secret History of Primitive Accumulation*, Durham: Duke University Press.

Pisanelli, S. (2017), Political Power vs 'Natural Laws': Physiocracy and Slavery, *History of Economic Thought and Policy*, 1: 67–85.

———. (2018), *Condorcet et Adam Smith. Réformes économiques et progrès social au siècle des Lumières*, Paris: Classiques Garnier.

Poivre, P. (1768), *Voyage d'un philosophe ou observations sur les mœurs et les arts des peuples de l'Afrique, de l'Asie et de l'Amérique*, Maastricht: Yverdon.

Rambaud, J. (1889), *Histoire des doctrines économiques*, vol. 1, Paris: L. Larose-A. Cote.

Ramos, A. (2011), Luxury, Crisis and Consumption: Sir James Steuart and the Eighteenth-Century Luxury Debate, *History of Economics Review*, 53: 55–72.

Ramos, A. & Mirowski, P. (2011), A Universal Scotland of the Mind: Steuart and Smith on the Need for a Political Economy, *Poroi*, 7(1): 3–44.

Salter, J. (1996), Adam Smith on Slavery, *History of Economic Ideas*, 4(1–2): 225–251.

Schumpeter, J.A. (2003), *Storia dell'analisi economica*, vol. 1, Torino: Boringhieri.

Sen, R.S. (1995), *The Economics of Sir James Steuart*, London: G. Bell & Sons Ltd.

Skinner, A.S. (1963), Sir James Steuart: International Relations, *Economic History Review*, 15: 438–450.

———. (1981), Sir James Steuart: Author of a System, *Scottish Journal of Political Economy*, 28(1): 20–42.

Smith, A. (1978), *Lectures on Jurisprudence*, Oxford: Clarendon Press.

———. (1979), *An Inquiry into the Nature and Causes of the Wealth of Nations*, Oxford: Clarendon Press.

———. (2004), *La Teoria dei Sentimenti Morali*, Milan: Bur Rizzoli.

Strangeland, C.E. (1966), *Pre-Malthusian Doctrines of Population*, New York: A.M. Kelley.

Voltaire, F.M.A. (1774), Questions sur l'Encyclopédie par des amateurs, in *Collection complètes des Œuvres de Mr De*, vol. 23, Genève: n.p.

Wakefield, E.G. (1929), *A Letter from Sydney and Other Writings on Colonization*, New York: Everyman Library.

Weulersse, G. (1910), *Le Mouvement physiocratique en France*, vol. 2, Paris: Félix Alcan.

4 Beyond Montesquieu

Scottish institutional legal thought and Steuart's spirit of the people

Aida Ramos[1]

Introduction

Sir James Steuart's concept of the Spirit of the People, a people's culture as expressed through their 'morals, government, and manners', is a unique aspect of his *Principles of Political Economy* that is absent from later economic treatises in English (10).[2] Steuart uses the 'spirit of the people' to contextualize and analyze a people's economic development and serve as a guide to the formation of the best policies to bring about a stable and satisficing outcome for a people. Studying the 'spirit of the people' is essential to both the economist and the statesman to comprehend how the current conditions in which people live came to be and the extent to which they can be bettered. Thus 'spirit' should form and inform the economic policy and the practice of political economy.

Steuart's historical method and historical consciousness in his use of the 'spirit of the people' has been recognized, particularly in Kobayashi (1999) and Skinner (1966b, 1962: 19), and attention has been given to its historical-evolutionary rather than mechanistic analysis of institutions and society in Caboret (2001) and Stettner (1945). Skinner and Kobayashi, as do several others such as Redman (1996), attribute the creation of the 'spirit of the people' mainly to Montesquieu's *Spirit of the Laws*. However, they also note that Steuart was steeped in the study of history while at university at Edinburgh. While Skinner further acknowledges a connection between Steuart's method and the contemporary study of law as a social science (1962: 19), he does not then explore how Scots law was taught and analyzed. Attributing the origins of the 'spirit of the people' to Montesquieu's influence alone elides the intellectual culture of Scottish legal study that fostered the historical approach and consideration of local approaches previous to Montesquieu's publication in 1748. The similar historical emphases found in the works of Steuart, David Hume, Adam Ferguson, John Millar, and Lord Kames are embedded in the methods of Scots legal thought. The goal of this chapter is to further contextualize Steuart's thought by examining the striking similarity between Scottish legal thought regarding custom and Steuart's use of the concept of the 'spirit of the people'.

I do not deny Montesquieu's influence; he is cited throughout *Principles*, and both use the word 'spirit' to speak of collective characteristics of human communities, and both emphasize differences in nations correlating to differences in conditions. However, Steuart's spirit does not depend upon geography and climate but is formed in history, and, as Robert Urquhart (1999) comments, is more dynamic than Montesquieu's. Spirit causes change and can itself change over time. Noboru Kobayashi (1999) has noted that the ways in which Steuart uses the spirit concept differently are innovations upon Montesquieu and are partially inspired by David Hume. However, Steuart's spirit is also influenced, I argue, by a common source within Scottish intellectual life, which also partially explains Montesquieu's warm reception amongst the Scottish literati.

One can see that Steuart's approach to the law and its application is the same as his approach to principles and their application in political economy. He comments to David Hume on November 10, 1767 that laws in general:

> ever have been and ever must be changing according to circumstances; and a law which is made this day must be as good and solid a law as any one which has subsisted for a thousand years. Nor are we to imagine that our ancestors had any more right to make laws and regulations for us, than we have to alter them and substitute others in their place.
>
> (in Burton 1849: 175–176)

Steuart remained consistent in this viewpoint when applying the methods of his legal study and Scots law to his study of economics and economic policy.

My purpose in this chapter is thus to demonstrate that Steuart is influenced by the treatment of custom, history, and adaptation in Scottish legal thought, which is the same as his treatment of the 'spirit of the people'. Key to this inquiry are the 17th- and 18th-century works referred to in Scots law as institutional writing, compendia of Scots law used for reference and instruction. Steuart studied the major institutional texts at Edinburgh from the late 1720s until he passed the bar in 1735. By exploring the similarities between the two, I demonstrate that Steuart applies the methods and practice from Scots law of how one is to analyze the development and conditions of any community and navigate different circumstances to arrive at an appropriate judgment into his method of political economy.

The institutional authors, and Steuart's familiarity with their work, are presented in Section 2. The dual role of custom/spirit in the institutional authors' views of the evolution of law and court decisions, as well as evidence of the institutional method in Scots law practice in the literature referred to as the 'practicks' is explored in Section 3. How Steuart utilized institutional views on custom and adaptation in *Principles* is demonstrated in Section 4. Concluding thoughts on the dynamism in both sets of writings are presented in Section 5.

Scottish legal thought and education: The institutional influence

While much attention has been paid to jurisprudence and political economy, as in the works of Knud Haakonssen, very little attention has been paid to Scottish legal thought in its instruction and practice and its influence on political economy. With the exception of Menudo (2013), none of the literature on law and economics has focused on Steuart, despite the fact that it was the focus of his study and imperative to his intended career as a politician. Therefore it is necessary to consider Steuart's intellectual background in the law. He came from a family long distinguished in Scottish legal circles. His grandfather was the Lord Advocate under Queen Anne, his father was the solicitor general and a minister of Parliament, and his Dalrymple ancestors included a number of jurists, the most notable being Viscount Stair (Skinner 1966a). However there is more to Steuart's connection to the law than his pedigree. His persistent and consistent view of the formation of laws and principles and how they are to be changed or applied according to circumstances, and methods regarding the use of custom in comprehending laws and their application are the same as the institutional writers. An exploration of Steuart's legal education and contemporary Scottish legal theory reveals a common intellectual culture regarding custom and thus provides a likely source for the methods he advocates in *Principles* for studying political economy and forming appropriate policy.

Scots law and institutional writing

English law and Scots law are two different systems that differ in their views of what law is based upon and how decisions are made. While English Common Law is based upon precedent, Scots law is influenced by a variety of sources, including Roman law, canon law, formal and informal custom, statutes, and prior decisions, and focuses on adaptation to circumstances over time. Collections of Scots law were slower to appear in print than those of English Common Law. This changed in the 17th century with the emergence of institutional writing, named for its reliance on the structure of Justinian's *Institutes* and intended for instruction and reference.[3]

James Dalrymple, Viscount Stair, great uncle of Steuart, published the first institutional work, *The Institutes of the Laws of Scotland* (1681). Following Justinian's outline, he delineates both Scottish legal principles and Scottish legal practice. George Mackenzie's *The Institutes of Laws of Scotland* (1684), which was based on Stair but contains a slightly different substructure, was the second institutional work and was followed by Lord Bankton's *Institute* in 1753. John Erskine's (1773) *An Institute of the Laws of Scotland,* based on the structure of Mackenzie, is considered to be the last major institutional work of the 18th century.[4] The works of Stair and Erskine are considered to be the most authoritative in modern Scots law and are still used to argue modern cases (Cairns 2000; Cairns 1983: 94; Walker 1982: 25–26).

The institutional works contain similar arguments and objects. While they vary in including, as Stair did, an introduction on natural law, all of them discuss the development of the Scots law from Roman civil law and canon law and adaptations to Scottish circumstance and accepted legal custom. They then discuss the application of the law in Scottish practice. Thus institutional writing was invaluable for the legal education of future jurists and public administrators.

Steuart's legal education

When Steuart was enrolled, law students at Edinburgh took courses in four areas: Universal history, which also included Roman antiquities, Roman law, and Scots law. These were useful for passage of the bar, which required an oral examination and a thesis on some aspect of the Roman law. Courses were also available in public law and the law of nature and nations, although these were not as popular. Although not needed for bar passage until after the 1740s, knowledge of Scots law was necessary for actual practice and understanding one's property rights. The Roman law class consisted of a two-course sequence comprised of 50 lectures on Justinian's *Institutes* and 100 lectures on Justinian's *Digest*. The Scots law courses used institutional works as their textbooks, and lectures consisted of the professor's commentary on these texts. Legal humanism, the study of Roman law in the context of Roman social, political, and legal life and institutions, was the dominant method of study of the institutional writers, and at the universities of Leyden and Utrecht that Scottish students most frequented and that their professors had trained in previous to the establishment of law curricula in the Scottish universities. Legal humanism thus easily became standard in the Edinburgh law curriculum (Cairns & Macqueen 2013: 3; Emerson 2016: 10, 111–113).

Steuart studied law at Edinburgh under Alexander Bayne, the first chair in civil or Roman law, and studied constitutional history with Charles Mackie (Skinner 1966a). According to Bayne's (1731, 1726) published notes, he used Stair and Mackenzie as his course's main textbooks. His lectures closely followed the outline of Mackenzie's *Institutions* with his added commentary on the institutes and new topics, and he required students to reference Justinian and Stair. His commentary is derivative of both Stair and Mackenzie and shows a unified approach to the study and application of the law. Bayne's discourse on the development of Scots law, published in 1726 and thus close to the time Steuart matriculated, stresses the importance of studying the Roman law because 'the *Spirit* of that Law . . . shines forth in our Law' (151; emphasis added).

Steuart spent much time in his courses immersed in the Roman law as a means of understanding the development of the Scots law and the laws of other nations. Intriguingly Steuart's nephew also says of his uncle's time at Edinburgh that he 'There taught and studied the Roman and Scoch [sic] Law' (Buchan 1787).[5] The Steuart literature has not previously mentioned that he taught law. This may mean tutoring other students or it was meant to be in the next sentence where Buchan mentions that Steuart had "occasional" tutoring from Hercules Lindsey, later Buchan's law professor at Glasgow. In addition to the institutional writers, Steuart had great familiarity with Justinian's works. He successfully passed his oral examination on Justinian's principles of restitution and published his thesis in 1735 (Buchan 1787). His thesis topic is unknown, but it was common practice to write on the same aspect of Roman law on which one had been orally examined.[6]

Steuart's further training at Leyden and Utrecht is also connected to Scottish legal theory, as the major institutional writers all studied at the Dutch universities. Dutch law similarly had its foundations in the Roman law adapted to Dutch needs and circumstances. The contemporary law textbooks most used in the Netherlands were those of Johann Heineccius and Tursellinus, both legal humanists who taught on Roman law and its adaptation in Dutch legal practice.[7] The student notes from John Millar's law courses on Heineccius reveal he used the same method of studying the law by understanding its evolution through history and its need for adjustment in application. Millar, reflecting on Heineccius, stressed that there are 'different systems in different countries from different circumstances at the same time [and] similar from similarity of character and situation' (1794: 1). While the Roman law is 'the groundwork of our reasoning and opinions', it is to be considered as a guide of 'written reason' rather than the sole authority in Scotland (1794: 12).

Steuart had great familiarity with the institutional and Dutch approach to the law, its development, and social change that was commonplace in contemporary Scottish intellectual life. The approach accepts that law contains many sources and that dynamic adaptation of general rules to specific circumstances is required. The dynamism of Scots law, due to the importance placed on custom in understanding of the law and decision making, is another common element between institutional methods and those in Steuart's *Principles*.

Custom and adaptation in institutional thought

Steuart's 'spirit of the people' is a multivaried thing: It both causes laws to be formed and requires changes in how one applies particular policies. Specific outcomes of particular actions depend upon the 'spirit of the people' rather than economic principles alone. This concept has antecedents in institutional legal writing, study, and practice in 17th- and 18th-century Scotland.

Custom in institutional thought

While all of the institutional texts first discuss the evolution of Scots law from the influence of Roman law, they also stress that Roman law is neither the only foundation nor authoritative source of the Scots law. Custom, also referred to as consuetude or a practice that continues to be in use, is recognized as a major formative source of the Scots law. The Roman law, they argue, was in some cases adapted to local Scottish practice, and in others is used when Scottish custom is deficient to settle a particular matter. Stair is clear that custom is one of the most important factors in the formation of Scots law: 'we are ruled in the first place, by our ancient and immemorial Customs, which may be called our Common Law' (1681: 12). MacKenzie says that Scotland adopted the Roman law as their own civil law, 'except where our own law or customs have receded from it' (1681: 3). Bayne stresses that the Roman and feudal laws, 'we have accommodated to the Genius and Manners of our Country', and to the needs of Scottish society, with a stress on adaptation to particular circumstance (1731: 6–7).

The *Oxford English Dictionary* defines consuetude as both 'custom, usage, habit (Chiefly in Scottish use)', and as 'Custom recognized as having legal force; the unwritten law of custom; use and wont' (2018). Institutional writing uses both definitions. Customs are practices or habits of thought that caused a law to form but are also equally be part of informal laws that are unwritten but accepted in a locality. According to Stair, consuetude establishes not only equity but also different property regimes: 'By this law is our primogeniture, and all degrees of succession' (1681: 10). Customs thus being 'anterior to any statute and not comprehended in any, as being more solemn and sure than these' are not necessarily to be found in the written law (*ibidem*).

Because custom exists previous to the law, according to Stair, some legislative authority is required to formalize custom into law. Using Emerson's phrase, Stair considered laws to be 'customs given sanction by those in power' (2016: 113). However, to Mackenzie, Erskine, and Bankton, the source of authority for custom is its established usage. Erskine lectured that 'consuetude makes law from the tacit consent of the People, which cannot here be alledged' (1787: 4). Customs gained their authority not through legislative dictates but through consistency, reasonableness, and long use. Thus customs had legal power because they were known, accepted, and considered appropriate by the community. The institutional writers may have disagreed on the source of the authority of custom, but they agreed on the influence of custom as a major source of the law and a force to change law.

Adaptation in institutional thought

Cairns (1983) notes that institutional writing was strongly influenced by sixteenth century humanism, which:

> demonstrated that Roman law was not immutable or a form of natural law, but rather was a law developed by and for a specific people. This resulted in the realisation that laws adapted to local conditions ought to be valued and in the encouragement of the study of local law.
>
> (1983: 78–79)

The idea that customs themselves evolve, resulting in necessary adaptations, just as various nations adapted the Roman law to their circumstances, was embedded in institutional thought.

A second key way in which custom enters Scottish legal thought is in the adaptation of formal laws to particular customs and circumstances, and thus has strong consequences both for how laws are formed and how legal decisions should be made, that adaptation is necessary.

A form of legal literature that shows the importance of adaptation to custom and circumstance are the practicks. Hector McKechnie (1936) categorizes these into decision practicks and digest practicks, which are collections of decisions made by the Court of Session. Digest practicks contain more material and references to the literature, statutes, and evidence upon which the court's decision was made. The purpose of the digest practicks is for the instruction of those in legal practice so that they can argue from like cases and so that they can see that although a law may apply in similar cases, there may be differing circumstances that cause the court's decision to change. Practicks first appeared in the sixteenth century as rudimentary textbooks for those studying the law before institutional writing was available, and were commonplace by the 18th century, with older practicks being reprinted and newer ones made available. In 1731, Alexander Bayne edited *Hope's Minor Practicks*, to which he appended a new introduction and the introductory notes to his class.

The practicks demonstrate a method by which lawyers and jurists were to apply and interpret the law. Digest practicks discussed the law of Scotland 'drawn from both written and unwritten sources, with the emphasis at least on the local sources of the law' (Ford 2007: 85). Practicks differed from legal theory and compendia of Scots law because they explained how particular decisions had been made, the legal principle at work in the decision and how particular laws and decisions had changed in their adaptation to conditions (Ford 2007: 82–85; McKechnie 1936).

The practicks demonstrate the understanding that laws and their application were based upon general principles and should be adjusted for circumstance. Custom was the main cause of adjustment. They also showed that the judgment of the Court of Session on how a law was applied could change. Judgments were to take the current situation, rather than precedents in case law unless extremely similar, into account. The practicks also demonstrated that while decisions of the Court of Session were binding on the participants at the time, a later session dealing with a similar case might rule differently, given some changed circumstance.

Lord Dirleton had questioned in the 17th century whether decisions of the Court of Session were laws and whether a judge was free to rule differently on a like case than he had previously. Lord Advocate Sir James Steuart answered that decisions were binding on those involved, but that they 'in no wise tie up the Lords dissenting, that they may not vote according to their own opinion in like cases occurring thereafter' (1715: 277).[8] This viewpoint, itself not in the written law, was customary law through the 18th century. As William Forbes commented, judges' decisions were examples of applications of rules and judges were to view cases not only with their own eyes but also 'with the eyes of their learned and judicious predecessors whose observations . . . they may improve to the best advantage. It's ridiculous to think that the subject of decisions is exhausted' (quoted in Walker 1998: 331). Fraser Tytler wrote in the *Dictionary of Decisions* in 1770 (quoted in Walker 1998: 332). He continues that, when a similar case is brought before a court old and new arguments must be considered and 'an examination of principle on which the judgment rested . . . and the ingenuity of lawyers is employed anew in canvassing their principle and foundations' (*ibidem*). Erskine concurred that custom shaped the decisions of the Session but only consistent, repeated decisions on like cases formed a new custom that could be a law.

ADAPTATION IN PRACTICE

The following provides an example of the twofold use of custom in Scots law. The first is how property law was affected by custom and the second is how a particular circumstance caused the property law to be adapted to that circumstance. Unlike English property law, which is based on the right to exclude others from one's property, Scots property law follows the Roman law, which is based on possession and concerned with the right of use and ownership of a thing. While English law would have focused on ownership of an entire building, due to the custom of construction of tenements in Old Town Edinburgh, it was customary Scots property law to grant horizontal rather than vertical ownership. In a tenement, one could claim ownership of one's apartment or floor in a tenement building but no one person owned the entire building. Top floor owners bore responsibility for upkeep of the roof and the ground floor owners were responsible for the foundation. From this custom, itself unique to contemporary construction practices, arose the formal law of tenement. The tenement custom eventually caused another law to emerge. Because all tenants benefitted from the roof, it was decided that all tenants should bear some burden for its upkeep, not just the top floor tenants. Just as the law of tenement arose from of the law of possession and custom, the law of burden developed to rectify the injustice to top floor owners (Reid 2000: 215–220).

Another example is the case of Learmonth versus Sinclair's Trustees wherein it was decided that the custom in Caithness that a landlord must repay a tenant for costs a tenant incurred to improve the landlord's wall had to be enforced as law, although not found in written law. The court ruled in the tenant's favour because the unwritten custom was proven to be well known, longstanding, and did not violate other principles of property law (Court of Session 1878: 549–552).

Although Scots laws had authoritative force, they were expected to adapt to different circumstances and changes in customs. As shown in the practicks, the laws had been applied and cases decided upon in a variety of ways. Jurists' decisions on individual cases could deviate from the strict written law or previous decisions. Custom formed the formal laws, but what made them just was their appropriateness to the situation at hand.

Both the practicks and institutional writing demonstrate the role of custom and adaptation in Scots legal thought and practice. Legal education in Scotland and the Netherlands both also stressed the role and rule of custom and variability of the law and judgments upon it. Therefore Steuart was part of an intellectual culture that stressed the role of custom and differing circumstances in the formation of institutions and that felt the proper method of study of such a vast collection of ideas and actions was to identify general principles in the law at hand and to take the history and present customs of a people into account when applying those principles and passing judgment on a case.

Legal humanism and adaptation in Mackie's courses

Charles Mackie is often remembered in the Steuart literature as Steuart's history professor and an important correspondent when he was on the Grand Tour (Skinner 1966a). However, the interconnection between Mackie's courses and Steuart's legal training has been understressed. Two of Mackie's history courses were part of the law curriculum at Edinburgh, and both evince an approach that is consistent with that of the institutional writers and Steuart. Mackie's method of study bore great relation to legal humanism, or the study of Rome and the evolution of the

Roman law in its social, political, and economic context, and was also applied to the study of the history of other countries after the Empire.

Mackie's course in universal history was a part of the law curriculum to instruct students in the development and conditions of different countries, in particular those that had developed their legal systems from the Roman law. The course in Roman antiquities was required for an understanding of the evolution and context of the Roman law. Mackie also covered the nature of the peoples of antiquity and how that nature caused changes in their institutions and then changes in their natures as their civilizations expanded and contracted. According to Emerson, 'Gregory of Tours was one of his guides for lectures on how the barbarians assimilated Roman manners and culture and changed both the Empire and themselves' (2016: 111). Mackie's course also included lectures on how the institutions of the Scots people in particular had changed with changes in their culture (2016: 112). Studying the evolution of Roman law from its beginnings to the works of Justinian had a larger purpose than instruction in Roman history. Studying history in this way was a practice in: 'tracing a changing society which was neither imperial nor commercial in the beginning to one which was both. Growing legal complexity was bred of economic and political changes. Those altered manners and customs and modified laws' (2016: 113).

Further, Mackie had studied at Utrecht and his lectures in Roman Antiquities at Edinburgh followed closely the notes he had taken in Utrecht. He assigned the same texts at Edinburgh that he had been instructed in at Utrecht: Tursellinus' universal history and Pieter Burman's *Roman Antiquities*, which studied the legal, civil, political, and social history and institutions of ancient Rome (Mijers 2012; Emerson 2016).

The institutional writers and their fellow Dutch scholars had already developed the idea that European countries, excepting England, had shaped aspects of the Roman law to their particular culture. Therefore in Scotland and elsewhere the notion that laws and people have a national character of laws existed previous to Montesquieu's book. As Cairns states:

> Scots Law had been reduced to an intelligible system in the writings of Stair and Mackenzie. Even before Montesquieu formulated such ideas in a coherent, theoretical way, Scots considered their law to be particularly suited and adapted to the 'genius' of the Scottish people.
>
> (Cairns 1986: 262–263)

Steuart agreed with the institutional and humanist view of customs, complexity, and adaptability when it came to legal institutions.

History, spirit, and adaptation: The institutional methods in *Principles*

Contextual and historical analysis, attention to custom and its affect on institutions, and adaptation of laws and judgment by legislators to circumstance and custom, are hallmarks of the institutional approach. Steuart applies this approach to the economic realm in multiple ways throughout *Principles* in his discussion of history and change of societies in general, the role of spirit, and analysis of the effects of principles, taking custom and adaptation into account. Both the way in which economic principles are to be used and the way in which economic policy is formed and adapted are the same as those in institutional writing and practice on drafting and analyzing legislation and how a jurist, or in Steuart's case a statesman, is to adapt policy.

History, change, and development

The study of society through the lens of changing institutions and viewpoints due to changed circumstances is an element of the stages explanation of economic development that recurs throughout Scottish Enlightenment writing (Skinner 1996). As we have seen, an historical approach dominated the Steuart's legal education. Mackie's and others' courses on the development of Roman law focused on the change of Roman society through time and how that led to different forms of government and social organization. Steuart applies the same analysis, and legal humanism in general, to the change of political and economic institutions.

He examines the economic development of Europe in context and the change of certain institutions given 'revolutions' in the circumstances of European states. The introductory material in Book I, Chapter 2 is a prime example of the use of this approach. Steuart attributes the shift from a feudal to a 'free and commercial' stage in European development to 'the discovery of American and the Indies, the springing up of industry and learning, the introduction of trade and luxurious arts, the establishment of public credit, and a system of general taxation' (I: 13). These economic changes drove the changes in political institutions. The industriousness of the lower classes allowed for their independency, which changed both government and the manners of the people. Under feudalism 'everything was brought about by numbers; now numbers of men cannot be kept together without money' (I: 14). The industrious spirit of the people caused the initial change, which eventually led to a change in circumstance and a further change in spirit. The timing of certain policies also influences the 'revolutions' that can impact political and economic institutions. He mentions the mistiming or mistemper involved in 'introducing popery into England' (I: 15) when the 'spirit of the people' did not want it or were not ready for it.

Steuart is upfront that his method has 'taken a hint' from the changes that have occurred in Europe, which 'have pointed out to be the regular progress of mankind, from great simplicity to complicated refinement' (I: 20). The 'historical clue' method is to examine the causes and effects of the changes in Europe in Book I 'from the cradle' to commercial modernity, in which 'the trade and industry of Europe has increased alienation and the circulation of money' (I, 20–21). How this improvement in exchange came about, and its effects, form the bulk of Books I and II. How these circumstances gave rise to the introduction of credit and the interrelation between credit, war, debt, and taxation form Book II. This method, as we have seen, is the same as that of the institutional writers tracing the evolution of Roman law and the Scots law: It had to be studied in the context of changing historical circumstance and the customs of the people, which could both alter over time.[9]

Custom and conditions

Customs as habits of thought are included in Steuart's definition of the 'sirit of the people'. The spirit is analogous to the use of custom in institutional thought, as it refers to informal practices of longstanding and accepted use in a community. Steuart's definition of the 'spirit of the people' in Book I, Chapter 2 is very similar to that of custom in institutional writing. He says the spirit is made of 'a set of received opinions' on morals, government, and manners and that these once established, 'confirmed by long and constant habit, and never called in question, form the basis of all laws, regulate the form of every government, and determine what are commonly called the customs of a country' (I: 10). The spirit is confirmed by the same elements that confirm a custom in legal theory: Long use and acceptability. Like the institutional writers, he asserts that the spirit determines the kind of government that prevails in a nation. What Steuart refers to as custom, as part of the spirit, is the same as the unwritten laws of consuetude in a country.

As in institutional writing, custom, or the 'spirit of the people', plays a twofold role in Steuart's economics. First, it shapes not only the economic conditions in which people live because it has shaped not only their history but also present and future conditions. Therefore Steuart asserts that the statesman must study the 'spirit of the people' to understand a nation's economic development, how well his policies will be received, and their likely results. Second, the able statesman should consider the 'spirit of the people' when forming new policies and interpreting the outcomes of the economic principles at work in his policies. The functions of custom are thus the same as in the writings of the institutional writers and the practice of Scots law as evinced by the practicks.

The 'spirit of the people' influences both the current and future economic conditions of a country. For instance, Steuart explains that it was the industriousness of the peoples of Europe that caused the movement from feudalism to commercial society. The industry and innovation in the character of the people caused this change. The rise of commercial society introduced luxury and credit, topics he deals with separately in Book I and then more connectedly in Book II, which introduced a change in the 'spirit of the people' because it changed their patterns of consumption. Whether luxury leads into more vice or more innovation on the part of the people depends on their own virtue, but the possibility is still open that the character of the people can change due to this economic circumstance. After all, 'Nothing is more certain than that the spirit of a nation changes according to circumstances', which itself leads to further economic changes (II, 20).

Spirit thus, like consuetude, both forms conditions but also affects how changes in circumstance should be analyzed by a judge, or, in Steuart's case, the statesman and the political economist. One of the complicating factors of *Principles* is that it is both a book of principles and a policy guide on how principles are to be interpreted and applied. However this is also modelled on institutional writing's study of the development of the Scots legal system, delineation of legal principles, and instruction in how jurists were to analyze them. The practicks literature demonstrates that the act of interpretation and judgment of a law in particular cases, considering different customs, often led to varied outcomes even when applying the same legal principle.

Custom, interpretation, and adaptation

Spirit and circumstance viewed through the lens of history therefore can lead one to understand why changes have occurred in a nation's institutions. This 'historical clue' in Steuart is essential not only for understanding a nation's current conditions but also for forming appropriate policy (I, 21). The idea that one must adapt the laws to the 'spirit of the people' is the same as the idea that interpretation and judgment of the law must take custom and circumstance into account. The 'laws' in *Principles* are the economic principles Steuart derives but also the economic policies in place. While the principles themselves, much like legal principles, refer to tendencies between persons or variables, their outcomes are variable. Similarly, policies or laws related to economics are also changeable. Indeed Steuart says of political laws that 'invariable laws, can never subsist among men, the most variable thing we know' (I, 9). The only unchanging law, according to Steuart, is *salus populii suprema lex esto*, that the wellbeing of the people is the supreme law. However, even this 'is a maxim rather than a law' (*ibidem*). Due to the changeability of people and their circumstances, economic policy must ever be ready to adapt.

Examples of adaptation to culture and circumstance abound in *Principles*, and those explored here are illustrative of the method but by no means exhaustive. That 'Wants promote industry, industry provides food, food promotes numbers' is Steuart's summary in Book I, Chapter 11 of the principles delineated in the preceding chapters (I, 77). These are the natural 'laws' in place in the economy. However he also devotes much space in those ten chapters examining the effects of different spirits on the outcomes of the principles. For instance, a people who are less industrious or who may have more nobility not raised to industrious labour will not necessarily be as productive in manufactured products as a society with a smaller number of nobles.

Similarly, the principle that the emergence of the freehands will cause the creation of manufactured goods – but what kind of goods and how many are determined by the spirit and demands of the society? (I, 81–86). In his explanation of the movement from a simple to the more complicated economy with three sectors, the 'law' is that the emergence of the freehands will cause production and circulation of goods and payments. How each community produces and distributes goods, and what kinds of goods are produced, depends on the 'circumstances relating to the extension, situation, and soil of the country, and above all, to the spirit of the people' (I, 87).

He provides a general example regarding taxation. It is accepted that taxes are necessary to fund public administration but how easily or how many taxes can be raised will depend on the 'spirit of the people' in relation to taxation. A land tax, he says, will be objected to in France whereas an excise tax will be resisted in England – both are taxes but the customs of the countries in relation to each are different and therefore the effect of the tax will be different (I, 17). He returns to this case later in the text, now including Germany and Scotland, but underscoring the effects of spirit not only in relation to the idea of taxation but on industry, which influences land values and thus the incidence of land taxes (IV, 277–288).

An early principle discussed is that an increase in the food supply will cause an increase in population. However the extent of the increase depends on both the food consumption habits of the people and other circumstances relating to soil and climate. The law applies but its outcome depends on circumstances and people, and therefore the rational statesman will take these into account in judging what policy should be applied when trying to boost numbers or increase the food supply. Steuart demonstrates the case of multiple outcomes using examples. He says that the lands of the Dutch, Germans, French, and English were all in a state of improvement compared to previous times and thus the population would increase, in keeping with Steuart's principle regarding the food supply and population. However he points out that if the English ate more bread rather than meat, their population would rise at an even faster level than presently. And if conversely the Dutch, Germans, and French would shift from their eating habits based more on grains, fruit, fish, and sauerkraut then the population would fall for having switched to beef and the land being unable to support more pasturage and tillage and maintain or grow the larger population. Improvement will increase population therefore, but it is important to know what the consequence is of a situation where the land will not support a greater population in the production of the foodstuffs that the people are accustomed to eat. If the people are resistant to change, then the population will decline, he predicts. If the people are open to innovation and changing their eating habits, then the population, industry, and trade of the country will increase (I, 156–158).

The spending habits of a people, influenced by their Spirit, likewise determine whether an increase in the money supply will actually cause inflation (I, 345). Steuart compares the grain market in Scotland, where prices cannot rise above the subsistence of the poor, and that of ancient Greece and Rome, which had more coin in circulation than Scotland but had less expensive grain than in modern Scotland. If money alone were the cause, then the price of grain would have been higher in ancient times than in Scotland (I, 345–349).

Another example is the principle that as wealth increases the price of money will fall in the same proportion. However, how the rate will change depends on the 'spirit of the people' in terms of their view of different kinds of consumption (Tortajada 1999: 242–250). To maintain a particular growth rate the statesman has to take action to ensure that interest rates do not rise too high. Again Steuart starts from a general principle and analyzes the effects of certain actions given that the local conditions and tradition may not be consonant with bringing about a particular change in interest rates.

Later in the text, Steuart posits the principle that the circulation of money times the number of transactions will have a proportional effect on taxation. He demonstrates that the effect of a proportional tax on consumption and circulation will depend on the customs of commerce of a particular location. Steuart's conclusion that 'taxes must come out of that money which exceeds what was necessary for carrying on alienation before they were imposted' holds true, but the amount that can be gathered in taxation depends on how people customarily hold their money (IV, 238–239). In Spain, the payment will come 'from the chests of the hoarders, and increase circulation for a while' (IV, 239). In England under William II's general taxation increase because the supply of money was low the tax on malt had to be drawn from funds people would have spent on barley and hence is why the price of barley fell in this period. French people, he argues, are more familiar with taxes, and the prices of agricultural products never fall in order to accommodate taxes that reduce profits and thus 'the diminution of the mass of coin must diminish consumption' (IV, 239).

Another factor to consider is that natural circumstances also determine the habit of living. Steuart explains that in France, due to denser forests, that farmers tend to be gathered in villages and in England it is customary to have many small farmers upon individual plots. The 'spirit of the people' determines, he says, 'the employment of the lower classes; the employment of these determines their usefulness to the state, and their usefulness their multiplication' (I, 138). If they are employed as cottars helping to bring in a small harvest that cannot support an increase of population, the lower classes will not thrive or improve. However, if the lower classes engage in other work, as freehands, or improvers of the land, then there is a possibility for their increase and improvement (I, 136–139).

Therefore the statesman has to assess external factors as well as people's inclinations, how this affects their current situation, what the best course to take is, and adjust policy accordingly, to either 'support and encourage' or curb them (I, 63). The plan of government must be consistent with the Spirit of the People, ' in order to make a people happy' and in order to bring about workable results (I, 9–10). The statesman, just like his good economist, is required:

> to become a citizen of the world, comparing customs, examining minutely institutions which appear alike, when in different countries they are found to produce different effects: he should examine the cause of such differences with the utmost diligence and attention.
>
> (I, 4)

As Urquhart says, Steuart's statesman must be able to view the world through the history of the people (1999: 126). Keeping the customs of only one's own country in mind will lead one astray in one's analyses of others. Steuart's view of the use the statesman must make of custom is yet another iteration of the Scottish institutional view that culture shapes the law and its application and interpretation, and the rational jurist must take these factors into account.

Conclusion: History, spirit, and dynamism

Kobayashi (1999) and Skinner (1996, 1966b) agree that Steuart's method is one of combined induction and deduction, based on initial empirical observation and that this is an attempt to follow Newtonian principles. At the same time Steuart's method evinces the observation, reflection, and judgment of Scottish jurists. The historical approach to development and the privileging of circumstances and Spirit is not something Steuart simply borrowed from Hume but something that both Steuart and Hume, as a fellow law student at Edinburgh, were both inculcated with in their legal studies, and that Steuart utilized to much a larger extent. Previous commentary that Steuart's methodology relies on the observation of historical phenomena and the dynamism of human communities is encompassed in the institutional approach. Viewing Steuart's method as institutional complements the existing narratives of Urquhart, Kobayashi, Skinner, Caboret, and others because it provides a context for his reliance on the historical method and a rationale for why he works from general principles and considers the application of them in particular circumstances.

To the modern reader, and to some of his contemporary English readership, tracing out the ramifications of every principle depending on culture and particular circumstances makes *Principles* somewhat cumbersome. However, to Steuart's 18th-century Scottish audience his method and use of the 'spirit of the people' is another version of the way in which Scots law was analyzed, applied, and interpreted. The institutional writers and the law professors and students who followed them viewed 'the study of law as a local, territorial, and historical phenomenon' (Cairns 1983: 79). Likewise Steuart creates a local and history-based political economy whose concerns are to understand the past, comprehend the present, and to accommodate for present and future peoples' quality of life.

The common foundations and methods of the institutional writers and Steuart's political economy focused on change and adaptability allows for dynamism in the crafting of both theory and practice. Such dynamism is necessary due to the subject matter at hand, the human person, 'the most variable thing we know' (I, 9). For both Steuart and the institutional writers, external factors could change and had to be taken into account when studying a community's evolution and when judging what new policy is best and what best avoided.

Thus both law and economics require flexibility to change with the needs of the people in order to satisfy what the institutional writers and Steuart both agreed should be the only goal of policymakers and judges: The wellbeing of the people must be pursued. Such dynamism is necessary also because individual and national wellbeing is contingent on a number of circumstances, besides basic satisfying of needs. Concern for the wellbeing of the people alongside satisfaction of material needs therefore is a guidepost for the statesman and the economist. The recognition that the wants and wellbeing of a people will change as their economic conditions and social lives change; thus their culture changes and imbues Steuart's work with the spirit of institutional thought. Just as the institutional writers sought to understand and adapt laws and decisions according to time and place, so too does

Steuart demonstrate why 'as one considers the variety to be found in different countries . . . one must conclude that the political economy in each must necessarily be different' (I, 3).

Notes

1 I wish to thank the conference organizers, the editors of this volume, and the special collections of the libraries of the University of Edinburgh and University of Glasgow. I am also thankful for the research assistance of Aaron B. Fricke, JD, who helped me navigate the realms of legal terminology and archival documents. The final version was also much improved due to comments by Christopher Berry, to whom I am grateful.

2 All page references to the *Principles of Political Economy* refer to volume I of the *Works*.

3 Sir Thomas Craig's *Jus Feudale* (1655) predates these. However because it focuses on feudal law and does not follow Justinian, it is not always considered an institutional work.

4 Although Henry Home, Lord Kames, contributed greatly to 18th-century Scottish legal writing, he is not traditionally considered to be an institutional writer because he did not produce a similarly structured compendium with commentary

5 This memoir contains some details not found in the memoir Buchan published in *The Bee*.

6 The thesis is recorded in the Minute Book of the Faculty of Advocates. However it is no longer in their collection, according to correspondence I had with members of the Faculty of Advocates Library in 2015.

7 John Millar, younger contemporary of Smith and Steuart, used Heineccius's text in his Roman law course at Glasgow. The student notes from Millar's lectures show the similarity between Heineccius's view of custom and law and MacKenzie's and the other institutional writers. (Miller [sic] upon Heineccius' Institutes 1794).

8 Skinner attributes this work to Steuart the Solicitor General (1966a, 1962: n13). However, the frontispiece of the first edition states that it is by Lord Advocate Steuart.

9 While Steuart was certainly influenced by Hume, and one can see the similarities here to Hume's discussion in 1752 in the *Discourses* and the attention to historical detail in the *History of England*, I contend that Steuart and Hume were both influenced by the institutional method. I thank Christopher Berry for the references to Hume.

Bibliography

Bayne, A. (1726), Discourse on the Rise of the Law of Scotland, in *Hope's Minor Practicks*, Edinburgh: Thomas Ruddiman.

———. (1731), *Notes for the Use of the Students of Municipal Law in the University of Edinburgh*, Edinburgh: Thomas & Walter Ruddiman.

Buchan, D.S.E.L. (1787), *Memoir of the Life of Chevalier Steuart*, Chalmers, MS: Edinburgh University Library Special Collections.

Burton, J.H. (1849), *Letters of Eminent Persons Addressed to David Hume*, Edinburgh: William Blackwood & Sons.

Caboret, D. (2001), The Formation and Development of Commercial Society in the Economics of James Steuart, in P.L. Porta, R. Scazzieri & A. Skinner (eds.), *Knowledge, Social, Institutions and the Division of Labour*, London: Edward Elgar: 264–284.

Cairns, J. (1983), Institutional Writings in Scotland Reconsidered, *Journal of Legal History*, 4: 76–117.

———. (1986), The Formation of the Scottish Legal Mind in the Eighteenth Century, in N. McCormick & P. Bierks (eds.), *The Legal Mind*, Oxford: Oxford University Press: 255–277.

———. (2000), Historical Introduction, in K. Reid & Zimmeran (eds.), *A History of the Private Law of Scotland*, Oxford: Oxford University Press: 14–184.
———. (2015), *Law, Lawyers, and Humanism*, Edinburgh: Edinburgh University Press.
Cairns, J. & MacQueen, H. (2013), *Learning and the Law: A Short History of the Edinburgh Law School*. Available online at www.law.ed.ac.uk (Last accessed 29 August 2018).
Court of Session, Scotland. (1878), *Cases Decided in the Court of Session: Court of Justiciary, and House of Lords*, Edinburgh: T. & T. Clark.
Emerson, R. (2016), *Essays on David Hume, Medical Men, and the Scottish Enlightenment*, London: Routledge.
Erskine, J. (1787), *Notes of Mr. Erskine's Praelections on Sir George Mackenzie's Institutions of the Law of Scotland, Sessions 1740–41*, Glasgow University Library Special Collections.
Ford, J.D. (2007), *Law and Opinion in Scotland during the Seventeenth Century*, Oxford: Bloomsbury.
Kobayashi, N. (1999), On the Method of Sir James Steuart's Principles of Political Economy, in R. Tortajada (ed.), *The Economics of James Steuart*, London: Routledge: 102–120.
MacInnes, A. (1999), Regal Union for Britain 1603–38, in G. Burgess (ed.), *The New British History: Founding a Modern State*, London: IB Tauris: 33–64.
———. (2015), *Union and Empire: The Making of the United Kingdom in 1707*, Cambridge: Cambridge University Press.
Mackenzie, G. (1684), *The Institutions of the Law of Scotland*, Edinburgh: George Reed.
McKechnie, H. (1936), *Sources and Literature of Scots Law*, vol. 1. Edinburgh: Stair Society.
Menudo, J.M. (2013), Sir James Steuart's Theory of Justice, *Economies et Societies*, 49: 1659–1679.
Mijers, E. (2012), Scotland's Fabulous Past: Charles Mackie and George Buchanan, in C. Erskine & R.A. Mason (eds.), *George Buchanan: Political Thought in Early Modern Britain and Europe*, London: Routledge: 249–268.
Miller upon Heineccius' Institutes. (1794), Copied from David Boyle's Copy. ML 4/6, s-264. Glasgow University Library Special Collections.
Oxford English Dictionary Online. Oxford: Oxford University Press, viewed April 2018.
Redman, D. (1996), Sir James Steuart's Statesman Revisited in Light of the Continental Influence, *Scottish Journal of Political Economy*, 43(1): 48–70.
Reid, K. (2000), Property Law: Doctrines and Sources, in K. Reid & R. Zimmerman (eds.), *A History of Private Law in Scotland*, vol. 1, Oxford: Oxford University Press: 185–219.
Richter, M. (1977), *The Political Theory of Montesquieu*, Cambridge: Cambridge University Press.
Skinner, A. (1962), Sir James Steuart: Economics and Politics, *Scottish Journal of Political Economy*, 9: 17–37.
———. (1966a), Biographical Sketch, in A. Skinner (ed.), *An Inquiry into the Principles of Political Economy*, Edinburgh: Oliver Boyd.
———. (1966b), Analytical Sketch, in A. Skinner (ed.), *An Inquiry into the Principles of Political Economy*, Edinburgh: Oliver Boyd.
———. (1996), *A System of Social Science: Papers Relating to Adam Smith*, Oxford: Clarendon Press.
———. (1999), Sir James Steuart and the Jacobite Connection, in R. Tortajada (ed.), *The Economics of James Steuart*, London: Routledge: 1–23.

Stair, V.J.D. (1681), *Institutions of the Law of Scotland*, Edinburgh: Andrew Anderson, 1693.

Stettner, W. (1945), Sir James Steuart on the Public Debt, *The Quarterly Journal of Economics*, 59(3): 451–476.

Steuart, Sir J.L.A. (1715), *Dirleton's Doubts and Questions on the Law of Scotland, Resolved and Answered*, Edinburgh: James Watson.

Tortajada, R. (1999), Rate of Interest, Profit, and Prices in the Economics of James Steuart, in *The Economics of James Steuart*, London: Routledge: 235–252.

Urquhart, R. (1999), Steuart's Method: Aristotelian Political Economy, in R. Tortajada (ed.), *The Economics of James Steuart*, London: Routledge: 121–136.

Walker, D.M. (1982), *Principles of Private Scottish Law*, Oxford: Clarendon Press.

———. (1998), *A Legal History of Scotland*, vol. 5, Edinburgh: T. & T. Clark.

5 The notion of political economy in Steuart's and Smith's main works

Francis Clavé[1]

The term 'political economy' was coined at the beginning of the 17th century at the time when the economic field was becoming increasingly important in societies. Also at this time, states were being established and England was experiencing the revolutions that would lead to the emergence of modern democracies, while France was moving towards royal absolutism. Finally, at the same time, the notion of interest took precedence over that of glory, while the concept of compensatory passion emerged. The term 'political economy' is very polysemous. In 1767, Steuart defined it as the field of activity that extends beyond the family. It is the concern of the state, whereas the economy concerns the family and its 'the art of providing for all the wants of a family, with prudence and frugality'. This seemingly technical definition nonetheless has political implications. Indeed, it revives one of the main problems of the 17th-century English revolutions, namely knowing whether the King should be considered the head of the family and the people as the children. This role distribution was highly disputed by revolutionaries. Moreover, the juxtaposition of the words 'economy and politics' in the phrase 'political economy' implicitly raises the issue of the link between the political and economic fields, at a time when politics is confronted with the necessity of placing more and more emphasis on the economic field. The purpose of this chapter is to compare what Steuart and Smith think about the relation between economics and politics. At the very moment when these two economists wrote their major works (Steuart's book, *An Inquiry into the Principles of Political Economy*, in 1767; *The Wealth of Nations*, by Smith, in 1776), several issues are yet to be dealt with:Should the economic remain dominated by politics? Is an economic science an instrument only at the statesman's service or, on the contrary, a tool able to emancipate it from politics? This chapter will show that, on these points, Steuart's and Smith's respective answers diverge strongly and have influenced future debates. It aims, moreover, at better defining both these authors' contributions to what is called classical political economy. To complete the proposed study, a first part is devoted to the presentation of the concepts of political economy and science, specially that of the economic, since the beginning of the 17th century until the time when both authors published their books. In the second part, three key points in Steuart's political economy will be analyzed: The way he envisions the science of political economy and the way in which the regulation of economic interests is carried out.

Finally, the third part is dedicated to the way Adam Smith addresses the question of the relations between economics and politics.

The rise of political economy in its context

In what context did the notion of political economy emerge in the early 17th century? What transformations marked the political and moral ideas of the 17th and early 18th centuries? How is the notion of political economy understood at the very moment when both economists under review wrote their major works? These are the points that this section aims to clarify.

The prospective joint rise of the notions of economy and of interest

From the 16th century onwards, the colonization of South America by the Spanish and Portuguese, as well as the opening of a new sea route to India and China, contributed to the economic development of Europe. In this respect, Smith notes:

> The general advantages which Europe, considered as one great country, has derived from the discovery and colonization of America, consist, first, in the increase of its enjoyments; and secondly, in the augmentation of its industry.
> (Smith 1976: IV, 104)

Steuart agrees with Smith on this point and highlights the impact of economic development on government affairs.

> The great alteration in the affairs of Europe within these three centuries, by the discovery of America and the Indies, the springing up of industry and learning, the introduction of trade and luxurious arts, the establishment of public credit, and a general system of taxation, have entirely altered the plan of government everywhere
> (I, 13)

The rise of economic concerns is accompanied by the decline of the notion of glory, which is mostly linked to the military domain and to the aristocracy. Faced with this withdrawal, on the contrary, the more bourgeois notion of interest, meant 'in the sense of concerns, aspirations and advantage' (Hirschman 2013: 32), asserted itself and became dominant. It is also in this period that the Duke of Rohan's book, *On the Interest of Princes and States of Christendom* (1638), contributed to the emergence of the idea of compensatory passion (i.e., a passion that comes to limit another one). For Spinoza (1632–1677), for example: 'nothing can oppose or delay the impulse of passion but a contrary impulse' (quoted in Hirschman 2013: 24–25). For his part, Boisguilbert (1646–1714), on Jansenist moral grounds, insists that the 'mechanics of individual interests', channeled into the markets, makes it possible to achieve opulence (Faccarello 1986: 216).

In the early 18th century, Bishop Butler (1692–1752) – who influenced Hume and Smith – argued that: 'reasonable self-love – that is, interest – is arrayed alongside morality against the passions' (Hirschman 2013: 35). Insofar as interest is seen as contributing to the world's predictability and constancy, both Steuart and Smith adopted this view the moment they made interest the key to their economy (Hirschman 2013). But, the prominence of economic issues also causes the evolution of the word economy and the emergence of the term political economy, as will be seen hereafter.

The notion of political economy until Steuart and Smith

The notion of political economy emerged in France around 1611, in a context marked by the Religious Wars and the assassination of Henry IV, king of France and Navarre (1553–1610). Louis Turquet de Mayerne (1533–1618), a Calvinist, was first to use the term political economy. He did so in The Aristodemocratic Monarchy (1611), a book which belongs to the tradition of Monarchical republicanism (Greengrass 2007: 7) and is opposed to Cardinal de Richelieu's idea of a centralized state (1585–1642) (Greengrass 2007: 8). Turquet de Mayerne, in the paragraph where he introduces the notion of political economy, insists on the notion of equal opportunities:

> we set ourselves, as a final goal for the citizen in our political economy, where everyone is given causes and means to obtain, by virtue and knowledge, without hindering or preventing anyone, depending on their capacities and scopes, by which they can improve their conditions, which is a requisite of equality that is essential to true royal and paternal government.
>
> (Turquet quoted in Barthas 2011: 116)

The second scientist who uses the expression 'political economy' (Groenewegen 2008: 2) is Montchrestien (sometimes spelled Montchrétien). He uses the term in a sense that reflects at least two important things in this chapter. First of all, for the author, the economy has become a major concern for statesmen; it is even 'the ultimate objective of a government' (Montchrétien 2017: 109, our translation). Montchrétien also insists on the importance of the 'public menagerie, which the State's needs and burdens oblige it to have mainly regard to' (Montchrétien 2017: 125, our translation). Guery (2011: 420) reminds us that the word 'ménagerie' or 'mesnagerie' is derived from the word 'mesnager', which refers to the house. In this sentence, Monchrétien extends to country level what, following Aristotle, still pertains to the family (Guery 2011: 424). It should be noted here that for him, and later for Steuart as well, the king, in an analogy with the head of the family, is considered as the father of the people (Guery 2011: 422). In Monchrétien's case, then, as Barthas (2011: 115) points out, while the economy weighs on politics, it does not emancipate itself from it. In fact, at that time, the field of the economic and politics were in some ways under construction.

Laudet (2017) points out that if the word 'politics' seems to derive from the Latin 'politicus' and from the Greek 'politikos', whose meaning reads 'which concerns the citizen, the State (qui concerne le citoyen, l'Etat)'. At that time, for an author like Monchrétien, the word 'politics' also had the meaning of 'police' (from the Latin 'politia') which meant the order or organization established in a geographical territory corresponding to a State – a political entity then in the making. On this point, we can note an opposition between Monchrétien and Turquet de Mayerne on the meaning of the word 'police' that they both use. For the Calvinist author, a little like Smith, the idea of the police is linked to the term 'policé' ('policed'). It is about civil virtue and the ability to govern oneself (Greengrass 2007: 10). In short, the police refers to a specific quality of the individual more than to an external order imposed by the Prince. However, during the period covering the 17th and early 18th centuries, economy did not really depart from politics when, with Pudendorf and Grotius, it became at odds with the religious, notably regarding the issue of the fair price concept (Tortajada 1992: 84–89). It can be noticed nevertheless that, at the turn of the 17th and 18th centuries, Boisguilbert's work heralded laissez-faire, releasing the grip of political control over the economy (Faccarello 1986).

The economy came back to the forefront with the publication, in 1748, of the *Esprit des lois* by Montesquieu. During this period – which lasted until 1756, and which Weulersse (1910: I, 23) described as pre-physiocratic – political economy issues were of great interest. Just after that, the physiocratic 'moment' began, which lasted until the early 1770s. In general, enthusiasm for the economy is also linked to the financial and economic problems faced by states in the second half of the 18th century (Machet 2015: 52). On this point, it is important for our purpose to remember that Steuart resided in France from about 1746 to 1755, during the pre-physiocratic period, while Smith lived there in 1764–1766, when the physiocracy was at its peak, as it were. The Physiocrats, at least Quesnay and Mirabeau, seem to use the term political economy relatively little. They prefer the term economics or economy.

Quesnay, for example, in his book *Maxime générale d'un gouvernement* économique (1758), uses the word economics, not political economy (Cannan 1929: 40). Moreover, in 1760, Mirabeau, in his explanation of Quesnay's economic table, speaks 'of political economy as if it consisted of a dissertation on agriculture, the public administration as well as on the nature of wealth and the means of procuring it' (Cannan 1929: 40). In fact, for Mirabeau, political economy provides a broader sense than 'a research on the causes and nature of wealth' and includes, as in Steuart, an administrative and political side. Moreover, it should be underlined that Mirabeau (1760) considers Quesnay discovered the 'principles of economics', not of political economy. It is just that his English translator, as Cannan (1929: 40) indicates, translated economics into political economy. It can therefore be affirmed that the physiocrats, at least Quesnay and Mirabeau, seem to distinguish between the principles of economics, understood as scientific matter and a broader field, political economy, which concerns both economic policy and public administration. Let us notice that Physiocrats were very sensitive to the idea of economic government. They think 'good government' is one that follows the natural economic order (Steiner 1998: 94) and is a matter of legal despotism (Steiner 1998: 94). So that next to, and in connection with, economics, physiocrats developed an institutional model, which Smith did not fail to point out.

> This sect, in their works, which are very numerous, and which treat not only of what is properly called Political Oeconomy, or of the nature and causes of the wealth of nations, but of every other branch of the system of civil government, all follow implicitly, and without any sensible variation, the doctrine of Mr. Quesnai.
>
> (Smith 1976: IV, 200)

Let us note that until Steuart, the Anglo-Saxons would scarcely use the term political economy. In a way, this term becomes popular thanks to him. For Steuart (I, 1), political economy is to the state what 'economy, in general', is to the family: 'the art of providing for all the wants of a family, with prudence and frugality'. Thus, can be found in Steuart, as Urquhart notes, 'the birth of a new sphere of social activity between that of the family and that of the State' (1998: 154). Say (2001: 9) reproaches Steuart and the Physiocrats with having confused the research of the principles that constitute a good government with those the growth of wealth is based on, whether public or private. He notes:

> In confounding in the same researches the essential elements of good government with the principles on which the growth of wealth, either public or private, depends, it is by no means surprising that authors should have involved these subjects in obscurity, instead of elucidating them. Stewart, who has entitled his first chapter 'Of the Government of Mankind,' is liable to this reproach; the sect of 'Economists' of the last century, throughout all their writings, and J. J. Rousseau, in the article 'Political Economy' in the *Encyclopédie*, lie under the same imputation.
>
> (Say 2001: 9)

Fortunately for Say (2001: 10),

> Since the time of Adam Smith, it appears to me, these two very distinct inquiries have been uniformly separated, the term political economy being now confined to the science which treats of wealth, and that of politics, to designate the relations existing between a government and its people, and the relations of different states to each other.

Skinner (2003: 104) seems to believe things are not so simple, when he notices that 'The analytic apparatus developed in *The Wealth of Nations*' first two books' is, if not Physiocrat-inspired, at least marked by Physiocrats. It is significant in this regard that, in Book I, Smith does not use the term political economy, which he used only once in Book II with the meaning it can have in physiocratic economics: The nature and cause of wealth. Moreover, if it is true, as Say points out, that Smith does not deal with political institutions in the same way as do Quesnay and the Physiocrats, he nevertheless dedicates Book IV to political economy, understood as systems linking economics, law, and politics. It is precisely in this part that he deals with commerce, as well as agricultural and natural liberty systems.

So, it can be said that if Smith did not use the term political economy in his major book title, it is not because the term was coined by Steuart, as Cannan (1929: 42–43) suggests, but because such a title would have misrepresented his own thinking. *The Wealth of Nations* deals both with economics and political economy while it avoids, unlike the Physiocrats, proposing a model of political government.

The emerging idea of economy as a science

Thanks to Descartes and especially to Newton, the idea of science became extremely popular during the 18th century. Redman (1997: 106) insists on the fascination shown by Scottish intellectuals between 1710 and 1730 for Newton and the theory of natural law. He points out that 'Francis Hutcheson, David Hume, and Adam Smith, were only three of a much larger group who set out to found a science of man by using Newtonian methods'. For them, Newtonian science was 'characterized by its empiricism and a parsimony and simplicity of organizing principles' (Redman 1997: 107). In France, this idea of parsimony and simplicity of principles is found in Etienne Bonnot de Condillac (1714–1780) (Steiner 1998: 12), an author that Smith and the Physiocrats have read. The idea of a science of economics spread in France from 1750 onwards and, in 1752, Carl von Linné (1707–1778), in *Le Journal oeconomique*, saw economics as the science 'that teaches us how to prepare things for our use' (Steiner 1998: 13). In 1753, Forbonnais (1722–1800) referred to 'the science of political commerce', which he understood as the way 'to guide the activity of merchants in a way that would benefit everyone' (Steiner 1998: 14).

The idea of an economic science based on calculations was developed by Mirabeau in *Rural Philosophy* (1763), a book written in close collaboration with François Quesnay (Steiner 1998: 17). Although, among Physiocrats, the idea of science is linked to that of an economic table and that of calculation, Quesnay nevertheless rejects the differential calculus (Steiner 1998: 21), which became the key tool of economic science, with Cournot and the neoclassics. Nevertheless, Victor Riquetti de Mirabeau views resorting to science as a way to weigh down onto political decision (Steiner 1998: 20). Hence, for him, there is at least willingness to strike again the right balance between economic science and politics.

While Steuart and Smith were writing their books, the reflection on the economic situation was well advanced in France, a country where they had both resided. Nevertheless their notion of science fit into a Newtonian perspective, if Chamley is to be believed, (1965: 48–49). But Smith's outlook, more influenced as he was by stoicism, is more liberal, while Steuart's is more marked by neoplatonism and the restoration of order. Smith belongs to a school that, according to Redman (1997), was convinced that the same order and harmony that Newton had found in the physical universe existed and had to be discovered as well in the social and moral universe. For them, disorder in this field was man-made and 'could be averted by studying human nature and ascertaining the natural laws or connecting principles that govern society' (Redman 1997: 111). It was Smith's project to discover the true principle of human nature and derive the true political economy or economics.

On the contrary, even if Steuart is also a Newtonian, as Chamley argues (1965: 48–49), he does not adopt a Newtonian approach in the classical sense of the term because his notion of science remains marked by Aristotle, as Urquhart (1998) points out. Aristotle and Steuart, unlike the Newtonian approach based on the search for a very small number of principles, emphasized the peculiarities and insisted on the fact that 'we cannot establish any principle, nor any set of general principles that can explain human behaviour in particular circumstances' (Urquhart 1998: 147). Smith, in *A History of Astronomy*, challenged this feature of aristotleism which in a way leads to the justification of a hierachical world. He accused Aristotle of considering that the only things settled by God or by the 'First Cause' pertain to the First Heaven, while 'the inferior Planetary Spheres derived each of them its peculiar revolution from an inferior being of the same kind' and that 'all other inferior things are unworthy of their consideration; and that, therefore, whatever was below the Moon was abandoned by the gods to the direction of Nature, and Chance, and Necessity' (Smith 1980: 115). In short, according to him, Aristotle, or at least the Aristotle understood by Smith and by those then interested in astronomy, developed a hierarchical vision of the world in which little attention is paid to what is below. On the contrary, with a Newtonian epistemology the whole world is governed by the same principles, and stars and planets are governed by the same law. As Koyré (1962) points out, with Newton, 'the Aristotelian view of space, a differentiated set of intramundane places' is succeeded by 'the space of Euclidean geometry – a homogeneous and necessarily infinite extension'. Smith's approach of science is part of a Newtonian perspective, where what matters most is to establish general relationships between facts. 'Philosophy', he wrote, is 'the science of the connecting principles of nature' (Smith 1980: 45). The purpose of observations is to integrate into a larger and more coherent system events or things that look incoherent at first sight; in short, the purpose is to unify things that are not hierarchical. With Smith, therefore, science seeks to make progress in coherence and explanatory power, based on parsimony of principles.

Steuart's political economy

Three key points in Steuart's political economy will now be analyzed in this section: How does Steuart want to determine the principles of political economy that he perceives both as a science and an art? How are interests harmonized? What links exist between politics and economics?

Political economy as science and art

For Steuart, political economy is both a science and an art. As a science, its purpose 'is to secure a certain fund of subsistence for all the inhabitants . . . to provide everything necessary for supplying the wants of the society, and to employ the inhabitants' (I, 3). It is a deductive science (Kobayashi 1998b: 124), which attempts to establish general principles by means of observation and reflection.

> The speculative person who, removed from the practice, extracts the principles of this science from *observation* and *reflection*, should divest himself, as far as possible, of every prejudice in favour of established opinions, however reasonable, when examined relatively to particular nations: he must do his utmost to become a citizen of the world, comparing customs, examining minutely institutions.
>
> (I, 4)

The statesman is not a speculative person but a man of the art who must adapt this science to specific countries:

> The great art therefore of political oeconomy is, first to adapt the different operations of it to the spirit, manners, habits, and customs of the people; and afterwards to model these circumstances, so as to be able to introduce a set of new and more useful institutions.
>
> (I, 3)

Steuart affirms that a statesman does not only have to adapt science to a country: He is also the one who must manage change. Steuart (I, 16) wrote:

> The great art of governing is to divest oneself of prejudices and attachments to particular opinions, particular classes, and above all to particular persons; to consult the spirit of the people, to give way to it in appearance, and in so doing to give it a turn capable of inspiring those sentiments which may induce them to relish the change, which an alteration of circumstances has rendered necessary.

This mixture of art and science allows achieving more grandiose works. This is how Steuart explains that, for example, with art and science you can build a military road through mountains and forests, whereas, with art, merely a communal road can be built (I, 87).

Reflecting on the reasons why the statesman is so important to Steuart, it can be deduced this is because he does not believe in invariable laws. Steuart warns the statesman of the responsibility of adapting to times that demand that legislation be modified according to each nation, particular circumstances and people's desires. Steuart (I, 9) wrote:

> All governments have what they call their fundamental laws; but fundamental, that is, invariable laws, can never subsist among men, the most variable thing we know; the only fundamental law, *salus populi*, must ever be relative, like other things. But this is rather a maxim than a law.

This approach of laws as variable as maxims opposes him to the Physiocrats. Victor Riquetti, Marquis de Mirabeau (1715–1789), the father of Honoré-Gabriel de Mirabeau (1749–1791), the French revolutionary, insisted on the immutability of laws and precisely subtitled his book (published in 1764) *La Philosophie rurale* (*Rural Philosophy*), *L'économie générale et politique de l'agriculture, réduite à l'ordre immuable des lois physiques et morale qui assurent la prospérité des empires* (*The General and Political Economy of Agriculture, reduced to the immutable order of the physical and moral laws that ensure the prosperity of empires)*. This way of understanding the law also sets him against Smith, who follows a more Newtonian scientific approach, based on much more fixed relations and laws. Somehow, this mistrust of invariable relations can be felt when Steuart deals with systems. Founded on deductions based on some fundamental maxims, he finds them unfit to account for reality.

> but, when inquiries are made concerning the complicated interest of society, the vivacity of an author's genius is apt to prevent him from attending to the variety of circumstances which render uncertain every consequence almost which he can draw from his reasoning. To this I ascribe the habit of running into what the French call Systèmes. These are no more than a chain of contingent consequences, drawn from a few fundamental maxims, adopted, perhaps, rashly. Such systems are mere conceits; they misled the understanding, and efface the path to truth.
>
> (I, xii)

So Steuart prefers establishing principles of political economy that leave more room for political initiative to adapt to circumstances, while providing guidelines to both people and politics.

> But when principles are not known, all inquiry is an end, the moment a nation can be engaged to submit to the burden. It is the same with regard to many other parts of this science: while people remain blind they are always mistrustful.
>
> (I, 5)

It should be noted here that there is reason to believe the word 'principle' is somewhat reminiscent of Newton's main work, which is, incidentally, entitled *Principia (Mathematical Principles of Natural Philosophy)*. As a conclusion to the preface, he still leaves some doubt as to whether or not he wants to create a system.

> I pretend to form no system, but, by tracing out a succession of principles, consistent with the nature of man and with one another, I shall endeavour to furnish some materials towards the forming of a good one.
>
> (I, 7)

However, what really matters to Steuart (I, x) are principles relating to 'the most interesting branches of modern policy, such as population, agriculture, trade, industry, money, the currency, interest, circulation, bank exchanges, public credit and taxes.' Steuart (I, x) adds, heralding all economics books, especially the classical political economists' who put the word *Principle* in their title:

> The principles deduced from all theses topics, appear tolerably consistent; and the whole is a train of reasoning, through which I have adhered to the connection of subjects as faithfully as I could; but the nature of the work being a deduction of principles, not a collection of institutions.

Control of the individual interest by the politic

As a general rule, institutions and the economic organization are intended to frame and harmonize men's personal interests so that they contribute to the general interest.

> The best way to govern a society, and to engage every one to conduct himself according to a plan, is for the statesman to form a system of administration, the most consistent possible with the interest of every individual, and never to flatter himself that his people will be brought to act in general, and in matters which purely regard the public, from any other principle than private interest.
> (I, 220)

Like Smith, Steuart (I, 218) makes interest the key element of his economics:

> The principle of self-interest will serve as a general key to this inquiry; and it may, in one sense, be considered as the ruling principle of my subject, and may therefore be traced throughout the whole.

Both of them assert men must follow their interests without any concern for the public good. While both, as argued by Redman (1996: 61), are in favour of a well-ordered society, they are opposed regarding the way to achieve this. While Smith claims 'economic forces should be left running their natural course' (Redman 1996: 61), Steuart on the contrary insists that statesmen have to harmonize interests and show that the common good is 'the combination of every private interest which forms the public good, and of this public good, that is, the statesman only, can judge' (I, 221).

For Steuart (I, 109; emphasis added), the social purpose of harmonizing interests is to promote a perfect free community, where everyone helps and assists the community in proportion to the assistance provided.

> The political oeconomy of government is brought to perfection, when every class in general, and every individual in particular, is made to be aiding and assisting the community, in proportion to the assistance he receives from it. This conveys my idea of a free and perfect society, which is *a general tacit contract, from which reciprocal and proportional services result universally between all those who compose it.*

The eminent position given to statesmen in the determination of general interest shows some propinquity with the Duke of Rohan's sentence 'Princes order their peoples and interest orders princes' (Cited in Hirschman 2013: 34) and provides a better understanding of why politics have to drive economics both domestically and internationally. As will now be seen, Steuart has little confidence in economic agents. For example, Steuart (I, 310–311) compares the trading nations of Europe to ships. According to him, victory depends not only on the crew's dexterity but on the captain's also, as compared to the statesman. Likewise, he is weary of the innovation introduced by men. He notes:

> In treating every question of political oeconomy, I constantly suppose a statesman at the head of government, systematically conducting every part of it, so as to prevent the vicissitudes of manners, and innovations, by their natural and immediate effects or consequences, from hurting any interest within the commonwealth.
>
> (I, 161)

The economic as a means of rationalizing the government and ensuring the subordination of men

Steuart believes liberty consists in being governed by general laws (I, 315). Thus a good government must be based on a regular administration applying general laws: 'I speaks of governments only which are conducted systematically, constitutionally, and by general laws; and when I mention princes, I mean their councils' (I,331). However, Steuart's thinking presents much ambiguity when defining the notions of liberty and of general laws. First, he doubts the existence of general laws, and that is why he prefers relying on politics. Second, it is difficult to imagine that a leader who decides on the general interest could have regard for general laws. The inherent temptation of such a system is to constantly intervene to achieve the goal. Finally, Steuart seems to assimilate the legislative and the executive, when he writes: 'The statesman is a general term to signify the legislature and supreme power, according to the form of government' (I, 2). This formulation seems to fly in the face of Montesquieu's precepts and be unable to contain the temptation of politics to fall into arbitrariness. So when Steuart notices that the statesman 'is neither master to establish what oeconomy he pleases, or, in the exercise of his sublime authority, to overturn at will its established laws, let him be the most despotic monarch on earth' (I, 2–3). Nevertheless, he does not indicate which device will prevent the government from yielding to passion and behaving in a despotic manner. In short, unlike Smith, where passions are contained through the market mechanism and the link between economics, politics and jurisprudence, Steuart does not suggest any mechanism able to balance passions. He merely postulates, as Redman (1996: 57) points out, that the statesman always shows an inclination 'to virtue and benevolence' (II, 69).

Concerning the government of men, Steuart (I, xi), in the preface to his book, insists on the need to make men understand the reasons for decisions 'in political questions it is better for people to judge from experience and reason'. However, for him as for Filmer,[2] which Locke (1632–1704) refutes in the *Two Treatises of Governement* (Carrive 1994: 33), ordinary men are children. Steuart writes: 'What Oeconomy is in a family, political oeconomy is in the state – with these essential differences, however, that in a state there are no servants, all are children' (I, 2). This perspective refers to the political commitments of Steuart, a Jacobite partisan of the Stuarts, to the dynasty that was removed from the throne during the Glorious Revolution. Steuart's commitment certainly jeopardized the success of his book. All the more so as Smith was considered whiggish (the party of the victors of the English revolutions) (Long 2006: 191). Smith is precisely opposed to Filmer on a crucial point of his thinking: Relating to the equality of men and their vocation – equal or almost equal to that of kings – to make decisions. While for Filmer the King is God's vice-governor ('vicegerent', according to the terminology at that time) (Carrive 1994: 65), and as such is above laws and men, for Smith ordinary men have in them moral faculties that he considers as vice-governors (vicegerents) because they 'are the sovereign principles of human nature' (Smith 1976: IV, 233). Men and the king are placed on an equal footing and both may legitimacy take part in political and economic decisions (Smith 1999: 233; Clavé 2005: 40–44).

For Steuart (I, 316–317), subordination is linked to dependency. He distinguishes three kinds of dependency: The natural dependence of children on parents; the political dependence between lords and vassals, princes and subjects; and the economic dependence between 'the rich and the industrious'. Although subordination also includes an element of authority, the major element of subordination is that the superior may be able to meet his subordinates' needs (I, 316). For Steuart, for subordination to be reasonable and just it must be proportionate to dependence. Thus the sovereign must be rich to maintain power. Steuart (I, 321) wonders, rhetorically: 'Do we not see how subordination rises and falls under different reigns, under a rich Elizabeth, and a necessitous Charles?'. To enforce subordination, the statesman has some sort of social duties. Redman (1996: 59) emphasizes Steuart's proximity to German cameralism and the 'paternalistic nature of the government's policy plan'. On this point, one could also say Steuart is not very far from the thought of Laud (1673–1645), a bishop of Canterbury, who is close, like Steuart, to the Stuart dynasty. For Weber (2002: 139), this adversary of the *Glorious Revolution* and of *the Puritans* aspired to establish a 'social Christian' economic organization that would have been governed by the King and the Church – an organization whose king expected some political and fiscal advantages.

Economics and political economic system in Smith's works

After considering how Steuart addressed the issue of the link between politics and economics, a similar analysis should be made of Smith. The study will be structured around three questions: What is the place of interest in its scientific approach? How do market mechanisms allow the economy to achieve an amount of autonomy in opposition to politics? What is the function of political economic systems with Smith?

Smith and the economic science

The Wealth of Nations is considered as one of the foundations of economic science, thanks to the concept of capital, profit, and value (Kobayashi 1998a: lxxxviii), all of which cannot be found in Steuart. For him, political economy helps the statesman lead people, while for Smith, it is intended to help the people obtain 'a revenue or subsistence for themselves; and furthermore, to supply the state or commonwealth with a revenue sufficient for the public services' (Smith 1976: IV, 449). For Smith, economics is also a moral science (Young 1997); therefore two principles, or two 'inclinations', of human nature – perceived by him as universal – support the construction of *The Wealth of Nations*, thanks to the propensity of men 'to truck, barter, and exchange one thing for another' (Smith 1976: I, 17) and 'the disposition to self-improvement' (Rothschild & Sen 2006: 324). These principles are at the foundation of the division of labour, the use of money, and the increase in the wealth of nations. However, interest is the key principle of *The Wealth of Nations*, as Heath (2013: 254) explains: 'Nonetheless, Smith's treatise reveals how economic interactions are governed primarily by a form of self-interest'. Mehta points out that, for Smith, it is because human beings are guided by their personal interests that consumers react to price, that entrepreneurs invest, and different economic agents work. Smith's focus on interest is the strength of his science project. Hirschman (2013: 112) has written about it,

> Moreover, the proposition and ensuing doctrine fulfilled another requirement of the highly successful paradigm: while it was a splendid generalization, it represented a considerable narrowing of the field of inquiry over which social thought had ranged freely up to then and thus permitted intellectual specialization and professionalization.

Indeed, interest is not necessarily prevailing in all social categories. For example, landowners – the category Steuart belongs to – are ignorant of their interests, and so are employees, often active and labourious but ignorant due to lack of time spent studying (Rothschild & Sen 2006: 328). On the contrary, interest is decisive for merchants and industrialists, the '"heroes" of *The Wealth of Nations*' (Rothschild & Sen 2006: 325). Even so, one of Smith's great forces is to deal with passions, without being obliged, like Steuart, to bring in another principle – subordination – from the field of politics. This allows him to remain in a Newtonian model, while Steuart adopts a more Aristotelian model, where each phenomenon can possibly have a different principle (Berry 2006: 125).

The role of interest in making economics independent from politics

For Steuart, the statesman controls individuals' interests and decides on the general interest, while, in Smith, the agents enjoy much greater freedom and are not as subordinate to the state. Mehta (2006: 251) notes:

> Too often, legislators or others presume to know best how interests are to be served. In attacking that presumption, Smith is not replacing a public-spirited

> motive with a self-interested one. Rather, he argues that relevant agents should be allowed to judge their own interests rather than having them judged by the powerful who, in any case, are likely to be guided by *their* interests.

Following from it, Mehta (2006: 252) cites 'the purpose of *The Wealth of Nations* is to redefine the public good, so that it reflects the *equality* of interests'. It seems that Smith also wants to show that economic agents are better able to achieve what is most effective for society. In this regard, comparing the analysis of agents' behaviours on the wheat market is enlightening. For Steuart (I, 373), the statesman's intervention is absolutely necessary. For Smith, on the contrary, intervention by the state is bad because it prohibits a rational organization of the markets and causes famine. Smith (1976: IV, 33) supports that 'Famine has never arisen from any other cause but the violence of government attempting, by improper means, to remedy the inconveniencies of a dearth'.

He also accuses governments of yielding to popular demagogy and of believing or pretending to believe that merchants constantly speculate. For him, on the contrary, the merchant has no interest in raising his price too high because then consumption falls, and the merchant may not sell everything. In short, it is the theme of interest as rational passion. Yet, while for Steuart only statesmen are able to make good use of them, Smith believes in a more egalitarian way, namely that all men can use this faculty.

The problem is that the economic agent, too, may not follow his personal interest and behave badly by following his passions. This is an important topic for Smith. For example, the slave owner does not cater to his own interest by resorting to slavery. It must be remembered here that Smith, unlike Steuart, believed that slavery was not profitable because it did not encourage the men and women subjected to this oppression to work. According to him, slavery could be practiced only where profits were very high, such as in sugar colonies. Thus, for Smith, slave owners do not follow their interests but endeavour to satisfy passions such as the urge to dominate, the eagerness to be noticed, etc. (Mehta 2006: 256). Similarly, merchants and manufacturers want to escape market laws to give free rein to their passion for gain. Like feudal vassals, they forget their long-term interests in associating with the rulers who are in a position to grant them monopolies.

For Mehta (2006: 257), '*The Wealth of Nations* is an account of how the interests of all might be harmonized, not a claim that they are always, or naturally, in harmony'. Smith finds that the market is one of the means of harmonizing interests. The market functions in two ways: On the one hand, it opposes merchants' interests competing with one another and, on the other hand, merchants' interests and consumers'. This results in a market price that does not necessarily maximize an agent's gains. Moreover, on the market one is obliged to take into account what the other participants think and intend to do, so that, in a certain way, the impartial spectator' speculating game comes to moderate passions in order to reach agreement. Furthermore, when the economic agents do not look for the big profits in the short term and are cautious, as is the case of the merchant who, out of prudence, to better control his affairs, invests in the domestic industry rather than the foreign industry, then, the Invisible hand helps them achieving the common good.[3] As Smith (1976: IV, 477) argues:

> By preferring the support of domestic to that of foreign industry, he intends only his own security; and by directing that industry in such a manner as its produce may be the greatest value, he intends only his own gain, and he is in this, as in many other cases, led by an invisible hand to promote an end which was not part of his intention. . . . By pursuing his own interest he frequently promotes society's more effectually than when he really intends to promote it.

Still, Smith does not only rely on the market to harmonize interests; he affirms that politics and legislation also have their roles to play, as will be seen in the next paragraph.

Political economy systems in Smith's works

Smith defines political economy 'as a branch of the science of a statesman or legislator' (Smith 1976: IV, 449). Two interpretations of this definition are possible. First, the solution of continuity, where *The Wealth of Nations* only deals with political economy, and second, the discontinuity solution. In Books I and II of *The Wealth of Nations*, Smith deals with economic science and in Book IV with the science of political economy. The second solution advocated in this chapter seems the most logical, and it is in any case the one that best takes into account Young's remark (1997: 19): 'science, for Smith, was a broader and less clearly focused activity than it is today'. It should be noted that Smith defines political economy in Book IV of *The Wealth of Nations*, where he deals with 'systems', a word Steuart was very reluctant to use, as seen earlier. To find the answer to what a Smith system is, one has to refer to the *History of Astronomy*, where he defines a system as 'an imaginary machine invented to connect together, in fancy, those different movements and effects that are in reality already performed' (Smith 1980: 66). It can be deduced that Smith, through the systems of political economy, might try to establish links between the economy and the legislators and/or statesmen. The hitch here is that he distinguishes three possible systems (mercantilism, the agricultural system, and that of natural fredom), while a Newtonian science might keep only one. Now, it would be possible to argue that one of the three, natural freedom, seems to be the best as he sees it because it is the most suited to the natural course of things. In support of this thesis it could also be recalled that Smith establishes a fairly strong equivalence between the natural and the best. For example, in *The Wealth of Nations* he considers that asserting that the development of trade and manufactures is the cause, not the result, of rural area improvement, does not correspond to the natural order, which would have resulted in things being done in the opposite way. He infers from this that not respecting the natural course of things leads to an order 'necessarily both slow and uncertain' (Smith 1976: III, 441).

The second problem posed by the definition of the political economy comes from the way of interpreting the 'or' set between the words 'statesman' and 'legislator' in the sentence where political economy is defined 'as a branch of a statesman's or legislator's science'. Should 'or' be read as an '*et* (and)' as in the French translation (Smith 1991: 11) or as an 'or', meaning that the statesman and the legislator were one and the same? The very fact that the question arises seems to reveal Smith's temptation to reduce the statesman's function to that of a legislator. It can also be noted that he prefers the legislator 'whose deliberations ought to be governed by general principles, which are always the same' (Smith 1976: IV, 490), rather than the statesman, who he considers an 'insidious and crafty animal . . . whose councils are directed by the momentary fluctuations of affairs' (Smith 1976: IV, 490). In connection with the enduring nature of the law cited earlier, Smith advocates for 'the laws of justice' that define the rules of the game, not 'laws of police' that attempt to direct the actual rule of the game, in order to affect the outcomes (Young 1997: 194). The laws of justice allow for creating a framework where the common good is achieved without being really sought after. In this respect, Young (1997: 177) notes: 'The law, especially the common law, may be able construct an institutional environment, in which individual incentives lead to the promotion of the common good as an unintended consequence of individual action'.

For Smith the virtue of justice is a vicegerent 'implanted in the human breast' (quoted in Long 2006: 306) that allows maintaining sociability, a concept he substitutes to Aristotelian teleology and Thomistic consciousness. The laws of commutative justice are also essential to the proper functioning of the market by setting the rules of the game and sanctioning those who do not respect them. It is now time to analyze the way Smith approaches politics.

In the political domain, Smith does not think self-interest necessarily leads to the common good (Young 1997: 178). Smith notes that businessmen hardly like competition that comes to curb their passion for profit. So for him 'the proposal of any law or regulation of commerce which comes from this order, ought to always to be listened to with great precaution' (quoted in Young 1997: 180).

For Smith, 'Politics is a matter of judgment' (Long 2006: 316), so that, in order to establish laws, the politician must arbitrate between different interests while committing to accountability to people. It can be noticed that many authors argue that in Smith, politics become less self-centred and more focused on the economy. For example, Wolin & Cropsey (*ibidem*) speak of 'a non-political model of society', while Long (*ibidem*) argues that it is a pragmatic approach that takes away the doctrinaire aspect of politics. Anyway, for Smith, a statesman must have both the necessary authority and the character as well as the sense of the public mind to fulfill his task successfully (Long 2006: 294–295), i.e., establish a framework in which economic agents can enrich themselves while enriching the state.

Conclusion

As a conclusion, while Steuart and Smith both set interest at the core of their economic thought, they, however, are opposed regarding the ways to harmonize economic players' divergent interests. Steuart affirms statesmen are in charge of this duty, whereas Smith believes market mechanisms may contribute to harmonization that promotes the autonomy of the economy from politicians. Although the two authors' political economies seek to increase wealth, they conflict on the way to achieve that objective. Steuart believes it is the duty of statesmen, while Smith feels it is economic agents' task. For him, the statesman is basically a legislator who has to create a framework favourable to economic agents' actions. The classics seem to pick up this theme, but they do so in the Bentham version of a dichotomy between what the statesman can do and what he cannot do (Clavé 2005a: 94). Classical economists also take from Steuart the notion of principles they often use in their major works titles (Deleplace 2007: 4). Likewise, they take up from Steuart the term of political economy and reject the notion of a system, dear to Smith. Concerning economic science, they also adopt the distinction established by Steuart between science and art. Nonetheless, they will refuse to see any amount of continuity between the *Theory of Moral Sentiments* and the *The Wealth of Nations*, thus creating the Adam Smith problem. This chapter emphasizes the possibility of considering that Smith is developing two close, but distinct, scientific projects. The first one set forth in Books I and II of the *Wealth of Nations* aims at establishing an economic science, while the second, explained mainly in Book IV, scientifically (or logically) establishes links between economics, legislation, and politics, through the notion of a political economic system.

Notes

1 Acknowledgement: I would like to thank Gilles Campagnolo for his comments and observations, which enabled me to greatly improve the chapter, the first part in particular. I would also like to thank Maria Knight and Dominique Macabies for contributing to the translation of this article.
2 Filmer is neither a traditionalist royalist nor a worshipper of the past; rather, this author strives at renewing a type of thinking, and in this respect as well, he is close to Steuart (Daly 1979: 155; Carrive 1994).
3 See Clavé (2005b: 61).

Bibliography

Barthas, J. (2011), Le Traicté de l'oeconomie politique est-il un anti-Machiavel? Note philologique, historiographique et critique, in A. Guery (ed.), *Monchrestien et Cantillon, le commerce et l'émergence d'une pensée économique*, Lyon: ENS Editions: 103–130.
Berry, C. (2006), Smith and Science, in K. Haakonssen (ed.), *Cambridge Companion to Adam Smith*, Cambridge: Cambridge University Press: 241–266.
Cannan, E. (1929), *A Review of Economics Theory*, London: P.S. King & Son Limited.
Carrive, P. (1994), *La pensée politique anglaise: passions, pouvoirs et libertés de Hooker à Hume*, Paris: P.U.F.
Chamley, P. (1965), *Documents relatifs à Sir James Steuart*, Paris: Librairie Dalloz.
Clavé, F. (2005a), Walter Lippmann et le néolibéralisme de la Cité libre, *Cahiers d'économie politique*, 48: 79–110.
———. (2005b), Smith face au système de l'optimisme de Leibniz, *Revue de Philosophie économique*, 12(2): 19–71.
Daly, J. (1979), *Sir Robert Filmer and English Political Thought*, Toronto: University of Toronto Press.

Deleplace, G. (2007), *Histoire de la pensée économique*, Paris: Dunod.

Faccarello, G. (1986), *Aux origines de l'économie politique libérale: Pierre de Boisguilbert*, Paris: Éditions anthropos.

Greengrass, M. (2007), The Calvinist and the Chancellor: The Mental World of Louis Turquet de Mayerne, *Startseite*, 34(2). Available online at https://journals.ub.uni-heidelberg.de/index.php/fr/article/view/45065.

Groenewegen, P. (2008), Political Economy, in S.N. Durlauf & L.E. Blume (eds.), *The New Palgrave Dictionary of Economics*, London: Palgrave.

Guery, A. (2011), L'honneur et le profit. Economie du pouvoir et économie de la richesse chez Montchrestien, in A. Guery (ed.), *Monchrestien et Cantillon, le commerce et l'émergence d'une pensée économique*, Lyon: ENS Editions: 417–439.

Heath, E. (2013), Adam Smith and Self-Interest, in C. Berry, M.P. Paganelli, & C. Smith (eds.), *Oxford Handbook of Adam Smith*, Oxford: Oxford University Press: 241–266.

Hirschman, A. (2013), *The Passions and the Interests*, Princeton, NJ: Princeton University Press.

Kobayashi, N. (1998a), Introduction, in J. Steuart, *An Inquiry into the Principles of Political Oeconomy*, vol. 1, London: Pickering & Chatto.

———. (1998b), De la méthode de sir James Steuart dans les principes d'Economie Politique, *Economies et sociétés, Oeconomia Série P.E.*, 27(11–12): 123–140.

Koyré, A. (1962), *Du monde clos à l'univers infini*, Paris: PUF.

Laudet, M. (2017), Introduction, in A. Montchrétien, *Traité de l'oeconomie politique*, Paris: Classiques Garnier.

Long, D. (2006), Adam Smith's Politics, in K. Haakonssen (ed.), *Cambridge Companion to Adam Smith*, Cambridge: Cambridge University Press: 288–318.

Machet, A. (2015), Vue d'ensemble, in P. Verri, *Méditations sur l'économie politique*, Paris: Classiques Garnier.

Mehta, P.B. (2006), Self-Interest and Other Interests, in K. Haakonssen (ed.), *Cambridge Companion to Adam Smith*, Cambridge: Cambridge University Press: 246–247.

Mirabeau, H. G comte de (1760) *Théorie de l'impôt*, n.p.

Montchrétien, A. (2017), *Traité de l'oeconomie politique*, Paris: Classiques Garnier.

Quesnay, F. (2014), *Philosophie rurale ou économie générale et politique de l'agriculture*, Genève: Slatkine Erudition.

Redman, D. (1996), Sir James Steuart's Statesman Revisted in Light of the Continental Influence, *Scottish Journal Of Political Economy*, 43(1): 48–70.

———. (1997), *The Rise of Political Economy as a Science*, Cambridge: The MIT Press.

Rothschild, E., & Sen, A. (2006), Adam Smith's Economics, in K. Haakonssen (ed.), *Cambridge Companion to Adam Smith*, Cambridge: Cambridge University Press: 319–365.

Rousseau, J.-J. (2002), *Discours sur l'économie politique*, Paris: Vrin.

Say, J.-B. (2001), *A Treatise on Political Economy, or the Production, Distribution and Consumption of Wealth*, Kitchener: Batoche Books.

Skinner, A. (2003), Adam Smith (1723–1790): Theories of Political Economy, in J. Warren, J.E. Biddle & J.B. Davis (eds.), *A Companion to the History of Economic Thought*, London: Blackwell Publishing Ltd.

Smith, A. (1976), *An Inquiry into the Nature and Causes of the Wealth of Nations*, Chicago: The University of Chicago Press.

———. (1980), History of Astronomy, in W.P.D. Whightman & J.C. Bryce (eds.), *Adam Smith Essays on Philosophical Subjects*, Oxford: Clarendon House.

———. (1991), *La richesse des nations*, vol. 2, Paris: GF-Flammarion.
Steiner, P. (1998), *La 'science nouvelle' de l'économie politique*, Paris: P.U.F.
Tortajada, R. (1992), La renaissance de la scolastique, la Réforme et les rthéories du droit naturel, in A. Béraud & G. Faccarello (eds.), *Nouvelle histoire de la pensée économique*, vol. 1, Paris: Editions La Découverte: 71–91.
Urquhart, R. (1998), La méthode de Steuart: économie politique aristotélicienne, *Economies et Sociétés, série PE*, 27: 141–158.
Weulersse G. (1910), *Le Mouvement physiocratique en France*, Paris: Félix Alcan.
Weber, M. (2002), *L'éthique protestante et l'esprit du capitalisme*, Paris: Champs Classique.
Young, J.T. (1997), *Economics as a Moral Science: The Political Economy of Adam Smith*, Cheltenham: Edward Elgar.

Part II

Money, prices, and production

6 James Steuart on John Law's system

The beginnings of a rational monetary analysis?

Jean Cartelier

Steuart devotes 12 chapters of his *Inquiry* to the system John Law has implemented in France at the time of the *Régence*.[1] His diagnosis about Law's system reveals a great intellectual proximity between the two authors that one cannot think that something more than a pure sympathetic attitude towards Law's action explains Steuart's favourable judgment.[2] My hypothesis is that Law and Steuart belong to an ancient and venerable tradition of economic analysis dubbed *monetary analysis* by Schumpeter in his *History of Economic Analysis*. That tradition has been superseded by another, dubbed *real analysis*, which encompasses all value theories, from Smith to Arrow-Debreu, passing by Ricardo, Marx, Walras, and Marshall. Although Schumpeter maintains that the opposition between real and monetary analysis is the main cleavage in our discipline, few economists are aware of the co-existence of these two paradigms during history. Consequently they hardly realize that Law's and Steuart's works cannot be read as if they were value theoreticians. Steuart, who published his *Inquiry* nine years prior to Smith's *Wealth of Nations*, could not help the modern reader to avoid the confusion.[3]

Taking seriously Schumpeter's opposition between real and monetary analysis helps to understand why Steuart may feel close to Law in spite of his reluctance towards many aspects of his system. It is even possible to suggest that Steuart's consciousness of his affinity with Law marks the birth of a rational monetary analysis. Before Law and Steuart, authors labelled 'mercantilists' by Smith had paved the way, but they had not offered a general framework, making their different contributions related to each other. It is only with Law and Steuart that a sound theoretical basis has been worked out. Although Smith and all value theoreticians after him have succeeded in making a real approach the dominant one, the theoretical basis of monetary analysis due to Law and Steuart was still available and has made later developments possible, Keynes being the most prominent (Sen 1947).

Problems raised by money are not at all the same in the two approaches. Identifying these problems as they appear in the text of the authors allows us to recognize the approach they belong to (or the one they are close to). Money enters Law's and Steuart's works in a very specific way, which differs radically from the so-called 'integration of money in value theory', the one that more than two centuries of domination of value approach have made us familiar with (Section 1). As far as money is concerned, a central proposition shared by Law and Steuart opposes them to all other theoreticians of the time: Money is issued through a sovereign transformation of some wealth item into means of payment (Section 2). That proposition comes along with a common view of what economics is about. In a nutshell, both authors conceived economic relations as monetary transfers of units of accounts and not as a permutation of commodities amongst individuals – in short, payments versus voluntary exchange. Thinking of economic relations as flows of payment leading to a restructuration of wealth is also shared by these authors (Section 3).

Law and Steuart as representatives of monetary analysis

A modern economic theoretician reading Law's and Steuart's works may notice the absence of any preoccupation concerning the so-called 'integration of money in value theory'. This comes as no surprise. Such a concern can be present in a theory only if its main propositions and results are obtained and make sense in a moneyless framework, as it is the case with Ricardo (rate of profit and prices of production determination) or general competitive equilibrium theory (existence and optimality of competitive general equilibrium). What backs that latter stance is the conviction that real wealth matters and that monetary phenomena hide the heart of the matter. As a consequence, money should be discarded at a first stage in order to grasp the essence of economic reality. Money has to be integrated at a second stage only, the crucial stakes being the conditions of its neutrality that could justify the neglect of money at the first stage.

Such a preoccupation is to be found neither in Law's nor in Steuart's writings. This is manifest when these authors deal with the determination of prices (although they call them values).

Law's value theory for commodities boils down to the following statement, recurrent in Essay and in Money and Trade.

> Goods have a Value from the Uses they are apply'd to; And their Value is Greater or Lesser, not so much from their more or less valuable, or necessary Uses: As from the greater or lesser Quantity of them in proportion to the Demand for them.
>
> (1934: 2)

Steuart is a little bit more explicit:

> The value of things depend upon the general combination of many circumstances, which however may be reduced to four principal heads: First, The abundance of the things to be valued; Secondly, The demand which mankind make for them; Thirdly, The competition between the demanders; and Fourthly, The extent of the faculties of the demanders. The function therefore of money is to publish and make known the value of things, as it is regulated by the combination of all these circumstances.
>
> (II, 271–272)

Temptation may be great today to read both statements as if they were a preliminary and crude version of modern 'supply and demand' theory.[4] Such a temptation ought to be resisted since modern supply and demand is not to be found neither in Law's nor in Steuart's writings. For both authors, prices are known as ratios between amounts of money and commodity quantities. Cantillon will make explicit that view a quarter of century after Law and prior to Steuart.[5] Keynes will take it again in the fundamental equations of his Treatise on Money.

Determining market money prices is the only way to assess the value of commodities. According to Law and Steuart there is no possibility to calculate prices without resorting to money and payments. In a rigorous meaning, there is no value theory properly speaking to be found in the writings of Law and Steuart. Their vision of prices deeply differs from the one centuries of domination of real analysis has accustomed us to take for granted. Contrary to what value theoreticians will do later, Law and Steuart presuppose money at the very starting point, and there is no meaning to ask for an integration of money in value theory or to inquire into a dichotomy between value and money theories. Attributing to Law and Steuart, a value theory or a quantitative theory of money value is not only an anachronism – a venial sin indeed – but also and mainly a misunderstanding of what is the common logical structure of their analysis – the original sin of most academic theoreticians.

But if money is at the very beginning of the theory, and if no proposition can be established without considering it, Law's and Steuart's money theory should be very different from that one associated to real analysis where money comes as an afterthought. It is effectively the case. Moreover, their theories of money are sufficiently closed to be considered as forming one unique and specific theory.

An original theory of money

Law and Steuart defend a view about money far more general than the one that could be derived from the mere observation of the current monetary systems at the time. Moreover, Law and Steuart are, to my knowledge, the only ones to do so. Even Cantillon, an outstanding thinker indeed, seems to restrict his reflections to metallic currency only, credit being for him just a means to increase money velocity of circulation. Even if Law and Steuart carefully study the working of metallic monetary systems (the latter more than the former), they are able to conceive of diverse organizations on the basis of an abstract and general money theory in which metallic money is only a special case.

Both consider that money results from a sovereign transformation of any kind of wealth into a means of payment. That basic idea not only avoids the absurd notion of 'money creation ex nihilo' (to be found in many modern text-books) but also the fetishism of precious metals.

According to Law and Steuart, money is not an item of wealth nor a commodity (this would oblige to add to 'commodity' the perilous adjective 'special' in order to explicit why and how money differs from other commodities). The notion of fiat money in modern theory is a good example of that procedure: fiat money is a 'special' commodity since (1) it is of no use in consumption and in production, and (2) its quantity is not privately determined. The consequence is that money quantity is treated as an arbitrary parameter.

For Law and Steuart, wealth is a necessary but not a sufficient condition of money existence. Wealth has to be transformed through a sovereign procedure in order to be used as a means of payment. The term 'sovereign transformation' makes the difference. First of all, the statesman is an integrated part of the economy; the statesman is in charge of maintaining its smooth operation. Adapting the quantity of money to the needs of trade is part of his duties. Issuing money is an endogenous procedure combining private agents and statesman actions. Sovereignty and, with it, some notion of power, find a legitimate place in economic thought, not as an afterthought, showing the regret not to have been able to think of them right from the beginning, but as a full and plain recognition of their central importance, on the same footing as market and prices.

In more concrete terms, gold and silver are not means of payment *per se*. They become so only when they are coined, i.e., transformed by a supra-individual institution – the mint – according to legal rules and statutes. The relation of precious metals to money is conditional to sovereign rules. Without such rules, gold and silver are nothing but commodities. That view opens up room for conceiving that monetary organizations may follow other rules. In his *Essay on a Land Bank* and in *Money and Trade*, Law advocates a system in which the means of payment are issued by a transformation of land into certificates of paper. Later on, in the system, means of payment are issued by a transformation of a company's shares (capital).

Law and Steuart have in common a dual view about money. It is characterized by a conceptual distinction between the item of wealth, which is transformed into means of payment, and the material means of payment are made of.

Table 6.1 illustrates that distinction, taking Law as an example:

Table 6.1 The virtual extension of the economic basis of money is also clearly perceived by Steuart, who takes John Law's ideas

Material minted wealth / *Means of payment*	*Metal*	*Land*	*Bonds (capital)*
coins	specie	xxxxx	xxxxx
paper (banknotes)	*Banque générale* (1716)	Land Bank	System

> Nothing is so easy as to invent a money which may make land circulate as well as houses, and every other thing which is of a nature to preserve the same value during the time of circulation. Whatever has a value, may change hands for an equivalent, and whenever this value is determined, and cannot vary, it may be made to circulate; and in the circulation to produce a vibration in the balance of wealth, as well as a pound of gold or silver made into coin.
>
> (II, 40–41)

Law and Steuart are able to free themselves from what they empirically observe and to realize that metallic currency is only a specimen of a general species. Metallic monetary systems are just characterized by the fact that the material used for the means of payment (coins) is the one that is minted by the coinage. Other monetary organizations do not exhibit that special characteristic. In our economies, for instance, means of payment are made of paper or are electronic impulses, while they are issued by a transformation of capital under the control of a monetary authority.

Although in complete agreement about what money essentially is, Law and Steuart may differ because they do not put the stress on the same aspects of a monetary organization. If both are interested in the elasticity of the means of payment issue and its adaptation to the needs of trade, Law is more attentive to the competition amongst means of payment, while Steuart emphasizes their differences.

For Steuart, coins are *real* money while other means of payment are *symbolical* money. Dealing with symbolical money, he carefully separates the different sorts of minted wealth or counterparts:[6]

> If they [banks] be considered relatively to the principles upon which their credit is built, they may be divided into banks upon *private credit*, banks upon *mercantile credit*, and banks upon *public credit.*
>
> First, private credit. This is established upon a security, real or personal, of value sufficient to make good the obligation of repayment both of capital and interest. This is the most solid of all.
>
> Secondly, mercantile credit. This is established upon the confidence the lender has, that the borrower, from his integrity and knowledge in trade, may be able to replace the capital advanced, and the interest due during the advance, in terms of the agreement. This is the most precarious of all.
>
> Thirdly, public credit. This is established upon the confidence reposed in a state, or body politic, who borrow[s] money upon condition that the capital shall not be demandable; but that a certain proportional part of the sum shall be annually paid, either in lieu of interest, or in extinction of part of the capital; for the security of which, a permanent annual fund is appropriated, with a liberty, however, to the state to free itself at pleasure, upon repaying the whole; when nothing to the contrary is stipulated.
>
> (III, 190; emphasis added)

That distinction between real and symbolical money raises a question distinct (but complementary) to that of competition: Does a hierarchy exist between the two types of money? The answer is positive:

> He who pays in intrinsic value [coins], puts the person to whom he pays in the real possession of what he owed; and this done, there is no more place for credit. He who pays in paper [convertible] puts his creditor in possession only

of another person's obligation to make that value good to him: here credit is necessary even after the payment is made.

(II, p. 269)

Were it inconvertible, paper would be legal tender and the distinction would be between legal tender and credit instead of between coin and credit. Steuart introduces a fundamental distinction in money theory: *money proper* (as Keynes will call it later in his *Treatise*), which is the only means of payment making the payer and the payee free from any obligation vis-à-vis each other, is *qualitatively* different from *credit money*, which only allows for postponing the ultimate payment without going out of debt.

This distinction, fundamental as it is, is also an element of the competition amongst means of payment at the disposition of the statesmen who may proceed by means of legal restrictions about their capacity to be legal tender (as exemplified in the system). It is why Law's and Steuart's views may be more complementary than opposed.

But, beyond these nuances in emphasis, Law and Steuart provide us with the analytical tools to be able to think about the multiplicity of the means of payment in general. It has been said earlier that sovereignty pervades the means of payment issue (Pesante 1999). Schematically, when it is issued through quasi-private agreements, credit money is submitted to its convertibility into money proper. The hierarchy is the one noted by Steuart in the quotation earlier. But when, as it is the case nowadays, credit money is issued in a regulated framework in which banks operate under a strict control of a monetary authority, the difference between the two types of money fades away. In short, the difference between the multiple means of payment may be measured by the degree of sovereignty involved in their issue. In modern terms, 'too big to fail' seems to be a property of systemic banks, which makes their liabilities almost as good as legal tender.

Law's and Steuart's unitary vision of money issue is unbelievably ahead of its time, given the state of development of the economies they could observe. Their vision is specific and cannot host the main theoretical proposition of mainstream monetary theory.

The famous equation (in fact an identity) of exchange ($MV \equiv PT$) will take different significations according to the different views about money issuance. It is only when MV is assumed to be independent (M being conceived of as a parameter and V being constant) that the quantitative theory of money makes sense: In that case causality univocally goes from money to economic variables (price- or quantity-effects according to the assumed elasticity of production).

Law's views are not compatible with a quantitative theory of money. His concern is more to lessen shortages in money, a major concern in his time. The remedies to that shortage are multiple: Credit, compensation, etc. Law more radically maintains that the solution is to institute a system, such that the availability of means of payment will be ensured at the level required by the economy. He examines at length in Chapters 3, 4, 5, and 6 of *Money and Trade* the diverse possibilities for increasing the quantity of money (changes in the unit of accounts, banks, etc.), but no one appears to him sufficient in comparison with the project of a land bank he develops in Chapter 7 of Money and Trade. His project is entirely conformed to the abstract view presented earlier.

Steuart is very clear about the quantitative theory of money he knew through Hume and Montesquieu. After having alluded to these two authors with great respect and civility, he goes on:

> Upon examining this theory, when I came to treat of the matters it is calculated to influence, I found I could not make it answer to the principles I had pursued, in the most natural order in which I had been able to deduce them: and this consideration obliged me, with regret, to lay it aside, and to follow another, much more complex. I have already expressed the mortification I have always, had upon finding myself forced to strike out a general rule, and this, of all others, had at first hit my fancy the most; but I am obliged to confess, that upon a close examination of the three propositions, I am obliged to range this ingenious exposition of a most interesting subject, among those general and superficial maxims which never fail to lead to error.
>
> (II, 85)

Steuart could not accept the idea of an exogenous quantity of money. This is the direct consequence of his original view about the issue of the means of payment, in the same spirit as that of John Law.

Their original theory of money prevents both authors from finding room for real analysis. Through their fundamental view about money and prices, they belong to another tradition. That tradition does not welcome a quantitative theory of money value. Because it is issued as a counterpart of a determinate amount of wealth, money quantity is necessarily endogenous, and prices are necessarily associate to that issue. There is no logical anteriority of money quantity to prices, contrary to what is implied by the quantitative theory of money value.[7]

A corollary of Steuart's position is the emphasis put on the international relations. Value of money (intended as purchasing power) makes sense only by a comparison with other monies, i.e., amongst units of account. Movements of money prices reflect the evolution of exchange rather than that of quantity. When he comments upon Law's system, Steuart does not point out the huge quantity of notes as a problem *per se*. He prefers to blame the bad management that has undermined confidence.

The originality of Law's and Steuart's money theory is not the symptom of a pathology (some commentators about Law use the term 'crank'). It comes from the specific approach they share about economics: Monetary circulation and its effects on relative and absolute wealth rather than permutation of commodities through exchange and production.

Economy conceived of as monetary circulation

Law's and Steuart's theoretical efforts converge without doubt. The way they define wealth is the same: Wealth is a quantity of units of account and not a vector of commodities; its amount is equal to the flow of income it yields divided by the rate of interest. In short, wealth is thought of as a quantity of *capital*, whatever its concrete form may be. The term 'capital' is not ideal since the form of production Law and Steuart consider is not a capitalist form properly speaking. When they deal with the payment of wages it is not to stress the importance of a wage relationship but only the level of employment. Free hands are more often mentioned than wage earners and wealth is thought on the mode of a land rent more than of a profit on capital. To put it briefly, for Law and Steuart wealth is the ratio of a flow of net payment to a rate of interest. It is a nominal magnitude, not the scalar product of a vector of commodity quantities multiplied by a price vector, as value approach has made us uncritically believe.

In relation to this common view about wealth, two basic elements, at least, characterize their common approach to economics:

1 *Money mediation is the fundamental form of economic relations*; there is no other way to support a high level of activity; basically this is so because money shapes the particular form of society in which people work more than their reproduction requires as a consequence of their submission to their own needs. Money mediation is the condition for an advanced division of activities and not its consequence, a fundamental and meaningful difference with Adam Smith (see Cartelier 2000)
2 *The entity or institution responsible for a smooth working of the economy is not the market but the statesman.* Two opposite views of economic dynamics correspond to that difference. 'Market' may be associated to the traditional dynamical methods relying on a Lyapunov spirit (the quest for asymptotic properties of stability), whereas the action of the statesman is well represented by the theory of viability (Jean-Pierre Aubin et alii). These two 'technical' approaches to dynamics differ deeply in their philosophical backgrounds. The first one corresponds to a determinist position (which often corresponds to a claim to be scientific, a common pretension of value theoreticians), while the second approach comes along a sceptical view about economic regulation, to a conception of economics as an art rather than a science. Rather than automatic rules, discretionary actions of the statesman are the mode of regulation spontaneously considered by Law and Steuart, both authors being well aware that the actions of the statesman use the voluntary reactions of free economic agents as a lever more than resort to an absolute power.

It may be useful to give a formal expression to that paradigmatic opposition, although it is obviously anachronistic. If $x(t)$ is the vector describing the state of an economy at time (t), supposedly influenced by control variables (prices for instance) $u(t)$, academic economists represent the dynamics of that economy by a system of the following type:

$$x'(t) = F((u(t), x(t))$$
$$u'(t) = G(u(t), x(t))$$

where $G(\cdot)$ has some *a priori* properties of the market that will hopefully ensure the global stability of the economy. Academic economists are interested in the asymptotic properties of the dynamical system. An automatic rule, the so-called "law of supply and demand" or the "gold specie mechanism", is designed to do the job without any arbitrary intervention of a policymaker.

Opposed is the theory of viability. Its starting point is a set of *a priori* workable states of the economy that encompasses equilibria and out-of-equilibrium situations as well. Let $K: = \{0 \leq x(t) \leq x_{max}\}$ be that *constrained set* and $U: = \{a \leq u(t) \leq b\}$ the set of all *a priori* actions the statesman can decide. The dynamical system is then:

$$x'(t) = H(u(t), x(t))$$
$$u(t) \in U$$

The issue is no longer the asymptotic properties of the system but the existence of situations such that it is ever possible for the statesman to fix $u(t)$, keeping the economy in the constrained set, i.e., keeping the economy viable. Formally, we are looking for the greater subset of the constrained set such that $x(t) \in K$ for all $t > 0$. Such a subset is called the *viability kernel*. While the economy is in the viability kernel there exists at least one action of the statesman that makes possible keeping the economy in a sustainable state forever. Of course, this does not guarantee that the statesman will effectively succeed: It may exist at time (t) only one appropriate decision among an infinity of others, all of which will be proved to be not successful. But at least one right decision exists, and the statesman may find out which it is.

On the whole, money and statesman are two unavoidable ingredients of the approach common to Law and Steuart, both ingredients making it clear that a market economy does not imply reciprocity only but also sovereignty and hierarchy; there is no bridge between monetary analysis and real analysis, whose basic propositions are established in a framework without money and without sovereignty (Menudo & Tortajada 2015). Representing economics as a combination of various forms of money circulation regulated by an authority (mint or statesman) instead of a generalized permutation of commodities rules by voluntary exchange goes along with a fundamental property: The *primacy of expenses*. There is no symmetry between expenses and receipts since the receipts of some agents are the consequences of the expenses decided by the other.

More precisely, preeminent people are those able to give a first move to money circulation. This is clear in the island parable Law presents in Chapter 7 of *Money and Trade* (see Figure 6.1). Land is the type of wealth that is transformed into means of payment. Consequently, landowners' decisions determine the level of circulation and employment.

The prime mover of that change is the landlord who asks the farmers to pay the rent in money. He monetizes one year's rent and pays his workers with that money. Law seems to assume that rent is equal to full employment wages. That

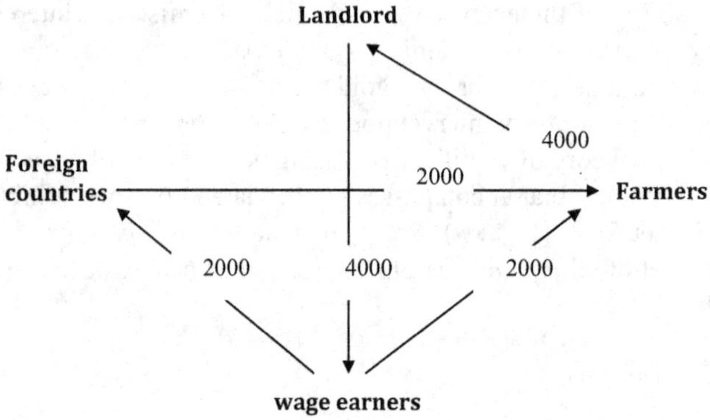

Figure 6.1 Steuart could endorse such a representation of economic activity

assumption is arbitrary. But what is interesting is that the quantity of money issued by the landlord is equal to the total wages, an endogenous variable. Workers spend the money towards farmers. Law assumes that only half the wages are spent. As a consequence, the farmers cannot pay all the rent. Law resorts to an ad hoc argument: An additional emission of money attracts additional consumers in the island. This is far from being clear. Law would have better assumed that workers spend the rest of their money abroad. Equilibrium of external balance requires that foreigners exactly spend towards farmers what workers have spent towards them. Farmers get in that way the whole of money and are able to pay the rent. Therefore, money achieves its circulation.

> By wealth, I understand this circulating adequate equivalent [consequence of liberty]. The desires of the rich, and the means of gratifying them [money], make them call for the services of the poor: the necessities of the poor, and their desire of becoming rich, make them cheerfully answer the summons; they submit to the hardest labour and comply with the inclinations of the wealthy, for the sake of an equivalent in money.
>
> This permutation between the two classes, is what we call circulation; and the effects produced by it upon the political situation of the parties, at the precise time of circulation, and the consequences, after it is completely effected, explain what is called the balance of wealth.
>
> (II, 32)

Unfortunately Steuart did not provide a detailed description of a circuit that could be compared with Law's schema. But, on an important point, the author of the *Inquiry* makes a step further. He is aware of what is implied by money mediation by comparison with a mere exchange economy. Circulation requires not only money but also a specialized class of persons: the *merchants*:

> This operation of buying and selling is a little more complex than the former [barter]; but still we have here no idea of trade because we have not introduced

> the merchant, by whose industry it is carried on. Let this third person be brought into play, and the whole operation becomes clear. What before we called wants, is here represented by the consumer; what we call industry, by the manufacturer; what we called money by the merchant.
>
> (I, 238)

Even more significantly, Steuart explicitly considers the effects circulation has on the structure of wealth anticipating to some extent the stock-flows consistent models. He devotes long developments to what he calls 'the balance of wealth'. The way settlements are carried on affects the relative wealth of people and their ability to run their activity in the next round of circulation.

Difficult to give is a more accurate view of what Steuart's theory is about: No absolute distinction between economy and society, hierarchy based on money, and wealth recomposed by circulation.[8]

To conclude

Listing the characteristics common to Law and Steuart is tantamount to sketching an alternative approach to that which dominates the history of economic thought after Smith, Ricardo, Malthus, and Say. These characteristics are:

- Taking for granted that economic relations are nothing but nominal; they are made of all the payments performed with the view of settling or postponing debts over time (by contrast with the exclusive consideration of goods and services).
- A dual theory of money; the wealth whose sovereign transformation into means of payment is conceptually distinct from the materials the means of payment are made of (by contrast with the idea of fiat money defined as a special good having special properties).
- The pre-eminence of money expenses and thus the strategic character of the procedure by which means of payment are issued (by opposition with the symmetric character of Walrassian budgetary constraints and with the quantity of money treated as a parameter).

Notes

1 I am grateful to an anonymous referee for his/her helpful remarks. The usual disclaimer applies.
2 A more detailed account of Steuart's appreciation may be found in a companion paper "James Steuart Comments on John Law's System: Steuart as a Virtual Money Doctor", in progress.
3 An interesting and different point of view is that of Eyüp Özveren. See this volume.
4 It is, for instance, Antoin Murphy's position concerning John Law.
5 Recall that the Essai sur la nature du commerce en général, although published in 1755, was written in circa 1730.
6 See Furuya (2008).
7 Note in passing that the quantitative theory of money does not hold valid for a metallic currency!
8 A detailed analysis is given in Cartelier (2015).

Bibliography

Aubin, J.P., Bayen, A. & Saint-Pierre, P. (2011), *Viability Theory, New Directions*, Berlin: Springer.

Cantillon, R. (1952), *Essai sur la nature du commerce en général*, Paris: INED.

Cartelier, J. (2000), Division of Labour and Money: Some Comments on Steuart, Smith and Their Legacy, in P.L. Porta, R. Scazzieri & A. Skinner (eds.), *Knowledge, Social Institutions and the Division of Labour*, Cheltenham: Edward Elgar: 285–300.

———. (2015), James Steuart: A Neglected Inspiration for an Alternative Economic Theory, in J. Steuart, *An Inquiry into the Principles of Political Oeconomy*, vol. 2, Napoli: Liguori Editore: xli–lxvii.

———. (2017), *James Steuart Comments on John Law's System: Steuart as a Virtual Money Doctor*, Lyon: Working Paper.

Furuya, Y. (2008), Construction of James Steuart's Monetary Theory, Prague: *Annual Conference of the European Society for the History of Economic Thought.*

Keynes, J.M. (1930), A Treatise on Money, in *The Collected Writings of John Maynard Keynes*, vols. 5–6, London: Macmillan.

Law, J. (1934), Money and Trade, in Oeuvres complètes, Paris: Sirey.

———. (1994), Essay on a Land Bank, Dublin: Aeon Publishing.

Longhitano, V. (2014), Steuart difensore di John Law, in S. Figuera & M. Grillo (ed.), *Un 'keynesiano' del secolo XVIII James Steuart (1713–1780)*, Napoli: Napoli Liguori editore: 47–66.

Menudo, J. & Tortajada, R. (2015), Double Competition and Stability in Sir James Steuart, *History of Economic Ideas*, 23(1): 39–58.

Murphy, A. (1997), John Law: EconomicTheorist and Policy-Maker, Oxford: Clarendon Press.

Pesante, M.-L. (1999), Steuart's Theory of Money and Sovereignty, in R. Tortajada (ed.), *The Economics of James Steuart*, London: Routledge: 186–200.

Schumpeter, J. (1954), History of Economic Analysis, London: Allen & Unwin.

Sen, S. (1947), Sir James Steuart's General Theory of Employment, Interest and Money, *Economica (New Series)*, 14(53): 19–36.

Ulgen, F. (1999), James Steuart's *Principles* as a Modern Analysis of Monetary Economy, in R. Tortajada (ed.), *The Economics of James Steuart*, London: Routledge: 253–274.

7 'Writings on money full of instruction'

Steuart and Ricardo as two squabbling bedfellows

Ghislain Deleplace[1]

Half a century after the publication of Steuart's *Principles*, David Ricardo's judgment on the monetary theory contained in this book was ambivalent:

> The writings of Sir James Steuart on the subject of coin and money are full of instruction, and it appears surprising that he could have adopted the above opinion, which is so directly at variance with the general principles he endeavoured to establish.
>
> (Ricardo 1816: 59)

This 'surprising . . . opinion' was the 'idea of a currency without a specific standard' (*ibid*) which Ricardo decidedly opposed. The celebration of the 250th anniversary of the publication of Steuart's *An Inquiry into the Principles of Political Oeconomy* (1767) and of the 200th anniversary of Ricardo's *On the Principles of Political Economy, and Taxation* (1817) offers an opportunity to inquire into the reasons of such ambivalence. Making a connection between these two books might look artificial, since Steuart does not appear in Ricardo's *Principles*, even on factual aspects. This does not mean that Ricardo, who had referred to him in previous writings, no longer considered him as having contributed to the progress of political economy. On the contrary, one may read in the 'Preface' to *Principles*:

> To determine the laws which regulate this distribution [of the whole produce of the earth], is the principal problem in Political Economy: much as the science has been improved by the writings of Turgot, Stuart, Smith, Say, Sismondi, and others, they afford very little satisfactory information respecting the natural course of rent, profit, and wages.
>
> (Ricardo 1817–1821: 5)

As emphasized by this quotation, the main subject of *Principles* was the distribution of aggregate income, and, according to Ricardo, Steuart – but not only him – did not provide 'satisfactory information' on this topic. In previous writings, as we will see, Ricardo always referred to Steuart on money. Although a whole chapter (27: 'On Currency and Banks') was devoted to money in Ricardo's *Principles*, this was only a side issue; the core of his theory of money had been exposed one year before in *Proposals for an Economical and Secure Currency* (Ricardo 1816), from which four full pages would be quoted by Ricardo himself in the 2nd and 3rd editions of *Principles*. It is in this pamphlet that Ricardo had clearly expressed his ambivalent judgment on Steuart's views on money, which is the subject of the present chapter.

Each of the first two sections of the chapter studies one side of this ambivalence, Steuart 'instructing' Ricardo (Section 1) but also 'surprising' him negatively (Section 2). I suggest in conclusion that Steuart and Ricardo were both at odds with monetary orthodoxy but in different ways (Section 3).[2]

Steuart 'instructing' Ricardo

The 'instruction' that Ricardo may have derived from Steuart on money was twofold. It dealt at the domestic level with the effect of the debasement of the coin on the market price of gold bullion and at the international level with the notion of real par of exchange and the effect of money on the exchange rate.

The effect of the debasement of the coin on the market price of gold bullion

At the domestic level, Steuart distinguished between two causes of 'imperfection' of a metallic currency, that is, of variation in its value. The first cause was that the *value* of the metal itself (gold or silver bullion) was variable:

> There is another circumstance which incapacitates the metals from performing the office of money; the substance of which the coin is made, is a commodity, which rises and sinks in its value with respect to other commodities, according to the wants, competition, and caprices of mankind. The advantage, therefore, found in putting an intrinsic value into that substance which performs the function of money of account, is compensated by the instability of that intrinsic value.
>
> (II, 288)

The second cause was that the *quantity* of the metal in the coin might be lower than the legal one (because of wear and tear or clipping) and this debasement of the coin was reflected in a high price of bullion:

> {*Why silver bullion is dearer than coin*} When you sell standard silver bullion at the mint, you are paid in weighty money; that is, you receive for your bullion the very same weight in standard coin; the coinage costs nothing; but when you sell bullion in the market, you are paid in worn-out silver, in gold, in bank notes, in short, in every species of lawful current money. Now all these payments have some defect: the silver you are paid with is worn and light; the gold you are paid with is over-rated, and perhaps also light; and the bank notes must have the same value with the specie with which the bank pays

> them; that is, with light silver or over-rated gold. It is for these reasons, that silver bullion, which is bought by the mint at 5*s*. 2*d*. [62 pence] *per* ounce of heavy silver money, may be bought at market at 65 pence the ounce in light silver, over-rated gold, or bank notes, which is the same thing.
>
> (II, 321–322)

With the first statement Ricardo agreed, but he derived opposite conclusions from it: Changes in the value of the standard of money were not a reason to advocate the 'idea of a currency without a specific standard', as Ricardo blamed Steuart for holding it (see Section 2), but were consistent with the adoption of a currency that would only vary in value with the variations in the value of the standard. To do so, according to Ricardo, one should prevent the *price* of the standard (as distinct from its *value*) from varying. One of the causes which raised the market price of gold bullion above the legal price of gold in money (hence depreciating the currency) was the debasement of the coin, and it is on this question that Steuart's second statement was 'full of instruction'. This was a lesson that Ricardo developed by advocating the complete substitution of banknotes for coins.

One of the few quotations from Steuart to be found in Ricardo's writings immediately follows the latter's statement that 'the exchange will, therefore, be a tolerably accurate criterion by which we may judge of the debasement of the currency, proceeding either from a clipped coinage, or a depreciated paper-money' (Ricardo 1810–1811: 72). Ricardo's quotation reads as follows:

> It is observed by Sir James Stuart,[3] "That if the foot measure was altered at once over all England, by adding to it, or taking from it, any proportional part of its standard length, the alteration would be best discovered, by comparing the new foot with that of Paris, or of any other country, which had suffered no alteration. Just so, if the pound sterling, which is the English unit, shall be found any how changed; and if the variation it has met with be difficult to ascertain, because of a complication of circumstances; the best way to discover it will be to compare the former and the present value of it, with the money of other nations which has suffered no variation. This the exchange will perform with the greatest exactness."
>
> (Ricardo 1810–1811: 72–73)

According to Ricardo, there was, however, a better index of the debasement of the metallic currency at home than the exchange rate, which also reflected the state of the currency in the other country. In accordance with Steuart's second statement, this index was a rise in the market price of the standard metal in bullion over and above its legal price in full-bodied coin. At the time of Ricardo, this causal relationship was disputed by nobody, whether the Bullionists – those (including Ricardo) who explained the depreciation of the pound by the overissue of Bank of England notes – or the anti-Bullionists – those who denied the Bank of England any responsibility in the high price of bullion and explained it by other factors. Among these factors some anti-Bullionists mentioned the debasement of the coins. Ricardo opposed them not on the general effect of debasement on the market price of bullion but on its relevance in the circumstances of the time, the divergence being about 'that coin which is the principal measure of value' (Ricardo 1951–1973: VI, 2) – the gold or the silver one – Ricardo arguing that it was the gold one and that it was not debased.

The reason why the causal relationship between the debasement of the coin and a high market price of bullion was common knowledge at the time of Ricardo is that it had been established by Steuart more than 40 years before. The relation illustrated by Steuart's quotation may be formalized as follows. Supposing gold is the standard, let $\overline{q_{GC}}$ be the intrinsic weight of the standard coin 'fresh from the mint' (undebased), that is, the quantity of gold (measured in ounces) legally contained in it, and q_{GC} the quantity of gold contained in the average circulating coin of the same denomination, with $q_{GC} \leq \overline{q_{GC}}$. One may define the rate of debasement D as the percentage difference between the legal gold weight of the undebased coin and the actual average gold weight of the debased one:

$$D = (\overline{q_{GC}} - q_{GC}) / \overline{q_{GC}} \tag{1}$$

Neglecting for the moment the coining and melting costs, let me suppose that the average circulating coin is debased by $D = 10\%$, but the law is such that it passes indifferently with an undebased one. If the seller of an ounce of gold bullion is paid £3. 17s. 10$^{1/2}$d. in such debased coins – that is, at a market price equal to the legal price of an ounce of gold in undebased coin – he really exchanges one ounce of gold bullion for 0.9 ounce of gold in coin. He may alternatively bring his bullion to the mint to have it coined in £3. 17s. 10$^{1/2}$d. in undebased coins. The diminished supply of bullion in the market raises its price, until one ounce of gold bullion exchanges at this higher price for one ounce of gold in debased coins. This occurs when the market price of gold bullion is 10% above the legal price of gold in coin. If this premium overtakes 10%, the owner of debased coins, rather than buying bullion at that price, prefers to melt them to sell the bullion thus obtained. The increased supply of bullion in the market sinks its price, until the premium falls back to 10%. Arbitrage thus sustains the market price of gold bullion above the legal price of gold in undebased coin, by a margin determined by the rate of debasement. In other words, £3. 17s. 10$^{1/2}$d. in debased coin buy in the market 10% less in gold bullion than it should according to the legal definition of the pound: Measured in gold bullion, the debased currency is depreciated by 10%, and this depreciation continues as long as the average circulating coin remains debased by 10%.

The relation between the rate of debasement and the rate of depreciation is as follows. By definition one ounce of gold contains $1 / \overline{q_{GC}}$ undebased coins, each one declared to be legal tender for £1, so that the legal price $\overline{P_{GC}}$ in pounds of one ounce of gold in undebased coins is given by:

$$\overline{P_{GC}} = 1 / \overline{q_{GC}} \tag{2}$$

In circulation, one ounce of gold contains $1 / q_{GC}$ debased coins, each one being also legal tender for £1. The no-arbitrage condition in the market for gold bullion states that one ounce of gold bullion exchanges for one ounce of gold in debased coins, so that, with P_G the market price in pounds of one ounce of gold bullion:

$$P_G = 1 / q_{GC} \quad (3)$$

By definition, the rate of depreciation d of money is equal to:

$$d = (P_G - \overline{P_{GC}})/P_G \quad (4)$$

Combining (1) with (4) gives:

$$d = D \quad (5)$$

The higher the rate of debasement of the coin, the higher the rate of depreciation of money. It should be noticed that the level of depreciation of the currency entirely results from the no-arbitrage condition in the market for gold bullion. It does *not* depend on any relation between the quantity of money, its value, and the aggregate money price of all circulated commodities (the so-called Quantity Theory of Money).

In practice convertibility of bullion into coin (minting) and of coin into bullion (melting) was costly. In England the delay to obtain the coin at the mint exposed the owner of bullion to a loss of interest; the legal prohibition of melting and exporting the coin exposed its owner to a melting cost that included the compensation paid to the intermediary for the risk of fraud. The market price of gold bullion P_G could thus vary around the legal price $\overline{P_{GC}}$ of gold in undebased coin between narrow limits corresponding to s_G the minting cost and m_G the melting cost (both in percentage of the price):

$$\overline{P_{GC}}\,(1 + m_G) \geq P_G \geq \overline{P_{GC}}\,(1 - s_G) \quad (6)$$

When the circulating coins were debased, the upper limit of the market price of gold bullion was augmented by the rate of debasement D:

$$\overline{P_{GC}}\,(1 + D)(1 + m_G) \geq P_G \geq \overline{P_{GC}}\,(1 - s_G) \quad (7)$$

The rate of depreciation could now be greater than the rate of debasement by a margin equal to the melting cost. When the circulation was composed of debased coins, they were all the more depreciated since their melting cost was increased by the prohibition of melting and exporting the coin. This is why Ricardo advised to make them free:

> The most perfect liberty should be given, at the same time, to export or import every description of bullion.
>
> (Ricardo 1816: 67)

On this point he was in agreement with Steuart, who had discussed at length the pros and cons of the prohibition of melting and exporting the coin (see III, 437–448) and concluded:

> On the whole, we may determine, that a flourishing commercial state, which has, on the average of its trade, a balance coming in from other countries, should lay it down as a general rule, to facilitate the exportation of its coin, as well as of bullion.
>
> (III, 446)

There were other points linked with international relations on which Ricardo could find Steuart's writings 'full of instruction'.

The real par of exchange and the effect of money on the exchange rate

At the international level there were two important points contended by Steuart. The first was that the state of the foreign balance should be ascertained by comparing the exchange rate with the *real* par of exchange and not the *legal* par. The second point was that monetary conditions at home and abroad could produce an unfavourable exchange of the pound, even when the foreign balance was in favour of England. These two points paved the way to Ricardo's contention that the deviations of the exchange rate from the real par reflected the depreciation or appreciation of the domestic currency.

At the time of Steuart, the legal par of exchange (the ratio of the weight of metal legally contained in the main coin of each respective country) was used to infer whether the balance of payments with a given foreign country was favourable or adverse and to calculate the import and export bullion points by which the variations in the exchange rate were constrained. This use was convenient because the legal price of gold in coin in each country was a given magnitude that was left unchanged by the state, except in extraordinary circumstances. The knowledge of this price in England and in each foreign country thus allowed calculating the legal par of exchange between the pound and each foreign currency. Supposing as earlier that $\overline{q_{GC}}^{£}$ and $\overline{q_{GC}}^{L}$ were the respective quantities of gold defining the English pound and the French *livre* at the mint, the legal par of exchange $\overline{R}^{L/£}$ of the livre in pounds was by definition equal to $\overline{q_{GC}}^{L}\,\overline{q_{GC}}^{£}$, that is, according to (2), $\overline{P_{GC}}^{£} / \overline{P_{GC}}^{L}$.

The use of the legal par of exchange nevertheless opened a margin of error, both for the diagnosis of the balance of payments and the calculation of the bullion points. The reason for this error was to be found in the inaccuracy of the circulating coins for calculating the par of exchange that equalized the quantities of gold contained in them. This was obvious when circulating coins were debased, that is, when wear and tear or clipping made them contain less pure gold than they legally should. The real par of exchange, as it was called – that is, the par that equalized the *actual* quantities of gold contained in the domestic and foreign coins – then differed from the legal par of exchange – calculated on the basis of the *legal* quantities.

Since, as seen earlier, the debasement of the coin raised the market price of gold bullion P_G above the legal price of gold in coin $\overline{P_{GC}}$, one should now consider the real par of exchange $R^{L/£} = P_G^{£} / P_G^{L}$ rather than the legal par $\overline{R}^{L/£} = \overline{P_{GC}}^{£} / \overline{P_{GC}}^{L}$. As Steuart emphasized:

> The general rule, therefore, I think, is, to settle the real par of different coins, not according to the *bullion* they contain, but according to the bullion they are worth in their own market at the time.
>
> (III, 30)

One should thus determine the par by calculating not the ratio $\overline{R}^{L/£}$ of the respective quantities of gold legally contained in the full-bodied coins in Paris and London but the ratio $R^{L/£}$ of the respective market prices of the same quantity of gold bullion in London and Paris. The diagnosis of the balance of payments and the understanding of the limits between which the exchange rate could vary then required the analysis of the factors that could make the market price of gold bullion diverge from the legal price of gold in coin – hence the real par of exchange diverge from the legal par. However, this was not common knowledge at the time of Steuart, even among specialists, as illustrated by his critique of a recent pamphlet:[4]

> Mr. Cantillon, in his *Analysis of Trade*, which I suppose he understood by practice as well as by theory, has the following passage in his 99th page: "The course of exchange between Paris and London since the year 1726, has been at a medium price of 32 pence sterling for the crown of three livres; that is to say, we pay for this French crown of three livres, 32 pence sterling, *when calculated on gold*, when in fact it is worth but thirty-pence and three farthings, which is giving four pounds in the hundred for this French money; and consequently, upon gold, the balance of trade is 4 *per cent*. against England in favour of France." In this place, Mr. Cantillon calculates the par of exchange according to the common rule, to wit, gold bullion against gold bullion in the coins of both nations, where both are supposed to be of legal weight; and he finds that there has been, these thirty-four years past, a balance of 4 *per cent*. against England. Now, according to my theory, this is exactly what the coinage in France ought to produce, supposing on an average that the trade had been at par.
>
> (III, 22; Steuart's emphasis)

An exchange rate of 32 pence sterling per French crown was above the legal par (then $30^{3/4}$), and this was interpreted as signalling an unfavourable balance of England with France. Steuart objected that this conclusion was in no way warranted since the par with which the exchange rate was compared was not accurate:

> To calculate, as every body does, the par of the French crown, either by the gold or the silver in the English *standard* coin, when no such *standard* coin exists; and to state all that is given for the crown above 29½*d*., if you reckon

> by the silver, or 30¾*d.* if you reckon by the gold, for the price of a wrong balance, is an error which may lead to the most fatal consequences.
>
> (III, 431)

Things changed when the exchange rate was compared with the real par, which could depart from the legal par in a still greater proportion according to the respective deviations of the market price of gold bullion from the legal price of gold in coin in each country:

> But suppose two cases which may happen, viz. 1. That gold bullion at Paris should be at the price of coin, while at London it may be at mint price; or, 2. That at Paris it may be at mint price, when at London it is at 4*l.* 0*s.* 8*d.* what will then the real par of exchange be? I answer, that on the first supposition, it will be [. . .] the crown of 3 livres equal to 30.076 pence sterling. In the other, [it will be] for the crown of 3 livres 33.728. A difference of no less than 8.9 *per cent.* Is it not evident that these variations *must* occur in the exchange between London and Paris? And is it not also plain, that they proceed from the fluctuation of the price of bullion, not from exchange?
>
> (III, 429–430; Steuart's emphasis)

In the first case, the market price of gold bullion was at its maximum in Paris (equal to 'the price of coin') and at its minimum in London (equal to 'mint price'); the real par $R^{L/£} = P_G^{£} / P_G^{L}$ was at its minimum, viz. 30.076 pence sterling per crown. In the second case, the market price of gold bullion was at its minimum in Paris (equal to 'mint price') and at its maximum in London (equal to £4. 0s. 8d., giving a melting cost of 3.6%); the real par of exchange was at its maximum, viz. 33.728 pence sterling per crown. An observed exchange rate of 32 pence per crown, which, compared to the legal par of 30.75, seemed to indicate a balance with France of 4% against England, really revealed a favourable balance for England when compared to a real par of 33.728.

Steuart's conclusion was that the monetary factors which, in each of the two countries, made the market price of gold bullion deviate from the legal price of gold in coin also made the real par of exchange deviate from the legal par and consequently affected the exchange rate, even if the balance of trade between the two countries was even. These monetary factors were those described in inequalities (6) and (7). In England, the debasement of the coin and the prohibition of its melting and exporting pushed the market price of bullion upwards, and in France the existence of seignorage pulled it downwards, both aspects raising the real par above the legal par. In particular, as mentioned earlier by Steuart when he criticized 'the common rule' of calculation of the par, 'according to my theory' the seignorage in France accounted for the rise of the real par (with which the exchange rate actually agreed), contrary to the wrong inference of an adverse balance of trade from the fall of the exchange rate below the legal par.

From this analysis Ricardo could derive two 'instructing' lessons. The first was that one should use the real par when evaluating the exchange rate. According to

Ricardo, when the domestic currency was neither depreciated nor appreciated, the market price of gold bullion was equal to the legal price of gold in coin and, supposing the same in the foreign country, the real par of exchange was consequently equal to the legal par. The exchange rate could then only diverge from the par in the limit set by the cost of transferring bullion from one country to the other:

> If the trade in the precious metals were perfectly free, and money could be exported without any expense whatever, the exchanges could be no otherwise in every country than at par. If the trade in the precious metals were perfectly free, if they were generally used in circulation, even with the expenses of transporting them, the exchange could never in any of them deviate more from par, than by these expenses. These principles, I believe, are now no where disputed.
>
> (Ricardo 1817–1821: 230)

When the domestic currency was depreciated, the discount on the banknotes paying for the bills of exchange opened an additional margin of variation in the exchange rate. This meant that to determine the actual limits set by the transfer costs to the variations of the exchange rate one had to substitute the market price of gold bullion in each of the two countries for the legal price of gold in coin. Instead of calculating the bullion points by adding to (subtracting from) the legal par the cost of importation (exportation) of bullion, one should calculate them on the basis of the real par of exchange, that is, the ratio of the market prices of gold bullion.[5] This is what Ricardo explained to McCulloch in a letter dated October 2, 1819:

> Instead of ascertaining the par by a consideration of what the pound sterling was formerly worth, it should be computed with reference to its present value, which is to be known by the value of the bullion which a pound can command. . . . The real par is justly estimated by the current value of the pound sterling – that current value is depreciated, hence a new real par is, or ought to be, established.
>
> (Ricardo 1951–1973: VIII, 87–88, 91)

Already in a practical example discussed in *Reply to Bosanquet*, Ricardo had mentioned: 'the par of exchange being calculated not on the value which the coin actually passed for in currency, but on its intrinsic value as bullion' (Ricardo 1811: 180).

The second lesson that Ricardo could derive from Steuart was that, to understand the movements of the exchange rate, one should concentrate on the monetary factors (such as the depreciation of the domestic currency), not on the state of the foreign balance. As early as *High Price*, Ricardo stated an opinion that he would maintain in all his subsequent monetary writings:

> While the circulating medium consists, therefore, of coin undebased, or of paper-money immediately exchangeable for undebased coin, the exchange can never be more above, or more below, par, than the expences attending the

> transportation of the precious metals. But when it consists of a depreciated paper money, it necessarily will fall according to the degree of the depreciation.
>
> (Ricardo 1810–1811: 72)

This statement was based on a conception of money that should now be contrasted with Steuart's because the latter conception, in Ricardo's words, 'appears surprising' – negatively.

Steuart 'surprising' Ricardo (negatively)

The basic point on which Ricardo disagreed with Steuart was on the relationship between money and the standard. This had two consequences for the design of the monetary system, on the question of seignorage at the domestic level and on the question of the exchange rate at the international one. Ricardo may have found Steuart's positions on these points 'surprising' and, in his view, contradictory to sound principles.

The relationship between money and the standard

Steuart extended the critique of variability of metallic money to any currency linked to a standard, whether coin or paper money. In contrast, Ricardo advocated that in order to be a nearly perfect currency the paper money should be regulated by a standard. In his *Proposals for an Economical and Secure Currency*, Ricardo's opposition to Steuart on this point was explicit, although, as noted earlier, he mixed a critique in the main text with a laudatory appreciation in a footnote. The full quotation is as follows:

> This idea of a currency without a specific standard was, I believe, first advanced by Sir James Steuart,* but no one has yet been able to offer any test by which we could ascertain the uniformity in the value of a money so constituted. Those who supported this opinion did not see, that such a currency, instead of being invariable, was subject to the greatest variations, – that the only use of a standard is to regulate the quantity, and by the quantity the value of the currency – and that without a standard it would be exposed to all the fluctuations to which the ignorance or the interests of the issuers might subject it.
>
> *The writings of Sir James Steuart on the subject of coin and money are full of instruction, and it appears surprising that he could have adopted the above opinion, which is so directly at variance with the general principles he endeavoured to establish.
>
> (Ricardo 1816: 59)

By the 'idea of a currency without a specific standard', Ricardo had in mind what Steuart called 'money of account' and defined as follows:

> Money, which I call of account, is no more than *an arbitrary scale of equal parts, invented for measuring the respective value of things vendible. Money* of

> *account*, therefore, is quite a different thing from *money-coin*, and might exist, although there was no such thing in the world as any substance, which could become an adequate and proportional equivalent for every commodity. . . . The degree [with regard to angles] has no determinate length, so neither has that part of the scale upon plans which marks the unit: the usefulness of all those inventions being solely confined to the marking of proportion. Just so the unit in money can have no invariable determinate proportion to any part of value, that is to say, it cannot be fixed to perpetuity to any particular quantity of gold, silver, or any other commodity whatsoever.
>
> (II, 270–271; Steuart's emphasis)

As illustration of such 'money of account' Steuart gave the *florin banco* of Amsterdam:

> That money, therefore, which constantly preserves an equal value, which poises itself, as it were, in a just equilibrium between the fluctuating proportion of the value of things, is the only permanent and equal scale, by which value can be measured. Of this kind of money, and of the possibility of establishing it, we have two examples: the first, among one of the most knowing; the second, among the most ignorant nations of the world. The bank of Amsterdam presents us with the one, the coast of Angola with the other. A florin banco has a more determinate value than a pound of fine gold, or silver; it is an unit which the invention of men, instructed in the arts of commerce, have found out. This bank money stands invariable like a rock in the sea. According to this ideal standard are the prices of all things regulated; and very few people can tell exactly what it depends upon. The precious metals with their intrinsic value, vary with regard to this common measure, like every other thing. . . . No adulterations in the weight, fineness, or denominations of coin have any effect upon bank money. These currencies which the bank looks upon as merchandize, like every other thing, are either worth more or less bank money, according to the actual value of the metals they are made of. All is merchandize with respect to this standard; consequently, it stands unrivalled in the exercise of its function of a common measure.
>
> (II, 276–277)

Since the *florin banco* of Amsterdam was defined as a given quantity of bullion, it may be surprising that Steuart rejected a definite quantity of metal as monetary unit while he illustrated his conception of a 'money of account' with the bank money of Amsterdam. What Steuart praised in the *florin banco* was its invariable definition, in contrast with the variable quantity of metal that circulating coins actually contained. However, this did not prevent it from varying in value with respect to every commodity. The monetary unit 'cannot be fixed to any particular quantity of gold, silver, or any other commodity whatsoever' because any such chosen 'substance' varies in value with all other commodities whose respective values are measured by money. The monetary unit could indeed be defined as an invariable *quantity* of metal, but its *value* was always changing:

> Money of account, therefore, cannot be fixed to any material substance, the value of which may vary with respect to other things. The operations of trade, and the effects of an universal circulation of value, over the commercial world, can alone adjust the fluctuating value of all kinds of merchandize, to this invariable standard. This is a representation of the bank money of Amsterdam, which may at all times be most accurately specified in a determinate weight of silver and gold; but which can never be tied down to that precise weight for twenty-four hours, any more than to a barrel of herrings.
>
> (II, 277–278)

It may be remarked that the *florin banco* of Amsterdam was also chosen by Ricardo as example of the 'nearly perfect' currency he was looking for. Already in his 'Notes on Bentham' written around Christmas 1810, Ricardo had mentioned the Bank of Amsterdam:

> In Holland and Hamburgh the advantages of the Banks is 1° in the use of paper instead of metals which has been admirably described by this author [Bentham], and 2° in having a uniform measure of value subject to no debasement or deterioration.
>
> (Ricardo 1951–1973: III, 288)

In the Appendix to the 4th edition of *High Price*, published in 1811, Ricardo outlined his Ingot Plan and again referred to the Bank of Amsterdam:

> The plan here proposed appears to me to unite all the advantages of every system of banking which has been hitherto adopted in Europe. It is in some of its features similar to the banks of deposit of Amsterdam and Hamburgh. In those establishments bullion is always to be purchased from the Bank at a fixed invariable price. The same thing is proposed for the Bank of England. . . . The currency could neither be clipped nor deteriorated, and would possess a value as invariable as gold itself, the great object which the Dutch had in view, and which they most successfully accomplished by a system very like that which is here recommended.
>
> (Ricardo 1810–1811: 126–127)

How was this convergence between Steuart and Ricardo on the *florin banco* possible? The answer appears when one reformulates Steuart's statements in Ricardo's terms. Fixing a given quantity of metal to define the *florin banco* amounted to fixing the *legal price* in *florin banco* of one unit of weight of bullion. But this was not enough to prevent the *market price* of this weight unit from varying, hence also the relative value of bullion in terms of all other commodities and the value of the monetary unit in terms of these commodities. One then discovers that Steuart and Ricardo had a common object: How does one build a monetary system so that the market price of the standard is kept at its legal level? However, there were two important differences.

First, for Steuart the metal could not be the standard because of its 'imperfection in performing the functions of money of account' (III, 10), namely its varying value in terms of all other commodities. For Ricardo, changes in the money *price* of the standard could be avoided thanks to the adoption of an appropriate monetary system (his Ingot Plan), which guaranteed that the value of money remained always equal to the value of the standard (both values in terms of all other commodities). Such conformity of the currency to the standard meant that it varied in *value* with changes in the *value* of the standard, but this was necessary to prevent the market *price* of the standard from varying. In other words, linking money to a standard prevented its value from varying for monetary reasons (such as 'the ignorance or the interests of the issuers' of notes), but this implied accepting that it varied for real ones (such as changes in the cost of production of gold): 'In a sound state of the currency the value of gold may vary, but its price cannot' (Ricardo 1951–1973: V, 392).

The second important difference between the two authors on the relationship between money and the standard concerned the design of the monetary system. This difference may be illustrated at two levels, domestic and international.

The attitude towards seignorage

An example of the difference between Steuart and Ricardo on the design of the monetary system was the attitude regarding seignorage. The two authors were in favour of a seignorage but for different reasons.

Steuart viewed seignorage as a way of sustaining the exchange of the pound against the French currency, and he advised to introduce it at a level as high as in France (around 8%). The reason was that when the French *aggregate* foreign balance was favourable, the inflow of gold bullion lowered its market price in Paris (in the limit set by the seignorage in France) and this raised the real par of exchange of the French currency against the pound. This depressed the exchange rate of the pound with the French currency, even if the *bilateral* balance between the two countries was in favour of England. The imposition of a seignorage in England would correct this bias each time the English aggregate foreign balance was favourable (see Deleplace 2015). Being advantageous in relations with abroad, this imposition would nevertheless have inconveniences at the domestic level, as a consequence of the coin 'being a metal as well as a money of account' (III, 7). The argument was the following.

When the aggregate foreign balance was in favour of England, the inflow of gold bullion lowered its market price in London below the legal price of gold in coin, in the limit set by the minting cost (now the suggested seignorage). If, for any reason, the aggregate foreign balance turned against England, the demand for gold to discharge it raised the market price of gold bullion, which equalized with the legal price of gold in coin. The money prices of all commodities rose with the price of bullion, since they were attached to a given quantity of grains of the standard:

> Here then is a case, where the coin is made to lose all its advanced price as a manufacture [as compared with bullion]; and this is owing entirely to its being a metal as well as a money of account. Now as the coin has lost this additional value, by a circumstance purely relative to itself as a metal, there is no reason why other merchandize should sink in value along with it. The consequence, therefore, of this revolution ought to be, that as the merchandize, *bullion*, has got up 8 *per cent.* with regard to the *coin*, and as the price of all merchandize ought to be in proportion to the grains of bullion to which that price amounts, the revolution having annihilated the 8 *per cent.* advance upon the coin, ought to have the same effect with respect to prices as if coinage were given gratis.
>
> (III, 6–7; Steuart's emphasis)

One would expect that when the aggregate foreign balance turned again in favour of England this disturbing effect would disappear. But, when the unfavourable balance persisted for long, this would not occur:

> We now proceed to another chain of causes, which tend greatly to destroy the due proportion of value between coin and merchandize. This with justice may be put also to the account of the imperfection of the metals in performing the functions of money of account. Universal experience shews that the prices of merchandize are so attached to the denominations of coin, that they do not fluctuate as principles point out, any more than projectiles describe parabolas, or that machines operate the effects, which by calculation they ought to do. The resistance of the air in one case, the frictions of the part in the other, tend to render theory incorrect. Just so here; our theory represents prices as rising and sinking in the most harmonious proportion together with the metals; but in practice it is not so. They have their frictions and political resistances, which render the theory delusive only when every circumstance is not combined. A good gunner must calculate the resistance of the air upon his bomb, or he never will hit the mark.
>
> (III, 10)

Monetary illusion would play its role: During the time of a persisting unfavourable foreign balance, and coin having become equal in price with bullion, all prices of commodities became 'attached to the denominations of coin':

> The imposition of coinage must, on many occasions, have the effect of attaching the price of commodities to the denominations of the coin, instead of preserving them attached to the grains of the metals which compose them, as in theory they ought to be.
>
> (III, 11–12)

Consequently, when the aggregate foreign balance turned again in favour of England and the market price of gold bullion fell down to its initial level, the prices of commodities did *not* fall with it but remained at the higher level reached when the balance was unfavourable. The coin 'being a metal as well as a money of account', the seignorage created an asymmetry: As long as the (market) price of coin as metal was below the (legal) price of coin as money of account (by the amount of the seignorage), the prices of commodities moved with the market price of the metal. But when the latter equalized with the legal price of the coin, as a consequence of the unfavourable foreign balance, the confusion between the two deprived the metal of its regulating role, and the prices of commodities became insensitive to the fall in the price of bullion when it eventually occurred. There was, however, one exception: The exported commodities were subject to foreign competition and hence regulated by their gold-prices. Their money prices had to fall with the price of bullion. As a result, the 'just equality of profit and loss among all the merchants, relatively to the real state of the balance' (III: 422) was broken: The profits of the exporters were squeezed between the falling price of the exportable commodities they sold and the persistently high price of the domestic commodities they purchased:

> When coin begins to rise above the price of bullion, the manufacturers stick to the denominations of the coin, instead of descending in value (as they ought to do by theory) along with the bullion. What is the consequence of this? It is that the prices of manufactures *for home-consumption*, and of *commodities peculiar to the country*, stand their ground; that is, prices do not descend, and cannot be brought down by merchants. But as to manufactures for exportation, which are not peculiar, but which are produced by different countries, the prices of these are violently pulled down by the force of foreign competition; and the workmen are obliged to diminish them. This hurts them effectually, not because of the diminution of the prices; because, properly speaking, this diminution is relative only to the denominations of the coin; their gains will purchase as many grains of bullion in the market as before, but not so much coin, and consequently not so much of any commodity which, by the principles just laid down, have attached themselves to the denominations of the coin, and have risen in their price along with it.
>
> (III, 12–13; Steuart's emphasis)

This was all the more to be regretted since the exporters were responsible for a favourable foreign balance, which enriched the nation as a whole. The imposition of seignorage had thus a pernicious effect on the profits of exporters, as compared with those of domestic traders. It reinforced the effect of foreign competition, which already explained 'why those who work for foreign exportation, are the poorest class of all the industrious of a state, although the most useful to it, at the same time' (III, 14).

The remedy suggested by Steuart was an intervention of the state, which should use the benefit of the seignorage to compensate the loss incurred by exporters because of its imposition:

> I shall here by the bye observe, that as the state is made to profit by the diminution of the gains of this most useful class; as she receives the coinage which strangers pay, and which is really deducted from the manufacturers who support exportation, she ought to indemnify this class (as may be done in a thousand ways, by premiums, for example, upon exportation) out of the profits arising upon coinage, instead of giving coinage free, to the evident loss of the nation, and benefit to strangers.
>
> (III, 14)

Ricardo was also in favour of a seignorage, provided it was small. As he wrote in *Principles*: 'To a moderate seignorage on the coinage of money there cannot be much objection' (Ricardo 1817–1821: 371). But his reasons were different from Steuart's ones. Being examined by the Secret Committee on Resumption on March 19, 1819, he stressed an inconvenience linked to the absence of seignorage: 'a great inducement offered to all exporters of gold, to exchange their bullion for coin previously to its exportation' (Ricardo 1951–1973: V, 401), since the advantages of the coins (certified fineness, divisibility) were not compensated by the cost of obtaining them. The imposition of a seignorage would thus induce exporters of gold to alter their behaviour and to export bullion rather than coin. However, even 'moderate', a seignorage on a coin 'has also its inconveniences' (*ibid*: 402): It opened a margin of fall in the market price of bullion – hence also in all other prices – when the Bank of England contracted its issues. It thus gave the Bank of England the opportunity of changing the value of the currency, a recurrent complaint by Ricardo.

Ricardo's ambivalent position on seignorage was entirely determined by his analysis of the requirements of a good monetary system. Preventing the actual exportation of the coin was in line with his wish to separate the domestic currency from the international means of settlement (what would be called a century later the gold-exchange standard). But this advantage of seignorage was counterbalanced by the possibility it gave to the Bank of England of changing at will the value of the currency. Hence this was a second best; a better solution was to eliminate the domestic circulation of coins altogether:

> I am still of opinion, that we should have all its advantages [of a seignorage], with the additional one of economy, by adopting the plan, which I had the honour of laying before the Committee when I was last before them.
>
> (*ibid*: 403)

Ricardo then referred to his Ingot Plan, in which the currency (composed exclusively of banknotes convertible into bullion) was to be obtained from the Bank against standard bullion at £3. 17s. 6d. per ounce, 0.5% below the price at which it was legal tender (£3. 17s. 10½d.) – a difference sufficient to cover the cost of management of the currency by the Bank of England while maintaining at a trifling level the margin of fall in the market price of bullion. Nowhere did Ricardo envisage, like Steuart, to use seignorage as a way of improving the exchange. This topic was another point of disagreement he had with his predecessor.

Correcting the exchange

As seen in this chapter, Steuart contended that the market price of gold could diverge from its legal price according to the monetary factors influencing the price at which bullion was transformed into coin and coin transformed into bullion. This aspect might be directly modified by decisions of the national and foreign states concerning money. The purpose of Steuart's inquiry was thus, not only to warn against a wrong evaluation of the state of the foreign balance but also to suggest remedies against an undue loss of precious metals:

> Since the loss upon high exchange against a country, affects principally the cumulative interest of the whole, relatively to other trading nations; it is the business of the statesman, not of the merchants, to provide a remedy against it.
> (III, 449)

Steuart's analysis of the real par of exchange thus did not only allow dispelling the confusion created by the use of the legal par and avoiding inappropriate and dangerous decisions about how to handle an adverse balance of trade. It also suggested means of practically influencing the exchange, so as to facilitate 'the business of the statesman'. One 'remedy' was as follows:

> If government should think fit to impose, in their own mint, a coinage, equal to that of France, and make all their coin of equal weight, and at the due proportion, it will take off all the loss we suffer by paying coinage to France (which we at present impute to the exchange) while she pays none to us.
> (III, 431)

Two measures were thus envisaged by Steuart: First, the imposition in England of a seignorage 'equal to that of France', and second, the recoinage of English coins at their legal weight and the suspension of the prohibition of melting and exporting them. On seignorage (although for different reasons) and on liberty of exporting gold in whatever form, Ricardo agreed. The disagreement was at a deeper level, that is, about the international adjustment of an adverse foreign balance.

For both authors the reference on this point was Hume who praised the metallic basis of money because international flows of metal automatically eliminated any positive or negative foreign balance (the so-called price-specie flow mechanism). On the contrary Steuart explained the absence of self-adjustment by the inconveniences attached to metallic money. International transfers of precious metals, which according to Hume adjusted the balance of trade, depended on the market prices of bullion in the various trading nations. These prices were affected by monetary factors such as the debasement of the coins by wear and tear and the existence of a seignorage on coining. A country could thus experience an outflow of bullion while the balance of trade was not against her. Even worse, such outflow had a negative impact on the domestic market for credit; in a country like England where gold to be exported was obtained at the Bank of England against convertible notes, the fall in its metallic reserve led the Bank to reduce its discounts, and this resulted in a shrinkage of overall credit that hurt the economy. Rather than relying on a self-adjusting mechanism that did not work because of the malfunctions of metallic money, it was the task of the state to intervene actively so as to prevent outflows of bullion, by adapting the domestic monetary system (recoinage, imposition of a seignorage when there existed one in the other trading nations) and by providing assistance when, in case of a temporary adverse shock on the foreign balance, 'banks ought to borrow abroad, and give credit at home' (III, 239):

> Were the bank of England to keep a subscription open, at all times, in Amsterdam, for money to be borrowed there, on the payment of the interest in that city, who doubts but loans might be procured at much less expence than at present, when we are beating about for credit every where, until by the return of a favourable balance upon the trade of England, she shall be enabled to fill up the void. (III, 466)

The interest on the money borrowed by the Bank of England in Amsterdam should be paid by the state, whose assistance was required to avoid the shrinkage of credit in case of an adverse foreign balance:

> We have abundantly explained the fatal effects of a wrong balance to banks which circulate paper; and we have shewn how necessary it is that they should perform what we here recommend. There is therefore nothing new in this proposal: it is merely carrying the consequences of the same principle one step farther, and making it a branch of policy, for government to be assisting to trade in the payment of balances, where credit abroad is required; and we have proposed that this assistance should be given out of the public money. (III, 465)

Again, the object was for the state to contribute to establishing 'a just equality of profit and loss' rather than having the burden of the consequences of the adverse foreign balance 'fall upon that part of the body politic from which the whole draws its vigour and prosperity [the exporters]' (III, 464):

> If this be a fair state of the case, I think we may determine that such balances ought to be paid by the assistance and intervention of a statesman's administration. The object is not so great as at first sight it may appear. We do not propose that the value of this balance should be advanced by the state: by no means.

> They who owe the balance must then, as at present, find a value for the bills they demand. Neither would I propose such a plan for any nation who had, upon the average of their trade, a balance against them; but if, on the whole, the balance be favourable, I would not, for the sake of saving a little trouble and expence, suffer the alternate vibrations of exchange to disturb the uniformity of profits, which uniformity tends so much to encourage every branch of commerce.
>
> (III, 465)

Steuart suggested that an unfavourable exchange could be corrected by borrowing abroad at interest paid by the state.

This was not Ricardo's view: according to him, the state should not interfere with the exchange, which could only be corrected through the domestic management of the note issue by an independent central bank. To arrive to this conclusion, Ricardo also departed from Hume. Contrary to what is commonly believed in the literature, Ricardo did not subscribe to the price-specie flow mechanism; his analysis of the international adjustment to a monetary shock made no room for the response of the balance of trade to price changes triggered by variations in the quantity of money. Ricardo nevertheless took another route than Steuart's. For him, in a mixed monetary system of coins and convertible notes, international bullion flows did play a role in the adjustment, but only inasmuch they led to corrective changes in the quantity of money, at the import through minting and at the export through forced contraction of the note issue (for details, see Deleplace 2017: Chapter 8). Such adjustment process was slow and harmful to the economy and 'the judicious management of the quantity' (Ricardo 1816: 57) of notes convertible into bullion (hence eliminating coins) was thus preferable. If this quantity was increased when the market price of bullion fell below its legal level and contracted when it rose above, the currency was prevented from being appreciated or depreciated. Consequently, inflows or outflows of bullion for monetary reasons would cease:

> The most perfect liberty should be given, at the same time, to export or import every description of bullion. These transactions in bullion would be very few in number, if the Bank regulated their loans and issues of paper by the criterion which I have so often mentioned, namely, the price of standard bullion, without attending to the absolute quantity of paper in circulation.
>
> (Ricardo 1816: 67)

This profound difference between Steuart and Ricardo as to their disagreement with Hume's price-specie flow mechanism raises the question of their respective attitude towards monetary orthodoxy.

Conclusion: Two forms of monetary unorthodoxy

The 'instruction' that Ricardo could derive from Steuart was common knowledge at his time, and it testifies to the influence of the Scottish author on the understanding of some technical aspects of the currency (such as the causal relationship between the debasement of the coin and the high market price of gold bullion) and foreign exchange (such as the use of the real par of exchange to evaluate the state of the foreign balance). This was the kind of influence Steuart was looking for when he wrote: 'I write not to instruct merchants, but to extract from their complicated operations, the principles upon which they are founded' (III, 448).

Fifty years after they were published, Steuart's *Principles* were thus 'full of instruction' for all authors writing on money (including Ricardo), whatever their particular monetary theory. However, at the same time, these authors could disagree with Steuart's theory of money and with the political consequences which he derived from it. This was the case of Ricardo, who rejected Steuart's 'idea of a currency without a specific standard' and was certainly at odds with Steuart's suggestion to correct the exchange through borrowing abroad at interest paid by the State. Ricardo's observation that Steuart's idea was 'so directly at variance with the general principles he endeavoured to establish' did not point to an internal inconsistency in Steuart's theory of money but to the coexistence between, on the one hand, 'general principles' (on currency and exchange) put forward by Steuart and denied by nobody 50 years later, and on the other hand an 'idea' of the currency that was rejected by the majority of writers on money.

Ricardo's judgment on Steuart thus reveals the latter's position towards monetary orthodoxy but also the former's. At the time of Steuart, as of Ricardo, monetary orthodoxy was represented by David Hume who, 15 years before Steuart's *Principles*, had advocated a quantity theory of money at the domestic level and the price-specie flow mechanism at the international one (Hume 1752). Steuart's and Ricardo's respective attitude towards monetary orthodoxy can thus be evaluated through their positions towards the quantity theory of money and the price-specie flow mechanism.

Against Hume's argument according to which rising domestic prices consequent upon an inflow of precious metals would prevent a favourable balance from lasting, Steuart contended that domestic prices would *not* be affected, since they were not regulated by the quantity of circulating money – as advocated by Hume – but ultimately by the supply of and the demand for labour:

> The price of articles of the first necessity regulates, in a great measure, the price of everything else. . . . The price of necessaries depends on the occupations of a people, and not on the quantity of their specie. The standard price of *subsistence* is in the compound proportion of the number of those who are obliged to buy, and of the demand found for their labour. . . . The price of subsistence must rise and fall according to the number of workmen, and demand for their work: that is to say, the price of subsistence must be in the compound proportion above mentioned. . . . Nothing can determine the value of a vendible commodity, any where, *but the complicated operations of demand and competition*, which however frequently *influenced* by wealth, yet never can be *regulated* by it.
>
> (II, 254–256; Steuart's emphasis)

Steuart thus rejected 'the opinion of Messrs. De Montesquieu and Hume, who think that the price of every thing depends upon the *quantity of specie* in the country' (II, 255; Steuart's emphasis). As for international adjustment, Steuart initiated a tradition which would later be illustrated by Thornton, Tooke, and Keynes of the 1920s. This tradition relies on short-term international capital flows as a stabilizing factor in case of an asymmetrical exogenous shock. For Steuart the cause of an unfavourable foreign balance was *not* a domestic monetary malfunction generating an excess quantity of money *but* an unusual circumstance affecting the country (this contrasted with the orthodox view which emphasized adjustment in case of a foreign deficit endogenous to the monetary system). The unfavourable balance was viewed by Steuart as *temporary*; the role of the international short-term capital market was then not to restore external equilibrium or to establish a new one but to overcome the consequences of the foreign deficit (this contrasted with a view in which the central issue was the determination of international equilibrium). The international adjustment responding to an asymmetrical and temporary exogenous shock relied on the *capital account* of the balance of payments, more precisely international short-term capital flows (this contrasted with a view – Hume's price-specie flow mechanism – in which the current account adjusted thanks to variations in the quantity of money). This adjustment required implementing a discretionary policy oriented towards the international short-term capital market (this contrasted with a view in which international adjustment was implemented by an automatic mechanism).

Ricardo is generally associated by commentators with the Quantity Theory of Money and an automatic international adjustment adapted from Hume to a mixed monetary system of coins and convertible banknotes. Things are not that simple (see Deleplace 2017). Ricardo's approach to money is *not* a quantity theory: 'in a sound state of the currency' the value of money is not determined by its quantity but by the value of the standard. The quantity of money only affects its value in disequilibrium, and it does so through changes in the market price of the standard, not real balance effects. The quantity of money is not exogenous but endogenously adjusted to 'the wants of commerce'. As for international adjustment, Ricardo rejected its dependence upon bullion flows and favoured an appropriate management of the note issue, which should operate before exports or imports of gold had the opportunity to occur.

In spite of deep theoretical disagreements, there are two points on which Steuart's insights may help understanding the specificity of Ricardo's approach to money. On the one hand Steuart was the first to distinguish clearly between money (coin) and the standard of money (bullion) and to derive from this distinction the conclusion that monetary disorder (such as the debasement of the coin) or monetary institutions (such as seignorage) were reflected in the market price of the standard. This paved the way for Ricardo's idea that the high price of bullion was a 'proof' of a monetary disorder (the depreciation of bank notes), *not* of real determinants of the supply of and the demand for bullion (such as an adverse balance of trade). On the other hand Steuart emphasized the monetary determinants of the exchange rate (such as the debasement of the domestic coin or the seignorage on the foreign coin). This paved the way for Ricardo's idea that the external depreciation of the currency (the lowering of its exchange rate below par over and above the cost of exporting bullion) was always caused by its internal depreciation (due to an excess quantity of money) and never by an exogenous foreign balance.

At the end of the day, Steuart and Ricardo appear as squabbling bedfellows, sharing an approach to money at variance with the quantity theory inherited from Hume but opposing each other on the question of the standard of money and on the relationship between money and capital.

Notes

1 I thank Paolo Paesani and Ramon Tortajada for their remarks, which contributed to the improvement of the paper. The usual disclaimer applies.
2 The present paper is based on my contribution (Deleplace 2015) to the new publication by Gino Longhitano of the 1767 edition of Steuart's *An Inquiry into the Principles of Political Oeconomy* and on my interpretation of Ricardo's theory of money in my book *Ricardo on Money. A Reappraisal* (Deleplace 2017).
3 The reference in Steuart is (II, 280–281).
4 Published in 1759 by Philip Cantillon under the title *The analysis of trade, commerce, coin, bullion, banks, and foreign exchanges.* Philip Cantillon was a cousin of Richard Cantillon, the author of the *Essai sur la nature du commerce en général*, published in French in 1755. The relation of the *Analysis* to the *Essai* has been a matter of controversy; see for example Van den Berg (2012).
5 As shown by inequalities (6), the market price of gold bullion in each country may vary around the legal price of gold in coin in a range determined by the respective minting and melting costs. Consequently, the real par of exchange may itself vary around the legal par between a minimum and a maximum determined by Steuart's method mentioned earlier.

Bibliography

Deleplace, G. (2015), James Steuart: An Unorthodox Monetary Approach to Exchange and the Foreign Balance, in J. Steuart, *An Inquiry into the Principles of Political Oeconomy*, vol. 1, edited by G. Longhitano, Napoli: Liguori Editore: lxix–xcviii.

———. (2017), *Ricardo on Money: A Reappraisal*, Abingdon: Routledge.

Hume, D. (1752), Political Discourses: Of the Balance of Trade, in *David Hume: Essays, Moral, Political, and Literary*, Indianapolis: Liberty Fund.

Ricardo, D. (1810–1811), *The High Price of Bullion: A Proof of the Depreciation of Bank Notes*, in Ricardo (1951–1973), vol. 3, 1951: 47–127.

———. (1811), *Reply to Mr. Bosanquet's Practical Observations on the Report of the Bullion Committee*, in Ricardo (1951–1973), vol. 3, 1951: 155–256.

———. (1816), *Proposals for an Economical and Secure Currency*, in Ricardo (1951–1973), vol. 4, 1951: 49–141.

———. (1817–1821), *On the Principles of Political Economy, and Taxation*, 1st edition: 1817, 2nd edition: 1819, 3rd edition: 1821, in Ricardo (1951–1973), vol. 1, 1951.

———. (1951–1973), *The Works and Correspondence of David Ricardo*, edited by P. Sraffa with the collaboration of M.H. Dobb, Cambridge: Cambridge University Press.

Van den Berg, R. (2012), Richard Cantillon's Early Monetary Views?, *Economic Thought*, 1: 48–79.

8 James Steuart

A modern approach to the liquidity and solvency of public debt

Nesrine Bentemessek and Rebeca Gomez Betancourt

Introduction

Sir James Steuart's analysis of public debt seems singular in the history of economic thought. Unlike David Hume (1752) and Adam Smith (1776), who saw public debt as a barrier to the process of capital accumulation, Steuart considered public debt to have many advantages for society, including a positive role in the promotion of economic growth.

Steuart's *Principal of Political Economy* (1767) was published during a period of intense debate on economic and political matters, particularly in England and France. For Steuart, public debt was the *balance wheel of the economy*, whereas Hume and Smith considered that the accumulation of debt must ever lead to bankruptcy. Smith (1776) argued that funds lent to the state constitute a loss for capital accumulation. In fact, instead of constituting advanced capital for 'future reproduction', these funds are transformed into income that reduces the share of the national product initially intended for growth.[1] For Hume the main problem of an increase in public debt is the weight it represents for the country. The augmentation of public debt necessarily leads to an increase of the interest payments on it, which in a certain point would make impossible the reimbursement and lead the country to default.

Steuart's view of public debt has been studied by several authors, such as Stettner (1945), Sen (1957), and more recently by Rutherford (2012) and Tiran (2014). We insist in this chapter that Steuart's analysis of public debt was not of his time, rather his position was quite heterodox and *avant-garde* and was to considerably influence future authors who recognized some of the advantages of public debt for the macroeconomic system.

We note here the main reasons that justify the originality of Steuart's analysis of debt, primarily in the links he made between: (1) public debt, bank liquidity and market liquidity; (2) public debt and the complementarity between liquidity and solvency; and (3) public debt and active banking activity. Moreover, Steuart was original because he considered (4) public debt as a useful macroeconomic policy tool, and (5) he also analyzed the conditions for the optimal functioning of the primary and secondary debt markets. His position on public debt was quite different to Hume (1752) and Smith (1776). Finally, we also note the importance

Steuart attributed to the management of public debt and to improving the solvency of the state; this made him a unique author of his time.

Our aim is to show the originality of Sir James Steuart's analysis of public debt and better understand his place in the history of economic thought between the mercantilist authors and the fathers of the classical political economics. In the first section, we present the link between public debt and liquidity that can be observed in Steuart's writings; and in the second part we analyze the relation he established between public debt and state solvency.

Public debt and liquidity

In his *Principles of Political Economy*, Steuart strongly criticizes Hume's and Montesquieu's vision of money. As shown by Gomez Betancourt and Pierre Manigat (2019), according to Marx, Steuart was the first to ask whether the amount of money in circulation is determined by the price of commodities or whether the price of commodities is determined by the amount of money in circulation. He called into question the belief of the time that the only explanation for an increase in price was a variation in the quantity of money and was one of the first authors to explicitly oppose what would later be called the quantity theory of money. Also according to Marx, Steuart was one of the fathers of the law of reflux, prior to Thomas Tooke.[2]

Similarly to his vision of money as a reflux, James Steuart analyzes economic growth as a dynamic process in which wealth is transferred from property owners, 'solid property', to merchants and industrialists,[3] what Steuart calls the *vibration of the balance of wealth*.[4] These transfers of wealth can only take place if they can flow easily from one agent to another and without loss of value, that is to say, if they are liquid.

Although he does not use the term, Steuart is particularly interested in liquidity. Instead, he uses the term 'circulation'[5] or the idea of the 'melting down of solid property' to express the transformation of assets into money.

According to Steuart, the process of the *vibration of the balance of wealth* (II, 37), the engine for economic growth, occurs when an agent *x* exchanges his money for a consumable good produced by agent *y*. As *x* consumes this good, he is impoverished compared to *y* because his initial cash contribution has disappeared and at the same time, once the product is totally consumed, he no longer has the counterpart of this cash. As for *y*, his absolute position remains unchanged since he has a quantity of cash equivalent to the consumable property he transferred to *x*. However, *y* is now relatively richer than *x*. These *vibrations of the balance of wealth* fundamentally represent opportunities for the transfer of wealth to tradesmen and industrialists, and they are induced, as we have seen, by the act of consuming: 'The consumption, therefore, is the only thing which makes the balance turn' (II, 43).

The transfer of wealth from this vibration, as we have said, is at the heart of the dynamic of economic growth. Indeed, as economic exchanges increase, industrial demand increases, and metallic money may no be longer sufficient to meet these additional needs. This is the point at which Steuart introduces the banks that provide 'paper money', or what he also calls 'symbolic money', through credit.[6] Consequently, by transforming (melting down) the 'solid property' of agents into 'paper money', banks provide the necessary liquidity for this growth in demand.

Steuart's definition of 'solid property' is quite broad.[7] Indeed, by 'solid property', Steuart means any real or financial asset that he qualifies as 'sure', and that agents can present as collateral to banks in order to obtain symbolic money, and therefore credit. Steuart does not limit the definition of solid property to land or commodities but extends it to financial assets whose value is linked to the income (funds) they generate. In this respect, Steuart attributes a fundamental role to public debt bonds issued by the state insofar as, like land ownership, they represent a solid guarantee that banks accept as collateral for obtaining credit.

From this, Steuart considers public debt bonds as solid property that can be 'melted down' into money by banks.[8]

However, it should be noted that, for Steuart, banks may only perform the role of transforming these bonds into symbolic money if the public debt to which they are linked is well managed. In other words, the solidity of these securities depends on the solvency of the state and therefore on the regular payment by the latter of interest on its debt.[9]

In addition, Steuart analyzes the way in which public debt may be used as a lever for providing bank liquidity. Indeed, as the vibration of the balance of wealth increases with the growth of exchange, the state makes public debt, a form of 'solid property' which banks accept as collateral for the introduction of symbolic money, available to agents.

In this respect, it should be noted that among the many functions that Steuart attributes to the statesman[10] is the role of providing necessary liquidity for economic growth, with the help of banks. As we have seen, public debt is the expedient implemented by the state to achieve this: 'it is, therefore, the business of a statesman who intends to promote circulation, to be upon his guard against every cause of stagnation' (II, 56). This explains why it is necessary to support banking activity by the state:

> The statesman's interest is supposed to be more closely connected with that of his banks. . . . If he does not support them by a systematical chain of conduct, he will drain the fund of circulation by his remittances.
>
> (IV, 123)

Moreover, before Smith (1776), Steuart was well aware of the need for state regulation of the banking system.[11] As we have seen, banks are central to his analysis of growth dynamic: they introduce endogenous money through a demand for credit in exchange for solid collateral. Being aware of the problems generated by the credit market (and this goes from liquidity to solvency risks faced by the banks), Steuart supported state regulation of banks.[12]

In addition, public debt is an economic policy tool that aims to ensure that an 'adequate circulating equivalent' is constantly aligned with economic needs. In fact, one of Steuart's major concerns is to ensure that there is full circulation between agents. In other words, it is the role of the state to ensure that appropriate measures are put in place to prevent any form of monetary stagnation. From there, the needs of all agents must be met through the availability of sufficient means of payment. Public debt is a means that the state uses for this purpose.

Indeed, on the one hand, by issuing public bonds, the state absorbs any excess liquidity in an industry and immediately directs it towards 'a new channel of circulation' (IV, 101, 104).

On the other hand, if a country's circulation is full, the public debt of 'small amounts' with foreign agents[13] remains advantageous because it gives the state room to manoeuvre, allowing it to inject these funds into the economy if necessary (IV, 103).

Thus, Steuart strongly believes that effective tools must be available for the state to regulate economic exchanges in order not only to avoid monetary stagnation but also to contribute to economic recovery. Without developing a complete theory of discretionary monetary policy, Steuart's vision seems singular in the history of monetary thought.

Moreover, the liquidity provided by public debt, through its support for banks, has the advantage of 'naturally' (III, 140) lowering the interest rate,[14] which Steuart considers to be 'the soul of trade'.[15] This is firstly the interest rate at which the government borrows, and then the rate at which individuals borrow from banks.

Indeed, public creditors expect not only certain and long-term, even perpetual, income but also a holding of easily transferable – liquid – assets such as public debt bonds. Hence, this reduction in the risk on these assets leads them to consent to the lowering of the interest rate (IV, 131). In addition, the development of banking and credit activity now places the process of dual competition between lenders and borrowers in favour of the latter, which causes the interest rate to fall in an endogenous way (IV, 131).

In this regard, Steuart takes the example of the Bank of England (IV, 40–41, 125), which from 1707 circulated short-term public debt, Exchequer bills, and contributed to an increase in liquidity of these securities on the secondary debt market and to lowering the interest rate on them. In fact, by assuring their subscription by the public and their redemption at par value at its counters, the Bank of England subsequently increased the liquidity of this debt (which had long been unattractive because it was exchanged at a price well below its nominal value), restored confidence in the state and its solvency, reduced the counterparty risk of public debt in general, and finally reduced the interest rate at which it lent to the state.[16]

We see here that the liquidity of public debt is a condition for its solidity. Moreover, Steuart points out that it constitutes a compensation for the non-repayment of the debt-principal which is frequently initiated by the state.[17]

> In deducing the principles of public credit, we suppose . . . that an easy transfer of the capital from hand to hand [should] be permitted, in order to indemnify every creditor for the loss of his capital, which is not demandable from the state, as is commonly the case in private securities.
>
> (IV, 279)

In short, this analysis is quite original; according to Steuart, banks introduce the liquidity needed to vibrate the balance of wealth by transforming solid properties, including public debt bonds, into symbolic money. At the same time, banks also contribute to the liquidity of public debt bonds (IV, 99) by accepting them as collateral in their assets.

Consequently, if the state wishes to issue public bonds that will attract subscribers, it must ensure that the secondary market for the exchange of the debt already issued is liquid. In other words, public debt bonds must be traded quickly and without impairment. We have seen that Steuart makes clear that the liquidity of public debt also requires an attractive valuation for subscribers. In fact, the valuation of debt at a price well below its nominal value dissuades subscribers and reduces its attractiveness, hence its illiquidity (IV, 41–42).

Steuart also highlights in an original way the two founding dimensions of liquidity: Rapid transformation and the valuation of assets.

Similarly, by liquidity of the public debt market, Steuart understands liquidity of the financial market as a whole. In fact, on many occasions he uses the term *stockholders* to describe the holders of public debt.[18] It is true that in the 18th century the market for public debt was a major component of the whole financial market. It was not until the end of the 19th century that the financial market partially freed itself from state debt.[19]

Finally, public debt also has a civic function that binds the state to its citizens through a set of rights and duties. In this respect, Stettner (1945) highlights the social function of public debt in Steuart's work,[20] insofar as it gives rise to the emergence of public creditors, a new social class of 'solid property' holders, whose financial interests converge with the collection of taxes by the state, contributing to consent to the payment of taxes and more generally to an understanding of the notion of common interest.[21]

With regard to the civic dimension, we have seen that the state initially uses public debt, with the help of banks, to introduce the necessary liquidity for the dynamic of economic growth; in return, agents must pay taxes, which allows the state to meet its obligations to public creditors by paying interest.

In summary, for Steuart, public debt is examined as an economic policy lever that the state uses to promote bank and market liquidity. In this respect, Steuart's originality lies in his analysis of liquidity as the keystone of the growth dynamic insofar as it makes it possible to transfer wealth from the class of solid property owners to the class of merchants and industrialists. However, according to Steuart, the use of this expedient can only be optimal if public debt is well-managed and issued by a solvent state. Steuart's analysis of the relationship between sovereign solvency and liquidity is very enlightening.

Public debt and sovereign solvency

In the Steuartian analysis, the liquidity of public debt cannot be obtained without the solvency of the state. In other words, public debt bonds will be circulated all the easier on the secondary market when the issuer, in this case the state, is solvent.

In that respect, the statesman must do everything possible to improve his solvency, or his 'solidity' (IV, 7). This requires an active public debt management policy that aims to homogenize debt and reduce its cost, which will improve the functioning of both the primary market, where debt is initially issued by the state, and the secondary market, where public debt already issued is exchanged between agents.

Moreover, sovereign solvency is closely linked to the confidence that economic agents have in the state. In this respect, in Book IV on 'Public Credit' the term 'confidence' is mentioned several times.[22] When it comes to public debt, the statesman, however strong he may be, must ensure that his lenders have ongoing confidence in him, and therefore in both his solvency and his ability to optimally manage debt.[23]

> Public credit we have defined to be, the confidence reposed in a state, or body politic, borrowing money, on condition that the capital shall not be demandable, but that a certain proportional part of the sum shall be annually paid, either in lieu of interest, or in extinction of part of the capital, for the security of which payment, a permanent annual fund is appropriated, with a liberty, however, to the state to free itself, by repaying the whole, when nothing to the contrary is stipulated.
>
> (IV, 6)

First, to ensure its solvency, and before issuing public loans, the state must set up a tax fund to pay public creditors, which is a necessary condition for the solvency of its debt and for improving confidence in the state: 'The first requisite for contracting public debts is to establish a fund for fulfilling public engagement. This procures the confidence of the lender' (IV, 288). And, 'the method, therefore, of borrowing money, to the best advantage, is previously to establish a fund of credit, arising from annual taxes' (IV, 120).

Similarly, the creation of a tax fund reassures public creditors that the state will pay the interest in their favour, while contributing to civil consent in the payment of tax.

In this respect, it should be noted that, according to Steuart, public credit differs from private credit or commercial credit for two reasons.[24] First, as Stettner (1945) points out, it is not a net debt because it is held by those who will pay future taxes. In addition, the borrowing state has the option of early repayment or non-repayment of the principal amount of the debt. As compensation, public creditors obtain perpetual or long-term interest from the state. This represents an additional divergence with Smith (1776). The latter considers the creation of a perpetual fund to be an illusory operation on the part of the state to artificially accommodate agents who would pay admittedly a moderate tax, but over a long period. Essentially, Smith (1776) favours the introduction of a high tax for a limited period, after which time public debt is repaid and tax is restored to its original level.

However, for Steuart, the payment of permanent or long-term income to public creditors is a fundamental element supporting his thesis that public debt promotes the injection of stable and regular income into the economy,[25] thereby increasing demand and promoting economic growth.[26] Of course, this can only be achieved if banking activity is able to support this increase in demand, via credit, in the case of a shortage of metallic money.

Indeed, for Steuart, it is appropriate for the state to issue loans that give rise to a long-term annuity payment. From there, these annuities may consist of interest and a minority portion to repay the principal, but they may be perpetual and in this case they will only consist of interest.[27]

We have seen that, for Steuart, public debt can only produce positive macroeconomic effects if the state sets up a tax fund to guarantee the payment of public creditors, but this is not enough! The second condition is the establishment of a credit system that can support the increase in demand: 'The next (*requisite*) is to establish an extensive plan of credit at home, which may be sufficient at all times to keep circulation full' (IV, 288).

In short, Steuart describes here 'a virtuous circle of public debt'[28] that can only work if each element is fulfilled.

Ultimately, confidence in the state, the starting point of this cycle contributes to promoting public debt, which in turn promotes liquidity and private credit by providing agents with a new form of 'solid property'. The additional demand is thus satisfied by the issuing of symbolic money, credit, with the help of banks, and the vibration of the balance of wealth is thus achieved and contributes to economic growth. From there, the payment of taxes is facilitated, which allows the state to easily pay the annuities due to its public creditors, resulting in an improvement in both confidence in the state and its solvency (IV, 120).

Moreover, the resolutely singular analysis of public debt explains Steuart's equally original examination of the financial experiences of the South Seas Company in England and that of the John Law Mississippi Company in France at the beginning of the 18th century.

Steuart was not opposed to these projects because their aim was to restore confidence in the state by restructuring public debt. Here, Steuart assigns an important function to the statesman's management of public debt. In fact, the state must put in place an effective debt management policy to ensure that the debt produces the expected positive effects.

Steuart perceived in these projects, which most 18th-century authors criticized, an attempt to improve confidence in the state and restore its solvency by homogenizing its debt, improving the liquidity of the debt already issued and reducing its cost.

It is worth recalling here that English and French financial experiences were based on the conversion of illiquid[29] and costly public debt into shares of commercial companies: The South Seas Company and the Mississippi Company.

For example, with regard to the experience of the South Seas Company, Steuart points out that the South Seas Company's public debt restructuring operations in England reduced the cost of public borrowing already issued, without the same reduction in market interest rates, as was the case in France.

> But one great difference between the South Sea and Mississippi, was this: That in France there was abundance of money in the hands of the public,

> for purchasing the actions, at the exorbitant price to which they rose; but in England there was not: consequently, in France, the rate of interest fell to 2 per cent and in England, the great demand for money to borrow, raised it beyond all bounds.
>
> (IV, 45)

It is within this context that Steuart considers the South Seas Company project '*an assistance to public credit*' (IV, 42).

With regard to the John Law system in France, Steuart sees not only the opportunity to restructure French public debt through the operations of the Mississippi Company, but above all, he notes Law's implicit objective of generalizing paper money and lowering the interest rate in an endogenous way:

> It is not this whole doctrine verified in the strongest manner by the operation of the Mississippi . . . . Paper money had not been introduced three years, when interest fell to 2 per cent.
>
> (IV, 120)

That said, he attributes the failure of these experiences to poor currency management and, more specifically, Steuart strongly criticizes John Law's various manipulations of the value of account money relative to metal during his system[30] and to the adoption of questionable dividend policies and financial contestability for both projects.[31]

In addition, still with a view to improving the solvency of the state, Steuart considers the establishment of a sinking fund as a useful instrument for strengthening confidence in public credit, allowing the government to borrow on favourable terms.[32]

As we have seen, Steuart attributes an important role to the solvency of the state, which enables it to make optimal use of its debt in order to introduce the necessary liquidity for economic growth. Moreover, he fully perceives the link between the solvency of the state and the reduction in the sovereign risk of default and consequently the fall in the interest rate on the issued public debt.

The following quote speaks volumes on this subject:

> The solidity of this security is essential to the borrowing upon the cheapest terms: let me suppose it to be as solid as land property, and as permanent as government itself.
>
> (IV, 7).

In other words, by putting in place what has been described earlier as a virtuous circle of debt, and, in particular, with the help of banks and the consequent introduction of symbolic money, the state improves confidence in itself, reducing its risk of default, and enabling it to issue new loans at a low rate (IV, 120).

Finally, Steuart argues that an active public debt management policy promoting the restoration of state solvency will have a beneficial effect on the complementarity between the primary and secondary markets. Here too, this author can attest to a modern vision of public finance theory.

In short, improving confidence in the state and restoring its solvency contributes to making the secondary debt market more fluid, where bonds already issued can be traded quickly and without impairment; in other words, it contributes to improving its liquidity by allowing the state to easily issue new loans on the primary market.

Conclusion

The reading of James Steuart's *Principles* has taught us that liquidity is crucial for the dynamic of economic growth, which is achieved when wealth is transferred from property owners to merchants and industrialists. It also makes clear that the development of private banks and the liquidity of public debt are mutually reinforcing forces. We have shown that for Steuart, public debt is not an obstacle to economy expansion provided it is backed up by reliable and permanent revenues. Steuart was aware that public annuities represent a permanent income for public creditors and that, at the same time, public debt facilitates the macroeconomic conditions for the development of symbolical money, namely credit.

One of the most significant contributions of Steuart's analysis is that well-managed public debt, issued by a solvent state, means liquid public debt. This is the way in which economic growth is achieved through 'the vibration of the balance of wealth'.

All of these original ideas on debt and the public finance system allow us to consider Steuart as an *avant-garde* author of the late 18th century.

Notes

1 See Smith's *Wealth of Nation*, Book V, Chapter 3.
2 See in Gomez Betancourt and Pierre Manigat (2019): 'In his Investigations into Currency Th. Tooke underlines that money in its function as capital flows back to its starting point (REFLUX OF MONEY TO ITS POINT OF ISSUE), but in its function simply as CURRENCY does not flow back. This distinction, noted by Sir James Steuart, among others, long before Tooke, serves the latter simply for a polemic against what the preachers of the CURRENCY PRINCIPLE claim to be the influence the issue of credit money (Banknotes, etc.) exercises upon commodity prices' (*Letters Marx to Engels*, may 23, 1868).
3 See Vickers (1959), Skinner (1981) and Akhtar (1978).
4 With regard to the notion of the vibration of the balance of wealth, we refer the reader to Diatkine and Rosier (1999).
5 The use of the term 'circulation' to express what is meant by liquidity today can be found in several authors, including David Hume (1752) and Adam Smith (1776).
6 See Diatkine and Rosier (1999)
7 See Steuart (III, 168).
8 See Steuart (IV, 640).
9 We analyze this point in the second section of this article.
10 On Steuart's 'statesman' figure, see Skinner (1993) and Urquhart (1996) and Pierre Manigat's article in this book.

11 'The best method to establish credit in an industrious nation, is a bank properly regulated' (III, 234).
12 We do not expand on this point in this article either. However, with regard to the regulation of the banking system by the state for Steuart, we direct the reader towards Diatkine and Rosier (1999), Piteau (2002) and Bentemessek (2012). On liquidity risk and banks, see De Boyer (2013).
13 When the circulation is full, the state should not ask for more debt through national agents in order to avoid an increase of the interest rate (IV, 103).
14 See Tortajada (1999) and Yang (1993).
15 Steuart argues that a lower level of interest rates is 'the soul of trade' (III, 146). However, this reduction must not be arbitrary or abusive. Steuart advocates for an endogenous reduction of the interest rates through a competitive relationship between lenders and borrowers and criticizes the arbitrary fixation by the state of the interest rate level. On this subject, see Tortajada (1999).
16 See de Boyer (2006) and Bentemessek and Boyer (2014).
17 Steuart is interested in the introduction of stable and regular income through public debt to public creditors in order to promote economic growth. Hence, it is appropriate for the state to issue loans that give rise to the payment of long-term annuities. These annuities may consist of interest and a minority portion of the capital, but they may be perpetual, and in this case they will only consist of interest (Steuart, Chapter 10, p. 666, in Skinner's edition).
18 Steuart, Book IV, Chapter 5, p. 640, p. 629 and p. 635 in Skinner's edition.
19 See Morgan and Thomas (1969).
20 Stettner (1945: 452).
21 On Steuart General Sales Tax and more generally on public finance in Britain, see Dome (2001).
22 The term 'confidence' has been used ten times in the 'On public Credit' section, in Chapters 1 to 3, Chapter 5, and Chapters 8 to 10 in Book IV of Steuart's *Principles*.
23 'Where the power of the statesman is unlimited, he may substitute his authority over the people who are to pay, instead of confidence, but with respect to those who are to lend, he will find no room for any substitution: confidence here is the only expedient' (IV, 119).
24 For Steuart, public credit does not crowd out private credit. At the macroeconomic level, both are accumulating. Economic agents with financing capacity are rational and therefore lend to the state when this strategy seems more profitable to them. 'We have said that loans are filled by money stagnating, which the owner desires to realize: if he cannot do better, he lends it to the government; if he can do better, he will not lend it' (IV, 450). See also Stettner (1945: 456) on this question.
25 'When a statesman, therefore, establishes a system of public credit, the first object which should fix his attention is to calculate how far the constitution of the state, and its internal circumstances, render it expedient to throw the revenue of it into the hands of moneyed interest. I say, this is the most important object of his deliberation; because the solidity of his credit depends upon it' (IV, 7).
26 On theoretical connections with Keynes, see Ülgen (1999) and Skinner and Eltis (2008).
27 Steuart, Book IV, Chapter 10, p. 666 in Skinner's edition.
28 See Bentemessek (2012).
29 Steuart also made reference to the devaluation of English and French public debt before the restructuring experiments.
30 For the examination of John Law's system in France, we have based ourselves on Rist (2002), Faure (1977), Murphy (1997), and de Boyer (2013).
31 For a detailed discussion of these aspects, see Bentemessek (2012).
32 See Stettner (1945: 470).

Bibliography

Akhtar, M.A. (1978), Sir James Steuart on Economic Growth, *Scottish Journal of Political Economy*, 25(1): 57–74.

Bentemessek, N. (2012), Public Credit and Liquidity in James Steuart's *Principles*, *European Journal of the History of Economic Thought*, 19(4): 501–528.

Bentemessek, N. & Boyer, J. de. (2014), Financial Institutions and Liquidity of National Debt in England [1694–1720], Lausanne: *Annual Conference of the European Society for the History of Economic Thought*.

Boyer, J. de. (2006), Dette publique, Banque d'Angleterre et taux d'intérêt: 1694–1800, *Économies et Sociétés: Histoire économique quantitative*, 34(2): 215–232.

———. (2013), Bank Liquidity Risk: From John Law (1705) to Walter Bagehot (1873), *European Journal of the History of Economic Thought*, 20(4): 547–571.

Diatkine, S. & Rosier, M. (1999), Steuart and Smith on Banking Systems and Growth, in R. Tortajada (ed.), *The Economics of James Steuart*, London: Routledge: 218–234.

Dome, T. (2001), Sir James Steuart and a General Sales Tax, *History of Political Economy*, 33(2): 345–367.

Faure, E. (1977), *La banqueroute de Law: 17 juillet 1720*, Paris: Gallimard.

Gomez Betancourt, R. & Pierre, M. (2019), James Steuart and the Making of Karl Marx's Monetary Thought, *European Journal of the History of Economic Thought*, 25(5): 1022–1051.

Hume, D. (1752), *Political Discourses: By David Hume, Esq. Edinburgh*, Edinburgh: A. Kincaid & A. Donaldson.

Morgan, E.V. & Thomas, W.A. (1969), *The Stock Exchange, Its History and Functions*, London: Elek Books.

Murphy, A. (1997), *John Law: Economic Theorist and Policy-Maker*, Oxford: Oxford University Press.

Piteau, M. (2002), Monnaie de compte et système de paiements chez James Steuart. Quel rôle pour la stabilité bancaire?, *Revue économique*, 53(2): 245–271.

Rist, C. (2002), *Histoire des doctrines relatives au crédit et à la monnaie depuis John Law jusqu'à nos jours*, Paris: Dalloz.

Rutherford, D. (2012), *In the Shadow of Adam Smith: Founders of Scottish Economics 1700–1900*, London: Macmillan International Higher Education.

Sen, S.R. (1957), *The Economics of Sir James Steuart*, London: Bell & Sons.

Skinner, A.S. (1981), Sir James Steuart: Author of a System, *Scottish Journal of Political Economy*, 28(1): 20–42.

———. (1993), Sir James Steuart: The Market and the State, *History of Economic Ideas*, 1(1): 1–42.

Skinner, A.S. & Eltis, W. (2008), Steuart, Sir James (1713–1780), in S.N. Durlauf & L.E. Blume (eds.), *The New Palgrave Dictionary of Economics*, 2nd edition, Basingstoke: Palgrave Macmillan.

Smith, A. (1776), *An Inquiry into the Nature and Causes of the Wealth of Nations*, Indianapolis: Liberty Fund, 1981.

Stettner, W.F. (1945), Sir James Steuart on the Public Debt, *The Quarterly Journal of Economics*, 59(3): 451–476.

Tiran, A. (2014), Dette publique et fiscalité chez James Steuart, in J.P. Potier (dir), *Les Marmites de l'histoire*, Paris: Classiques Garnier: 41–53.

Tortajada, R. (1999), *The Economics of James Steuart*, London: Routledge.

Ülgen, F. (1999), James Steuart's Principles as a Modern Analysis of Monetary Economy, in R. Tortajada (ed.), *The Economics of James Steuart*, London: Routledge: 253–274.

Urquhart, R. (1996), The Trade Wind, the Statesman and the System of Commerce: Sir James Steuart's Vision of Political Economy, *European Journal of the History of Economic Thought*, 3: 403–404.

Vickers, D. (1959), *Studies in the Theory of Money, 1690–1776*, Philadelphia: Chilton Company.

Yang, H.-S. (1993), *The Political Economy of Trade and Growth: An Analytical Interpretation of Sir James Steuart's Inquiry*, Doctoral Thesis, Durham University.

9 Steuart's naïve theory of money and credit

A macroeconomic perspective

Shigeki Tomo[1]

Introduction

This chapter clarifies, from a modern macroeconomic perspective, the naïveté of Sir James Steuart's theory of money and credit. As is understood, the interest rate – an additional variable pertaining to the demand function of money – is the breakthrough by which the investment/saving – liquidity preference/money supply (*IS – LM*) model was established as modern macroeconomics' fundamental model. Crucially, the liquidity-preference theory reveals the linkage of money at hand and the existence of its alternative interest bearing asset: The Consols (an abbreviated name for the Consolidated Threes). Although an available source exists (authorized by the state) which always warrants a positive return, people keep money in amounts following the price of the Consols' return rate. Keynes, offering a convincing explanation of human motives, concluded the demand function of money depends on interest rates. Thus theoretical economists like John Hicks formulated general equilibrium models of product and money markets.[2]

Following England's 1751 creation of the Consols (and before publishing *An Inquiry Into the Principles of Political Economy*), Steuart confronted the same economic institutions John Maynard Keynes would. Nevertheless, Steuart's masterpiece contains almost nothing concerning ideas or philosophies leading to the liquidity-preference theory. The following proposes a reason for this omission, considering Steuart's statesman philosophy and an observation concerning the era's complicated Sinking Fund measures. The way Keynes, beyond Steuart, could value probable knowledge (including the liquidity or use of money) is derived from Hume's viewpoint on scepticism.

'The Hayekian Perspective', used in this chapter's original title, was replaced with 'A Macroeconomic Perspective'. Obviously, Hayek did not found modern macroeconomics. Nevertheless, his understanding of the liquidity-preference orientation (expressed in his 1939 reproduction of Henry Thornton's *Paper Credit*), while questionable, helped the present author detect the naïveté inherent in Steuart's theory of money and credit. Hayek's interpretation of Thornton's phrase 'loss sustained by keeping money' – the precursor to Keynes's liquidity-preference theory – was, from a modern macroeconomic viewpoint, incorrect. It lacks the connotation of portfolio selection among assets, especially money and Consols.

However, Hayek was correct to exclude Steuart as a forerunner of the liquidity-preference theory. Steuart scholars, like S.R. Sen, should have attached significant importance to the preface to Hayek's 1939 edition of Henry Thornton.

Sen (1957: 102–103), asserting that Keynes had overlooked Steuart, suggested ready money demands as an element of liquidity preference – a notion seen frequently in Book IV of Steuart's *Inquiry* (III, 225, 235, 408). The term 'ready money', used by writers since the early 15th century (per the *Oxford English Dictionary* and the Eighteenth Century Collection Online), cannot serve as a 'signpost' for economic historians to pinpoint the forerunners of liquidity-preference theory. Furthermore, Steuart used the term nonspecifically, suggesting that he cared not about precise meanings, using it in its wider sense. Adam Smith's use of the term is remarkable; the phrase 'ready money for answering occasional demands' appears at least ten times in *The Wealth of Nations*. Smith's specification 'for answering occasional demands' indicates that ready money has many demand-oriented purposes – including those pertaining to today's specified payments – that are altogether excluded from the explanatory scope of liquidity preference arising from speculative motives.

If this is so, shouldn't the work of Smith, not Steuart, be the precursor to Keynes's liquidity-preference theory, given its specification? The answer is 'no', merely because Smith's (as well as Steuart's) work lacks fundamental discussions of the modern feature of liquidity-preference theory – namely, portfolio selection between Consols and ready money for answering occasional demands.

Steuart's naïveté

In 1751, Henry Pelham issued 3% annuities to consolidate the nine stocks (securities) issued for national debts in 1721, 1736, 1738, 1742–45, and 1750 (Dickson 1967: 242, Table 30) with interest payments from the Sinking Fund. These formed the original Consols. Pelham's project provided the institutional setting, potentially leading to Steuart's and Smith's observations of the close relationship between ready money and the Consols' perpetual interest yield. However, neither mentions the Consols' liquidity-preference connotation, save for the Sinking Fund. The Sinking Fund was established in 1717 by Robert Walpole, without reducing fiscal spending or introducing additional excise duties (*ibidem*. 88–89; 212–214). Walpole's intention was to use the surplus from previous commodity taxes in the consolidation, as well as the excess from the former conversion from short-term to long-term debts. After the Sinking Fund's establishment, the South Sea Bubble occurred, and Steuart suggested measures to prevent 'the abuses in the rising of the South Sea' (Steuart Vol. II 389). Thus management of the Sinking Fund was a major issue in the spheres of public credit and finance. Following the Consols' birth, the Sinking Fund's function did not turn out to be 'sinking' in nature, but a perpetual source of interest payments. This led to high confidence in Consols and, by extension, their continuing existence. The 'funding' system in the title of Ricardo (1820) reflects the perpetuity of the Consols.

The Consols' function, then, is to consolidate many former securities, while perpetually postponing their liquidation by providing constant, stable interest payments. Their remarkable merit warrants theoretical consideration of the Consol system. However, neither Steuart nor Smith estimates the Consols' excellence – nor do they anticipate their projection into today.

The Consols' 1751 introduction marked the first state institutionalization of money's positive, *perpetual* interest bearing nature. This was a historical watershed, as the 18th-century Catholic Church still prohibited the taking of interest. The Anglican Church's opposite stance is traceable to Henry VIII, who abolished the Catholic usury-prohibition policy, introducing a maximum 10% interest rate as early as 1545. Thenceforth, major 17th-century writers on money interest – including Thomas Culpeper, Josiah Child, Thomas Manley, and John Locke – concerned themselves with clarifying causalities among low interest rates, trade, and the quantity of money. England's reduction of legal interest rates culminated in the Consols, which supplied the Seven Years' War (1755–63) with lower interest rates than previous war-finance measures.

Following England's February 1763 triumph, Steuart returned to Scotland, staying at Newmains until early 1765. While there he worked on Book IV, *Of Credit and Debts of Inquiry*.[3] Writing Part I, 'Of the Interest of Money' – comprising nine chapters – Steuart emphasizes applicability of the principles of double competition (Book II, Chapter 2)[4] to the regulation mechanism of interest rates in the money market:

> The borrowers desire to fix the interest as low as they can; the lenders seek, from a like principle of self-interest, to carry the rate of it as high as they can. From this combination of interests arises *a double competition*, which fluctuates between the two parties. If more is demanded to be borrowed, than there is found to be lent, the competition will take place among the borrowers. Such among them who have the most pressing occasion for money, will offer the highest interest, and will be preferred. If, on the contrary, the money to be lent exceeds the demand of the borrowers, the competition will be upon the other side. Such of the lenders, who have the most pressing occasion to draw an interest for their money, will offer it at the lowest interest, and this offer will be accepted of.
>
> (III, 154–155; emphasis added)

However, applying double competition on both sides of the money market (i.e., borrowers and lenders) does not sufficiently explain the equilibrium interest rate's uniqueness in an economy, since another interest rate exists in the Consols' market. Nothing verifies their identicalness. The duality of money's price doesn't enter Steuart's theoretical discussion; he defines interest as the price of money in the singular form (III, 155).

Double competition and competitive arbitrage regarding money and the Consols would give an economy a single interest rate. Steuart fails to offer explanatory behavioural principles among 'all monied people'.[5] He outlines generally the Consols' institutional authority over money's interest bearing, defining public credit as 'the confidence reposed in a state, or body politic, borrowing money, on condition that the capital shall not be demandable, but that a certain proportional part of the sum shall be annually paid' (IV, 2). He doesn't highlight implications of the Consols' emerging market, whose price calculates their real yield rate. Before the Consols, underwriting jobs were executed by so-called moneyed interests (e.g., the East India and South Sea companies). Thereafter, the Bank of England became a monopolistic underwriter, providing the Consols greater liquidity for future transactions.

The Steuart doctrine's naïveté on money and credit lies in its lack of insight into (1) revolutionary changes[6] prompted by the Consols; (2) their market role in creating an environment where every money holder could earn interest at will;[7] and (3) their interest rates' role in providing ready money for answering occasional demands (particularly from the viewpoint of liquidity preference due to speculative motives).

Steuart's naïveté (or prematurity) is evident in his critique of de Montesquieu-Hume's quantity theory of money.[8] Contradicting their proposition that 'The prices of commodities, [sic] are always proportioned to the plenty of money in the country' – a proposition he also summarized (I, 289) – Steuart asserted 'there is no real or adequate proportion between the value of money and of goods; and yet in every country we find one established', raising the question: 'How is this to be accounted for?' (II, 79). The answer is in his effective-demand theoretical statements: 'The direct principle which has influenced them [prices], and which will always regulate their rise and fall, is the increase of demand' (I, 75). 'I propose another doctrine, which is, that nothing can determine the value of a vendible commodity, any where [sic], *but the complicated operations of demand and competition*, which however frequently *influenced* by wealth, yet never can be regulated by it'. (II, 255–256; emphasis in original)

Steuart's emphasis on the operation of demand allows his evaluation as a forerunner to Keynes; however, this is only somewhat accurate. By this logic, there is no clear insight into the path of interest rate movements from increased money supply to greater investment spending, thus leading to an increase in effective demand.

Declining interest rates due to increased money supply would be wholly explained by Steuart's principles of double competition in the money market, unless other interest bearing institutions or assets existed. Criticising the quantity theory of money, Steuart should have elaborated on interest rates' long-term effects, as affected by the Consols' market. Surprisingly, on this point, he had nothing to say.

Steuart's *Monetarsystem* – celebrated by Karl Marx in *Grundrisse* – was somewhat premature compared to Keynes, evidenced by its insufficient ideas on parameters for a monetary economy. In two 1932 drafts (reproduced in Volume 13 of *The Collected Writings of John Maynard Keynes* (CWJMK)), he first refers to the notion of liquidity preference as a monetary economy parameter (396 ff). Keynes's parameter emphasis can be understood like this: He saw the schedules of liquidity preference as major disrupting factors in the quantity equation of money. Fisher's $MV = PT$ assumes neither any background movements of interest rates, nor their repercussions regarding the volumes of T and P. Steuart's critique of the quantity theory reveals that his *Inquiry* foreshadowed Keynes's *The General Theory*.

The philosophy of statesman

Why could neither Steuart nor the classical economists (including Smith) conceive of the Consols' liquidity-preference connotation?

Ostensibly, the contemporary milieu offers an answer. Pelham's consolidation was considered a mere conversion, executed previously and repeatedly. This is seen in cyclical episodes of over nine issues of stocks for national debt. These financed the wars, plus their conversions in English Parliament, between the late 17th and early 18th centuries. Contemporary public concern regarding national debt concentrated not on the brand new function of Consols (intended to benefit later generations); rather, it focused on traditional interest burden reduction through the Sinking Fund. This point appears in Smith's reference to interest reduction legislature:

> In 1727, the interest of the greater part of the publick debts was still further reduced to four per cent. and in 1753 and 1757, to three and a half and three per cent; which reductions still further augmented the sinking fund.
>
> (Smith 1979: II, 915)

Smith offers no special description of Pelham's consolidation project; rather, he focuses on the interest paying source: The Sinking Fund.

However, these matters address our question incomprehensively. Keynes, the leading economist propounding the liquidity-preference theory, also discusses the effects of the Sinking Fund, including an attenuation of the propensity to consume (Keynes 1987: VII, 95). The liquidity-preference perspective is thus completely compatible with economic thinking vis-à-vis the Sinking Fund.

A more convincing answer can be derived from the particularity of Steuart's definition of 'political economy' as the statesman's science of control. In expounding (Book II, Chapter 27) on the statesman's objectives, Steuart writes that the statesman 'ought at all times to maintain a just proportion between the produce of industry, and the quantity of circulating equivalent, in the hands of his subjects, for the purchase of it' (II, 53). The statesman's superior conception is found in this sentence – especially considering today's monetary control by the central banking system[9] – even as the Bank of England was still a mere joint stock company whose major chartered business was discounting bills and notes (III, 276). Steuart supposed that in a time with no open-market operation, a statesman would have it 'in his power to increase or diminish the extent of credit and paper money in circulation, by various expedients, which [would] greatly influence the rate of interest' (III, 175). The 'various expedients' of this sentence could be replaced with 'skilful hands' (I, 431), contrasting remarkably with Smith's 'invisible hands'[10]

Thus Steuart's theory of money and credit is a good example, indicating the clear distinction of two systems of political economy at its emergence.

However, the parameters of a monetary economy – like the psychological schedules of the liquidity preference of 'subjects'[11] – is largely outside the statesman's purview, as is its prudent control or management.[12] Steuart's conclusion that 'Money which does not circulate is of no use to the proprietors' (II, 260) is a by-product of his statesman viewpoint. Doubtless, it prevented Steuart from deeper considerations of the money market's demand side, as influenced by interest rates.

It is clear that Steuart directed his concern towards the arts of the statesman in 'promoting equable circulation' (I, xxiii), but he didn't neglect the psychological factors of a people. Rather, following de Montesquieu's concept of the *esprit général*, he wrote:

> THE spirit of a people is formed upon a set of received opinions relative to three objects; morals, government, and manners: these once generally adopted by any society, confirmed by long and constant habit, and never called in question, form the basis of all laws, regulate the form of every government, and determine what is commonly called the customs of a country.
>
> (I, 10)

Had Steuart noticed that schedules of liquidity preference align with a people's manners and customs, and the non-neutral role of money out of circulation, monetary economics would likely have had a different starting point.

Hume's scepticism

French Philosopher de Montesquieu (not the Scottish Enlightenment dominant in Steuart's homeland) influenced the plan for Steuart's *Inquiry* during his mid-18th-century exile in Southern France (Skinner 1966: xxxvi). In 1759 Tübingen, far from Scotland, Steuart finished *Inquiry*'s first two books. The years between 1763 (when he was pardoned and could return to Scotland) and 1767 (when *Inquiry* was published) were too short a period to revise *Inquiry*'s whole system in consideration of the Scottish Enlightenment's common sense philosophy.

The scepticism of David Hume (who graduated from Edinburgh before Steuart) provides a frame of reference for comparing Steuart and Keynes on the nature of liquidity and the use of money. Steuart supports Hume in his 1771 pamphlet criticizing James Beattie's common sense philosophy (VI, 3). Keynes deeply understood Hume's scepticism through close conversations with his father during revision of the 4th edition of *Formal Logic*[13] (begun on September 7, 1905 (Keynes 1994: ADD 7855, 246)). As early as February 1876, Neville Keynes wrote extracts from Hume's *A Treatise of Human Nature* in his private notebook, which was given to his son, Maynard.[14] It is likely that, during *Formal Logic*'s revision process, Neville taught Maynard the limit of formal logic's ability to resolve Hume's scepticism. The wider notion of probability in Hume's proposition – 'All knowledge degenerates into probability'[15] – was not in traditional theories of probability.

Maynard faced a challenge in his fellowship dissertation: Extend logic or replace the frequency theory with a wider theory of probability by formulating rational belief in terms of mathematics. This was so intellectually attractive that he left the Economics Tripos in May 1906 (Moggridge 1992: 97), despite Marshall's strong endorsement.

Hume's scepticism – which awakened the works of Immanuel Kant and Karl Popper – was summarized by Keynes's Cambridge senior Bertrand Russell as the proposition that 'nothing can be known a priori about the connection about cause and effect' (Russell 1912: 129–130). Nonetheless, Hume did not apply his scepticism to causal discussions of interest phenomena. Otherwise, he would have contributed nothing to the 17th-century controversy on the meanings of 'low interest'. Hume is regarded as a mechanical or naïve quantity theorist of money due to his proposition 'All augmentation [in the quantity of money] has no other effect than to heighten the price of labour and commodities', (Hume 1752: 62). Milton Friedman quotes this atop his *New-Palgrave* article on the quantity theory of money. It assumes a causal relation between the plenitude of money and price levels. If one is so sceptical as to doubt the existence of causality itself, one could not be a quantity theorist.

Hume thus referred to several causalities of historic events in his *Political Discourses*. His doubts in *A Treatise of Human Nature* were not directed to causality but to the uncertainty of future events. Keynes appropriately summarized that 'Hume's sceptical criticisms are usually associated with causality; but argument by induction – inference from past particulars to future generalisations – was the real object of his attack' (Keynes 1987: VIII, 303). Keynes references the famous proposition that 'All swans are white' (Keynes 1987: VIII, 247) as an example of drawing generalizations from one's experiences or observations. Countering Hume's attack, Keynes sought to introduce the concept of subjective probability and show that 'the success of induction in the past can certainly affect its probable usefulness' (*ibidem*, 272).

Struggles with Hume's scepticism unrefuted so far triggered Keynes's 1907 fellowship dissertation.[16] Perhaps they brought Keynes to the idea of liquidity preference or holding money as an answer to practical questions about accepting the uncertainty of future economic events (the initial reason for Hume's scepticism). Keynes restated the significance of holding money in summarizing the contents of *The General Theory* in 1937: 'our desire to hold money as a store of wealth is a barometer of the degree of our distrust of our own calculations and conventions concerning the future' (Keynes 1987: XIV, 116). Instead of underlining the power of *a priori* judgements in human reason as Kant's answer to Hume's scepticism, Keynes relied on individuals' observable behaviour to provide for future uncertainty, viz. holding money.

Regarding interest phenomena, besides the prospect of swans' colour, Keynes reconciled the Aristotelian generalization 'money itself is sterile for ever' with another future generalization – namely, that as long as the Consols were supported by the government, money is prolific, with certainty of them bearing a positive return. With the idea of portfolio selection between money and Consols according to their returns, Keynes could introduce that money demand depends on interest rates. Although Steuart saw the same institution (Consols) as Keynes, he did not reach Keynes's conclusions. This diversity was explained by their differing attitudes towards Hume's scepticism. Steuart remained a supporter, whereas Keynes shifted from supporter to challenger.

Something must have stimulated the metamorphosis of Keynes's economic thoughts and attitudes towards Hume's scepticism. Friedrich Hayek triggered Keynes towards the monetary theory of production[17] by criticizing Keynes's *A Treatise on Money* and by publishing his London School of Economics (LSE) lectures as *Price and Production* in 1931.

Price and Production brought Hayek attention for locating in Hume's *Political Discourses* the successive effects of an increase or decrease of the amount of money. Quoting from Hume: 'it is only in this interval or intermediate situation, between the acquisition of money and the rise of prices, that the increasing quantity of gold and silver is favourable to industry' (Hume 1752: 47; c.f., Hayek 1931: 9).

Hayek's quotation must have revived Keynes's intellectual discussion of Hume because Keynes quoted the same sentence (and the three which followed) in *The General Theory* (Keynes 1987: VII, 343). There, Keynes replaced Hayek's interpretation of Hume as 'the successive effects' with his own: Hume stressed the importance of the equilibrium position as compared with the ever-shifting transition towards it. More importantly, Keynes added before the quotation that Hume didn't overlook 'the fact that it is in the [shifting] transition that we actually have our being'. This addition evinces Keynes's new conceptualization of the nature of uncertainty, which had caused Hume's own scepticism: we exist in a changing, shifting world. Consequently, he reached one of *A Treatise on Money*'s major revisions. 'When I began to write my *Treatise on Money*', confessed Keynes,

> my lack of emancipation from preconceived ideas showed itself in what now seems to me to be the outstanding fault of the theoretical parts of that work (namely, Books III and IV) that I failed to deal thoroughly with *the effects of changes* in the level of output.
>
> (Keynes 1987: VII, xxii, my emphasis)

The notion of living with uncertainty allowed Keynes to conceptualize money as a link between present and future, with ideas on the theory of shifting equilibrium. Namely, he proposed 'the theory of a system in which changing views about the future are capable of influencing the present situation' (Keynes 1987: VII, 293) Money as 'a subtle device for linking the present to the future' (Keynes 1987: VII, 294) can be a super asset for the shifting future or uncertainty in our economic lives, going beyond Hume's scepticism.

Per Hicks's 1962 research, the concept of money as liquidity became commonplace in the present business world following Keynes's 1930 definition of liquidity.[18] An analogy from 18th-century Scottish philosophy seems applicable: Keynes could be seen in the extended line of the common sense school of the

Scottish Enlightenment, represented by Thomas Reid, as a counterpoint to Hume's scepticism.

Economically, Keynes's contribution was far more than common sense. His idea of holding money as keeping liquidity premium brought a revolution with a corollary, viz. his conceptualization of interest as a reward for parting with money for a specified period (Keynes 1987: VII, 167, 174). This allows regarding interest rates as independent variables of the demand function for money (Keynes 1987: VII, 199). Since interest rates adjust savings and investments in the product market, the general equilibrium linkage with the money market is established in a macroeconomic model through the interest rate. The *IS-LM* model, regardless of whether it represents Keynes's desired structure, now inevitably helps economics students discuss effects of fiscal and monetary policies on national income, viz. employment levels.

Concluding remarks

When Austrian Eugen von Böhm-Bawerk criticized Steuart's theory of interest (Chapter 3 of his *Geschichte und Kritik der Kapitalzins-Theorien*), he did not address Steuart's careless attitude towards the Consols' introduction. This seems a reasonable criticism of past interest theories. In his opening chapter, Böhm-Bawerk declares that social policies must be excluded from theories investigating interest phenomena. The Consols and their institutionalization of positive interest rates (as parts of social policy) were not subjects of Böhm-Bawerk's critical project. Independent of English political measures of interest rates, he theorizes in *Positive Theorie des Kapitals* three reasons for the existence of positive interest rates.

Böhm-Bawerk's distinction between theory and practice became a yoke for Hayek, who was not to be the founder of modern macroeconomics. As early as 1931, Hayek (having read Böhm-Bawerk's earliest 1876 draft on interest (Yagi 1983), plus his major work, *Kapital und Kapitalzins*) – concerned himself with money's influence on production. In 1934 (when Hayek edited Menger's collected works at LSE), he underscored the importance of Menger's definition of 'money' as the commodity with the highest marketability (*Absatzfähigkeit*) (Hayek 1934: 403, 414). Nonetheless, Hayek couldn't further develop the liquidity-preference line of thought as Keynes did.

Hayek's major concern was explaining the trade cycle in terms of velocity differences in the circulation of money and commodities.[19] While the velocity of commodity circulation was present in Böhm-Bawerk's notion of roundaboutness in capitalist production, money circulation is the V in the quantity equation. Hayek, therefore, could not target the quantity theory of money for criticism. His examination could not see preferences for the highest marketability or liquidity as crucial elements. Keynes's liquidity-preference theory showed the reverse effect of interest rates on the demand for money in the context of a variety of assets (such as money and the Consols). In contrast, Hayek did not develop any extended theory of interest and could not emerge from the intellectual perspective Sir James Steuart used to criticize the quantity theory of money.

Notes

1 My many thanks go to professors and young scholars in Japan who helped me by giving comments and opportunities for my access to materials: Messrs José Manuel Menudo at Sevilla, Shin Kubo at Kwansei-Gakuin, Nobuhiko Nakazawa at Kansai, Taro Hisamats at Dohshisha, Yuji Sato at Rikkyo, and Shinji Nohara at Tokyo University. This chapter is supported by JSPS Kakenhi, Grant-in-Aid for Publication of Scientific Research Results, 16HP3005, 2016–2020, via the Jshet Scheme to Promote International Activities (2017).

2 We should note here that the present author's purpose is not to assert that the *IS – LM* model represents what Keynes really wanted to build but to highlight his liquidity-preference theory as a fundamental piece of that model, especially compared to Steuart's doctrines of money and interest.

3 'I write in 1764' (III, 166). See also Skinner (1966: 44).

4 I once reported on my interpretation that Steuart's principles of double competition presage the double-auction system seen in today's continuous trading (Tomo 2010).

5 This expression is found in Steuart (III, 169).

6 Dickson sees the financial 'revolution' taking place in England in the early 18th century. This seems to me to be an overly long period. From the macroeconomic viewpoint presented herein, the revolution took place with the introduction of the Consolidated Threes.

7 Keynes points out that 'the existence of an organised market gives an opportunity for wide fluctuations in liquidity preference due to the speculative-motive' (Keynes 1987: VII, 170–171).

8 Steuart summarizes the history of the quantity theory of money: 'I find it in Mr. Locke, and in the Spectator for the 19th of October, 1711; but they have been beautifully illustrated by Monsr. de Montesquieu; and Mr. Hume has extended the theory, and diversified it prettily in his political discourses' (II, 84). This summary was adopted in Marx's *Grundrisse* (666).

9 King (1936) recognizes a milestone – namely, the 1825 crisis – after which the Bank of England was considered a central bank. It would be difficult to find any scholar before 1825 who had asserted that the bank was already behaving as the central bank.

10 On this contrast, see Omori (1996).

11 Keynes (1987: VII, 202) asserts that 'It is evident, then, that the rate of interest is a highly psychological phenomenon'.

12 The phrase 'prudent management' is referenced by Steuart (II, 172).

13 Neville writes 'I have received helpful comments from J. S. Mackenzie and from my son, Mr. J. M. Keynes' in 'Preface to the Fourth Edition of Neville's *Formal Logic*'. This was pointed out by O'Donnell (1989: 15).

14 *Keynes Papers*, King's College Library, UA/2A/7. This is a bound manuscript of five notebooks. The fourth one contains the extract: 23–147.

15 Hume 1739 – Green edition 472. John Neville Keynes copied this proposition quoted from the Green edition of Hume in his notebook. *Keynes Papers*, King's College Library, UA/2A/7 77.

16 *Keynes Papers*, King's College Library, TP/A/1. It is entitled *Principles of Probability*.

17 This is the title of his article contributed to *Festschrift für Spiethoff*. (Keynes 1987: XIII, 408–411)

18 'More certainly with short notice without loss realizable', in Volume II of *A Treatise on Money*.

19 Hayek's first initiation for this line of thought was his encounter with the paragraph in Foster and Catchings' *Money*: 'When money is spent faster than the commodities reach the retail markets, business booms forward. When commodities continue to reach the retail markets faster than money is spent, business slackens' (Foster & Catchings 1923: 277). See Tomo (2017).

Bibliography

Böhm-Bawerk, E. (1884), *Kapital und Kapitalzins*, Innsbruck: Wagner'schen Universitätsbuchdruckerei.

Dickson, P.G.M. (1967), *The Financial Revolution in England: A Study in the Development of Public Credit 1688–1756*, London: Macmillan.

Foster, W.T. & Catchings, W. (1923), *Money*, Boston: Houghton Mifflin Company.

Friedman, M. (1987), Quantity Theory of Money, in J. Eatwell, M. Millgate & P. Newman (eds.), *The New Palgrave: A Dictionary of Economics*, vol. 4, London: Macmillan: 3–20.

Green, T.H. & Grose, T.H. (1874), *A Treatise on Human Nature*, London: Longmans, Green, and Co.

Hayek, F. (1931), *Price and Production*, London: Routledge.

———. (1934), Carl Menger, *Economica*, 1: 393–420.

———. (1939), *An Enquiry into the Nature and Effects of the Paper Credit of Great Britain (1802), by Henry Thornton*, London: George Allen & Unwin.

Hicks, J. (1962), Liquidity, *The Economic Journal*, 72: 787–802.

Homer, S. (1963), *A History of Interest Rates*, New Brunswick: Rutgers University Press.

Hume, D. (1752), *Political Discourses: By David Hume, Esq. Edinburgh*, Edinburgh: A. Kincaid & A. Donaldson.

Keynes, J.M. (1937), The General Theory of Employment, *Quarterly Journal of Economics*, (51): 209–223.

———. (1987), *The Collected Writings of John Maynard Keynes*, Cambridge & London: Macmillan.

Keynes, J.N. (1906), *Studies and Exercises in Formal Logic, Including a Generalisation of Logical Processes in Their Application to Complex Inferences*, London: Macmillan.

———. (1994), *The Diary of John Neville Keynes, 1864–1917*, London: Adam Matthew Digital Ltd.

King, W.T.C. (1936), *History of the London Discount Market*, London: Routledge.

Marx, K. (1857), *Grundrisse*: *Foundations of the Critique of Political Economy*, Harmondsworth: Penguin Books, 1973.

Moggridge, D.E. (1992), *Maynard Keynes: An Economist's Biography*, London: Routledge.

Murphy, A. (1997), *Monetary Theory: 1601–1758*, vol. 4, London: Routledge.

O'Donnell, R.M. (1989), *Keynes: Philosophy, Economics and Politics*, London: Macmillan.

Omori, I. (1996), *Steuart and Smith, Skillful and Invisible Hands*, Tokyo: Minerva.

Ricardo, D. (1820), *Funding System*, Edinburgh: Constable.

Russell, B. (1912), *The Problems of Philosophy*, London: Williams & Norgate.

Sen, S.R. (1957), *The Economics of Sir James Steuart*, London: Bell & Sons.

Skinner, A. (1966), Introduction, in *Sir James Steuart: An Inquiry into the Principles of Political Oeconomy*, vol. 1, Edinburgh: Oliver & Boyd.

Smart, W. (1890), *Capital and Interest: A Critical History of Economical Theory*, London: Macmillan.

Smith, A. (1979), *An Inquiry into the Nature and Causes of the Wealth of Nations*, Oxford: Clarendon Press.

Tomo, S. (2010), Steuart as a Theorist of Double Auction, Sydney: *Annual Conference of the History of Economic Thought Society of Australia.*

———. (2017), The Hayek Code, Antwerp: *Annual Conference of the European Society for the History of Economic Thought.*

Yagi, K. (1983), *Böhm-Bawerk's First Interest Theory with C. Menger-Böhm-Bawerk Correspondence 1884–5, Study Series*, vol. 3, Tokyo: Hitotsubashi University: 5–40.

10 Determination of prices in the economic theory of James Steuart from a modern classical perspective

Alexander Tobon

Introduction

The aim of this chapter is to contribute to the understanding of Sir James Steuart's work, using some elements of modern classical theory. In particular, his intuitions about the role of prices of goods in a commercial economy are proposed to be formalized. To achieve this objective, we start with the standard formalization in the perspective developed by Von Neumann, Leontief, and Sraffa, which allows determining an equilibrium price vector, in order to show the compatibility of manufacturers' production decisions.

Although Steuart focuses his analysis around commerce and not production, the method of modern classical theory allows introducing additional hypotheses capable of describing commercial activity. In effect, commerce constitutes an intermediate economic activity between the purchase of production and subsequent sale as means of production. The difference between the prices involved in both commercial operations is one of the ways to make the profit obtained by the merchants visible. Thus an interpretation of the theory of prices emerges that allows us to understand one of Steuart's greatest concerns: The phenomenon of merchant enrichment.

The reconstruction of Steuart's theory of prices rests only on some aspects of his work, which is why there is no intent to be faithful to all his proposals, which would not only be innocuous but perhaps impossible. Two aspects of his work are particularly discussed: First, the role played by merchants as the individuals spreading the information related to prices is formalized; and second, Steuart's idea of the statesman or Prince being the one who determines the 'best possible state' of the economy, since he establishes the rule for the distribution of the social surplus and fixes its level, is formalized. Under the latter, Steuart's theory of prices is limited to the mercantilist thought, not to Smith's classical tradition, since in the latter it is the market itself, not the Prince, which ensures coordination of production decisions, the generation of social surplus, and its distribution amongst individuals.

A discussion context

The mercantilist thinkers of the 17th and 18th centuries share their concern for international trade. In the context of a European society transitioning from feudalism to capitalism, mercantilists note that the economic activity of cities accelerates the enrichment of some merchants. This enrichment comes from changes in the level of international competitiveness of exported goods. Said changes would be the result of variations in the nominal value of the metallic coins minted by the Princes of the different kingdoms. Gold and silver are the measure of wealth, so enrichment would be explained by the variations in the circulating quantities of these metals.

However, a select group of mercantilists, among them William Petty, Richard Cantillon, and Steuart, believe this proposition is not evident, suggesting in their works to seek an explanation in the most profound conditions of commercial activity. They suggest that the explanation for merchant enrichment lies in the determinants of the prices of goods, regardless of the fact that their measure corresponds to the quantities of precious metals. In this way, the essential aspects that explain the operation of commerce have to be sought in the circulation of goods, not the circulation of metals. The most novel feature of these thinkers' analyses is that they conceive of a general interdependence between commercial activity, production of manufactures, and use of free labour. There's therefore the notion of 'economic system'.

Unfortunately, the current economic theory does not offer a single reference model that allows discussing, consistently, the main thesis consigned in the works of those three thinkers. This problem comes from the difficulty in distinguishing the activities of mercantile capitalism from those exclusive of servile feudalism. Indeed, liberal economic activities have the greatest scientific interest, since they are voluntary and spontaneous, that is, they are not coordinated *a priori* by the Prince, religion, or any other institution.

Some contemporary economists have proposed to overcome these and other difficulties. In particular, a suggestive interpretation of Steuart's work is presented by Aspromourgos (1995). In Chapter 8 of his work, the author proposes a 'rational reconstruction' of Steuart's theory of equilibrium prices. His model assumes that two goods (outputs) are produced – corn (agricultural good) and iron (the manufactured good) – based on the use of three types of inputs: Means of production (corn and iron), land, and labour; the latter is considered heterogeneous, since two kinds of labour are assumed: Primary and secondary. Likewise, two types of wages are presumed: On the one hand, the wage equivalent to the value of a basket of consumer goods composed of both types of goods and, on the other hand, this same wage but with an added a surplus, defined as the part of the wage that *exceeds* the value of consumer goods, called 'surplus wages'.

The pricing model is composed of two equations. The first one determines the relative price of the iron in terms of corn. This equation is a formalization of the classical cost-plus-profit hypothesis, where surplus wages are explicitly introduced. The second equation determines the real land rent. Given the technical conditions – input and output quantities – the relative price and real land rent are determined *only if* the profit of the corn producer, the profit of the iron producer, and the surplus wages are given exogenously (Aspromourgos 1995: 138). Thus the determination of the relative price is independent of both profits and surplus wages. The confusion in Steuart of the concepts 'wages' and 'profits' becomes evident.

Aspromourgos recognizes that Steuart does not offer alternatives to determine the profit. However, a vague reference is identified in some passages where 'the possibility of profits being "consolidated" is mentioned in the real value of commodities' (Aspromourgos 1995: 139). The 'consolidation' is an idea that involves the fusion of wages and profits; thus there is a single distributive variable. In his effort to link Steuart to the classical tradition, Aspromourgos fails to resolve the indeterminacy of this variable. This chapter proposes a solution, linking Steuart to the mercantilist thought.

The role of merchants

Regarding Steuart (1767), the main elements that allow him to carry out a reconstruction of his theory of prices are in Chapters 1, 2, 3, 4, 7, and 10 of Book II. It is about a society in transition from feudalism to capitalism, where the most important economic activity is trade, which is evident in the ports and cities of a country.[1]

There are three types of economic agents. First, there are the manufacturers or industrious men, those individuals capable of producing goods based on their willingness to assume production costs. These costs consist of the payment of wages to workers and the purchase of other goods (means of production) produced by other manufacturers. The sale of produced goods provides each manufacturer with an income at least sufficient to replenish the initial production costs and to ensure a profit that compensates their productive ingenuity. If at the end of the production process there is a surplus, this can be allocated to accumulation (payment of new workers, acquisition of new means of production) or to unproductive consumption.

Second, there are the workers free of serfdom, who survive in the cities by offering their labour force to manufacturers in exchange of wages. Third, there are the merchants who are individuals seeking to generate commercial profit. They buy final goods from manufacturers and resell them to other manufacturers as means of production, so that the commercial profit corresponds to the difference between incomes from sales and costs of purchases.

Under these considerations, how are the prices of manufactured goods determined? According to Chapter 4 of Book II of Steuart (1767), prices depend on the real value of the good or the production cost, determined by three elements: (1) the amount of goods produced by workers in production, (2) the value of wages paid to the workers, and (3) the value of the means of production.[2] 'There are three articles being known, the price of manufacture is determined' (I, 245). But, who calculates the prices for which the three elements constituting the cost of production have been established? Steuart's answer is surprising:

> By the extensive dealing of merchants, and their *constant application* to the study of the balance of work [supply] and demand, all the above circumstances are known to them, and are made known to the industrious, who regulate their living and expense according to their certain profit. I call it certain, because under these circumstances the seldom overvalue their work,

and by not overvaluing it, they are sure of a sale: a proof of this may be had from daily experience.

(I, 246; emphasis added)

In this way, Steuart states that it is the merchants who, through the constant exercise of their activity, can determine the prices of goods and then transfer this information to the manufacturers. Once prices are known, the merchants become aware of their economic situation. This 'communicator role' of the merchant appears much more explicitly in Book II, Chapter 3:

> Trade produces many excellent advantages; it marks out to the manufacturers when their branch is under or overstocked with hands. If it is understocked, they will find more demand than they can answer: if it is overstocked, the sale will be slow.
>
> *Intelligent men, in every profession, will easily discover when there appearances are accidental, and when they proceed from the real principles of trade; which are here the object of our inquiry.*
>
> Posts, and correspondence by letters, are a consequence of trade, by the means of which *merchants are regularly informed* of every augmentation or diminution of industry in every branch, in every part of the country. From this knowledge they regulate the prices they offer; and as they are many, they serve as a check upon one another, from the principles of competition which we shall here after examine.
>
> From the *current prices the manufacturers are as well informed.*
>
> (I, 242; emphasis added)

Based on these arguments, merchants, not manufacturers, are the ones who concentrate relevant information on the economy.[3]

Determination of prices

Let us suppose an economy without money, described by a production system in the classical perspective. It is assumed that production methods are invariable, the means of production implicitly include the number of free workers, and production takes place in a single period. Likewise, n manufacturers are assumed, but each of them produces a single good with a single production technique, which is why the number of manufacturers coincides with the number of goods. The known technical data are the following. On the one hand, let y_i be the quantity produced of i, with $i = 1, 2 \ldots n$ and, on the other hand, let y_{ij} be the quantity of means of production j that is used as an input to produce good i, with $j = 1, 2 \ldots n$. Under these hypotheses, the concrete production system is represented as:

$$y_{ij} \rightarrow y_i$$

The symbol → means 'produces'. By writing the production system in value, the price system becomes visible:

$$y_{ij}p_j \rightarrow y_i p_i$$

where p_j is the absolute price of a unit of means of production j, while p_i is the absolute price of a unit of good i. Both types of prices are unknowns of the system. The expression $y_{ij}p_j$ is in accordance with Steuart's indication that production costs determine prices. However, this indication is not enough because Steuart (I, 244) himself states that the 'profit upon alienation' of the manufacturer is another determinant of prices, defined as the average remuneration derived from the invested capital that is represented by production costs. This manufacturers' profit 'will ever be in proportion to demand, and therefore will fluctuate according to circumstances' (I, 245).[4]

Since r_i is the profit rate of each manufacturer i, then the value production system can be written in matrix form as:

$$(1+\mathbf{r})\mathbf{Yp} = \mathbf{yp} \tag{1}$$

where (1 + **r**) is a null matrix that contains the profit factors $(1+r_i)$ in its main diagonal, and **Y** is the square matrix containing the physical means of production y_{ij}, **p** is a column vector containing the list of prices, and, finally, **y** is a column vector that contains the quantities of goods produced y_i.

It should be noted that the **Y** matrix contains the goods demanded as inputs or physical means of production in the economy as a whole. Let x_j be the total quantity demanded of the means of production j by the manufacturers as a whole, obtained by adding in column the elements of said matrix:

$$x_j = \sum_{i=1}^{n} y_{ij} \tag{2}$$

The system of equations (1) involves n production equations and $2n$ unknowns, namely: n absolute prices and n profit rates, which is why this system is undetermined. As shown, the endogenous determination of prices will be linked to the introduction of a price as a numeraire and, above all, to the existence of a social surplus or net product and its respective rule for distribution among manufacturers.[5]

Equilibrium with social surplus

The discussion of the existence of the social surplus and its distribution among capitalists is essential in the classical theory of prices. Social surplus is understood as the quantity of goods resulting from the difference between the total supply of a good (production) and its demand in the form of physical means of production.[6] In short, an economy as a whole generates a social surplus if the supply of products is greater than its own demand, for each good j:

$$x_j < y_j \tag{3}$$

According to the arguments presented in Book II, Chapter 10, Steuart accepts the existence of a social surplus but is not explicit in proposing a rule for its distribution among manufacturers. Even more, according to Cartelier (1981: 155), Steuart tries to deny it. According to Steuart, if there are eventual increases in production as a result of the accumulation of capital from a productive use of social surplus (Steuart prefers to say it is the result of the intervention of the Prince), then nothing would happen, and the economy would return to the 'perfect' situation. The following quote makes the author's denial explicit:

> Now if, after a short vibration, the supply comes to be increased by the statesman's care, no harm will ensue, competition will change sides, and profits will come down again to the *perfect standard.*
>
> (I, 295; emphasis added)

However, the idea of a 'perfect standard' of profits is indicative that there is a rule for distribution.[7] Cartelier (1981: 155) suggests that a rule for distribution in Steuart is found in the following proposition:

> Here is the criterion of a perfect balance: *A positive moderate profit must balance a positive moderate profit; the balance must vibrate, and no loss must be found on either side.*
>
> (I, 294; emphasis in original)

One possible interpretation of this proposition is as follows: In the French edition of Steuart's 1789 work, the expression 'perfect standard' was translated as 'taux exact', which means 'exact rate'. Thus, the concepts of 'perfect balance' and 'perfect standard' of profits can be interpreted as a uniform profit rate or equilibrium profit rate, as conceived in the classical theory, that is to say: $r_1 = r_2 = \ldots = r_n = r^*$. In this way, and following Steuart, if at any time there are high rates of profit with respect to the equilibrium level, then it is expected that these equilibrate or balance with respect to the low profit rates, achieving at the end of the process the 'perfect balance' level among all of them.[8] The introduction of this distribution rule allows the system (1) to have a solution, and once the relative prices are determined they allow the calculation of the social surplus value, so that it will be distributed in the proportion r among all the manufacturers.

The necessary analytical structure to discuss the role of merchants is now available. For this purpose, let's return to the intuition explained earlier, according to which merchants concentrate the relevant information in the economy. Merchants carry out three economic actions. First, using the private information available to them, each merchant can anticipate independently the prices at which they believe they will sell goods (the physical means of production) to the manufacturers. This anticipated calculation is carried out based on the three elements of production cost indicated by Steuart and formalized in the production system (1). Second, once these anticipated selling prices are known, the merchants as a whole competitively determine the prices at which each of them buys the goods that will later be resold to the manufacturers. Finally, merchants determine the actual selling prices, which allow their profits to be realized. Let's review these three economic actions.

Determination of anticipated selling prices by each merchant

Suppose that there are m merchants type H, with $H = 1, 2, \ldots m$. Each one carries out their activity in all markets. Due to the 'constant application' in their commercial activity, they all know the same matrix $\mathbf{Y}$ that contains the demand for physical means of production that manufacturers will make. Likewise, merchants know the rule for the distribution of the social surplus that prevails in the economy, that is to say the 'perfect standard' of profits so that $r_1 = r_2 = \ldots = r_n = r^*$. It is assumed that it is an exogenous variable imposed by the Prince.[9] Finally, it is assumed that each merchant knows the quantities of goods produced, which are contained in the vector $\mathbf{y}$. In this way each merchant H has his own vector $\mathbf{y}$. By hypothesis, it is assumed that these quantities are such that the existence of a social surplus is verified, that is, condition (3) is fulfilled.

With this information, each merchant H has the capacity to construct the production system (1), which then involves n production equations and $(n-1+1) = n$ unknowns, namely: $(n-1)$ anticipated relative selling prices (since there is no money a price is chosen as numeraire)[10] and a single uniform profit rate. However, since r is fixed by the Prince, then one of the equations is redundant, which is why we have finally $(n-1)$ production equations and $(n-1)$ unknowns.[11] The solution of the system (1) for each merchant H is a vector $\mathbf{p}$ of relative prices whose components are of the type:

$$\frac{p^e_{j,H}}{p^e_{i,H}} = p^e_{ji,H}, \text{ for each } H.$$

This is the anticipated relative selling price at which each merchant H is willing to sell to the manufacturers the goods contained in their respective vector $\mathbf{y}$.

Determination of purchase prices amongst all merchants

The quantities of goods contained in the vector $\mathbf{y}$ are not offered immediately for sale to the manufacturers at the anticipated prices, since it is necessary to know the value at which these quantities are acquired by the merchants. It is then necessary to previously determine the purchase price of each good, for which it is assumed that these are determined by the set of demand and supply all merchants have.

The relative purchase price or relative market price of good j in terms of good i, denoted as p^m_{ji}, is determined by the comparison between, on the one hand, the demand for each good j known to all merchants (a technical data), valued at the different anticipated selling prices for each merchant *H*, determined endogenously by the solution of the system (1)[12] and, on the other hand, the sum of the quantities offered of the same good *J* contained in the vector **y**, that is:

$$p_{ji}^{m} = \frac{x_j\left(p_{ji,H=1}^{e} + p_{ji,H=2}^{e} + \ldots + p_{ji,H=m}^{e}\right)}{y_j^{H=1} + y_j^{H=2} + \ldots + y_j^{H=m}}, \text{ for each } j = 1,2,\ldots n$$

This relative market price formalizes Steuart's persistent idea of a single average price as a result of a balance between supply and demand. In turn, the determinants of this price show the phenomenon of 'double competition' among merchants, subject of a wide discussion in Book II, Chapter 7 of Steuart. With these elements, it can be stated that this price corresponds to the concepts of 'current prices' (I: 242), 'adequate value' (I, 263), and 'intrinsic value' (I, 309).[13]

Determination of effective selling prices informed to manufacturers

Merchants now set effective selling prices. A simple fixing rule implies, assuming that the effective selling prices correspond to the anticipated selling prices, since these were estimated endogenously from a system of equations that takes into account the technical conditions of production, i.e., the structure of demand for goods. If $\frac{p_{j,H}^{*}}{p_{i,H}^{*}} = p_{ji,H}^{*}$ is defined as the relative effective selling price, then the rule stablishes that:

$$p_{ji,H}^{*} = p_{ji,H}^{e}, \text{ for each } H.$$

It is interesting to note that merchants have different effective selling prices for the same good but assume a single purchase price for that good as a cost. From all available information, merchants can now estimate their profit. Let π_j^H be the value of profit (measured in numeraire *i*) of merchant *H* for the purchase and subsequent resale of good *J*. This magnitude is calculated by the difference between the income received from the sale of *J* to the manufacturers at the effective selling price and the values paid for the previous purchase of that same good in the market:[14]

$$\pi_j^H = p_{ji,H}^{*} x_j - p_{ji}^{m} x_j$$

Since x_j is constant (technical data), a positive commercial profit is only possible if $p_{ji,H}^{*} > p_{ji}^{m}$, that is, if the effective selling price is greater than the market purchase price. The total commercial profit of each *H* is:

$$\Pi^H = \sum_{j=1}^{n} \pi_j^H$$

Equilibrium without social surplus

Let's suppose the extreme case in which all merchants own the same quantities of goods contained in the vector **y**, so that these quantities satisfy the following condition:

$$x_j = y_j \tag{3)'}$$

This means that there is no social surplus. In this way, all merchants have a single system (1) that involves n production equations and $2n$ unknowns, namely: n absolute prices and n profit rates, which is why there is no solution. Now, since there is no social surplus, the determination of anticipated relative selling prices makes it possible to distinguish two interesting situations.

First, if the Prince is supposed to set the 'perfect standard' of profits equal to $r_1 = r_2 = \ldots = r_n = r^* > 0$ and the numeraire is added, there are n production equations and $(n-1)$ anticipated relative selling prices. Thus for there to be a solution it is necessary to delete any of the equations, however, the system yields different relative prices each time one of the equations is alternately removed. Under these conditions, the system of anticipated relative selling prices is indeterminate because there is no redundant equation.

Second, if the Prince sets the 'perfect standard' of profit as $r_1 = r_2 = \ldots = r_n = r^* = 0$ and we assume a price known as a numeraire, the system of equations yields a coherent solution:[15] One of the equations turns out to be effectively redundant, in such a way that we have $(n-1)$ production equations and $(n-1)$ anticipated relative selling prices. Since there is only one system (1) for all merchants, the components of vector **p** are of the type:

$$\frac{p_j^e}{p_i^e} = p_{ji}^e, \text{ for all } H.$$

Under these conditions, manufacturers would receive zero profit, and this unfavourable situation is transferred to merchants. Indeed, the forces of 'double competition' no longer manifest in the market, since the purchase prices correspond exactly to the anticipated selling prices determined by the system (1):

$$p_{ji}^m = \frac{x_j\left(p_{ji,H=1}^e + p_{ji,H=2}^e + \ldots + p_{ji,H=m}^e\right)}{y_j^{H=1} + y_j^{H=2} + \ldots + y_j^{H=m}} = p_{ji}^e$$

If merchants set the effective selling prices at the same level as the anticipated selling prices, then it's clear that $p_{ji,H}^* = p_{ji,H}^e = p_{ji}^m$, for each H. In this way, the commercial profit for each merchant H derived from the sale of each good is null:

$$\pi_j^H = p_{ji}^* x_j - p_{ji}^m x_j = 0$$

The total commercial profit of each H will also be zero.

$$\Pi^H = 0, \text{ for each } H$$

In short, when a 'perfect standard' of profits equal to $r_1 = r_2 = \ldots = r_n = r^* = 0$, then Steuart's theory of prices becomes irrelevant, since the stimulus of commercial activity as a whole disappears.

Example

Let's suppose an economy without money composed of two types of individuals. On the one hand, there are three manufacturers seeking a profit upon alienation, through the production of three goods: Yarn (good 1), oil (good 2), and flour (good 3). It is assumed that each manufacturer produces a single good from using the same good they produce and the two other goods of the economy. On the other hand, there are three merchants identified as A, B, and C, who seek commercial profits as a result of the purchase of goods from others and the subsequent resale to the manufacturers.

Because of their 'constant application' in the markets, the three merchants know the quantities demanded by the physical means of production used by each manufacturer, which are measured in meters (mt), gallons (gl), and kilograms (kg). These quantities are the components of the matrix **Y**:

Table 10.1 The components of the matrix and the total demand

	Components of Y	*total Demand*
Demand for yarn by manufacturers 1,2 and 3	$y_{11} = 18$ mt $y_{21} = 100$ mt $y_{31} = 70$ mt	$x_1 = 188$ mt of yarn
Demand for oil by manufacturers 1,2 and 3	$y_{12} = 50$ gl $y_{22} = 30$ gl $y_{32} = 12$ gl	$x_2 = 92$ gl of oil
Demand for flour by manufacturers 1,2 and 3	$y_{13} = 10$ kg $y_{23} = 20$ kg $y_{33} = 25$ kg	$x_3 = 55$ kg of flour

Economy with social surplus

Determination of anticipated selling prices

It is assumed that each merchant knows the quantities of goods produced (supply), so that there is a social surplus. For example:

Table 10.2 The quantities of goods produced

	Merchant A	*Merchant B*	*Merchant C*
Yarn supply	$y_1^A = 291.2$ mt	$y_1^B = 235.2$ mt	$y_1^C = 375.2$ mt
Oil supply	$y_2^A = 126$ gl	$y_2^B = 182$ gl	$y_2^C = 112$ gl
Flour supply	$y_3^A = 72.1$ kg	$y_3^B = 61.32$ kg	$y_3^C = 68.04$ kg

It is possible to verify the existence of the positive social surplus, estimated by each merchant, based on the difference between the quantity of products (supply) and the quantity of each good demanded by each manufacturer:

Table 10.3 The social surplus estimated by each merchant

	Merchant A	*Merchant B*	*Merchant C*
Social surplus of yarn sector	291.2 – 188 = 103.2 mt	235.2 – 188 = 47.2 mt	375.2 – 188 = 187.2 mt
Social surplus of oil sector	126 – 92 = 34 gl	182 – 92 = 90 gl	112 – 92 = 20 gl
Social surplus of flour sector	72.1 – 55 = 17.1kg	61.32 – 55 = 6.32 kg	68.04 – 55 = 13.04 kg

With this information, each merchant builds his own production system (1) in order to calculate the anticipated selling prices, at which they will be willing to sell their goods to the manufacturers. For each merchant there is a system of three production equations and six unknowns (three absolute prices and three rates of profit), which is why each system is indeterminate. However, they know that the Prince has set the 'perfect standard' of the profits as $r_1 = r_2 = r_3 = r^* = 40\%$. Also, since there is no money, they take the yarn price as a numeraire,[16] so $p_1 = 1$. In this case, one of the three equations is redundant, so there are two linearly independent equations and two unknowns: The anticipated relative selling price of oil in terms of yarn, p_{21}, and the anticipated relative selling price of flour in terms of yarn, p_{31}.

Table 10.4 Production and anticipated selling prices calculated by each merchant

	System of production equations	*Anticipated relative selling prices*
Merchant A	$(1+r_1)(18p_1+50p_2+10p_3)=291.2p_1$ $(1+r_2)(100p_1+30p_2+20p_3)=126p_2$ $(1+r_3)(70p_1+12p_2+25p_3)=72.1p_3$	$p^e_{21,A}=3$, 1 gallon of oil costs 3 meters of yarn. $p^e_{31,A}=4$, 1 kilogram of flour costs 4 meters of yarn.
Merchant B	$(1+r_1)(18p_1+50p_2+10p_3)=235.2p_1$ $(1+r_2)(100p_1+30p_2+20p_3)=182p_2$ $(1+r_3)(70p_1+12p_2+25p_3)=61.32p_3$	$p^e_{21,B}=2$, 1 gallon of oil costs 2 meters of yarn. $p^e_{31,B}=5$, 1 kilogram of flour costs 5 meters of yarn.
Merchant C	$(1+r_1)(18p_1+50p_2+10p_3)=375.2p_1$ $(1+r_2)(100p_1+30p_2+20p_3)=112p_2$ $(1+r_3)(70p_1+12p_2+25p_3)=68.04p_3$	$p^e_{21,C}=4$, 1 gallon of oil costs 4 meters of yarn. $p^e_{31,C}=5$, 1 kilogram of flour costs 5 meters of yarn.

Determination of purchase prices

With the previous information, merchants can estimate the relative market prices in which they incur:

$$p_{11}^{m} = \frac{x_1(p_{11,A}^{*} + p_{11,B}^{*} + p_{11,C}^{*})}{y_1^A + y_1^B + y_1^C} = \frac{188(1+1+1)}{291.2+235.2+375.2} = \frac{564}{901.6} = 0.625$$

$$p_{21}^{m} = \frac{x_2(p_{21,A}^{*} + p_{21,B}^{*} + p_{21,C}^{*})}{y_2^A + y_2^B + y_2^C} = \frac{92(3+2+4)}{126+182+112} = \frac{828}{420} = 1.971$$

$$p_{31}^{m} = \frac{x_3(p_{31,A}^{*} + p_{31,B}^{*} + p_{31,C}^{*})}{y_3^A + y_3^B + y_3^C} = \frac{55(4+5+5)}{72.1+61.32+68.04} = \frac{770}{201.46} = 3.822$$

The purchase price of oil is 1.971, which means that 1 gallon of oil costs 1.971 meters of yarn in the market. Likewise, the purchase price of flour is 3.822, meaning that 1 kilogram of flour costs 3.822 meters of yarn.

If merchants set the effective selling prices at the same level as the anticipated selling prices, we have the following comparison of different prices:

Table 10.5 Selling prices and purchase price

	Effective selling price to manufacturers	*Purchase price incurred by the merchant*
Merchant A	$p_{11,A}^{*} = 1$	$p_{11,A,B,C}^{m} = 0.625$
	$p_{21,A}^{*} = 3$	
	$p_{31,A}^{*} = 4$	
Merchant B	$p_{11,B}^{*} = 1$	$p_{21,A,B,C}^{m} = 1.971$
	$p_{21,B}^{*} = 2$	
	$p_{31,B}^{*} = 5$	
Merchant C	$p_{11,C}^{*} = 1$	$p_{31,A,B,C}^{m} = 3.822$
	$p_{21,C}^{*} = 4$	
	$p_{31,C}^{*} = 5$	

The commercial profit of each merchant is calculated by the difference between their income from the sale of each good (the value of the demand of manufacturers at the effective selling price) and the cost incurred in the purchase of the good (the value of the demand at the purchase price):

Table 10.6 The commercial profit of each merchant

	Profit for each type of good sold to manufacturers	*Total commercial profit*
Merchant A	$\pi_1^A = 70.5$ mt yarn	$\Pi^A = 174.9$ mt yarn
	$\pi_2^A = 94.668$ mt yarn	
	$\pi_3^A = 9.79$ mt yarn	
Merchant B	$\pi_1^B = 70.5$ mt yarn	$\Pi^B = 137.9$ mt yarn
	$\pi_2^B = 2.668$ mt yarn	
	$\pi_3^B = 64.79$ mt yarn	
Merchant C	$\pi_1^C = 70.5$ mt yarn	$\Pi^C = 321.9$ mt yarn
	$\pi_2^C = 186.668$ mt yarn	
	$\pi_3^C = 64.79$ mt yarn	

Economy without social surplus

Let's assume the same technical data contained in matrix **Y**, that is, the same quantities demanded. Now let's assume that all merchants have the same amounts of goods, so that there is no social surplus, for example:

Table 10.7 The amounts of goods of each merchant

	Merchant A	*Merchant B*	*Merchant C*
Yarn supply	$y_1^A = 188$ mt	$y_1^B = 188$ mt	$y_1^C = 188$ mt
Oil supply	$y_2^A = 92$ gl	$y_2^B =92$ gl	$y_2^C = 92$ gl
Flour supply	$y_3^A = 55$ kg	$y_3^B = 55$ kg	$y_3^C = 55$ kg

It can be verified that the social surplus is null:

Table 10.8 Social surplus if all merchants have the same amounts of goods

	Merchant A	*Merchant B*	*Merchant C*
Social surplus of yarn sector	188 – 188 = 0 mt	188 – 188 = 0 mt	188 – 188 = 0 mt
Social surplus of oil sector	92 – 92 = 0 gl	92 – 92 = 0 gl	92 – 92 = 0 gl
Social surplus of flour sector	55 – 55 = 0 kg	55 – 55 = 0 kg	55 – 55 = 0 kg

With this information, it is evident that all merchants have the same system (1), which involves three production equations and six unknowns (three absolute prices and three rates of profit), which is why the system is indeterminate. However, in the absence of a social surplus, two very specific situations are differentiated.

On the one hand, if the Prince is supposed to have set the 'perfect standard' of profits as $r_1 = r_2 = r_3 = r^* = 40\%$ and we assume the numeraire $p_1 = 1$, the system of equations has no solution. Indeed, we have three equations and two unknowns (two relative prices). However, it is not possible to eliminate any equation since none is redundant. Thus, whenever an equation is eliminated two different relative prices are obtained, that is, the relative price system is undetermined.

On the other hand, if the Prince is supposed to set the 'perfect standard' of profits as $r_1 = r_2 = r_3 = r^* = 0$ and we assume the numeraire $p_1 = 1$, the system of equations yields a consistent solution. In this case, one of the three equations is redundant, so we have two linearly independent equations and two unknowns: The two anticipated relative selling prices.

Table 10.9 Production and relative selling prices

	System of production equations	*Relative selling prices*
Merchants A, B, C	$(1+r_1)(18p_1+50p_2+10p_3)=188p_1$	$p_{21}^* = 2.716$
	$(1+r_2)(100p_1+30p_2+20p_3)=92p_2$	$p_{31}^* = 3.419$
	$(1+r_3)(70p_1+12p_2+25p_3)=55p_3$	

It can be verified that the purchase prices are equal to the anticipated selling prices:

$$p_{11}^m = \frac{x_1(p_{11,A}^* + p_{11,B}^* + p_{11,C}^*)}{y_1^A + y_1^B + y_1^C} = \frac{188(1+1+1)}{188+188+188} = \frac{564}{564} = 1$$

$$p_{21}^m = \frac{x_2(p_{21,A}^* + p_{21,B}^* + p_{21,C}^*)}{y_2^A + y_2^B + y_2^C} = \frac{92(2.716+2.716+2.716)}{92+92+92} = \frac{749.616}{276} = 2.716$$

$$p_{31}^m = \frac{x_3(p_{31,A}^* + p_{31,B}^* + p_{31,C}^*)}{y_3^A + y_3^B + y_3^C} = \frac{55(3.419+3.419+3.419)}{55+55+55} = \frac{564.135}{165} = 3.419$$

Likewise, it can be verified that the commercial profits from the sale of the good are null, so that in the aggregate it's also shown that $\Pi^A = 0, \Pi^B = 0, \Pi^C = 0$.

Conclusions

The present reconstruction of the theory of prices in Steuart's work reveals two interesting aspects. First, formalizing the classical perspective leads us to discuss the formation of the social surplus and the respective rule for its distribution. It has been shown that the traditional classical rule of a uniform rate of profit is compatible with Steuart's arguments. However, the acceptance of this rule does not bestow this thinker a place in the classical theory of prices. In effect, it is the Prince who arbitrarily fixes it; that is, it does not arise from the spontaneous interaction of capitalists in the markets as considered by the classical tradition. Steuart's theory of prices remains circumscribed to mercantilist thought. It has also become clear that in an economy without surplus, Steuart's theory of prices is irrelevant because merchants receive zero profits.

Second, by emphasizing the importance of commercial activity, a very fertile intuition has been identified: Merchants concentrate the most important economic information for the performance of economy as a whole. This information is essentially made up of prices. It is the merchants who determine them through three economic actions: (1) a private action that determines the anticipated selling price of the goods, (2) a collective action that determines the purchase price, and, finally, (3) an action that determines the effective selling price. The collective action is a basic way of understanding the mercantilist concern of competition among merchants in the goods market, by means of the balance between supply and demand, without the need to resort to an analysis of the money market (precious metals). However, the fact that prices are measured in quantities of traded goods and not in money leaves the 'door open' for the widely known discussion of the scope of barter models, in terms of the choice of the numeraire and its variation.

Notes

1 In the countryside feudalism still prevails, which is not a field of study of this chapter.
2 These same three elements are considered by Aspromourgos (1995: 135).
3 'Steuart conceives of the process of competition and price formation occurring in large measure via specialist 'merchants' who intermediate between consumers and producers' (Aspromourgos 1995: 129).
4 Another quote about it: 'The industrious man is recompenced in proportion to his ingenuity' (I, 298).
5 Aspromourgos (1995: 145) recognizes that if costs and prices are interdependent, then both magnitudes must be simultaneously determined.
6 For a simple explanation of the determination and use of the social surplus, see Bolaños (2012: 67–72, 89).
7 Aspromourgos (1995: 139) also finds in the concept of the 'perfect standard' the evocation of a norm of profit distribution.
8 It is important to note that in the mercantilist view, obtaining profits is a zero-sum game: The earnings of individual mean losses for another individual somewhere in the economy. It is for this reason that the idea of a positive and uniform profit rate is forced into Steuart's view. Aspromourgos (1995: 144) is explicit in pointing out that there is absence of profitable arbitraging opportunities in equilibrium. In fact, the expression 'profit of alienation' has the same connotation: Something that belonged to another individual is alienated. Now there's no need to exaggerate this point of view. Steuart believes that the increase in manufacturing work and ingenuity can also generate profits without this meaning loss somewhere in the economy.
9 According to Steuart, the Prince imposes equilibrium or harmony in a society: 'I have sufficiently shewn the difference [. . .] between the *vibrations* of this balance of work and demand, and the *overturning* of it. When it vibrates in moderation, and by short alternate risings and sinkings, then industry and trade go on prosperously, and are in harmony with each other . . . . This happy state cannot be supported but by the care of the statesman' (I, 308).

10 For an analysis of the numeraire hypothesis in Steuart, see Rebeyrol (1982: 8–9).
11 The system (1) can endogenously determine a uniform profit rate without considering the intervention of the Prince. However, it would be different for each merchant, which is why there would be a considerable divergence between the vectors of anticipated selling prices, which would be too far from the single purchase prices determined in the market.
12 Book II, Chapter 2 of Steuart's work is entirely dedicated to demand in commerce.
13 Another reinterpretation of the market operation and the role of the merchants in Steuart is found in Rebeyrol (1982). According to this author, this mercantile mechanism is close to a Smithian price gravitation model, whose purpose is to explain the stability of a classical equilibrium when the rule for distribution is precisely the uniformity of the rates of profit.
14 'Steuart conceives of two distinct categories of profits: profits of producers and profits of specialist merchants . . . . Furthermore, it is evident that the latter class of agents are arbitrageurs; so their profits are brought into systematic relationship with interest conceived of as the alternative rate of return, including an accounting for differential risk' (Aspromourgos 1995: 142).
15 In some parts of his model, Aspromourgos (1995: 140, 145) also assumes that profits are zero.
16 It could be assumed that the Prince also establishes this numeraire.

Bibliography

Aspromourgos, T. (1995), *On the Origins of Classical Economics: Distribution and Value from William Petty to Adam Smith*, New York: Routledge.

Bolaños, E. (2012), *Lecciones de teoría clásica de los precios*, Medellín: Universidad de Antioquia.

Cartelier, J. (1981), *Excedente y reproducción: La formación de la economía política y clásica*, México, DF: Fondo de Cultura Económica.

Rebeyrol, A. (1982), Marché et marchands chez Sir James Steuart, *Cahiers d'économie politique*, 7: 5–29.

Part III

Readers and readings of James Steuart

11 James Steuart versus Adam Smith

Tempest in a teapot?

Eyüp Özveren

Introduction

It is usually taken for granted that Adam Smith's *An Inquiry into the Nature and Causes of the Wealth of Nations* (1776) eclipsed Sir James Steuart's *An Inquiry into the Principles of Political Œconomy: being an Essay on the Science of Domestic Policy in Free Nations* (1767). This perception emerged long after the fact and by no means reflects the public perception that prevailed in the late 18th and early 19th centuries. Smith's persistent silence concerning the work of his predecessor played a significant role in burying Steuart's legacy into the bygone age of mercantilism. It was quite unusual that Smith did not refer to his fellow countryman Steuart's work not even once in his *Wealth of Nations*. It was also deliberate,[1] all the more so if the following belief holds: 'It has generally been believed that he wrote *WN* with the strong but implicit aim of refuting Steuartian political economy' (Omori 2003: 103). For example, Smith wrote:

> The public funds of the different indebted nations of Europe, particularly those of England, have by one author been represented as the accumulation of a great capital superadded to the other capital of the country, by means of which its trade is extended, its manufactures multiplied, and its lands cultivated and improved much beyond what they could have been by means of that capital only.
>
> (Smith 1976: II, 460–461; emphasis added)

The reference to unnamed 'one author' was likely to remind the initiated reader of Steuart, and not of a certain Melon who was later introduced into the references. Smith could have easily refuted this position by citing Steuart. He deliberately did not. Last but not least, Smith disclosed his secret in his correspondence, in a letter he addressed to William Pulteney in 1772, thereby providing us with the single strongest piece of evidence to date:

> In the Book which I am now preparing for the Press I have treated fully and distinctly of every part of the subject which you have recommended to me; and I intended to have sent you some extracts from it; but upon looking them

> over, I find that they are too much interwoven with other parts of the work to be easily separated from it. I have the same opinion of Sir James Stewart's Book that you have. Without once mentioning it, I flatter myself, that every false principle in it, will meet with a clear and distinct confutation in mine.
>
> (Smith 1978: 163–164)

Smith's tactic served his purpose well for more than a century. In a Smithian world the economists increasingly found themselves in, it became more and more difficult to make sense of Steuart's work. What defined such an intellectual environment in theoretical sense was the overwhelming presence of a 'real analysis' at the expense of 'monetary analysis', which was reduced to an epiphenomenon, if not being outright denied. As Smith became the stepping stone for the then advancing 'real analysis', Steuart's sin was identified as too much interest in money and credit, which was indeed unpardonable in an age of 'real analysis'. In fact, his comparative strength rests on money, and when it came to paper money even Smith sang praises to government regulation.

To put the matter in a novel perspective, we are quite handicapped with the legacy to begin with. In addition, to the best of my knowledge, we do not have at hand a copy of Steuart's work either underlined or with Smith's handwritten notes on it.[2] This makes our task all the more difficult. In the absence of firsthand sources, much of what is argued in this chapter remains conjectural and commonsensical. Fortunately, while historians are quite distrustful of conjectural argumentation, they, at least, hold a more favourable attitude towards common sense than most economists. Given the previous limitation, in the rest of this chapter we will not compare and contrast Steuart with Smith but rather their two major works of immediate economic relevance.

We will proceed with the interpretation of what is available in those very texts in order to support the hypothesis that the two works had much more in common than is usually acknowledged, and in fact, this would have been even more so if only Smith's work did not succeed Steuart's by about a decade, during which Smith gave a final shape to his *Wealth of Nations*. In the first section of this chapter we will trace the changing fortunes of Steuart and Smith over time in the history of economic thought, a theme to which we will return at the very end. In the second section we will compare the two books in general. A brief third section conceived as a digression will focus on how Smith's legacy was reconstructed by his two major successors. The fourth section will focus on the time effect to which we give critical importance from the viewpoint of the differentiation of the two works. We caution the reader that we do not argue that Smith changed his mind after reading Steuart's book. He was his own man and developed his way of thinking in a consistent way throughout a long career. A comparison of his Glascow lectures with his magnum opus suffices to demonstrate that. We insist that while his ideas and way of thinking did not change but only became more elaborate, he may have changed the structure, more specifically the order of presentation in the *Wealth of Nations*, in reaction to reading Steuart's book. As we will see, the structure of *The Wealth of Nations* has been characterized as confusing by some of Smith's loyal followers.

As it stands, the book is a bizarre conjoint presentation of what later came to be known as microeconomic theory with what was conceived as political economy. It is also suggested here that Smith's rhetorical style may also bear some mark of, and insinuations to, Steuart's work that breach his enduring silence concerning his predecessor. We then concentrate specifically on the contentious role of the statesman as conceived by the two authors in the fifth section. The sixth section returns to the texts with an emphasis on their conceptions of the nascent field of inquiry. In the last section, we conclude by recourse to a concept of 'Smithian Vice'. Our contention is that there exists a potential for a synthesis of the two works once we approach them from a contemporary heterodox, more specifically, historical institutionalist viewpoint.

Fortunes of Smith, misfortunes of Steuart

Histories of economic thought consider Smith's magnum opus as either implicitly or explicitly outperforming Steuart by a wide margin. Whereas Smith is extensively covered as a towering height or a turning point in the history of economic thought, Steuart is merely touched upon, if at all, as one of the many obscure names on the sidelines. In this respect, Ernesto Screpanti and Stefano Zamagni are more sparing than others,[3] as they include Steuart among the many economists belonging to 1750–80, when 'a first great theoretical revolution' giving birth to 'modern economic science' originated, yet also identify *The Wealth of Nations* as the climax of it and 'the supreme synthesis of all this work' (Screpanti & Zamagni 1993: 1). They then dedicate a subsection to Steuart, along with David Hume, before treating Smith in an extensive whole section (*ibidem*: 52–54). Alessandro Roncaglia treats Steuart in a subsection entitled 'The Scottish Enlightenment: Francis Hutcheson and David Hume' of the encompassing chapter 'From body politic to economic tables', which precedes his chapter exclusively on 'Adam Smith' (Roncaglia 2005: 111–114). In principle, the shorter the histories get, the more likely that Steuart will be entirely omitted (Sandelin et al. 2014; Kurz 2016).[4] This applies equally across the spectrum, irrespectively of whether the author in question belongs to the mainstream or is more open-minded and/or heterodoxy leaning.

As a consequence, Smith has been baptized as the one and only founding father of modern economics. By analogy, this approach characterizes Steuart as being one of the Last Mohicans belonging to a distant past *pace* James Fenimore Cooper[5] (2001), and paraphrasing the immortal first sentence of L. P. Hartley's *The Go-between* (1953) to a foreign country where they did things differently, and unfortunately this time, also pseudo-scientifically. For example, Screpanti and Zamagni credit Hume for 'the first systematic attack on mercantilist thought', while attributing 'its no less important' 'last defense' to Steuart (Screpanti & Zamagni 1993: 53). According to these co-authors 'Steuart also put forward an interesting historicist theory of economic growth which has rightly been considered as the best historical justification of mercantilism' (Screpanti & Zamagni 1993: 53). In a similar vein, Roncaglia insists that

> Steuart is not to be seen as one of the protagonists of the Scottish Enlightenment, but classed rather among the representatives of mercantilism given the role he attributed to active public intervention in the economy and the protection of manufactures with duties, together with the place he ascribed to demand in macroeconomic equilibrium.
>
> (Roncaglia 2005: 112–139)

Last but not least, the verdict is announced: 'Steuart remains a halfway house between mercantilism and classical political economy, in some respects he is the last of the mercantilists, no matter how advanced part of his work is' (Vaggi & Groenewegen 2003: 90) The counter-positioning of Steuart and Smith has indeed been extremely unfair to Steuart, who has been overlooked even by specialists of economic thought, whereas Smith has become a household name. Fortunately Steuart has recently improved his position considerably in the eyes of at least a few distinguished scholars. It has been observed: 'It was Steuart who initially made political economy stand on its own legs, independent from politics and jurisprudence. Smith followed close behind him in this respect' (Omori 2003: 103).

Joseph A. Schumpeter, in his voluminous classic history of economic analysis, presents the only formidable exception to the trend that commands our attention. He treats Steuart extensively, with 17 references, in the same chapter, entitled 'Consultant Administrators and Pamphleteers', along with Smith. More importantly, because he scales down the role of Adam Smith by emphasizing his synthetic ability at the expense of any originality, Steuart's treatment benefits from a relative improvement:

> England was still more immune to 'systemitis' than was France, Excepting the *Wealth* itself, there is but one book of the strictly systematic type to mention, but this one is of first-rate importance, Steuart's *Principles*. It was intentionally and labouriously systematic: what he wanted was to consolidate the factual and analytic knowledge of his time into a 'regular science,' that is to say, he clearly aimed at the same goal as A. Smith. Comparison with the *Wealth of Nations* is rendered difficult by two facts. In the first place, Steuart's work did not ride, like Smith's, on the wave of a single and simple policy that was rapidly conquering public opinion. On the contrary, he grouped all that really interests the public around the old-fashioned figure of an imaginary patriot statesman who in infinite wisdom watches the economic process, ready to interfere in the national interest – a conception that recalls Justi's and was quite out of contact with England's humor. But this should not weigh with us. In the second place, when one surveys (as the reader should) the five books into which the work is divided – Population, Trade and Industry, Money and Coins, Credit and Debts, and Taxes – one cannot fail to be struck by the number of points that indicate more originality and deeper thought than does the *Wealth of Nations*; but also by the number of definite mistakes and infelicitious formulations. In the theories of population, prices, money, and taxation Steuart went much below the smooth surface on which A. Smith happily sailed his course. But only in the

> first of these did he make a significant contribution . . . in the others it is a hard job to get the wheat out of unpromising chaff or even, in some instances, to be quite sure that there is any wheat at all.
>
> (Schumpeter 1954: 176)

Notwithstanding Schumpeter's ultimate verdict, Steuart scored high in this comparison and contrast, a viewpoint to which we could subscribe. The fact that they shared the same goal of system building as well as the same milieu as represented in the structure of *History of Economic Analysis* we find suggestive of the course we will follow in this investigation.

We do not know for sure if Steuart and Smith met in Scotland,[6] or for that matter, abroad, but it is highly likely that they did in the former (Skinner 1966: lii) and not in the latter. Be that as it may, Steuart and Smith were two intellectuals of the 18th-century Scottish Enlightenment.[7] The Scottish Enlightenment was a response to the conflict between economic development and moral corruption. As such, the earth under their feet, peripheral Europe yet rapidly moving ahead, provided Steuart as well as Smith with a constantly shifting original perspective on the past as well as future.[8] Hence even when they looked for the 'old', they could see it in a different if not new light. Moreover, moving out of the narrow confines of a change and growth-ridden provincial environment, they travelled far and wide – one much more and much longer than the other[9] – in continental Europe and benefitted from this experience. Irrespectively of what they thought about each other, they have had much in common. If this is so, then this shared heritage must be identifiable in their works and will offer us important clues as to how we can bridge their supposedly disparate approaches.

Comparing the two books in general terms

There exists a consensus that *An Inquiry into the Nature and Causes of the Wealth of Nations* is a classic cornerstone, in fact a pathbreaking achievement in economics. Given this consensus, there exists also a commonly observed truth that no one hardly reads the complete *Wealth of Nations* nowadays. This is as widespread among mainstream economists who trace their genealogy back to Smith as common folks. The former occasionally cite, if not quote, Smith to their advantage, but it is quite evident that their reading of Smith's canonical text has been selective, if not also superficial. In fact, among academics, it is often the case that sociologists and social scientists read Smith's text in its entirety more often than economists *per se*, a few historians of economic thought withstanding. Behind this there exists a discernable deeper cause that applies equally well, in fact, even more to the neglect of Steuart's *An Inquiry into the Principles of Political Economy*. While both books are little read, at least Smith's text in its complete version is more readily available in printed form, though the 'Chicago' edition is fast approaching half a century. It is not only the titles of the two works that are long but also the texts themselves. They are illegibly long by contemporary standards, Stuart's more so than that of Smith. They are in this sense like some

19th-century novels, now classics of literature, particularly the Russian novels of Dostoyevsky and Tolstoy, *Crime and Punishment*, *Brothers Karamazov*, *War and Peace*, and *Anna Karenina* that were deliberatively written to be read during long winter nights[10] that succeeded one another for many months. Whereas these are still legible for the privileged few, the works of Steuart and Smith are also almost 'illegible', reminding us of the distinct quality of modern novels of the twentieth century such as the *Ulysses and Finnegan's Wake* of James Joyce and *Remembrance of Things Past* of Marcel Proust, which test and try the patience as well as the capabilities of the reader. Steuart's and Smith's books privilege unintendedly the 'act of narration' over the 'structure' of the development and presentation of the overarching argument. Once the joy of reading, which is associated one to one with the narrative pulse, is lost from one generation to another, reading loses much of its attraction.

What makes these two texts vulnerable in this respect has to do with their content. They were intended as compilations of the state-of-the-art knowledge in one particular and then emergent intellectual domain. They were conceived by their authors as compendiums of some sort, encyclopedic in scope. Even if the original motive of the respective authors was system building in the first place, they also wanted to construct and avail a 'repository' of existing knowledge. This secondary and potentially transitory motive at work is traceable to two factors. First, what was at work was a transmission of the existing body of literature from the Mediterranean world and continental Europe to Scotland, where it was little known. This would have sufficed to legitimize this whole enterprise. The second factor at work was that the respective authors conceived their works as 'inquiries' with the indefinite article attached in either case. Not only were Steuart and Smith relatively modest in this sense, but they also had a notion of their individual works as works in progress. This was a good reason why they could easily lose their way within their narrative, as they did not know fully where they were heading – Steuart less so than Smith, a price he paid for being the firstcomer. Both texts are thus infected by numerous digressions – be they explicitly labelled as such or not – surprisingly Smith the successor's is more so than that of Steuart.

A 'digression' on Smith's two successors: Say and Ricardo

The proof of the previous thesis is most manifest in the posthumous attempts to reformat Smith's work. There were two critical readings of Smith that were vastly consequential in reformatting his analytical apparatus. One was by Jean-Baptiste Say. Say adopted and spread Smith's message, albeit in a modified way, in the continent and well beyond, by deploying French as the universal lingua franca of the time. The other was by David Ricardo, his disciple on his native soil, who was an autodidact in economics and explored new horizons after reading the *Wealth of Nations*. Say considered 'himself as *the* interpreter and *the* modernizer of Smith's thought' (Vaggi & Groenewegen 2003: 119), Although Say preferred Smith to all previous political economists, French or otherwise, and championed his cause, this did not mean he agreed with him fully (Faccarello & Steiner 2002: 102). The way

Say thoroughly reworked Smith can be discerned from his own acknowledgement, which contains a strong verdict on Smith's *Wealth of Nations:*

> L'ouvrage de Smith n'est qu'un assemblage confus des principes les plus sains de l'économie politique, appuyés d'examples lumineux et des notions les plus curieuses de la statistique, mêlées des reflexions instructives; mais ce n'est un traité complet ni de l'une ni de l'autre: son livre et une vaste chaos d'idées justes, pêle-mêle avec des connaissances positives.
>
> (Say 1841: 5)

Say's tacit comparison and contrast of his own work with that of Smith casts a further light on his assessment of the latter:

> L'excellence d'un ouvrage littéraire se compose autant de ce qui ne s'y trouve pas que de ce qui s'y trouve. Tant de détails grossissent le livre, non plus inutilement, mais inutilement pour son objet principal, qui est le développement des principes de l'économie politique.
>
> (Say 1841: 37)

It was but natural that Say would purge Smith's discussion of all its *non sequitur* elements and digressions and give it a new format that became more or less universally acceptable by the mainstream. As for Ricardo, he carved out of Smith's chaotic and somewhat crude work a gem by way of abstraction that could serve classical political economy as an analytical device for the deduction and demonstration of basic principles and universal laws, as would befit the needs of the classical surplus approach. In his work, Ricardo took off from Smith's seemingly commonsensical[11] assumptions and inferences only to reach opposite conclusions. The high level of abstract modelling and the blinding priority of deductive method inevitably led in the end to the accusation of the so-called 'Ricardian Vice'. Whereas Say's reformulation was worldwide received as an improvement of Smithian economics over Smith's *Wealth of Nations*, Ricardo's remained deeply entrenched in Britain. It was focused almost exclusively on the distribution of surplus among the contesting classes and the implications for economic growth of alternative ways of distribution; a problem that did not yet relate to the realities of other countries lagging behind in economic growth by way of industrialization.[12]

The difference time made

To his credit, Steuart did not pretend or write as if he were omniscient. He was well aware of his limitations and shared it with his reader. It was as if he felt himself launched on a discovery voyage, a feeling to which Smith might have been no stranger either:

> I am also a dauber; for I frankly acknowledge my own incapacity to treat this subject with all the perspicuity it deserves: my frequent repetitions, and

> my often returning to it at different times, in order to clear up my ideas and those of my readers shews plainly, that I am sensible of my insufficiency. By setting it, however, in different lights, and viewing it as it were from different stations, perhaps both my reader and I may come at last to see a little clearer.
>
> (I, 89)

He was more humble than the self-confident Smith and perhaps more frank. In contrast, Smith shifted the responsibility onto the part of the reader in one of the very few instances when he addressed him directly early on in his *Wealth of Nations*:

> I shall endeavor to explain, as fully and distinctly as I can, those three subjects in the three following chapters, for which I must very earnestly entreat both the patience and attention of the reader: his patience in order to examine a detail which may perhaps in some places appear tedious; and his attention in order to understand what may, perhaps, after the fullest explication which I am capable of giving it, appear still in some degree obscure. I am always willing to run some hazard of being tedious in order to be sure that I am perspicuous, some obscurity may still appear to remain upon a subject in its own nature extremely abstracted.
>
> (Smith 1976: 33)

Even so, he admitted in a letter of January 15, 1769, to Lord Hailes the very nature of the spell he was caught in: 'My own schemes of Study leave me very little pleasure, which go forward too like the web of Penelope, so that I scarce see any Probability of their ending' (Smith 1987: 115).[13] In much the same spirit, Steuart 'wrote very much in the style of a man finding his way through a new field',[14] and moreover, 'he consciously sought a thread which could run through the whole work' (Skinner 1966: lviii–lix). He did not find one. Moreover, 'The arrangement of the *Principles* may be defective, but the work is a monument of consistency with respect to purpose, plan and method' (Skinner 1966: lx).[15]

Smith enjoyed a great advantage over Steuart. Because his book came out later he had a chance to read Steuart's *Principles* and see where it went either wrong or fell short of achievement. Accordingly, he could take additional steps to improve the structure of his work that has otherwise matured over 'twenty-seven years from 1749 to 1776' (Cannan 1976: liii). Obviously, Smith also consistently preserved his silence over the Steuart effect. Even so, there is one rhetorical piece of convergence where it became discernible in *The Wealth of Nations*. This is the additional piece of evidence unearthed by the close reading of the two texts in the research undertaken for this present work. Smith virtually mimicked Steuart, in my view, unknowingly, in a rare instance during his discussion of the bounties, a subject of major importance for mercantilist policy. He adopted a polemical dialogue style where he made the case through the third person and then went on with 'I answer' twice in a row (Smith 1976: II, 13–14). This is not the usual way Smith presents his arguments, and to the best of my knowledge it appears nowhere else in his published works. On the other hand, this other point-of-view question versus the 'I answer' format is quite characteristic of Steuart's style of presentation (III, 239–262). Hence I find this involuntary stylistic borrowing by Smith of Steuart's time-and-again extensively exploited rhetorical device as evidence of a 'Steuart effect'. Be that as it may, the Steuart effect might have been present only in the period 1767–1776, that is the much shorter yet more recent, and therefore, possibly the more important part of this long gestation period. Obviously, it was not the only factor that impacted on Smith's mind during this all-important phase. Moreover, it was preceded by the visit Smith made to France in 1764–66 when he met members of the Physiocratic 'sect', including their master Quesnay, to whom Smith might have dedicated his *Wealth of Nations*, if only he had not been dead (Viner 1965: 77). This visit has been attributed as a major influence when his previous work is compared with *The Wealth of Nations*, and one major line of possible discontinuity may concern his commitment to free trade as distinct from his earlier position when he was not perhaps yet 'entirely free of protectionist fallacies' (Cannan 1976: xxxv–xxvi and xxxv). Even so, the publication of Steuart's work was a very important factor. In any case, we have good reason to believe 'the chief cause of the four years' delay [1772–1776] was the revision and alteration to which it was being incessantly subjected during that whole term' (Rae 1965: 257). As for Steuart, he also learned by doing. It is no coincidence that he inserted summary statements and connecting threads in his revision from one edition of his text to the next in order to overcome some of the ambiguities of his loosely knit work.

Despite Smith's advantage we referred to earlier, the difference would have remained one of degree, if Smith had sufficed himself with stylistic makeup instead of taking due action, which he actually did. This made a major difference in Smith's favour, even if it was not exactly an absolute success. Smith made one idea the support, the pillar, and the skeleton of his textual edifice that also serves as the connecting thread of his argumentation: Division of labour. No economist overloaded this concept as much as Smith did, and he placed it in as central a position in his analytical construct as he could. Smith used the same concept as covering both what we understand from it today as 'specialization'. This helped reinforce its uniquely central role and yet at the same time preserve its simplicity:

> [i]t is sufficient to look at the table of contents of *WN* to appreciate that the order of presentation of the various economic topics is rather *novel with respect both to Smith's previous work in the Lectures and to that of all of his predecessors*. (A comparison of the economic contents of Smith's *Wealth of Nations* and that of Sir James Steuart's *Principles of Political Œconomy* illustrates this particularly well. In Book I, a major cause of productivity, the division of labour, is followed by chapters on money and value, including discussion of the relationship between market and natural price, and concluded with chapters dealing with the three distributive categories: the rate of wages, profits and rent. Book II deals with the second great cause of labour productivity and growth of wealth: accumulation of capital or the proportions of productive and unproductive labour in society. No such emphasis given to the

> division of labour as the main principle of national wealth was ever repeated in later volumes of economic principles.
>
> (Vaggi & Groenewegen 2003: 107; emphasis added)

In retrospect, we may well say Smith exaggerated the role of the division of labour, but it served his intention of holding his work together. Steuart had no equal tool at his disposal. It is not that he overlooked the importance of division of labour-cum-specialization – far from it.[16] Yet he did not bestow upon it the central role of an organizing principle for the whole edifice. Contrary to Smith's faith in it, 'division of labour' as the beast of burden could not carry the heavy load and ultimately collapsed under its weight. The concept of 'division of labour' gradually lost ground within economics and was eventually expulsed to the neighbouring domain of sociology, as a founding father of it, Émile Durkheim, made it a now-classic book title in 1893 (Durkheim 2014). By then more than a century had lapsed, and Smith had consolidated his status as the founding father of modern economics in the wake of the Marginalist Revolution.

Figure and function of the statesman as the addressee

If the two books competed for a commanding height in the development of a new science, moreover, if in this rivalry they adopted an encyclopedic strategy of encompassing all accumulated knowledge in the field, then a good starting point is to identify the different mixes of the 'old' and the 'new' that characterize Steuart's and Smith's books. Of particular relevance in this regard is the status of sovereign vis-à-vis the two respective discourses. First of all, as we have already emphasized the encyclopedic preference of the two authors, it is but natural that much that is 'old' will naturally find its way into the books. In addition to much that is 'old', there can be relatively small amounts of what is 'new'. It would be farfetched to expect much originality from either author, as Schumpeter has already forewarned us in relation with Smith, whose predominant academic qualification was 'synthetic' ability rather than originality. Therefore, we need to turn our attention away from content to form and style involved in presentation.

As far as *Wealth of Nations* is concerned, it is addressed first and foremost to the sovereign. It is no coincidence that after a long detour, the fifth and last book that gives the final touches to the erected edifice and squares off Smith's system by prescribing for it a set of suitable policies is entitled 'Of the Revenue of the Sovereign or Commonwealth'. Smith gives advice to the sovereign as to how he should act. The book is reminiscent in this respect of the long tradition of advice literature, the origins of which are Asian; the practice had been transmitted via the Mediterranean world to Europe (Darling 2013). The best known early modern example of this genre of literature is the Mediterranean masterpiece of Niccolò Machiavelli, *The Prince*, first published in 1512 (Machiavelli 1992). Smith repeats the conventional style of this genre. In this sense, he is within the domain of the 'old'. Yet he gives the sovereign a 'new' piece of advice. The safest way to higher revenue is not necessarily the shortest. The poor performance of some despotic regimes in Asia that opted for confiscation and excessive taxation, as well as some mercantilist regimes of the European past that worked with outright prohibitions, attest to this. Rather than poking his nose into everything, the sovereign should let the 'natural system of liberty' follow its own course. He recommends the relatively 'little' that the sovereign should do in order to put his house in order and to increase his revenue:

> The sovereign is completely discharged from a duty, in the attempting to perform which he must always be exposed to innumerable delusions, and for the proper performance of which no human wisdom or knowledge could ever be sufficient; the duty of superintending the industry of private people, and of directing it towards the employments most suitable to the interest of society. According to the system of natural liberty, the sovereign has only three duties to attend to; three duties of great importance, indeed, but plain and intelligible to common understandings.
>
> (Smith 1976: II, 208)

Smith then goes on to enumerate the three basic duties that have since then become the sine qua non functions advocated by the liberal doctrine of the night watchman state, namely, defence of the country from enemies, the institution and enforcement of law and order, and the setting up of infrastructure and services necessary for public benefit that private enterprise would not undertake either because of its lack of resources or low profitability. By interfering less, in this sense, the sovereign will in fact make more. There is a limit to this 'less'. Let us remind ourselves that Smith saw the state as also responsible for public elementary education as well as for regulating the conventional liberal conception of the night watchman state (Kurz 2016: 33). This position would make Smith a post-mercantilist, but not a liberal, or for that matter a 'neoliberal' of contemporary vintage. Even though Smith addressed the sovereign several times in the *Wealth of Nations*, it was as if these lines were deliberately intended to combat Steuart's excessive treatment of the very same sovereign:[17]

> The uniform, constant, and uninterrupted effort of every man to better his condition, the principle from which public and national, as well as private opulence is originally derived, is frequently powerful enough to maintain the natural progress of things toward improvement, in spite both of the extravagance of government, and of the greatest errors of administration. Like the unknown principle of animal life, it frequently restores health and vigour to the constitution, in spite, not only of the disease, but of the absurd prescriptions of the doctor.
>
> (Smith 1976: I, 364)

Ultimately,

> It was the task of the statesmen to create the kinds of institutions and laws that made it in the interest even of bad people to act for the good of all. The science of the legislator, Smith elaborated, was designed to show the way to good government.
>
> (Kurz 2016: 29).[18]

Smith's discussion of the East India Company rule reveals that he had second thoughts concerning the relationship between good government and self-interest: 'But a company of merchants are, it seems, incapable of considering themselves as sovereigns, even after they have become such' (Smith 1976: II, 154).[19] He maintained a difference in attitude between the merchants and statesmen: 'No two characters seem more inconsistent than those of trader and sovereign. If the trading spirit of the English East India company renders them very bad sovereigns; the spirit of sovereignty seems to have rendered them equally bad traders' (Smith 1976: II, 343). He went further, however, when he stated 'Every man too is in some measure a statesman, and can form a tolerable judgment concerning the interest of society, and the conduct of those who govern it' (Smith 1976: II, 303).

As for Steuart, pursuit of self-interest was no less important in the construct. This might be surprising, but he stated his case in an even more straightforward manner:

> The principle of self-interest will serve as a general key to this inquiry; and it may in one sense, be considered as the ruling principle of my subject, and may therefore be traced throughout the whole. This is the main spring, and only motive which a statesman should make use of, to engage a free people to concur in the plans which he lays down for their government.
>
> (I, 218)

However, the statesman was to incarnate public interest as distinct from, and in addition and prior to, his self-interest. He had to cultivate people's 'trust' in him by doing so, without which he could not act otherwise.

In comparison with Smith, Steuart seemed even more modern in form. His advice was not directed to the sovereign, as he explained in his preface:

> If it should be asked, of what utility a speculation such as this can be to a statesman, to whom it is in a manner addressed from the beginning to the end: I answer, that although it seem addressed to a statesman, the real object of the inquiry is to influence the spirit of those whom he governs.
>
> (I, xviii)

Unlike Smith, Steuart directly addressed the reading public at large. He entered into a dialogue with his 'reader', who he appealed as an 'individual' time and again throughout his discourse. Writing before Smith, Steuart was in fact more contemporary with us in this respect. At the same time, the figure of sovereign (or even that of the Prince) appears quite frequently throughout his voluminous work.[20] He is not the addressee of the discourse but a true subject in political and economic life. In Steuart's work what the sovereign does matters significantly. There is much he can do in all domains, and the more he knows what he can do, the better he as well as the political economy in question will perform. At first sight it seems that this is 'old' wine in a 'new' bottle, as Steuart's sovereign is proactive in a way reminiscent of the sovereigns of the mercantile era who were called to step in whenever the interest of either state or business could benefit from it. But this first impression is quite misleading.

According to Steuart, as economic systems advanced from simplicity to complexity,[21] the power of the sovereign was greatly constrained, ripped from arbitrariness, and in some ways greatly reduced. In other words, the sovereign was far from being either omniscient or omnipotent. He was of limited capacity as well as capability, and it would be best if he came to terms with his limitations and made the best use of them:

> A great political genius is better discovered by the extent of his perceptions, than by the minute exactness of them in every part of the detail. It is far better for a statesman to be able to discern (though superficially) every object of government under all its relations, than to be able to trace any one with the greatest accuracy.
>
> (II, 55)

Steuart summarized his position neatly, and by recourse to appropriate imagery, in relation with the complexity and constraints characteristic of the modern times:

> The power of a modern prince, let it be by the constitution of his kingdom, ever so absolute, immediately becomes limited so soon as he establishes the plan of oeconomy which we are endeavouring to explain. If his authority formerly resembled the solidity and force of the wedge . . . it will at length come to resemble the delicacy of the watch, which is good for no other purpose than to mark the progression of time, and which is immediately destroyed, if put to any other use, or touched with any but the gentlest hand.
>
> As modern oeconomy, therefore, is the most effectual bridle ever was invented against the folly of despotism; so the wisdom of so great a power never shines with greater lustre, than when we see it exerted in planning and establishing this oeconomy, as a bridle against the wanton exercise of itself in succeeding generations. I leave it to my reader to seek for examples in the conduct of the modern Princes, which may confirm what, I think, reason seems to point out: were they less striking, I might be tempted to mention them.
>
> (I, 426–427)

To drive his point forcefully, Steuart approached the issue from a slightly different viewpoint:

> So powerful an influence over the operations of a whole people, vests an authority in a modern statesman, which in former ages, even under the most absolute governments, was utterly unknown. The truth of this remark will appear upon reflecting on the force of some states, at present in Europe, where the sovereign power is extremely limited, in every *arbitrary* exercise of it, and where, at the same time, it is found to operate over the wealth of the inhabitants, in a manner far more efficacious than the most despotic and arbitrary authority possibly can do.
>
> (I, 425)

In numerous instances, Steuart felt compelled to differentiate himself from mercantilism, of which we only cite a few. In his discussion of money and credit, which was of vital importance for conventional mercantilism, Steuart reached radically different conclusions:

> It would require a separate treatise, to investigate the artifices which have been contrived, to make mankind lose sight of the principles of money, in order to palliate and make the power in the sovereign to change the value of the coin, appear reasonable. But these artifices seem to be at an end, and Princes now perceive that the only scheme to get money, when occasion requires, is to preserve their credit, and to allow the coin, by which their credit is reckoned, to remain in a stable condition.
>
> (II: 306)

Moreover, he was in a 'Smithian' spirit when he affirmed: 'No fundamental law can bind up a Prince's hands so effectually as his own interest' (II: 296). Once again, Steuart went beyond standard mercantilism when he assessed the implication of chartered companies:

> The very jealousy and dissatisfaction, conceived by other merchants, equally industrious and equally well deserving of the public, because of the great advantages enjoyed by those who are incorporated, under the protection of exclusive privileges, is a hurt to trade in general, is contrary to that principle of impartiality which should animate a good statesman, and should be prevented if possible.
>
> (II: 185)

For Steuart, the role of the Sovereign vis-à-vis the market is essentially one of 'fine-tuning':

> It is not too much to say that Steuart identified as the fundamental problem of modern 'industrious society' the subtle and tense relationship between

> economic equilibrium and 'an artful hand'. Never denying the law of market mechanism in its entirety, he aimed at recovering, in accordance with that law, the autonomy of the market from possible malfunction. A statesman therefore should not intervene in the economic process in an arbitrary and direct fashion but should carefully adjust it to remove the disorder of the market. 'With an artful hand, he must endeavor to load the lighter scale' in the unbalance of 'work and demand' (I, 308) in order to maintain the 'double competition in the market. Accordingly, the 'small vibrations in the balance' are kept within the range.
>
> (Omori 2003: 113)

Steuart was a 'post-mercantilist' in the sense that, even when he turned his attention to the benefit of international trade from the viewpoint of a specific sovereign and his country, his concern was primarily economic and to do with wealth, rather than political and to do with power. Furthermore, Steuart did not see international trade as a zero-sum game but upheld the view that it was beneficial to mankind (Skinner 1966: lxxiii).[22]

The definition of the emergent field of inquiry

There exists a hearsay that because Steuart as the firstcomer called his book *An Inquiry into the Principles of Political Economy*, Smith was possibly compelled to react by naming his book otherwise (Cannan 1976: xxiv; Vaggi & Groenewegen 2003: 87), and adopted the title of *An Inquiry into the Nature and Causes of the Wealth of Nations* in order to differentiate his work from that of his predecessor. The implication is clear: Under ideal circumstances, had it not been for his relative latecoming, Smith would have taken up a title with 'political economy'. He was thus forced into a second-best as the price he paid for his delay. Although there could possibly be a grain of truth in this characterization, the whole truth is far more complicated. First of all, because the name 'political economy' was in wide circulation since the beginning of the early modern period, it was but natural for Steuart as first in line to call his book by reference to 'political economy', thereby earning also public recognition as the author of the first book on this subject in English. Moreover, Steuart was truly interested in analyzing how politics and the economy as two separate domains interacted. He saw various possibilities of this interaction, the success or failure of each being determined by time and place. The term 'political economy' had been popularized along with the spread of nation-states where the metaphorical household of the king was differentiated from the 'traditional' household of the family, in order to explore the further consequences of national economic policy in conjunction with governmental practice as would develop gradually into the mercantile system. For Steuart, there was nothing wrong with that, provided one could be aware of the number of possible 'combinations'[23] of the state and the economy. Hence he was quite at home with this concept, only elaborating on it further than it was originally intended for. The fact that, after Smith, the new discipline was conveniently called as 'political economy' attests to the wisdom in Steuart's judgment as well as the durability and adaptability of the concept concerned.

If Smith had wished first and foremost to differentiate his work from that of his predecessor, he would not opt for 'wealth of nations' as it was also widely used – albeit in the singular – in Steuart's book. If anything, Steuart saw the subject of his inquiry as the study of the 'wealth of a nation' just as he saw the objective of economic policy as the increase of this wealth of the nation as expressed time and again in *Principles*. Had this motive been all, Smith would have searched an altogether different title. Smith's definitive choice for the plural form was intentional, even if he were at first sight more focused on determinants of the process at work within a single state, just as was the case with Steuart. The use of 'wealth' had to do with a continuity with the so-called mercantilism that both authors shared. They were concerned with defining wealth in a new way that would be distinguishable from the crude original bullionist conception. As for Smith's preference for the plural, he must have seen that a lasting reality of the mercantile era that still concerned the sovereign was interstate competition and rivalries. This backdrop to his work would render it more attractive to the sovereign as well as the reading population. We see this international setting of the question as gradually receding to the background only with Ricardo's more abstract resetting of the question by economic modelling within the confines of a single state that would then enter into trade with others. In this respect, the perception and definition of the problem as one of international dimensions was a legacy of the mercantilist thought and was far more realistic. It is no coincidence that both Steuart and Smith subscribed to it, even though Smith went further and carried it to the title of his work.

Smith had a much more important reason for deliberately avoiding 'political economy' in his choice of title than his reluctance to remind the reader of his predecessor and thereby remain in his shadow. A careful reader of the *Wealth of Nations* will notice that Smith called the Book IV 'Of Systems of Political Economy'. He had in mind two such systems, namely, the physiocratic system and the mercantile system. Both systems combined politics and the economy because, to a large extent, they depended on policy choices and human design. As Smith put it, whereas the physiocratic system was largely a result of human design that had so far found little chance of application, the mercantile system had evolved from the very long gestation of the historical circumstances that obtained in Europe after the fall of the Roman Empire under the impact of barbarian invasions. He contrasted the 'logical' nature of the physiocratic system with the 'historical' character of the mercantile one, which in his view distorted the 'logical' sequence of history and substituted in its place a 'historical' sequence.

In a nutshell, cities and towns, as 'islands' in a feudal countryside that was Europe, preserved the Roman legacy, and when the time came, by reinforcing long-distance trade among themselves, impacted upon their hinterlands, and by virtue of their market function helped spread commercialization. The new patterns of luxurious consumption they could foster attracted the landlords' attention, who felt the need for cash to realize their aspirations. It was thus the dynamic role of markets that helped transform the countryside and stimulate both the commercialization of agricultural surplus and the spread of private property on land.

This historical process placing priority on manufacturers and foreign trade is diametrically opposite of what Smith saw as the 'logical' sequence characteristic of the physiocratic system stemming from agriculture. Simply put, division of labour in agriculture leads to creation of a surplus that then allows a segment of the population to specialize in nonagricultural activities, and the local trade among the two parties then gradually grows in concentric circles. For Smith, both the widely seen mercantile system and the rarely seen physiocratic system combined politics with the economy albeit differently and were thus 'systems of political economy' that contrasted sharply with what he cast against them as the alternative, 'the system of natural liberty'. The former two were highly artificial in comparison with the latter he characterized as 'natural'. Precisely because the 'system of natural liberty', serving as his lodestar, weighed heavily in comparison with the other two, 'political economy' occupied a secondary place in his scheme of analysis.

> All systems either of preference or of restraint, therefore, being thus completely taken away, the obvious and simple system of natural liberty establishes itself of its own accord. Every man, as long as he does not violate the laws of justice, is left perfectly free to pursue his own interest his own way, and to bring both his industry and capital into competition with those of any other man, or order of men.
>
> (Smith 1976: II, 208)

It was with this particular differential definition with important ontological implications and the treatment thereof in mind that Smith approached reluctantly to 'political economy' as a potential candidate for characterizing his intellectual undertaking.

We have seen the way Smith contrasted his 'system of natural liberty' with the other two systems of political economy, one based on agriculture and the other on commerce. The system he singled out as 'natural' served as his yardstick in the evaluation of the other two systems he qualified as artificial. However, Smith also acknowledged that a prerequisite of the 'system of natural liberty', and therefore the system itself, was far from being realizable:

> To expect indeed, that the freedom of trade should ever be entirely restored in Great Britain, is as absurd as to expect that an Oceana or Utopia should ever be stablished in it. Not only the prejudices of the public, but what is much more unconquerable, the private interests of many individuals, irresistibly oppose it.
>
> (Smith 1976: I, 493)

Hence he worked as lodestar with an 'ideal type' that was far from realizable and was hence even more 'artificial' than the other two systems of political economy, which he did not spare from his criticism. Smith's commitment to this idealized model, as well as his periodic return to his contention that self-interested agents in a market setting could produce an equilibrium coincident with the general welfare, combined with his powerful metaphor of 'invisible hand', attest to his inclination towards a mechanical automatism. This was as much his 'natural' inclination as it was learned from predecessors such as Richard Cantillon, who had also professed a Newtonian proclivity.[24] Even so, it is highly plausible that Smith accentuated this tendency in response to his reading of Steuart's work in order to deliberately differentiate his approach as more 'modern' from that of his archrival. He thereby tilted the balance in favour of this automatism, which bestowed upon his economic apparatus the inherent dynamics of a promising 'model' derived from his inspirational lodestar. This was a tactical move on his part, the full implications of which he might not have anticipated in his time, but they became clear retrospectively, when he was crowned as the founding father of modern economics.

Conclusion: Steuart as a beneficiary of the Smithian Vice

William Stanley Jevons, one of the three masterminds of the Marginalist Revolution, in a revoltive mood against the British tradition, wrote in his *The Theory of Political Economy* (1871), 'that able but wrong-headed man, David Ricardo, shunted the car of economic science on to a wrong line'. Schumpeter delved into Ricardo's disservice to economic science and coined the term 'Ricardian Vice' in order to characterize his method of abstract model-building as basis for simple policy derivations (Schumpeter 1954: 473).[25] Fortunately he elaborated his conception of the vice as 'the habit of piling a heavy load of practical conclusions upon a tenuous groundwork, which was unequal to it yet seemed in its simplicity not only attractive but also convincing' (Schumpeter 1954: 1171). If the Ricardian Vice as such was greatly responsible for 'shunting the car of economic science on to a wrong line', then we may also apply the same characterization to the role Smith – with his lodestar-inspired model of automatism – played in relation with the trajectory of economics and hence we can arguably speak of a Smithian Vice.

In retrospect, his tactical move benefitted Smith greatly over his rival. Whereas the differences between these two 'post-mercantilist' economists were greatly reconcilable and thus would not serve to cast them as two opposite poles of a nascent science,[26] thanks to Smith's deliberate deployment of this pseudo model of spontaneity and automatism, along with the strawman he made of mercantilism, the public perception of the picture changed considerably.[27] Thus Smith became increasingly a shining star, the brightness of which left Steuart in the dark until recently. However, as the Smithian Vice became increasingly a target for criticism by a variety of heterodox approaches, the tables started turning in favour of Steuart. It is no coincidence that Steuart, time and again, was rejoined by a set of heterodox orphans throughout the 19th and 20th centuries.[28] The ongoing renewal of interest in his *Principles* attests to a deeper process at work.

The resurrection of Steuart is imminent. However there is another side to this story. Smith is also being liberated from the neoclassical straitjacket. Renewed attention on Smith (Tribe 1999) reveals that there can be heterodox interpretations of Smith's work that emphasize other aspects of his approach that have until recently been either overlooked or considered of secondary influence. For example, the influence Smith put on historical and institutional factors of primary importance has recently been remembered[29] and links him directly with institutionalist approaches of either the original or the new institutional bent. The 'political economy' interpretation of *The Wealth of Nations* as based on a global perspective of comparative economic development, a very good example of which is Giovanni Arrighi's *Adam Smith in Beijing* (2007), is in greater conformity with Smith's original motivation, as manifest in his choice of 'nation' in the plural for his title. The process at work is undoing the stereotypical image of Smith and finally revealing the richness of *The Wealth of Nations* that cannot be reduced to the equilibrium model as characteristic of the neoclassical mainstream interpretation. In fact, in light of new developments, hitherto idolized automatism associated with market equilibrium appears more like a quick and uneasy patch forced upon the otherwise vastly expansive texture and themes of the book. This supports our contention that by reading Steuart's *Principles*, Smith may have deliberately further developed and foregrounded this aspect of his work in order to outperform his archrival.

In short, a Smith rid from the Smithian Vice is also in the wings. The coincident parallel developments are likely to bring Steuart and Smith far closer than they ever were. The Smithian Vice, by its once timely rise as well as its ongoing prolonged demise, has played a decisive role in all of this. In the first place it helped turn the balance in favour of Smith, and in its current phase it is serving Steuart's once seemingly lost cause. It should be noted that to foster heterodox proliferation as well as to show Steuart in a new light, the Smithian Vice was essential. Without its rise and fall, as well as the refraction in economic thinking it brought about, a linear cumulative development from Steuart to current heterodox economics could have been highly unlikely. Sometimes the shortest route is not the best one, and a roundabout alternative has blessings in disguise. If Smith deliberately promoted the Smithian Vice in order to overtake his archrival, without foreseeing its future consequences, this is indeed another, and this time ironic, example of his much renowned 'unintended consequences' thesis. Be that as it may, it is high time that they finally partake in a common – albeit different from the mainstream – lineage of contemporary political economy.

Notes

1 Although Smith ignored Steuart's book, it is noted that Smith's book borrowed the concept of 'effectual demand' from that of Steuart, though he used it differently (Kobayashi 1999: 116). Keynes allegedly repeated the same ostracism towards Steuart, who was his forerunner as an advocate of full-employment economy (Chamley 1962).

2 If only we had something remotely comparable to the printed manuscript of T.S. Eliot's *The Waste Land* with Ezra Pound's notes and recommendations on it, we would be moving on a much more solid ground (Eliot 1971).

3 Steuart is only mentioned once, and not in the text itself but in the 'Notes for Further Reading', while summarizing the content of a recommended article along with, not surprisingly, Richard Jones and Karl Marx in the widely used textbook with an international edition (Ekelund & Hébert 1990: 257). It has also been noted impartially and without further assessment that '[l]ike Galiani, Steuart strongly opposed the idea of

"general rules"' in political economy (Roncaglia 2005: 113). In this respect, it is no coincidence that Steuart's work 'received rather more than its due from some of the Germans' (Schumpeter 1954: 176n). Hegel devoted some three months to the study of this work and benefitted from it in formulating his notion of the economic basis of social structure (Caboret 1999: 57). It did not however enjoy the same success in France except for its influence over Etienne Sénovert (Albertone 1999: 41, 45).

4 Gianni Vaggi and Peter Gronewegen's, *A Concise History of Economic Thought: From Mercantilism to Monetarism* (Hampshire: Palgrave Macmillan, 2003) is a formidable exception. However, this 'concise' history is far from being 'short' and benefits further from its narrower time scope. Even so, the authors qualify Smith as one of the two 'masters' in contradistinction to Steuart, whom they characterize as one of several 'minor' contributors (Vaggi & Gonewegen 2003: 9).

5 Cooper was the popular writer of the shifting American frontier. His book was published in 1826, but set earlier as its subtitle, 'A Narrative of 1757' indicated, at about the same time as Steuart worked on his manuscript.

6 Smith was among the founders in 1762 of the Edinburgh Poker Club, a committee for political agitation of which Steuart is also listed as a member (Rae 1965: 134–136).

7 Steuart is usually not seen as such (Roncaglia 2005: 112). In contrast, he is treated as one of three pillars of the 'Scottish Triangle', along with David Hume and Adam Smith, a formidable constituent of the political economy of Scottish Enlightenment (Omori 2003: 103).

8 Smith benefitted from observations on the Scottish environment in general, and the highlands-versus-lowlands comparisons in his work (Smith 1976: 21–22; Ross 2010: 287). Steuart, being forced to remain on the continent, was more restrained in such benefits. As if to highlight his favourable difference, Smith wrote 'In the new town of Edinburgh, built within these few years, there is not, perhaps, a single stick of Scotch timber' (Smith 1976: 185).

9 Steuart spent the period 1735–40 travelling in Europe. He went to Holland and studied in the Universities of Leyden and Utrecht for about two years. He then went to Spain and spent time in Cadiz and Madrid. He visited Southern France and settled in Avignon. By way of Lyons he proceeded to Rome. In 1746, he was in Paris for about a year and moved to Angulême, where he started his study of political economy, only to return to Paris in 1754. In 1756–57, the family was in Frankfurt. They then spent four years in Tübingen, where he wrote much of his *Principles* – Book IV was written only after his return to Scotland in 1765–66 – in touch with university professors. He toured Tyrol and Padua and Verona in 1758 on his way to Venice. The family moved to Holland and stayed in Rotterdam and Antwerp. All in all, his book was the product of 'eighteen years' thought and travel' (Skinner 1966: xxiv–xxvi, xxxiv–xlii, xliv, xlvi), and Steuart had spent 22 years of his life abroad as a student and as an exile (Kobayashi 1999: 105). Compare with Smith's only two-and-a-half year long visit to France (mostly Paris but also Toulouse where he first started writing *Wealth of Nations*, and travel in the south of France, including Marseilles and a two month stay in Geneva, Switzerland) as the tutor of the young Duke of Buccleuch (Rae 1965: 174 and 284), during which he was fortunate enough to actively take part in society and meet leading influential French philosophers and Physiocrats along with other economists including Turgot (Ross 2010: 209–248). Steuart's long absence from home meant that Smith, before the publication of his *Wealth of Nations,* had converted Glascow merchants to the cause of free trade (Rae 1965: 61, 197).

10 As Smith put it: 'In countries where the winter nights are long, candles are a necessary instrument of trade' (Smith 1976: 403). So were long books.

11 Whereas Smith worked largely with common sense, Ricardo thought science started where common sense was questioned. Steuart shared a similar opinion, all the more so, when common sense coincided with popular opinion: 'The wandering and independent life I have led may naturally have set me free, in some measure, from strong attachments to popular opinions' (I, xv).

12 Ricardo is best known for his theory of international trade outside Britain. In a similar fashion to his fortunes with trade theory, Ricardo received more praise for his work on money than his original economic theory of value and distribution (Faccarello & Izumo 2014: 4).

13 He felt obliged to justify his order of presentation: 'Some of the foregoing reasonings and observations might perhaps have been more properly placed in those chapters of the first book which treat of the origin and use of money, and of the difference between the real and the nominal price of commodities' (Smith 1976: II, 65).

14 'But I insensibly wander from my subject' (I, 433).

15 It is contentious that the same could be said of Smith's *Wealth of Nations*.

16 Steuart wrote: 'When he provides food, he surely provides for a want; and experience shews, that it is better for a man to apply close to one trade, than to turn himself to several' (I, 110). Smith repeated Steuart: 'But when the improvement and cultivation of land and labour of one family can provide food for two, the labour of half the society becomes sufficient to provide food for the whole. The other half, therefore, or at least the greater part of them can be employed in providing other things, or in satisfying the other wants and fancies of mankind' (Smith 1976: 182). Both traced 'surplus' or 'superfluity' to this origin.

17 'England, however, as it has never been blessed with a very parsimonious government, so parsimony has at no time been the characteristical virtue of its inhabitants. It is the highest impertinence and presumption, therefore, in kings and ministers, to pretend to watch over the oeconomy of private people, and to restrain their expence, either by sumptuary laws, or by prohibiting the importation of foreign luxuries. They are themselves always, and without any exception, the greatest spendthrifts in the society. Let them look well after their own expence, and they may safely trust private people with theirs. If their own extravagance does not ruin the state, that of their subjects never will' (Smith 1976: I, 367).

18 Smith's distinction is notable in distancing himself from Steuart's concern: 'To judge whether such retaliations are likely to produce such an effect, does not, perhaps, belong so much to the science of a legislator, whose deliberations ought to be governed by general principles which are always the same, as to the skill of that insidious and crafty animal, vulgarly called a statesman or politician, whose councils are directed by the momentary fluctuations of affairs' (Smith 1976: II, 490).

19 See also (Smith 1976: II, 277)

20 Steuart's long stay in the continent may have been partly responsible for this over-presence of the sovereign in the book, which, with its resonating government intervention, alienated critics and readers in Britain when the book was published; but Steuart 'knew little of England' and much more of the 'Continent' that had practically become his background (Skinner 1966: xlvi–xlvii, lxxxii–lxxxiii). Steuart turned the tables round in his revised preface: 'If, from this work, I have any merit at all, it is by divesting myself of English notion, so far as to be able to expose in a fair light, the sentiments and policy of foreign nations, relatively to their own situation' (Steuart 1966: I, 5).

21 'However refined an economic theory may become, the growth in complexity of economic mechanisms will outstrip it, so that the need for careful amendment will never cease to exist' (Kobayashi 1999: 115).

22 In a far more specific case – the determination of the interest rate – similar propositions have been observed in greater detail, in Steuart as well as Smith, and thoroughly interpreted by recourse to the requirements of a historical turning point (Tortajada 1999: 250).

23 Smith also reasoned in terms of 'combinations' in much the same way though fewer times than Steuart: 'These three seem to exhaust all the possible combinations of events which can happen in the progress of improvement' (Smith 1976: 196). It should be noted that his important large-scale comparisons of Europe and China rest on this conception.

24 Same was true of Steuart who had not only worked on Newton but also was familiar with the work of Richard Cantillon, albeit indirectly (Groenewegen 1999: 34). This placed him at a disadvantage vis-à-vis his contemporaries, most of whom had read Cantillon's *Essai.* It would not be farfetched to argue that whatever temporary superiority

Smith had over Steuart aside from the tactical deployment of the concept of 'division of labour' was largely because of a Cantillon effect on his mind.

25 Schumpeter also characterized Say as 'also an addict to the Ricardian Vice' because 'he was much more anxious to exploit [economic analysis] for practical purposes than to formulate it with care' (Schumpeter 1954: 618). Schumpeter thought the vice infected many economists including his archrival John Maynard Keynes. This gives us a clue to what exactly he had in mind.

26 The term 'science' is employed in a loose sense here. Steuart used both 'science' and 'art' to characterize political economy. When his emphasis was more on the equivalence of political economy with economic policy, he preferred 'art', whereas when he focused on the underlying principles he opted for science (Sen 1957: 31). On the other side, Karl Polanyi, otherwise a vociferous critic of 'political economy', spared Smith at the expense of his alleged followers: 'A broad optimism pervades Smith's thinking since the laws governing the economic part of the universe are consonant with man's destiny as are those that govern the rest. No hidden hand tries to impose upon us the rites of cannibalism in the name of self-interest . . . Political economy should be a human science; it should deal with that which was natural to man, not to Nature' (Polanyi 1944: 112). In this sense, Smith and Steuart find themselves, once again, on common ground.

27 This viewpoint is supported by another study: 'The gulf between Political *Economy* and *WN* may not be as wide as is often assumed' (Omori 2003: 115).

28 It is no surprise that an early article associated Steuart with Richard Jones and Karl Marx on the basis of their evolutionist ideas (Grossman 1943). The connection would have been even more convincing if it was pursued along the lines of comparative historical institutional economics.

29 As summarily put, 'In order for the pursuit of self-interest to promote rather than damage the general interest, Smith insisted, certain institutional preconditions need to be met' (Kurz 2016: 28).

Bibliography

Albertone, M. (1999), The Difficult Reception of James Steuart at the End of the Iegteenth Century in France, in R. Tortajada (ed.), *The Economics of James Steuart*, London: Routledge: 41–56.

Arrighi, G. (2007), *Adam Smith in Beijing: Lineages of the Twenty-First Century*, London: Verso.

Caboret, D. (1999). *The market economy and social classes in James Steuart and G. W. F. Hegel*, in Tortajada, R. (ed.), *The Economics of James Steuart*, London: Routledge: 57–75.

Cannan, E. (1976), Editor's Introduction, in A. Smith, *Wealth of Nations*, Chicago: The University of Chicago Press: xix–liv.

Chamley, P. (1962), Sir James Steuart: inspirateur de la Théorie Générale de Lord Keynes, *Revue d'économie politique*, 72: 303–313.

Cooper, J.F. (2001), *The Last of the Mohicans*, New York: Modern Library.

Darling, L. (2013), Mirrors for Princes in Europe and the Middle East: A Case of Historical Incommensurability, in A. Classen (ed.), *East Meets West in the Middle Ages and Early Modern Times: Transcultural Experiences in the Premodern World*, Boston: De Gruyter: 223–242.

Diatkine, S. & Rosier, M. (1999), Steuart and Smith on Banking Systems and Growth, in R. Tortajada (ed.), *The Economics of James Steuart*, London: Routledge: 218–234.

Durkheim, E. (2014), *The Division of Labor in Society*, New York: Free Press.

Ekelund, R.B. & Hébert, R.F. (1990), *A History of Economic Theory and Method*, New York: McGraw-Hill.

Eliot, T.S. (1971), *The Waste Land: A Facsimile and Transcript of the Original Drafts Including the Annotations of Ezra Pound*, New York: Harvest Book.

Faccarello, G. & Izumo, M. (2014), Introduction: Ricardo's Travels into Several Remote Nations, in *The Reception of David Ricardo in Continental Europe and Japan*, London: Routledge: 1–9.

Faccarello, G. & Steiner, P. (2002), The Diffusion of the Work of Adam Smith in the French Language: An Outline History, in K. Tribe & H. Mizuta (eds.), *A Critical Bibliography of Adam Smith*, London: Pickering & Chatto: 61–119.

Groenewegen, P. (1999), Sir James Steuart and Richard Cantillon, in R. Tortajada (ed.), *The Economics of James Steuart*, London: Routledge: 27–40.

Grossman, H. (1943), The Evolutionist Revolt against Classical Economics: II. In England-James Steuart, Richard Jones, Karl Marx, *Journal of Political Economy*, 51(6): 506–522.

Hartley, L.P. (2002), *The Go-between*, New York: New York Review of Books.

Kobayashi, N. (1999), On the Method of Sir James Steuart's *Principles of Political Œconomy*, in R. Tortajada (ed.), *The Economics of James Steuart*, London: Routledge, 102–120.

Kurz, H.D. (2016), *Economic Thought: A Brief History*, New York: Columbia University Press.

Machiavelli, N. (1992), The Prince, New York: Dover Publications Inc.

Omori, I. (2003), The 'Scottish Triangle' in the Shaping of Political Economy: David Hume, Sir James Steuart, and Adam Smith, in T. Sakamoto & H. Tanaka (eds.), *The Rise of Political Economy in the Scottish Enlightenment*, London: Routledge, 103–118.

Polanyi, K. (1944), *The Great Transformation*, New York: Rinehart & Company.

Rae, J. (1965), *Life of Adam Smith*. New York: A.M. Kelley.

Roncaglia, A. (2005), *The Wealth of Ideas: A History of Economic Thought*, Cambridge: Cambridge University Press.

Ross, I.S. (2010), *The Life of Adam Smith*, Oxford: Oxford University Press.

Sandelin, B., Trautwein, H.M. & Wundrak, R. (2014), *A Short History of Economic Thought*, London: Routledge.

Say, J.-B. (1841), *Traité d'économie politique, ou simple exposition de la manière dont se forment, se distribuent, et se composent les richesses*, Paris: Guillaumin.

Schumpeter, J.A. (1954), *History of Economic Analysis*, New York: Oxford University Press.

Screpanti, E. & Zamagni, S. (1993), *An Outline of the History of Economic Thought*, Oxford: Clarendon Press.

Sen, S.R. (1957), *The Economics of Sir James Steuart*, Cambridge, MA: Harvard University Press.

Skinner, A. (1966), Analytical Introduction, in *An Inquiry into the Principles of Political Oeconomy*, Edinburgh: Oliver & Boyd: lviii–lxxxiv.

———. (1966), Biographical Sketch: The Life of Sir James Steuart-Denham, in *An Inquiry into the Principles of Political Oeconomy*, Edinburgh: Oliver & Boyd: xxi–lvii.

Smith, A. (1976), *An Inquiry into the Nature and Causes of the Wealth of Nations*, Chicago: The University of Chicago Press.

———. (1987), Letter n. 132 to William Pulteney, in E.C. Mossner & I.S. Ross (eds.), *The Correspondence of Adam Smith*, Oxford: Clarendon Press: 163–164.

Steuart, J. (1966), *An Inquiry into the Principles of Political Oeconomy*, Edinburgh: Oliver & Boyd.

Tortajada, R. (1999), Rate of Interest, Profit and Prices in the Economics of James Steuart, in *The Economics of James Steuart*, London: Routledge: 235–252.

Tribe, K. (1999), Adam Smith: Critical Theorist?, *Journal of Economic Literature*, 37(2): 609–632.

Vaggi, G. & Groenewegen, P. (2003), *A Concise History of Economic Thought: From Mercantilism to Monetarism*, Hampshire: Palgrave Macmillan.

Viner, J. (1965), Guide to John Rae's *Life of Adam Smith*, in J. Rae, *Life of Adam Smith*, New York: Augustus M. Kelley: 5–145.

12 Steuart and Davenant on financing wars

Yutaka Furuya

Introduction

James Steuart and Charles Davenant shared a similar view that financing wars are a vital issue for a nation and its economy. Davenant published *An Essay upon Ways and Means of Supplying the War* (hereafter *Essay*) in late 1694 (Waddell 1956: 207), during the war with France, when there was a pressing question of whether and how England can collect money to continue the war. Steuart prepared much of the latter volumes of *The Principles of Political Economy* (hereafter *Principles*) during the Seven Years' War and placed war finance at the core of public finance and evolvement of credit in a nation.

The approach they took when discussing how to finance the war was also very similar. Hoppit (1996) adequately named Steuart as one of the writers 'who explicitly attempted political arithmetic' in the latter half of the 18th century (Hoppit 1996: 520). Steuart and Davenant both regarded 'the Art of Reasoning, by Figures, upon Things relating to Government' (Davenant 1701: 2) as an effective approach to discussing the economy and public finance. Steuart's endorsement of political arithmetic makes a decided contrast with Adam Smith, who famously wrote: 'I have no great faith in political arithmetic' (Smith 1776: II, 121).

Steuart and Davenant's opinion on financing wars, however, differed on most decisive points: The method for financing wars and the influence of this financing on the nation's economy. Davenant was against borrowing on perpetual interest; he argued that if the King repeatedly borrowed on perpetual interest it will do great damage and hazard to the Kingdom. Steuart, on the other hand, was of the opinion that the nation should take advantage of this long-term credit in times of war; he argues that collecting tax and paying interest for the long-term debt does not necessarily mean a hazard to a nation; it may, on many occasions, give positive effects to the economy of the nation.

The similarity between Steuart and Davenant on treating war finance and the critical difference of opinion between the two on the method and influence of financing deserves more than a passing notice. Did Davenant's idea on financing wars have any influence on Steuart? How did Steuart come up with opposite conclusions from Davenant on some central issues regarding war finance? Answers to these questions are vital to larger questions such as the development of political arithmetic in the 18th century just before Smith's *Wealth of Nations*.

This chapter shows how Steuart learned from Davenant and how decisive an impact Davenant's arguments on public revenues and war finance had on Steuart. Steuart, when reading Davenant's arguments on the topic, did not hastily deny Davenant's conclusions on preferable ways to finance wars; rather, he attempted to trace carefully how Davenant came up with his conclusions by examining the circumstance and the spirit of the people at the time when Davenant was writing. And by doing so Steuart was able to shape a clear understanding of how credit drastically developed in Britain since Davenant's time; he explains that the difference in opinions between Davenant and him on how to finance wars was due to this drastic change in circumstances and the spirit of the people. The way Steuart dealt with Davenant's discussion was a reflection of the core methodology Steuart laid down in *Principles*: '[t]imes and circumstances must always be examined, before any decision can be passed in political matters' (Steuart 1760: 12).

This is important particularly because between the time when Davenant wrote *Essay* and the time when Steuart wrote *Principles* England went through the financial revolution; the establishment of the Bank of England in 1694 and the expansion of government long-term borrowing enabled the British government to fund the intermittent war with France. This development of Steuart's theory on public finance marks how the revolution was assimilated and integrated into economic theory in the 18th century.

Continuity between Steuart and Davenant

In Part IV 'of public credit' in Book IV of *Principles*, Steuart explains the historical development of public credit in England and France. He begins his explanation on England's public credit by referring to Davenant's writing; when he explains France's public credit he begins by referring to Cardinal de Richelieu's *Testament Politique*. The reason why he begins with the writings of these two writers was that according to Steuart, the two were the most qualified writers on these topics. Referring to Davenant, Steuart writes:

> No person at that time, whose writings I have seen, appears to have so thoroughly understood those matters [public credit] as Davenant. He was a man of theory, as well as knowledge of facts: he had an opportunity which few people have, to be well instructed in the one and the other; and he turned his talents to the best advantage for promoting the interest of his country. He has writ many tracts on political subjects, which, when carefully read and compared with what experience has since taught us, cast great light upon many questions relative to the subject of this inquiry.
>
> (IV, 12–13)

The fact that Steuart highly praised Davenant for his understanding of public credit is especially important in the light of political arithmetic. Davenant and Steuart both used political arithmetic chiefly to reveal the extent, the method, and the influence of war finance – in the same way Petty used it.[1] Davenant wrote his *Essay* and

Discourses on the Public Revenues, and on the Trade of England (hereafter *Discourses*) when England was fighting a war against France. Ito points out that '[t]he war against France was the starting point' of Davenant's political economy (Ito 2011: 41), which started with his *Essay* in 1694. Steuart echoes Ito and says 'This revenue of 1.570.318. l. [in 1694] was so inconsiderable, and so unequal to the expences [expenses] of the war, that other ways and means were sought after; and this gave occasion to Davenant to write upon that subject' (Steuart 1760: 154). Likewise, Steuart was preparing for the latter half of *Principles*, mostly during the Seven Year's War with France, and he explained public credit and taxes by contrasting those of Britain with those of France. Although *Principles* was published after the war, the potential rivalry between Britain and France remained. Steuart writes: 'Britain and France are two nations, rivals in every thing worthy of emulation' (IV, 26).

Personal circumstances in which Davenant and Steuart applied political arithmetic were also very similar.[2] Davenant lost his political position after the 1688 revolution; he wrote *Essay* and *Discourses* as a part of an effort to gain a place in the government service.[3] Similarly, Steuart's political ambition was scattered after the Battle of Culloden in 1746; he wrote *Principles* in an attempt to obtain his full pardon and a better future for his son.

Another similarity between Davenant and Steuart regarding public finance is their appraisal of Cardinal et Duc de Richelieu, Armand Jean du Plessis (1585–1642), chief minister to King Louis XIII of France, on this topic and their opinion about the authenticity of Richelieu's posthumously published *Testament politique d'Armand Du Plessis, cardinal duc de Richelieu* (hereafter *Testament*).

On Richelieu, Steuart says:

> Having laid before my reader the sentiments of Davenant on the subject of public credit, which were analogous to the then state of England, it may be instructive to compare them with those of another very great man, in a rival nation; I mean the Cardinal de Rich[e]lieu.
>
> (IV, 25)

The authenticity of *Testament*, however, was fiercely attacked by Voltaire, François-Marie Arouet, in 1749, and later again in 1764. Voltaire insists that numerous evidence shows that Richelieu cannot possibly be the author of *Testament*. Steuart, fully aware of Voltaire's attack, nevertheless held an unshakeable belief that *Testament* was written by Richelieu. He says anyone who insists that *Testament* was not written by Richelieu lacks either the effort or the ability to understand what is written in *Testament*.

> Let us now take a view of the sentiments of a great minister, delivered in writing by himself, in his political testament; the authority of which would never have been called in question, had the matter it contains been properly attended to, and well understood.
>
> (IV, 26)

This strong statement was Steuart's direct response to Voltaire's *Printed Lies and the Political Testament of Cardinal Richelieu* (*Des mensonges imprimés*). We know this because in his manuscript Steuart writes: '[H]ad he [Voltaire] been at the trouble to examine before he refuted, he would not have said so much against the 9th chapter [of *Testament Politique*], which he has not understood'.

Davenant had an identical opinion about Richelieu and his *Testament*. He highly praises Richelieu in *Essay* that 'the foundation of the present Greatness of that Monarchy [France], were laid by Cardinal Richelieu' (1701: 8). Ito (2011) describes that 'Davenant therefore turned to Cardinal Richelieu, particularly his posthumous *Testament Politique* (published in 1688) as a guide to good management in financing the war against France', and that '[a]lthough Davenant credited William Petty as the founder of political arithmetic in his Discourses on the Public Revenues, and on the Trade of England (1698), his conception of political arithmetic as an instrument of the able statesman comes from Richelieu' (Ito 2011: 42). This further confirms that Steuart and Davenant shared the common basis for their argument on public credit. We may, therefore, point out a clear connection between Richelieu, Davenant, and Steuart in terms of political arithmetic.

Disparity between Steuart and Davenant

Steuart's hearty applause for Davenant, however, does not mean that Steuart agreed with most of Davenant's arguments. In fact, Steuart differed from Davenant on numerous points, such as the reasonable base for taxation or estimation of the amount of debt the French government owed in 1697. The most notable difference between Steuart and Davenant, on the principles of public credit and public finance, was their views on the appropriate method of financing wars and its influence on the economy.

According to Davenant, a government may raise money for the war by:

- raising necessary amount of money within the year.
- anticipation, which is borrowing money for a few years.
- funding, which is borrowing money upon perpetual interest.

Davenant strongly supports the state to repay its borrowing within the year; he, on the contrary, strongly opposes borrowing upon perpetual interest, calling it cancer that will eat into the body politic.

> 'Tis true, sinking the Principal, or long Fonds, may give us present Ease; but they are a Canker, that in process of Time, will eat into the Body-Politick.
>
> In all probability, for the foregoing Reasons, it will be better Thrift, to exert our selves strongly, in the beginning, to pay off the Principal Debt, than to leave it a constant Burthen upon the Land, and Trade of *England*.
>
> (Davenant 1698: 202)

> Giving the King Money by Anticipating the Customs, or by Credit, upon distant Fonds, does apparently consume the Public with Usury: The new Fonds entail upon us a heavy Debt of perpetual Interest.
>
> (Davenant 1701: 39)

Steuart, on the other hand, had a fundamentally different view. He highlights in his definition of public credit that a state does not necessarily have to pay back the money she borrowed.

> *3tio*, Public credit. This is established upon the confidence reposed in a state, or body politic, who borrow money upon condition that the capital shall not be demandable; but that a certain proportional part of the sum shall be annually paid, either in lieu of interest, or in extinction of part of the capital; for the security of which, a permanent annual fund is appropriated, with a liberty, however, to the state to liberate itself at pleasure, upon repaying the whole; when nothing to the contrary is stipulated.
>
> (IV: 2)

As to the influence of public debt on the economy, Steuart says that 'the debts they [states] owe, *when due to citizens*, are on the whole, rather advantageous than burdensome: they produce a new branch of circulation among individuals, but take nothing from the general patrimony' (IV, 362).

But how did Steuart, starting from common grounds with Davenant on public credit, end up with conclusions on these core issues opposite from Davenant? To answer this question we need to follow Steuart's footsteps and see how Steuart absorbed and assimilated the writings of Davenant in order to develop his theory of public credit.

Steuart's departure from Davenant's reasoning

Steuart began his study on French government's revenue and expenditure in 1748, when he was settled in the province of Angoumois, France. This study eventually lead to his *Principles*.[4] He had started writing *Principles* by June 1756.[5] But it was not until 1760 that Steuart had a chance to closely study Davenant's *Essay* and *Discourses*. This can be confirmed from two sources.

First, in 1759, Steuart completed his first draft of Books I and II of *Principles*. In this draft, Steuart cites Davenant four times, and all four of those were taken from the same secondary source.

> As I write under circumstances not the most favourable for having recourse to books, I must imploy those I have. The article of Mr. Chambers's Cyclopedia furnishes me with some extracts from Sir Will: Petty and Dr. Davenant in the article *Political Arithmetic*, which I here intend to imploy, towards pointing out a solution of the question proposed.[6]

Internal evidence suggests that the original manuscript of this passage was written in or before 1757.

Second, after he completed his first drafts of Books I and II of *Principles*, in 1760, Steuart was preparing for the latter half of *Principles*, where he discusses money, credit, and taxes. During that year he wrote an extensive annotation on Davenant's *Essay* and *Discourses*.[7] We may, therefore, conclude that in 1757, Steuart did not have *Essay* and *Discourses*, but by 1760 he obtained his copy[8] of the two books so he could use them to prepare for his theory on credit and taxes.[9] Steuart carefully examined Davenant's argument and made nearly 20,000 word annotations.[10]

Although Steuart did not agree with everything Davenant wrote, he was aware of the importance of Davenant and his works. Steuart wrote, after reading *Essay*, that '[u]pon the whole, Davenant is an excellent writer for the age he lived in' (Steuart 1760: 122). What this annotation reveals is that Steuart, as he reads Davenant's *Essay* and *Discourses*, learns the circumstance and the sentiment of Davenant's time; by doing so, Steuart re-examines and gradually refines his understanding of how trade and credit developed during the last six decades.

For instance, by examining Davenant's passage where he laments how money is not circulating, Steuart learns how interests were not regularly paid, how tallies and wooden exchequer notes were heavily discounted, and how money was locked up and not lent.

> Upon the conclusion of the war with france [France] by the peace of Ryswic[k 1697], I find that Credit in England was very low. Interest had not been regularly pay'd [paid], which is reason enough for such an event. The consequence of this was that the public paper and tallies sold at discount, and money was locked up.
>
> (Steuart 1760: 123)

This was strikingly different from the reality of Steuart's age. Steuart applies here the historical framework he presented in Book I and Book II and understands the difference between credit in Davenant's time and credit in his time in the context of the development of the system of modern political economy. '[O]nce Credit, trade & industry are introduced', says Steuart, 'no body keeps money'. Instead, they will lend the money and get interest for it. '[M]oney, now, can never lye dead'. And by the same token, it will be much easier for the borrower to get money (1760: 154–155).

As credit was not yet established, it is no surprise that people's common understanding about public debts at this time was 'very ill disgested [digested]'. Steuart judges, by the calculation of debts and Davenant's effort to correct people's misunderstanding, that

> I must here observe that it must have been a common opinion at this time, with many people, that when a state borrowed money upon an assignation, to

> the creditor, of some sort of duty imposed on the people; that such borrowing did not constitute a debt.
>
> (1760: 133)

One important issue that is brought to the surface, by examining Davenant's criticism against long-term borrowing, is the development and the function of one key class in the modern society: Monied interest. Davenant, in his *Discourses*, says 'tis probable' that there are group of lenders who 'would be willing to supply the Government with a considerable Loan, and to stay for their Principal the whole Eight Years' (1701: 260). Steuart cites this passage and candidly expressed his amazement: 'how matters are changed! no moneyed interest here surely' (1760: 149). By noting that if, between Davenant's time and Steuart's time, the British government did not engage in long-term borrowing, there would still be no monied interest, Steuart says:

> [W]hat would he [Davenant] have said, had he lived in our days! [H]e argues against that Scheme [long-term borrowing], and is for falling vigorously to work, and paying off the Capital as fast as possible.
>
> The discussion of that question is a curious problem in politics. A nation who would follow Davenants opinion could never have a monied interest. We must therefore . . . examine all the Consequences of having a monied interest in a state.
>
> (Steuart 1760: 138–139)

Steuart reasons that monied interest, credit, huge long-term government borrowing, and the extensive tax system all needed to grow hand in hand; this growth, by degrees, formed Great Britain's system of economy in Steuart's time. It is a system of economy that can smoothly process the fluctuation of the demand for government borrowing, which is caused by alternating between war and peace. According to Steuart, huge long-term government borrowing is not an isolated variable in an economy; government borrowing cannot simply be removed from or attached to an economy without reshaping the whole structure of that economy.

Rational assimilation of the financial revolution

Through the perusal of Davenant's *Essay* and *Discourses*, Steuart was able to understand why Davenant opposed to long-term government borrowing at the time he wrote. In the printed edition of *Principles*, Steuart summarized the circumstances that lead Davenant to oppose long funds into four points. First, the interest rate was high. At the peace of Ryswick in 1697, England had 3.5 million pounds sterling debt in long funds. More than one-third of this debt was to be paid in a lifetime annuity of 14% and the rest of the debt was borrowed in the perpetual interest of over 11%. Second, it was still difficult to raise taxes in Davenant's time. Third, the supply of money did not meet the demand mainly because circulation was confined to the coin. Fourth, trade at that time was only beginning to take root in England; it demanded money, and profits on trade were great. All these circumstances altered during the following six decades and led Britain to a different stage of the economy.

Steuart also came to clearly understand that it was the time when Davenant was writing that the significant development in public finance started to take place. In the manuscript, Steuart already used an expression such as '[i]t is not as yet 60 years, that states have begun to borrow in a regular manner' (1760: 155). In the printed edition of *Principles*, he takes a step further and calls it the era of public credit: 'about the time of the revolution in 1688, which I may take to be the æra of public credit in England' (IV, 12).

And Steuart endorsed this new system of public finance not only from an economical point of view. He also stresses the political significance of this new system where the government was regularly engaged in long-term borrowing. He regarded this long-term borrowing as a vital innovation, an innovation that may serve to a nation as a decisive tool to out win her opponent in a war and survive as a nation.

> The borrowing of states (who have no provision made) and the expense of their war, being therefore pretty near equal; that state whose credit fails the first, must succumb.
>
> (Steuart 1760: 155)

Seven years later, in the printed edition of *Principles*, Steuart elaborates this point and underlines that the innovations on ways to further finance wars are a matter of important national competition:

> As long as nations at war observe the same policy in their methods of raising money, the ways in which they proceed are of the less importance: but when any one state makes an alteration, by which more money is thrown into their hands than they could formerly obtain; this circumstance obliges every other state to adopt the same method. Thus while Princes made war with the amount of their treasures and annual income, the balance of their power depended on the balance of such resources: when they anticipated their income on both sides, for a few years, the balance was in proportion still: when, afterwards, they adopted long funds and perpetual interest, the supplies increased; but still the balance was determined as formerly.
>
> (IV, 15–16)

Concluding remarks

In the year 1760, when he was preparing for the latter half of *Principles*, where he intended to write on money, credit, debts, and taxes, Steuart studied the writings of Davenant attentively. Steuart regarded Davenant as the ablest writer on public credit in his time, and Davenant's writings had a decisive impact on Steuart's theory on public credit. The two shared some important ideas regarding public credit: They both regarded that war finance is central to the topic, it is critical to reason by figures, and the argument must include or imply a comparison with rival nations.

By examining why his opinion differed with Davenant's on how war should be financed, Steuart learned how the credit in England developed in conjunction with the development of the trade, industry, and class structure of its society. Steuart was able to clearly understand that, starting from 1688, a decisive development in public credit took place in England that enabled the government to borrow more extensively. This development, according to Steuart, was a huge asset for England (or Britain) to fight wars against other nations. Thus Steuart's *Principles* was the first economic theory to positively assimilate and integrate the financial revolution in England.

Notes

1 Although I agree with Hoppit 1996 in categorizing Steuart as a political arithmetician, I do not fully agree with his explanation of Steuart's use of political arithmetic analysis. Hoppit refers to Book I 'Of Population and Agriculture' in *Principles* and says, 'Sir James Steuart thought that political economy must include demographic issues within its remit and, in turn, that demography had to be addressed largely in statistical terms'. Steuart, however, does not make much use of statistics and figures in Books I or II of *Principles*. Steuart's use of political arithmetic is most remarkable in Part IV, Book IV, and Part V of *Principles*, where he discusses public credit and taxation. The most important point to be noted, when referring to Steuart as a political arithmetician, is that the use of political arithmetic in Steuart's work was first and foremost in the context of pursuing the means, the extent, and the influence of public finance.

2 The fact that Davenant was a Tory and Steuart was a Whig bears little relevance to the matter in hand. The political situations of England and Scotland in mid-18th century are different from those in late 17th century, and moreover, both Davenant and Steuart had ties to different political groups. As for Davenant, '[a]s his positions in the 1680s suggest, by nature and temperament Davenant was in many (though not all) respects a tory and, as with many tories between 1697 and 1701, he was also happy to put his weight behind aspects of the "country programme" that sought to limit the executive power of William III and the whig junto' (Hoppit 2004). See also Ito (2005). As for Steuart, despite being a Whig, he was deeply involved in the Jacobite uprising of the 45.

3 See Waddell (1958) and Hoppit (2004). '[H]e was very perilously placed at the revolution of 1688 and lost all his positions with the advent of the new regime of William and Mary in 1689' (Hoppit 2004).

4 Steuart writes to Sir George Colebrooke in October 1780: 'I had the misfortune to live in Exile many years in that Country [France], and having nothing to do, I devoted myself to study. The Political Œconomy contains most of the fruits of it. / As you wish an Idea of the present resources of France, I can only recommend to you the same Method which I followed myself in complying the list of the Revenue and of the expenditure to which I have alluded' (Furuya 2014: 8).

5 Steuart most likely started writing *Principles* when he was in either Brussels, Liege, or Spa. Steuart, together with his family and friends, left Brussels on June 7, 1756. They stayed in Liege for a few days and arrived at Spa in the latter half of June.

6 Steuart (1759). This passage corresponds to Steuart (I, 53).

7 The manuscript was held privately until 1988, and it has hardly been considered.

8 At least *Discourses* was Steuart's own copy. 'I have made some small observations upon the margin of my copy, which require to be extended' (Steuart 1760: 116).

9 I conjecture that *Essay* and *Discourses* were included in the set of books he asked his friends in Paris to buy and send to him in Tubingen. According to Charles Whitworth, Davenant's works were 'so very scarce and valuable' in those days (1771: v).

10 The original annotations were written in 1760 in Tubingen. This year Robert Darcy, 4th Earl of Holderness, then Secretary of State for the North Department, worked hard to bring Steuart back to Britain. Steuart sent a petition to King George II by way of Lord Holderness, but unfortunately the King deceased in October. In 1765, when Steuart was writing his fnal draft of the *Principles*, he asked his amanuensis to transcribe these annotations into one notebook; this notebook is the manuscript we have today.

Bibliography

Chalmers, G. (1805), Anecdotes of the Life of Sir James Steuart, Baronet, in *The Works, Political, Metaphysical, and Chronological, of the Late Sir James Steuart of Coltness, Bart*, London: T. Cadell & W. Davies.

Chambers, E. (1751–52), *Cyclopaedia: Or, an Universal Dictionary of Arts and Sciences*, London: W. Innys, J. & P. Knapton & Others.

Davenant, C. (1698), *Discourses on the Public Revenues, and on the Trade of England*, vol. 1, London: James Knapton.

———. (1701), *An Essay upon Ways and Means of Supplying the War*, London: Jacob Tonson.

Furuya, Y. (2014), Manuscript of James Steuart: Steuart's Discussion on Finance, *Discussion paper. Tohoku Economics Research Group Discussion Paper*, 322.

Hoppit, J. (1996), Political Arithmetic in Eighteenth-Century England, *Economic History Review*, 49(3): 516–540.

———. (2004), Davenant, Charles (1656–1714), *Oxford Dictionary of National Biography*, online edn.

Ito, S. (2005), Charles Davenant's Politics and Political Arithmetic, *History of Economic Ideas*, 13(1): 9–36.

———. (2011), The Ideal Statesman: The Influence of Richelieu on Davenant's Political Thought, in H.D. Kurz, T. Nishizawa & K. Tribe (eds.), *The Dissemination of Economic Ideas*, Cheltenham & Northampton: Edward Elgar.

Smith, A. (1776), *An Inquiry into the Nature and Causes of the Wealth of Nations*, London: W. Strahan & T. Cadell.

Steuart, J. (1759), *An Enquiry into the Principles of Political Œconomy: Book First and Book Second.* Manuscript. Copy of the First Draft of the First Two Books of Steuart (1767) Dedicated to Charles Margrave of Baaden [sic]. Badische LandesBibliothek, Karlsruhe.

———. (1760), *Notes upon Davenant*. Manuscript. Edinburgh University Library.

Voltaire, F.M. Arouet. (1749), Des Mensonges Imprimés, et Du Testamen Politique du Cardinal de Richelieu, in *Œuvres complètes de Voltaire*, vol. 23, Paris: Garnier.

Waddell, D. (1956), The Writings of Charles Davenant, *The Library: Transactions of the Bibliographical Society*, 5–11(3): 206–212.

———. (1958), Charles Davenant (1656–1714) a Biographical Sketch, *The Economic History Review*, 11(2): 279–288.

Whitworth, C. (1771), Preface to This New Edition, in *The Political and Commercial Works of That Celebrated Writer Charles D'avenant*, London: Horsfield.

13 Steuart, a late mercantilist?

Mauricio C. Coutinho

Introduction

James Steuart (1713–1780) has been frequently designated a 'late mercantilist', or at least singled out as an economist who, in the second half of the 18th century, supported old-fashioned mercantilist principles. As his *Principles of Political Economy* (Steuart 1767) was published not too many years before the *Wealth of Nations* (Smith 1776), comparisons became inevitable. While Smith's work was assumed as the definitive argument against mercantilism, Steuart was taken by many critics as an author who defended outdated mercantilist policies, the merits of his work notwithstanding.

John Rae's (1895) account has contributed to spread among 20th-century readers the view that the absolute lack of references to Steuart in the *Wealth of Nations* should be interpreted as a rebuttal of Steuart's supposed endorsement of the 'mercantile system'. In fact, Rae's version echoes ideas that were already in circulation in the beginning of the 19th century, as reinforced by a suggestive passage of the *Discours Préliminaire* of Say's *Traité d'Économie Politique* (Say 1814) that refers to Smith's silence on Steuart.[1]

Even though not endorsing Rae's presumption, Johnson (1937) proposes that Smith's silence on Steuart, and his obsession for Thomas Mun, represented instead a sort of literary stratagem: Smith concentrated his criticism on an 'easy' target – Mun – thus avoiding the immense complexities associated to a criticism of Steuart.

Indeed, it may be assumed that, at least from the early 1800s until 1950, a strict connection between Steuart mercantilism was taken for granted by the history of economics literature. In his seminal work on the economics of James Steuart, Sen (1957) refers to two important general history of economic thought books – J.K. Ingram's *History of Political Economy* (Ingram 1888) and E. Roll's *History of Economic Thought* (Roll 1938) – representative of different times and traditions that held that Steuart's *Principles* shared outdated mercantilist principles. Effectively, Ingram considered *Principles* an 'unfortunate' book, inferior to the *Wealth of Nations* in 'style' and 'soundness' (Ingram 1888: 87), whereas Roll simply dispelled Steuart's contributions as rough mercantilism.

But even admirers commented on Steuart's mercantilist leanings. Marx, who extolled Steuart's precise insights into the structure of capitalist society, asserted that even though rejecting the mercantile conception that profit 'creates' surplus value, Steuart ultimately admitted the possibility of getting profit from external trade.[2] For this reason, by sharing the mercantilist dogma that profits arise not within a country, but in external exchange, Steuart would represent 'the rational expression of the Monetary and Mercantile systems'. (Marx 1863: 43).

It is true that in the 1950s a couple of books shedding light on Steuart's monetary theory evidenced that positioning Steuart's contributions under the umbrella of 'mercantilism' represents an oversimplification. Sen's (1957) and Vicker's (1959) compelling rehabilitations of Steuart's monetary theory are good examples of these efforts.[3] In the roll of general history of economics books, *History of Economic Analysis* (Schumpeter 1954) contributed to rehabilitate Steuart and to dispel the ambiguities of analyzing his work from the point of view of the adherence to mercantilism. Schumpeter not only avoided classifying the theoretical contributions of *Principles* under a unified label but also praised Steuart's 'systematic treatment' of relevant economic topics, in contrast to Smith's lack of depth in economic analysis. Moreover, under the heading 'Consultant Administrators and Pamphleteers' we learn that Steuart's insistence on the old-fashioned 'statesman' was just a reminiscence of von Justi. We will come later to Steuart's frequent appeals to the 'statesman', but the point is that Schumpeter (1954) seems to have drawn a division line, inducing more cautious, and less simplistic, appraisals of Steuart's theoretical merits.

Despite this sort of post-1950 rehabilitation of Steuart's work, a characteristic feature of general history of economics texts is the scarcity of mentions to Steuart's contributions to money and external trade. Bowley's (1973) review of the pre-1870 economic theory is representative of the propensity to understate Steuart's efforts in monetary analysis. Whereas acknowledging contributions to topics such as value and price, labour supply, and salaries, Bowley bypasses external trade, money, and credit, undoubtedly major contents of *Principles*. In this sense, Bowley reenacts Johnson's (1937) choice of taking into consideration only Books I and II (Population and Agriculture; Trade and Industry), leaving aside Steuart's complex incursions into money, credit, and taxes, in Books III, IV, and V of his *Principles*.

From another point of reference – pre-Ricardian approaches to distribution and value – Aspromourgos (1996) also emphasizes passages from Books I and II, leaving aside Steuart's treatment of money and external trade. The problem is that price formation is one of Aspromourgos' targets, and it's impossible to exclude money and exchange rate from Steuart's arguing on prices.

Even Hutchison (1988), whose authoritative review of pre-Smithian economics is much broader than Bowley's in the sense of considering elements of Steuart's approaches to money and external trade, does not emphasize money and credit as central elements of Steuart's system. In what refers to 'mercantilism', Hutchison contests the liberal usage of this term by the history of economics literature, going so far as to exclude from the set of mercantilist policies the defence of public granaries, an 18th-century policy supported by Steuart, many times assumed as representative of mercantilism. On the other hand, Hutchison considers that the fact of accepting gold as a 'true reserve stock of a state' (Hutchison 1988: 178) indicates that Steuart remained a mercantilist in policy issues.

Hutchison's comments deserve attention for another reason: They apparently endorse the view that it exists mercantilism in theory and mercantilism in policy. The defence of granaries is situated within the set of 'mercantilist policies'. All in all, Hutchison rejects positioning Steuart within the set of disciples of mercantilism under the argument that *Principles*' general approach to international trade is far more advanced than any favourable balance of trade interpretation, usually associated to mercantilism. Anyhow, Hutchison's references to 'mercantilist policies' seem to indicate the existence of differences between mercantilism in policy and mercantilism in theory, a subtlety – already admitted in Smith's criticism of the 'mercantile system' – that has pervaded the 20th-century theoretically informed commentaries on mercantilism.[4] The conundrum, to be developed later, is that Steuart's main policy proposals are attuned to his economic analysis of external trade, money, and credit. At least in Steuart's case, there is a convergence between theory and policy recommendations, which means the distinction between mercantilism in policy and mercantilism in theory seems to represent an inadequate criterion either to include Steuart in the set of mercantilist economists or to exclude him from it.

At any rate, being money and external trade are crucial components of Steuart's system, it is necessary to relate our leading question – Steuart, a late mercantilist? – to the development of money and external trade issues in *Principles*. Under this perspective, it must be admitted that Schumpeter himself, although acknowledging Steuart's precocious anti-metallism, did not emphasize the enormous inroads of *Principles* into monetary theory. Schumpeter, like other history of economics reviewers, opted instead for stressing topics such as population, salaries, the pioneering utilization of the expression 'balance of payments', the 'infant industry' argument, decreasing returns in agriculture.

It cannot be forgotten that one of the obstacles to the assessment of Steuart's approximations to mercantilism is the relative fuzziness of concepts such as 'mercantilism', 'mercantilist policies', and 'mercantile system'. This subject, covered by a varied literature, from Heckscher (1935) to Magnusson (1994), was obviously sharpened by Adam Smith's attack to the mercantile system and by the reception to the *Wealth of Nations* in the 19th century (Coutinho & Supryniak 2017).[5] In other words, the inclusion of Steuart in the mercantilists' cohort is subject to justified controversies, given the simple fact that the concept of mercantilism allows variations. Skinner (1991), for instance, adverts us that, although Steuart had been under the influence of mercantilist authors in his approach to external trade (themes and political analysis), his system was most of all indebted to Montesquieu and to the Scottish theory of economic evolution. Anyhow, external trade and bullion are central elements of any 'mercantilist' approach to the economy. Certainly, Steuart was extremely concerned with both elements.

The other dimension of Steuart's approximation to mercantilism is simply temporal. If we put the great mass of the 1620–1750 economic literature under the heading 'mercantilism', Steuart will be considered a mercantilist, simply because

Principles can be taken as a great synthesis of one and a half centuries of economic debates on money and balance of trade. Being money and external trade the common topics of most of the 1620–1760 economic debates, anyone who accepts these topics to define mercantilism will necessarily situate Steuart inside mercantilism.

To these two substantive dimensions we should add a third one that, notwithstanding its less substantial meaning, has frequently had a bearing on the assessment of Steuart's proximity to mercantilism: the frequent appeals to the 'statesman'. Steuart repeatedly exhorts the 'statesman', even though he does not seem convinced that the stateman's actions will be always efficacious, or even undertaken.[6] It is tempting to interpret the appeals to the statesman as an evidence of the weakness of Steuart's liberalism, even though he did not conceive the 'statesmen' as all powerful actors, and even though the principle of self-interest is as active in Steuart's *Principles* as it is would be in Smith's *Wealth of Nations*.

In my view, we'd rather take into consideration that Steuart frequently advocates actions that are, by definition, public. For instance, and as it will be seen, the 'balance of work and demand' requires an adequate provision of subsistence. Lack of food disrupts the basic social equilibrium portrayed by this 'balance', and – Steuart adverts – failures in local production can and should be countervailed by imports. Provision of food is a matter to be projected towards external trade, which implies associated matters, such as rate of exchange, tariffs, licenses, etc.; that is, provision of food implies variables necessarily affected by governmental action. The same applies to many extensively debated monetary issues, such as coinage rate, debasement, paper money, credit, and mortgages. All of them pertain to the realm of money and credit policies, which means they are, by definition, part of the 'statesman's' set of attributions.

Having situated the variety of senses that may be applied to the assessment of the relations between Steuart and mercantilism, and having assumed that responses will be necessarily dependent upon one's understanding of what mercantilism is or, at least, of which policies can be defined as 'mercantilist policies', the following sections will proceed the other way round: To propose Steuartian approaches that might be considered relevant to our motivating question – Steuart, a late mercantilist? These approaches encompass external trade and statesmanship (Section 2); money or, more properly, rate of coinage and its impacts on exchange rate (Section 3); credit in its relations to external trade (Section 4). In the conclusions, in Section 5, we return to the 'statesman', and to mercantilism.

External trade and statesmanship

Steuart examines external trade among countries in similar levels of development, as well as among states differing in their levels of development. Effectively, a great part of Steuart's considerations on external trade envisages the asymmetric relation between 'industrious' states and primitive people. This situation is not static and may evolve, in the sense that competition among suppliers of manufactured products or advantages somehow gathered by the exporters of natural products may overturn the initial dominance framework. Nonetheless, the basic or initial situation describes asymmetric relations.

Book II, Chapter 5 of *Principles* is specifically addressed to an 'active foreign trade', that is, a trade stimulated by the exporting drive of national merchants in search of new markets. Merchants, the leading characters of this active foreign trade, play a decisive role in Steuart's vision of the commercial system in general. Merchants seek profits and, most of all, they personify money.[7] As trade between producers of manufactures and providers of natural products involves states in different conditions, 'merchants profit at first of the ignorance of their correspondent' (II, 217). Steuart's profits from external trade suggest, at least under these conditions, an asymmetry in values. Effectively, the importer of manufacturing products is in this context denominated a 'not-trading country' (I, 246,248), an expression that suggests the inexistence of systematic production on this side of the exchange relation, and that there's no value equivalence in this exchange. Merchants will profit fixing prices according to the ability to pay off potential buyers, rather than to the cost of commodities, on both sides: Selling manufactured products to primitive states and selling natural products in the advanced states markets.

It's worth noticing that leveling mechanisms, whenever considered, differ from automatic adjustments similar, for instance, to Hume's (1752) specie flow mechanism. Effectively, though personified by merchants, money is hardly mentioned in the passages concerning trade between manufacturers and producers of natural products. Furthermore, the adjustments and departures from the initial situation discussed by Steuart affect both sides of the external trade relation. For instance, traders may feel tempted to reap the extra gains arising from exports to a new market, engaging in a price depressing competition. Or, on the other side, natural products sellers will strive to enhance their sales once they get accustomed to manufactures.

Anyhow, this asymmetric process ends up generating unilateral 'profits', to the benefit of the manufacturing country. In this case, it seems that natural products are not exchanged by their 'real value' – if it is appropriate to use 'real value' as a parameter of this sort of transaction.[8] The situation is not static. Profits may eventually disappear, either by competition among suppliers or by commercial expertise acquired by the 'not-trading country'. In the meantime, however, merchants and the exporting country would have profited from external trade.

Yet, when analyzing the trade among similarly developed European countries, Steuart's approach changes. Under this framework, industry and frugality are assumed to be evenly distributed, a condition that would in principle eliminate the necessity of surveillance by the statesmen: Trade could be left free. Steuart goes as far as pondering that, in the absence of specific advantages, external trade would tend to be extinguished. Nevertheless, in the real world, 'industry and idleness, luxury and frugality, are constantly changing their balance throughout the nations of Europe' (II, 10), so that 'able merchants' and 'able statesmen' will reengage in commerce and profit again. As a sort of last resource alternative, a nation could profit from its engagement in the carrying trade. That is, even trade among 'industrious states' does not eliminate the possibility of getting profits.

Self-correcting mechanisms are not the core of Steuart's analysis. In fact, in his criticism of Hume's quantity theory, Steuart overtly disputes Hume's thesis that there's a natural movement able to correct disequilibrium in balances and in the distribution of wealth among nations; in synthesis, Hume's proposition, 'that wealth may, like a fluid, come to an equilibrium' (II, 424). Indeed, the duty of the statesman is to 'cut off the communication of hurtful trade' (*ibidem*), so that the nation preserve its ability to keep its wealth 'above the level of the surrounding element' (*ibidem*).

Steuart's criterion in examining trade among European countries is the preservation of the 'balance of work and demand', the basic social equilibrium that provides employment and food for the industrious people, preserving the circulation of surplus and access to some superfluity. Success in the export of manufactures may draw population from agriculture, imperiling the production of food. The excess of money may induce an excessive import of luxury goods. For all these reasons, the 'statesman' must keep a 'watchful eye' upon importations, controlling excessive buying of luxury goods and preserving the provision of natural products that may be transformed at home – more precisely, feeding the population (when necessary) or providing raw materials to be transformed by local manufacturers. The ultimate criterion is the discouragement of the import of labour, and the encouragement of the export of labour – a balance of work, or of paid income, akin to Cantillon's (1755) approach to external trade.[9]

For Steuart, external trade's final purpose is the 'preservation of numbers', that is, the multiplication, or at least the maintenance, of the existing population. It is well known that population, as well as the preservation of internal 'work', was at least since Petty assumed as a sign of wealth. Intrinsically Steuartian is the 'balance of work and demand', a social equilibrium that envisages the stimulation of 'industry' and the circulation of surplus from agriculture towards cities, as well as from agricultural workers towards 'free hands'. This mechanism is activated by the demands of urban dwellers, especially those in conditions of consuming superfluous goods.

Even leaving the 'balance of work and demand' aside, there is no doubt that an 'active' foreign trade brings advantages to a country. Steuart's point of departure is neither a theoretical nor a logical examination of the mechanism of external trade. To the contrary, as an empiricist (Skinner 1966), his point of reference is the conflictive reality of competition among the trading European countries of his times. For him, 'the whole system of modern politics is founded upon the basis of an active foreign trade . . . A nation which remains passive in her commerce, is at the mercy of those who are active' (II, 276), unless favoured by natural advantages or by its mines.

Besides, wealth can effectively be drawn from foreign nations. It is this possibility, open to any manufacturing nation, which provides guidelines for the 'statesman'. Even admitting that competition and the many maladjustments to which the 'balance of work and demand' is subject may impel the nation towards a withdrawal into 'inland trade', Steuart clearly holds that drawing wealth from other nations is a proper means for the 'augmentation' of national wealth. In Book IV, in the debate of topics related to money, credit, and balance of payments, Steuart concludes that the acquisition of coin or specie, as a result of a positive 'grand balance',[10] 'adds to the intrinsic value of a country' (III, 217). It is out of the question that metals drawn into the country through external transactions are envisaged as effective national wealth.[11]

Metals are a special element in Steuart's reasoning, and possibly for this reason many critics were prone to consider him a mercantilist. I think one of the reasons for Steuart's emphasis on metals lies on the distinction (and opposition) between consumables and durables. Like many other economists of his time,[12] Steuart emphasizes this opposition. The consumption of a non-durable implied the extinction of its worth, so that, for instance, in the aftermath of an exchange of money for food, one of the traders would extinguish the worth of his commodity, via consumption, whereas the other would keep a durable in his hands. The exchange of consumable commodities, a sort of primitive stage of trade, does not accrue to the state's wealth.[13] Contrariwise,

> so soon as the precious metals became an object of commerce, and when, by being rendered an universal equivalent for every thing, it became also the measure of power between nations, then the acquisition, or at least the preservation of a proportional quantity of it, became, to the more prudent, an object of the last importance.
>
> (I, 433)

This is the reason why foreign trade 'has the effect of drawing wealth from all other nations' (II, 433). These passages add up two components of Steuart's approach to wealth, in its relations to external trade: On one side, and as mentioned, the ancient quest for durables (versus extinguishable matters); on the other side, the perception that international trade implies flows and accumulation of specie. Specie is simultaneously the ultimate durable, and a commodity able to perform crucial functions in external trade.[14]

I will conclude with a note on statesmanship.[15] As we have seen, external trade is not a matter to be left for the account of individual or independent traders only, for several reasons. First, monopolies attributed by the state are in some situations useful and even commendable – for instance, when seeking to avoid competition among suppliers from the same country to reduce the price of commodities exported to primitive nations. Second, even trade among developed countries involves national differences in industriousness, inclination for luxury, natural endowments, etc. Third, provision of food is always a strategic goal, having in view the 'balance of work and demand'. All these matters stress the necessity of an able surveillance by the statesman. Statesmanship is indispensable in both environments, trade confronting manufacturing countries and primitive states, and trade among developed countries. A lyric passage of *Principles* (II, Chapter 12) situates the necessity of statesmanship:

> The trading nations of Europe represent a fleet of ships, every one striving who shall get first to a certain port. The statesman of each is the master. The

same wind blows upon all, and this wind is the principle of self-interest, which engages every consumer to seek the cheapest and the best market. No trade wind can be more general, or more constant than this; the natural advantages of each country represent the degree of goodness of each vessel; but the master who sails the ship with the greater dexterity, and who can lay his rivals under the lee of his sails, will, ceteris paribus, undoubtedly get before them; and maintain his advantage.

(II, 310–311)

Money

The entirety of Steuart's approaches to monetary questions lies on his basic definition of money – 'an arbitrary scale of equal parts, invented for measuring the respective value of things vendible' (II, 270) – and on his insistence on the economic consequences of the 'realization' of money in coins, pieces of metals stamped by the sovereign. The 'realization' confounds the perception of what money effectively is, since people will tend to identify prices with specific metallic pieces of a given denomination, and not with the unit of account. The oscillation of the relative price of gold and silver, and the instability of the value of all metals, submit the monetary systems to additional hazards. Besides, the inexistence of uniformity of pieces under the same stamp (due to wearing and clipping) and debasement imposes further challenges upon national monetary systems.

It is important to stress that, if the consistency and completeness of Steuart's value and price theory is debatable,[16] the several conclusions on relative prices throughout *Principles* go well beyond a price theory strictly. Apart from the dependency upon demand, and from the subtle distinction between 'great' and 'high' demand (Book II, Chapter 2), Steuart's disquisitions on relative prices are connected to his understanding of money, and of the characteristics of metallic monetary systems themselves. In short, prices depend on money and on coining practices, as much as they depend on demand and competition, on different leveling mechanisms – for instance, the reactions in prices of different classes of commodities according to their sensibility to external trade – on specific types of commodities (necessaries or luxury goods) on credit.

Besides, and following a tradition of debates on the relation between 'value of money' and exchange rate that goes back at least to Locke, Steuart's approach encompasses three basic features of national monetary systems: debasement, the heterogeneity of pieces under the same stamp, and coinage rates. The economic literature of the 1700s had already submitted debasement to repeated screening, but Steuart dedicated his strongest efforts to incorporate the heterogeneity of the circulating media and the coinage rates into debates around the exchange rate. Of course, any examination of the connections between Steuart and mercantilism must have in view these monetary topics, that have an effective bearing on the exchange rate, thus on external trade.

In directing his investigation towards the several elements affecting the exchange rate, Steuart fled from an old known economic common sense, according to which the 'exchange' (exchange rate) was determined by the effective weight of the national metallic pieces, and not by their stamp; that is, weight versus weight ultimately establishes the ratio between two different national monetary units. First of all (in Book III, Chapter 7), Steuart tries to explain how is it possible that we arrive at an uniform exchange rate, in spite of the physical heterogeneity of coins under the same stamp. According to him, either the unit of account is also affected by this heterogeneity or the physical state of all coins in circulation makes an imprint on the value of the pound sterling.[17] As far as the exchange rate is sensible to the difference in the state of the real coins, 'Exchange . . . is one of the best measures for valuing a pound sterling, present currency' (II, 331).

The general principle is:

> That in countries where the money-unit is entirely affixed to the coin, the actual value of it is not according to the legal standard of that coin, but according to the means proportion of the actual worth of those currencies in which debts are paid.
>
> (II, 332)

This general principle accounts for two phenomena, the 'realization' of money in coins and the effective material condition of the coins. This sort of correction that the exchange rate imposes on the officially established value of money, leads Steuart to diverge from an epochal common sense, which held that the exchange rate in some circumstances did not reflect the 'real' value of the national currency. Those who propose the exchange rate to be wrong, concludes Steuart, simply take as a parameter the legal table of conversion of coins into units of account, leaving aside the effective state of the coins in circulation, and the fact that the official rate of conversion of coins into the legal standard might misrepresent the market value of gold and silver. In the end, external trade (the exchange rate) corrects the idiosyncrasies of national monetary systems.

So far, Steuart has related the exchange rate to the effective state of the circulating media. Going further, he introduces another variable, the fluctuations of the balance of trade. The basic formula – to take into consideration the average standard of the coins – is valid only under the assumption that the balance of trade oscillates around average values. Indeed, a consistently unfavourable balance of trade elevates the price of bullion, thus affecting the exchange rate. Nonetheless, a deeper approach to the relation between the value of the monetary unit and the price of bullion depends on a further examination of coinage, a crucial issue in England since the country did not directly charge coinage.

Steuart clearly advocates the imposition of a rate on coinage in England, as part of his appreciation of the commercial contest between England and France. In order to substantiate his proposal, he developed further studies on the relation between specie and coin in Part II of Book III of *Principles*.

Steuart's solution is simple: The rate of coinage affects the price of bullion. Commodities, by their turn, follow the price of bullion – in this case, it is commodity versus commodity. Since the rate of coinage raises the price of the coin relatively to bullion, there will be a reduction in the price of all commodities. It is this solution that ultimately reinforces the conception that the stamp, and not the metallic content of the coin, determines the value of money. Steuart qualifies an old dictum, which had Barbon (1690) as his foremost proponent, according to which the value of money is determined by official authority (by stamp), and not by the coin's real metallic content.[18]

By this confront between value of money and value of bullion, Steuart envisages the establishment of the limits to the variation of the price of bullion in order to assess the effects of a possible coinage rate. His conclusion is that the superior boundary would be established by the value of the coin, including coinage, remaining the price of bullion as the inferior boundary. Steuart also warns that once the exchange market is entirely controlled by experienced merchants – in addition, they are confronted to ordinary people ignorant of the subtleties of coinage and exchange rate, – the value of the merchandises does not follow the value of bullion. Value of merchandise and price of bullion may remain apart, which opens new arbitrage opportunities to merchants. To add complexity to the result, Steuart differentiates the effects of frequent balance of trade oscillations and of enduring 'wrong' balances. Enduring 'wrong' balances make people accustomed to prices determined by the high price of bullion, delaying any possible corrective move.

Prices do not react automatically to changing circumstances. As a rule, Steuart does not adhere to the idea of automatic adjustments. A passage reminding the effect of friction on parabolas described by projectiles calls attention to the attachment of prices to the stamp, an inescapable consequence of the 'realization' of money in coins: 'A good gunner must calculate the resistance of the air upon his bomb, or he never will hit the mark' (III, 10).

Steuart's conclusion is coherent: since the price of coinage affects the exchange rate, the 'par of exchange' – an old expression that equates bullion to bullion in different national moneys – is also affected by it, by means of its impacts on the price of bullion. Additionally, prices of commodities transacted in the internal market only are much more attached to the denomination of the coin than prices of commodities connected to external markets that are much more sensible to movements of the exchange rate. What Steuart denominates 'real par of exchange' is thus affected by three factors: The weight of gold or silver in each coin, the state of the balance of trade (which explains the demand for exchange), and coinage. The imposition of a rate on coinage in England would immediately affect the exchange rate, favouring the country's perspectives in external trade, not to mention the positive effects on public revenue. Traditional protective measures, as clogs and duties upon the French trade, are improper, harming a trade that is anyway favourable to England. The elimination of all traditional instruments of protection and the simple establishment of coinage rates, concludes Steuart, would in the end favour the English trade. It is visible that the addition of monetary instruments to the analysis of external trade builds a wall between Steuart's approach and any variant of 'mercantilism'.

Credit

Steuart's meticulous examination of credit, in Book IV, settles several points that had remained open in his analysis of external trade, money, international flows of specie and assets. It is worth reminding that 'credit' is an issue that crosses the whole extension of *Principles*, repeatedly coming to surface in Book II; that is, before a proper treatment of money. There are many reasons for this precocious appearance of credit. To begin with, 'anticipations' are a common trace of Steuart's narrative. Even before receiving a proper treatment, a topic may surface in the form of illustrations, theoretical insights preceding its proper development, indispensable complement to the exposition of another topic. Additionally, Steuart's conception of money and monetary relations pertain to the family of 'credit theories of money' (Schumpeter 1954). Credit relations are envisaged as inherent in trading societies, money naturally arising from them. Thus, credit drifts towards any consideration on trade, exchange, division of labour, and the structure of society. Finally, Steuart is insistent on the possibility of creating money upon land mortgages, or on the openness of land property to liquefaction. This matter, that was in debate at least since the mid-17th century (Potter 1650), and that had received a full treatment in Law's proposals on land banking (Law 1705), was by Steuart associated to the 'balance of wealth', *Principles of Political Economy's* framework involving the distribution of assets and social positions across the social spectrum. The 'balance of wealth' would be especially affected by the possibility of liquefying solid property, once this operation, on the one hand, conferred the agrarian elites the possibility of anticipating revenues, thus favouring expenditure in luxury goods; on the other hand, could ultimately impose the transfer of land from idle indebted landlords to industrious owners, a favourable move well suited to a thriving economy.

But what is somehow surprising, and certainly important in Steuart's presentation of credit in Book IV, is the combination of a sophisticated approach to the rate of interest with the old established dictum that metals are 'true wealth'. In other words, there are many evidences that Steuart combines his advanced perception of a credit economy with a reiterated insistence on the special role of metals. For instance, in Chapter 7 (Book IV), a bold conclusion is added to an unpretentious comment on the extinction of an operation of credit: 'This realization is commonly made in the metals; because they are the money of the world; they are the real and true riches, as much as land' (III, 176). Metals and land as 'true riches' is consistent with Steuart's preoccupation with 'liquefying' solid property, being also entirely connected to his perception of international credit, as it will be seen. Yet, metals as 'money of the world' – in contrast to the national currencies – was a simple international trade fact. To what extent it can be assumed that the admission of metals as 'real and true riches' – a sort of common sense shared among others by Petty (1899) – indicates adhesion to mercantilism is a question to be developed later.

Anyway, external credit would provide Steuart a new angle to the examination of the ebbs and flows of riches into and from a country. Now, international lending and borrowing complement exports and imports of commodities as a source of metals and riches. Credits against external debtors, due to their capacity of dragging money (in the form of interest) from another country, are in this context seen as elements of power and potential access to foreign riches.

Additionally, and given the dependence of foreign lending on the rate of interest, a decrease in the national rate of interest inhibits external lending into the country, at the same time enticing national lenders to send their money abroad.[19] Steuart asks if a country could 'enrich' by means of borrowing, to conclude (III, 178–179) that lending to foreigners and paying off external creditors are operations that counterbalance each other, being associated to the level of the interest rates. It's worth noticing that the unveiling of the importance of external credit and its basic mechanisms adds another element to the generic 'balance of trade', until then taken as responsible for attracting or repealing metals into and from the country. Indeed, Steuart is acknowledged (Viner 1937; Schumpeter 1954) as the first economist to consolidate under the denomination 'balance of payments' – or 'grand balance' – the totality of flows that have an impact on a country's ability to attract or dispatch specie abroad.

The rate of interest and the banking activities also play a crucial role in the establishment of internal monetary equilibrium and disequilibrium, all its implications upon economic activity implied. Persistent balance of trade deficits lead those who have a liability abroad to drain their deposits in order to pay what is due. Banks are in the end 'obliged to make good in coin' (III, 216) any payment to be made to foreigners. Since the national paper money does not fulfill any role in external transactions, external obligations in the end create an extra demand for coin. It is in this precise context that Steuart denominates notes 'money of the society' and coin 'money of the world' (II, 216).[20] Within this framework, payments abroad are connected to the possibility of contracting internal circulation, with the subsequent risk of retracting economic activity and imperiling the banks.[21] In this situation, in moments of unexpected contractions of the circulating media, assisting the banks becomes a 'national concern'. Losses would either raise the exchange rate (raising prices) or raise the interest rate, both consequences to be paid out of the 'solid property of the country'.

According to Steuart, metal 'adds to the intrinsic value of a country, as much as if a portion of territory were added to it' (II, 217). 'Symbolical money', contrariwise, does not add to the wealth of a country, but 'provides a fund of circulation out of solid property' (II, 217). Nations unable to settle their 'grand balance' with coins melt down solid property in order to pay their debts. In other words, credit may temporarily fulfill the role of metals, which implies the transfer of interests to foreigners. Steuart's synthesis is:

> either the grand balance must be paid out of the national stock of coin, or it must be furnished by foreigners upon a loan from them; the interest of which must be paid out of that part of the solid property of the nation which has been melt down into paper.
>
> (II, 219)

The melting down of solid property, a possibility opened by lending upon land mortgages, ultimately connects international lending to (national) property. Knowing that external trade would not even exist in the absence of international credit, Steuart connects solid property to international lending and to the subsequent flows of resources, and of specie. In the presence of credit, the indebted country pays either in coin or in solid property, and in both cases the operation is intermediated by banks. Whenever coins are unavailable solid property must step in. In either situation banks are the intermediaries, which explains the possibility of draining internal circulation by means of external loans. In the end, the possibility of substituting land for metals (via credit), and vice-versa, or of liquefying solid property by means of credit, enhances the range of credit and its role of provider of circulating media but at the same time places national territories – by means of loans – at the mercy of foreigners. Steuart's understanding of the implications of credit, and of the meaning of a credit economy, associates metals to other forms of national wealth, and at the same time stresses the special role of specie in an economy open to international trade.

Despite the full acknowledgement of the role of international finances, Steuart admits that the main use of money is internal.[22] His advice, against those who fear the consequences of having to settle international compromises, is appeasing: 'If the country owes a balance to other nations, let it be paid' (II, 291). The advice, a corollary of Steuart's belief in the immense dimensions of internal activities, is expressed by a sentence that could not be more alien to the spirit of mercantilism: 'What a trifle is a foreign balance, let it be ever so great, compared with the whole alienation of the country' (II, 291).

To complement, it is interesting to observe that despite Steuart's confidence in the much greater importance of internal trade he insists on the importance of skipping the permanent attempts, by exchange merchants, to corner the nation and the national businessmen when the balance of payments is in dire conditions. An additional argument in favour of the imposition of a rate on coinage lies in its capacity of imposing an extra charge on the activities of arbitragers. In the end, Steuart concludes, precious metals are a minor part of the national circulating media; let them be sent away in order to settle balances but let us not facilitate the activities of money dealers.

Conclusion

In the review of the possible interfaces between Steuart and mercantilism, we went from Steuart's innumerous and apparently naïve or outdated references to the 'statesman' to his sophisticated approach to credit and balance of payments, with its many implications upon monetary policy. References and appeals to the 'statesman', abundant in Books II and III of *Principles*, are less frequent in Book IV. It seems that the ubiquitous presence of the 'balance of work and demand' and of the 'balance of wealth' in Books II and III stimulated Steuart's inducements to social order, as well as his appeals to the character – the 'statesman' – responsible for the preservation of social stability, as well as for assuring the nation's independence and competitiveness in a world characterized by permanent inter-nation strife. It is interesting to note that it is less likely to identify recurrences to the statesman in Steuart's reiterated arguing in favour of the imposition of a rate on coinage in England.

In what refers to specie, Steuart's advanced understanding of balance of payments, all its components and monetary dimensions accounted for, do not dismiss the importance of metals and coins in monetary systems in general, and in international transactions specifically. That is, the broad understanding of the role of credit, as well as the admittance of several forms of 'symbolical money', do not efface – on the contrary, they enhance – the practical and even symbolical presence of metals and coins in Steuart's system. As seen, even being aligned with the political economy old motto that identifies wealth with commodities in general, Steuart in many passages individualizes metals as riches, not to mention the role of specie in settling balance of payments unbalances. Three possible reasons for this emphasis on metals will be addressed.

The first reason respects Steuart's methodology. As known (Kobayashi 1999; Urquhart 1999; Skinner 1965), although Steuart aims in *Principles* at 'a clear deduction of principles', applications are utilized 'in order to avoid abstraction as much as possible' (I, 5–6).[23] In short, principles must be confirmed by examples, a major reason for the abundance of illustrations. The possibility of dismissing general principles, simply because they have not been ratified by true facts, is real. The necessary confront with reality explains why the crucial understanding of money as 'money of account' does not efface the consequences of the 'realization' of money in metals, which brings to the fore all hazards of metallic pieces – debasement, oscillations in value, effects of coinage. Monetary upheavals, such as scarcity of metallic circulating media, over-speculation with specie, not to mention the troubles brought about by the utilization of two metals (gold and silver) in coinage, were trivial in England and abroad. To the extent that precious metals were universally accepted as means of exchange and store of riches, and that in some circumstances determinate coins were singled out as units of account within the boundaries of specific national monetary systems it was simply impossible to evade the hazards inherent to the 'realization' of money in metals.

Second, the international monetary and trade system operated under the aegis of gold. As Steuart said, gold was 'international money': It could to a certain extent be replaced by paper money in internal trade, but it kept its status as the only international reserve, as well as the universal denominator to settle accounts among trading countries. Additionally, and as Steuart emphasizes, specific coins were in some circumstances utilized as units of account. In short, the role of precious metals in monetary systems based on metals, most of all in systems subject to international trade, is unique. We must be careful in order not to confound the acknowledgement of this irreplaceable role of precious metals with 'mercantilism'.

The third reason to connect metals to wealth lies on the insistence on some elements that were part of the many economic policy platforms sustained by Steuart. A typical case was the imposition of a rate on coinage in England; another, the correct angle to assess (and to determine) the exchange rate and its role in external trade. In what refers to the rate of coinage, Steuart brings a very sophisticated explanation of the possible impacts, once England, adhering to the continental pattern, imposed a specific rate to its mint activities. In Steuart's view, by the absence of a coinage rate, England was losing some opportunities in trade, not to mention the loss of a straightforward public revenue instrument. In order to reaffirm his argument, Steuart was led to emphasize the distinction between coin – a monetary device – and bullion – a commodity – and its implications upon the exchange rate, thus upon external trade. Moreover, the assessment of the impacts of the coinage rate on the price of bullion required the full application of Steuart's perception of how the price system operated; especially the consequences of the 'realization' of money in coins upon prices.

I think that the clear differentiation between coin and bullion is one of the distinguishing marks of Steuart's contribution. Of course, many predecessors had already differentiated coin from bullion,[24] but the fact that, in metallic systems, money relies on metal, has many times blurred the distinction between money and metal, a distinction always evident for Steuart. If we add to this distinction another specificity of metallic systems, the coexistence of a national unit of account, and a range of coins with specific stamps,[25] which implies the establishment of numerical relations between material money (coins of specific stamps) and the unit of account, it will become clear that Steuart's effort in stressing 'unit of account' in distinguishing unit of account from coin and in averting the hazards imposed by the 'realization' of money in coins, goes well beyond any approach to money and monetary systems before his. Needless to say, Steuart's vision of the monetary system remains leagues ahead those of the emblematic 'mercantilists', such as Mun, Malynes, and Misselden. More impressive is that it is far superior to contemporaneous contributions, such as, for instance, Harris's superb *Money and Coins* (Harris 1757–58).

The fact that Steuart applied his monetary theory achievements to the assessment of how the exchange rate was effectively determined can be seen as another distinction between his and many other contributions to debates on external trade, 'mercantilist' or non-mercantilist. As mentioned, the epochal common sense was that 'bullion to bullion' was the ultimate criterion to determine the exchange rate. Steuart defended the thesis that factors other than the bullion content of the coin (and its correspondence in units of account) had an incidence upon the exchange rate, which led him to diverge from those who either considered the actual exchange rate as the ultimate sign of the state of external trade, or, the other way around, credited the exchange rate for the dire state of external trade. The coinage rate was, again, part of Steuart's approach, which also included the distinction between permanent or transitory balance of payment states (deficits or surpluses) and the price mechanisms peculiar to different sorts of commodities. It must be reminded that Steuart's 'grand balance' included non-commodity flows, which imposes a consideration on the effects of external lending. Ultimately, and once Steuart's treatment of the exchange rate implies commodities and non-commodities, his considerations on external trade intertwine with credit, interest rates, and external lending. Which, by means of his defence of land banking, and of his appreciation of the 'liquefaction of solid property', points at a possible emulsion of the monetary aspects of a mercantile economy with its social and economic background, involving trade, social structure, and manufacturers versus agriculture.

Of course, it always remains that Steuart attributed to metals a special status, defended external trade policies supposedly favourable to the nation – at least, favourable to the 'industrious' states – and insisted on the duties of the 'statesman'. Irrespective of the various meanings attributed to 'mercantilism', and even to 'mercantilist policies', it seems that the simple alignment of Steuart's system or of his policy prescriptions to the mercantile creed evades the sophistication of his monetary economics, which, as we see, has a definite bearing on his approach to external relations.

Notes

1 'On a dit que Smith avait de grandes obligations à Steuart qu'il n'a pas cité une seule fois, même pour le combattre. Je ne vois pas em quoi consistent ces obligations. Il a conçu son sujet bien autrement que Steuart; . . . Steuart a soutenu um système déjà embrassé par Colbert'(Say 1814: 1).

2 On profits from external trade, see Section 2.

3 *The Economics of Sir James Steuart* (Sen 1957) is a path breaking reappraisal of Steuart's contributions to economic theory as well.

4 See for instance Viner (1937).

5 Magnusson (1994) emphasizes the impropriety of considering Steuart a disciple of the 'mercantile system'.

6 'When principles are well understood, the real consequences of burdensome institutions are clearly seen; when the purposes they are intended for are not obtained, the abuse of the stateman's administrations appears palpable' (I, 5).

7 'The Merchant here represents the Money, by substituting credit in its place, and as the Money was invented to facilitate barter, so the Merchant, with his credit, is a new refinement upon the use of Money' (I, 239). Marx remarks on this passage in his *Grundrisse*.

8 On prices and 'real value' in Steuart, see Marx (1863), Johnson (1937), Hutchison (1988). Johnson argues that in the analysis of external trade Steuart abandoned his general price theory.

9 'The matter exported from a country, is what the country loses, the price of the labour exported, is what it gains' (II, 2). On the balance of labour in Steuart, see Viner (1937).

10 The 'grand balance' is the general balance of foreign payments, including merchandise and transfers associated to external loans.

11 Magnusson (1994) thinks differently, based on Steuart's warning on the difference between the specie gathered by a positive balance of trade and national wealth.

12 Including Smith. From the distinction between productive and unproductive labour: 'But the labour of the manufacturer fixes and realizes itself in some particular subject or vendible commodity, which lasts for some time at least after that labour is past' (Smith: II, 330).

13 'Consumption then was equal on both sides; and no balance was found upon either' (II,433).

14 Marx (1857–58) associates Steuart and the mercantile system in this precise connection: As soon as precious metals become an object of trade and a universal equivalent, they become a measure of power among nations.

15 A thorough appreciation of Steuart's 'statesman' is in Eltis (1995).

16 Hutchison (1988): 'Real value' includes cost of production and profit. Simultaneously, prices and profits are dependent upon demand. Marx (1863): Price comprises real value and profit upon alienation, which means, price exceeds real value.

17 'There are as many different pounds Sterling as there are guineas of different weights' (PPE,II,330).

18 In the English debates on debasement and value of money in the 1690s, Barbon (1696) confronted Locke, holding that the stamp determined the value of money. Locke (1696) held that the value of money depended on the metallic content of the coin.

19 In the English debates concerning the establishment of a legal ceiling to the interest rate, Locke (1691) was already attentive to the possibility that low rates of interest inhibited external lending into the country.

20 Smith (1776) denominates coin 'international money'.

21 A 'Keynesian' contraction of economic activity in Steuart, by means of shortage of money (and reduction of lending) is a point stressed by Sen (1957) and Vickers (1959).

22 'To keep accounts clear . . . within the country' (III, 290).

23 'Every supposition must be considered as strictly relative to the circumstances presupposed'(I, 7).

24 For instance, Barbon (1696), Locke (1696), and Harris (1757–58).

25 'Ideal money' versus 'real money', as reminded by Galiani (1751).

Bibliography

Aspromourgos, T. (1996), *On the Origins of Classical Economics: Distribution and Value from William Petty to Adam Smith*, London: Routledge.

Barbon, N. (1690), *A Reprint of Economic Tracts: Nicholas Barbon on a Discourse of Trade*, Baltimore: The Lord Baltimore Press, 1905.

———. (1696), Discourse Concerning Coining the New Money Lighter: Answer to Mr. Lock's Considerations about Raising the Value of Money, in L. Magnusson, *Mercantilism*, London: Routledge, 1996.

Bowley, M. (1963), *Studies in the History of Economic Theory before 1870*, London: Macmillan, 1973.

Cantillon, R. (1755), *Essay on the Nature of Trade in General*, Indianapolis: Liberty Fund, 2015.

Coutinho, M. & Supryniak, C.E. (2017), Steuart, Smith, and the 'System of Commerce': International Trade and Monetary Theory in Late-18th Century British Political Economy, Toronto: *History of Economics Conference*.

Eltis, W. (1995), Sir James Steuart's Corporate State, in *Collected Works of James Steuart*, vol. 7, London: Routledge & Thoemmes Press.

Galiani, F. (1751), *On money: a translation of Della moneta*, Chicago, University of Chicago, 1977.

Grampp, W.D. (1993), An Appreciation of Mercantilism, in L. Magnusson (ed.), *Mercantilist Economics*, Boston: Kluwer: 59–86.

Harris, J. (1757–1758), *An Essay upon Money and Coins*, London: Hawkins.

Heckscher, E. (1935), *Mercantilism*, London: Allen & Unwin.

Hume, D. (1752), Of Money, in D. Hume (ed.), *Essays, Moral, Political and Literary*, Indianapolis: Liberty Fund, 1985.

Hutchison, T. (1988), *Before Adam Smith: The Emergence of Political Economy, 1662–1776*, Oxford: Basil Blackwell.

Ingram, J.K. (1888), *A History of Political Economy*, Cambridge: Cambridge University Press, 2013.

Johnson, E.A.J. (1937), *Before Adam Smith: The Growth of British Economic Thought*, New York: Prentice-Hall.

Kobayashi, N. (1999), On the Method of Sir James Steuart's Principles of Political OEconomy, in R. Tortajada (ed.), *The Economics of James Steuart*, London: Routledge: 102–120.

Law, J. (1705), Money and Trade Considered with a Proposal for Supplying the Nation with Money, in A. Murphy (ed.), *Monetary Theory: 1601–1758*, Routledge: London, 1997.
Locke, J. (1691), *Some Considerations of the Consequences of the Lowering of Interest, and Raising the Value of Money*, London: Rivington, 1824.
———. (1696), *Further Considerations Concerning Raising the Value of Money*, London: Rivington, 1824.
Magnusson, L. (1994), *Mercantilism: The Shaping of an Economic Language*, London: Routledge.
Marx, K. (1857), *Grundrisse*, London: Penguin Books, 1973.
———. (1863), *Theories of Surplus Value*, Amherst: Prometeus Books, 2000.
Petty, W. (1899), *The Economics Writings of Sir William Petty Together with the Observations Upon the Bills of Mortality, vol. 1*, Cambridge: Cambridge University Press.
Potter, W. (1650), The Key of Wealth, in A. Murphy (ed.), *Monetary Theory: 1601–1758*, London: Routledge, 1997.
Rae, J. (1895), *Life of Adam Smith*, London: Macmillan.
Roll, E. (1938), *A History of Economic Thought*, New York: Prentice-Hall, 1942.
Say, J.-B. (1814), *Traité d'Économie Politique*, Paris: Antoine-Augustin Renouard.
Schumpeter, J.A. (1954), *History of Economic Analysis*, London: Allen & Unwin, 1986.
Sen, S.R. (1957), *The Economics of Sir James Steuart*, Cambridge: Harvard University Press.
Skinner, A. (1965), Economics and the Problem of Method: An Eighteenth Century View, *Scottish Journal of Political Economy*, 12(3): 167–180.
———. (1966), Analytical Sketch, in A. Skinner (ed.), *An Inquiry into the Principles of Political Economy*, Edinburgh: Oliver Boyd.
———. (1991), Sir James Steuart: Economics and Politics, in M. Blaug (ed.), *David Hume (1711–1776) and James Steuart (1712–1780)*, Aldershot: Edward Elgar, 1991.
Smith, A. (1776), *An Inquiry into the Nature and Causes of the Wealth of Nations*, Indianapolis: Liberty Fund, 1981.
Urquhart, R. (1999), Steuart's Method: Aristotelian Political Economy, in R. Tortajada (ed.), *The Economics of James Steuart*, London: Routledge: 121–136.
Vickers, D. (1959), *Studies in the Theory of Money, 1690–1776*, Philadelphia: Chilton Company.
Viner, J. (1937), *Studies in the Theory of International Trade*. New York: Harper.

14 Steuart, Hegel, Chamley

A case upon the nature of 'influence'

Gilles Campagnolo

> At the time when Hegel's political economy is born, there is no other example that a full-fledged economic system may have been built outside the Classical orthodoxy without falling into utopia; in line with its own times, Hegel's economic doctrine is still surprising with its clarity and openness.
>
> (Chamley 1963: 54; our translation)

Introduction

One methodological reminder is in order in beginning this chapter: In the history of economic thought, like in other fields, the notion of 'influence' is a rather slippery notion. Many Hegel scholars have sought out 'influences' that had been exerted upon 'their' philosopher. It can safely be argued that it was much less often the case though when it concerned economics. That being granted, however, one should ask about many influences, whether one either strictly confines oneself within philosophy or attempts at bridging fields, in this case between philosophy and economics. Paul Chamley surely did when relating Sir James Steuart and Hegel. We intend to discuss his views and his results, so we should also abide by the terms of the research thus undertaken: 'influence' remains a fragile concept and depends on which evidence can be delivered. How this is about Steuart is the theme of the present chapter. Indeed, the Scotsman himself got influenced as he notably visited Germany. He stayed in Tübingen for its famous university. One wonders whether Steuart actually encountered German Cameralists during his stay, what he read from earlier writers, like so-called 'Imperialist Cameralists' (Becher, Hörnigk and Schröder) or *jus naturalis* authors (like Justi and Sonnenfels). Can this influence be sourced?[1]

In the case of Hegel, some views can fortunately be clearly traced down. His library helps. It was catalogued by Seebeck (1832) and there are also biographies that may serve as pieces of evidence. To begin with his first biographer Karl Rosenkranz (1844) despite unfortunate gaps. Now, can we point at some 'triangular' relationship between Hegel's early endeavours in economics, the German version of Steuart's *Principles* and other influences, namely British incipient political economy and/or German older Cameralism? It is tempting to think Steuart *influenced* directly Hegel: This is Chamley's view. A more realist stand might be that both Hegel and Steuart found similar views in earlier elements (like those provided by Cameralist literature) for them to elaborate in their own way – while Hegel also found more material in economists coming after Steuart. This would explain that Hegel and Steuart partly shared some perspective – while *caveats* about the notion of 'influence' and the importance of common German sources are tracks to consider and welcome carefully and cautiously.

Hegel's journey in the Bernese Alps

From July 25 to 31, 1796, Hegel, then working as a private tutor for the aristocracy in Bern, took a mountain hike in the neighbouring Alps. His diary shows that the grand scenery left him unmoved. After contemplating 'the two famous glaciers at Grindelwald', he wrote:

> Their view offers nothing of interest. One may call this *a new way of sightseeing*, yet *one that provides nothing new for to the mind*. . . . We just passed by this mountain on the right hand-side: indeed nothing extraordinary in it, only a rocky cliff and we had already seen more than enough of that for the day.
>
> (Hegel 1796: 56–57; our translation)

The remaining days of Hegel's journey were in keeping with this remark. He deliberately neglected what Kant had called the 'sentiment of the sublime'[2] and would rather pay attention to the local activities of men and women living on those desolate premises. Hegel travelled from Thoune to Altdorg via the *Jungfrau* and the Uri, a land of glaciers. Yet he enjoyed neither tourism nor alpinism.[3] With regard to the Rousseau-like pre-Romantic feel pervasive to his times, this would concern a milder landscape and not the severe highlands and strenuous climbing that Hegel went through. The aesthetic approach that Albrecht von Haller had sung in his poetic narrative *Gedicht* (1732) did not obtain there.[4] Nature was neither charming nor generous when seen in real life of these higher mountain dwellers. Hegel witnessed them. His diary tells of his boredom in front of nature[5] and of his interest in the strenuous fight for survival by locals; having reached a desolate place, where nothing grew but sparse lichens and nothing blossoms but gentian plants, he saw them deprived as they actually were and depicts their condition, endowed only with a few goods:

> This family picks up roots that they burn to produce 'gentian' alcohol. The whole family lives here during summer, without any contact with the rest of mankind: they have built a distillery under granite blocks that nature unintendedly dumped in great numbers in a tower-like shape: the human beings were able to use this incidental position of things. I doubt indeed that even the most credulous theologian would dare assign to a set plan by nature any intentional goal for the utility of men in these mountains. . . . Poor dwellers are never guaranteed in the least their miserable work done by his own hands, hut and a miserable stable, shall not be destroyed overnight.
>
> (Hegel 1796/1988: 76; our translation)

In this desolate place, Hegel discovered two themes he would recall in further works:

1 Nature was *not* created for Man, whatever theologians may say. No Providence from divine source intervenes to help. On the contrary, human beings must abstract from nature the little they can use for a living.
2 In the heart of Europe, at the end of the 18th century, this fight for survival remains a sheer reality. The urge to develop the economy is obviously a duty and any delusion about some past 'Golden age' of 'life in the wild' is a ridiculous tale.

In his theological writings, Hegel already stated in full some 'socio-economic' aspects related to the Ancient world and it is clear he had never espoused the 'Golden Age' myth. What he saw confirmed his views and these ideas from his alpine journey would remain until his last works, for instance his *Elements of the Philosophy of Right* (1821) as well as passages on 'objective spirit' in the *Encyclopedia.* The few hand notes he wrote in his diary heralded early interest in economic themes that he would always maintain. Yet were discussing gentian alcohol distillery, making cheese and marmot meat already 'economic' ideas? Hegel indeed touched upon a theoretical topic: How do prices get fixed, even (seemingly) *out* of economic circulation?[6] Thus he recollected:

> A cowherd offered us to drink milk-cream and the boy let us decide how much we would be willing to pay for it. . . . These cowherds hope they will receive more than the value of their merchandise. [Hegel imagined testing the boy:] Let you give less than what they esteem to be the value for their good and one can rest well assured that they will immediately leave out any hesitation they may have displayed beforehand as to the value of their good, and ask for the price.
> (Hegel 1796/1988: 53–54; our translation)

Now, what is *this* price? Hegel was on the verge to ask. This important issue in economic analysis can be summed up as follows: how can anyone, out of the usual supply chains of a good, estimates its price? This cannot possibly be the fruit of one's own personal wonderings. Conversely it implies some preexisting network of trade relationships.[7]

Later on, as Hegel began studying economics for good, the query would reappear: in his reading of Sir James Steuart's *Inquiry into the Principles of Political Oeconomy*, Hegel would make his first step into economic *theorizing*. That happened when he transferred from Bern to Frankfurt/Main. In any case, although quite brief, his alpine hike displayed his budding interest for the necessities of life. Hegel was back to real life matters in a concrete way, his wish, as he wrote in a letter to his friend and fellow philosopher Schelling (with which we shall conclude this chapter).

Hegel realized that the use of scarce resources was key to economic thinking. Toil and misery of most of the people (especially poor mountain dwellers) were serious concerns and one puts aside divine Providence *ad hoc* explanations, one should study 'economic' doctrines.

In the following part, we show Hegel read Sir James Steuart's *Principles* in Frankfurt. Hegel then left for Jena, and later Nuremberg and Berlin. There, he read Adam Smith and David Ricardo. He would also mention Jean-Baptiste Say: We assess this influence in later sections of this chapter, with a qualified comparison of some economic and philosophical notions. We conclude by asking whether a 'Hegelian system of political economy' indeed ever existed as such – and, if so, whether it could have been inspired by Steuart or rather by other sources.

Hegel reads Steuart in Frankfurt/Main

In Frankfurt, Hegel was not yet a tenured *Gymnasium* professor (he would become so in Nuremberg a few years later). He was again a private tutor, experiencing hardships of a salaried life – though in wealthy families. We just saw that he had already abandoned any belief in Providence regarding economic matters. He started reading Steuart's *Inquiry* there, in the German translation published between 1769 and 1772.[8] His path into economic literature would later lead him to other authors, but this was a seminal start for major traits of understanding in economics. Chamley provided some sound evidence for this in Chamley (1963). We shall ask again whether Hegel would come into possession of a 'System' in this field like the system that represents the apex of German Idealism.

Yet, at this early stage, Hegel had none of that. He reached Frankfurt in January 1797. One may see his interest in economics indeed as a first attempt to build a system of 'objective spirit' in its own right. Chamley thinks so – see the sentence we put as an epigraph. Later on, this would only be one facet of the Hegelian doctrine, embedded into an enlarged 'objective spirit'. In any case, it plays a significant role and became essential to later thinkers like Marx. This encounter (philosophy *and* economics) was a milestone in Modernity – this is our view. This aspect is crucial because Hegel was naturally already aware of the 'economics' of the ancients, whether in Aristotle's *Politics* (Book I) or Xenophon – it is unclear whether Hegel knew of the three apocryphal Aristotelian books of *Economics* (and not yet known as apocryphal until the beginning of the 20th century).

In any case, ancient literature must be taken into account, while Chamley blatantly thought only of 'economics' dating from the 18th century on. Hegel had written about economic matters in theological texts as well, debating Ancient Hebraic law as well as the tragic loss of freedom in the 'beautiful totality' *(schöne Totalität)* of the Greek *polis* subdued by Romans. Imperial Rome fell in turn, due to the rise of Christian faith that impacted socioeconomic life and slave behaviour. In Bern, Hegel read the work by Gibbon on Roman decadence. He reflected upon this world history during his *Stift* seminary years in Tübingen, where he discussed it with Hölderlin.

In Bern and in Frankfurt, both friends eventually worked as private tutors.[9] Frankfurt was a whole new world: First, it was a city so different from both the seminar schooling and the society of aristocrats and peasants in Bern. Frankfurt was thriving with trade and economic life. There, plutocrats went alongside workers, tradesmen of all sorts of business, and banks and fairs were regularly held (two *Messe* per year). Those impacted well beyond southwest German provinces. Goods carried on the Main (for instance, wines of the Rhine and Moselle valleys), products both of local and of remote parts, manufactured goods from incipient factories and the *Verlags* system (home-spinning industry). This plenty marvels the observer: Another dweller, Goethe, a native from the city, indeed bore witness.

> The town where I was born enjoyed a very specific position, one that remains insufficiently noticed to this day, . . . One may observe in Frankfurt-am-Main a specific complex life where all get entangled: trade, personal movable property, realty and household wealth as well, with a taste for knowledge and to build up collections of products and objects.
>
> (Goethe 1811–1833/1941: 455–456; our translation)[10]

Hegel saw the trade going on and even lived a mundane life, as his letters show.[11] Rosenkranz pointed in his biography this change 'from an aristocratic patriarchate in Bern [to] a city of trade and the merchants' plutocracy [*Geldaristokratie*]' (Rosenkranz 1844: 85; our translation). Even more, French Hegel scholar Bernard Bourgeois writes:

> The realm of private life, where one lives according to this religion of love which Christ realized (as Hegel discovered in Frankfurt), is essentially a realm of private *properties* whose interconnection makes up the *bourgeois* civil society as it develops. Now, it is precisely during his stay in Frankfurt than Hegel took the time to dive into the study of political economy.
>
> (Bourgeois 1970: 31; our translation)

Bourgeois adds that 'in Frankfurt, young Hegel became a man' (Bourgeois 1970: 30). Hegel's philosophy changed indeed: he turned his early notion of reflection into an act of thought beyond mere understanding *(Verstand)* and found the identity between the rational (dictated by *Vernunft)* and the really effective. This new stand included worldly maters: Hegel left Kant aside and engaged, beyond criticism, into inserting 'reason within history' (he put together these words as soon as 1797). Reason emerges from within life that includes economic life. Once Providence and the theologians' casuistry are set aside (because they always come *ad hoc*), then it is still necessary to explain phenomena: This is how Hegel met the study of political economy and next the role of reading Steuart.

The idea to ground knowledge of economic life in rational life was a starter. Surely, Hegel would later quote less of Steuart than other economists (including Smith, Ricardo and Say in his 1821 *Elements of the Philosophy of Right*), but the issue is whether in 1797, his first experience of a doctrine of the experience of material life was based on the book by Sir James Steuart. And this might well be the case to some extent that we aim to determine. To that effect, let us consider as many elements as are available. Steuart's text was published in 1767 first in

London (a revised Scottish edition is dated 1770). Archives show that the first German translation (1769–1772 version) was found in Hegel's library. Not so much through what Chamley found (although he explored the archives of Steuart for the French public with their listing; see Chamley 1965), but with the catalogue of Hegel's books done by Seebeck in Berlin. Hegel owned 1606 volumes. His copy of the translation of Steuart's *Inquiry* surely dates back to his life in Frankfurt, given the date of publication and, above all, the following testimony:

> All ideas by Hegel on the essential nature of civil society, about the needs and labor, about the division thereof and the distribution of wealth between estates [*Stände*], about the poor and the police, about taxes, etc. all finally found their way into a commentary that he wrote about the German translation of the book of political economy written by Steuart. The commentary he must have written between February 19 and May 16, 1799 and *it is still now* [in 1844, when Rosenkranz writes] *in its entirety*. One can find there the greatest viewpoints about politics and history, with remarks fully appropriate.
>
> (Rosenkranz 1844: 86; our translation and our emphasis).

Rosenkranz probably had the commentary in hands since he speaks about it 'in its entirety', probably a notebook, to judge by the German word *Heft* following the whole of Steuart's *Principles*. This was probably a lengthy text since, in contradistinction with the alpine diary, Rosenkranz did unfortunately not edit it as an annex to his *Hegels Leben*. Because of that and the fact that the commentary was unfortunately lost afterwards, we lack those precious hints – probably forever, given the amount of work by specialists on the remaining papers by Hegel. However, this is how Hegel stepped into the science of political economy. Rosenkranz goes on calling Steuart a 'mercantilist' and we shall come back on that later. Now one should also take Rosenkranz' views with caution as he delivered his own interpretations, which may be arguable – like the following:

> Steuart was still a proponent of the Mercantilist system. With noble feelings and through an abundance of interesting examples, Hegel fought what he thought was indeed dead in this doctrine, while he made all endeavors to rescue the soul [*Gemüt*] of men, amidst the trials and tribulations of competition and of mechanization, in the world of labor as in trade.
>
> (Rosenkranz 1844: 86; our translation)

Steuart has often been called a 'late mercantilist' by historians, just like Rosenkranz does here. Yet this calls into question the relationship between the Scotsman and the notion of a 'mercantile system' in German-language provinces: did Steuart meet Cameralists while he sojourned in Tübingen? Texts by Steuart remain almost mute about his trip, so this issue cannot be settled easily. A personal encounter between Steuart and some representative of Cameralism was possible. But scholars lack factual evidence and material again – which remains a fact even if some among them consider their intuitive insights are strong enough to make bold claims in that regard (Skinner 1993; Redman & Starbatty 1993).

According to Rosenkranz, Hegel dedicated his attention to Steuart at a detailed and critical level 'with an abundance of interesting examples', probably taken from topics related to 'modern' economic life. Rosenkranz was closest to the source, trust is in order. Yet caution should prevail as shows the fact that Rosenkranz bases his judgment of Steuart solely on the arguable assessment of him being a mercantilist.[12] In any case, the ultimate evidence will still be lacking as the commentary disappeared. What Rosenkranz gives cannot be fully satisfactory. As a consequence, only inner textual evidence can set the higher or lesser plausible level of 'influence'. Comparing texts is required. Chamley conscientiously attempted it[13] in a minute undertaking, although he was perhaps sometimes somewhat too assertive:

> It was enough to put side by side the *Inquiry* [by Steuart] . . . and the System, in its completed form, by Hegel – if ever it reached such a completed form – to make obvious stand out close correspondence between the two.
>
> (Chamley 1963: 123; our translation)

One may point that some criteria that Chamley applied in his 1963 book may estrange today's scholars (Ege 1999). In putting side by side texts in the original, Chamley certainly paid much attention in the various sections he listed, like the 'elements and perspective in economic activities', the 'forms of the production process', 'needs' and 'value', and so on (Chamley 1963). Chamley chose to quote Steuart in the German version that Hegel used (Chamley's comments and narrative are otherwise in French).[14] Using the original in English may have been useful since the translation was arguably bad. But Hegel depended on the *German* translation so that key notions, when translated, could convey a (sometimes slightly, sometimes largely) different meaning. The first translation he used, published in Hamburg by Dr Büsch was, for instance, later heavily criticized by Marx for lacking in quality.[15]

A parenthesis: A few caveats

Besides translation issues regarding Steuart's *Principles* into German, a few caveats are in order regarding the Steuart-Hegel relationship based on Chamley's works as well as Marx (which we shall purposely limit to his observations on Steuart's translation) and also Cameralism. The non-specialist reader may skip them. We shall in any case keep them short. The expert reader may yet want to bear these in mind to avoid hasty objections, as well as the fact that we purposefully cut those while they perhaps raise too many questions to be dealt with in this chapter.

Besides the issue of the quality of the translation that Hegel could use, the risk is to extrapolate too far from Chamley's comparative literal analysis when putting side by side the texts, even in good faith. Moreover, we recalled in the Foreword how delicate it is to trace 'influence'. Even for Hegel to have Steuart's *Inquiry* in his library could neither suffice to prove that he read it all through, nor to what extent this reading was influential, although one may admit that Rosenkranz's testimony should set aside doubts. It should be granted that Hegel paid much attention to the book, and Rosenkranz insists on Hegel using examples and so on. Qualms about the extent of the influence should also be quieted. However Rosenkranz' vagueness unavoidably carries indetermination and frustration. But it seems reasonable to think Hegel actually debated the contents for himself. That he built from there a whole system of political economy could however be excessive – this is Chamley, once again the passage we chose as an epigraph to this chapter.

It is more helpful to note with many Hegel scholars that the interest taken in the objective spirit throughout Hegel's works marks a turning point in Modern philosophy: the mundane 'objective spirit' matters as much as metaphysical contents. Hence the heritage that followed from his Idealist systematic body of knowledge. What Steuart and Smith did was to form a body of positive knowledge that was distinct – as well as built against the background of British (sometimes sentimental) philosophy of sensualism (Hume, Shaftesbury, and Hutcheson) and liberal political philosophy (Locke, Hume).[16] In Germany, there was a different background; 'German Mercantilism' or 'Cameralism' thus requires debate as such since its notions were reworked by the German historicists somehow in opposition to the classics – but not to Steuart. So there is much in retrospect to take into account about 'Hegelian economics' at the moment when the *Inquiry* by Steuart came in a German translation.

If one compares how the works by Steuart and Smith penetrated Germany, the original *Principles* published by both authors were nine years apart in England (even six years apart if one counts the Scottish edition by Steuart of 1770). The time spanned much longer for translations: 1769–1772 for Steuart's five volumes and only 1794–1796 for Smith to be translated by Garve. Steuart's influence came earlier and until Smith caught all the attention and overshadowed him, Steuart was more influential, especially when Hegel got interested into economics. Hegel acquired later his translation of Smith, which he quoted in Jena as manuscript marginalia show in his *Realsystem* (1800–1802). Hence, Hegel found his way into political economy through Steuart.

Those were Hegel's first thoughts on a *doctrine* of political economy. When he later developed in the *Realsystem*, as well as his long essay on natural law (*Naturrecht*), Hegel gave weight to views developed when the reading of Steuart prevailed (Bourgeois 1972). Now, was Steuart himself conversely indebted to some German influence acquired during his stay a couple of decades before? Would those impregnate his views once back to Scotland? This is difficult to assess as well: Commentators are mute because Steuart himself was mute. The context was clearly of a both deep and partly variable movement of ideas, what is often labelled as 'mercantilism'. To describe this notion, which was born when it was put forth by hostile parties (to begin with Smith coining the word in the last chapters of his *Inquiry*), is always difficult. Similarly, it is often said that *Kameral-wissenschaften* (Cameral sciences) or Cameralism, are its 'German form': What does this say, though, besides excessively simplifying the issue? For 'mercantilism' not to be a 'catch-all' term, loaded with polemical intent, one must go beyond the pejorative service to fight precursors and opponents.

With very different writers being called 'mercantilists', could both Hegel and Steuart be seen as part of the movement? In some parts their views may look as if they inherited them, but sometimes they have rather little to do with that at all. It is thus questionable to unite all under one term, which may in the end be illegitimate.

However, this default comes as a convenient feature in one way at least for the historian of economic thought: It reminds us how later reconstructions function. Mostly in the 19th century (and into the 20th century), the so-called German Historical School labelled this 'Cameralism' as they sought to ground a tradition of German economics.[17] But German 'historicists' themselves were less of a formal group than a range of disciples with variants, relating to scholars Wilhelm Roscher and Gustav von Schmoller with criticisms of Classical political economy (Campagnolo 2010). Main themes like law, monetary issues, and the treasure of the Prince bring the issue of German 'Cameralism' as a case for lawyers and financiers rather than contributions to what was later labeled 'economics'.

One more case that is relevant, especially when taking into account the 'Preface' to the 1821 *Principles of the Philosophy of Right* and Hegel's contemporaries is that where the notion of *Volksgeist* emerged (and Hegel used it indeed), one should take it into account, even while pieces of evidence like commentaries on economics as such are clearly missing, that part of the German tradition is that perpetuated by the German Romanticists. One may think of Adam Mueller, who targeted Smith (Meyer 2009). One may also see Hegel's interest in the rational within economics, or the understanding aspect (*das Verständliches*) within its incipient science, as one more argument of the rational nature of knowledge and a rebuttal of Müllerian romanticism.[18] In the end, caution should prevail together with attention. Thus we shall explore how Hegel would later stress Smith or Ricardo over Steuart or German Cameralism. The following part discusses convergences and limits.

Philosophical notions between Hegel and Steuart: Convergences and limits

The caveats set forth in the previous section were necessary before examining texts. Otherwise, Hegel's views in the light of Steuart's notions may be cause to assess a reading where one puts one's own perspective forth. More than translation issues (however important), the role notions/concepts (*Begriffe*) play in Hegel remains key: Hegel had to distinguish between rationality and understanding to elaborate on his concept of reason. As he considered them uniformly, he increasingly felt that view was insufficient to reach the philosophy he sought. In Frankfurt, Hegel started talking about 'unconceivable concepts' (*unbegriffliche Begriffe*). He called for a 'religion of love to mend any scission, to make actually real freedom and happiness together' (Bourgeois 1970: 31; our translation). Concrete life, when based on love for universal values (an ideal abstraction to realize) would not suffice to fill claims such as those now including private property and self-love matters. In Jena, Hegel discovered this wish for freedom would account for full acceptance of the 'rational' (*die Vernunft*) and effectively real (*die Wirklichkeit*). From there, Hegel actualized ideas from his readings in Frankfurt, including his readings in political economy: Thus the material life of the people is a matter of public administration, private possession, and philosophical thought. While Chamley assesses mere continuity in Hegel's views, his strong conviction needs qualification:[19]

> From the beginning, in his [Hegel's] System, one may merge in one whole set all materials contained in his various works, provided that one would indicate doing so and . . . provide the original context of the various elements, as well as which peculiar point was modified, from one stage of the System to another stage.
>
> (Chamley 1963: 14–16; our translation)

Chamley confesses that he simply assumed unity and continuity in Hegel's philosophy (Chamley 1963), while it would be necessary to check various stages in the building of the philosophy of right. Now, Ilting (1973) did exactly that and traced all writings on the topic. The conclusion is that Chamley was insightful but that it was a bet on his part more than the result of his analysis by putting side by side excerpts by Hegel and Steuart. It is here impossible to detail all and why Chamley is convincing in the end on that point but extrapolates much too much on the influence by Steuart on Hegel. Yet we shall identify a few notions philosophical and economic that illustrate the common notional frame.

Trade and the exchange of goods and services are the engine of civilization. Trade and the exchange of goods and services are motivated by desire, or appetite to use Steuart's wording. The individual in modern society is determined by 'possessive individualism'.[20] This explains economic growth in Steuart and Hegel as well. The German word *Begierde* translates the Steuartian word (see the German translation, 1767/1770: 253 and *passim*). This very word is key in Hegelian philosophy: *Begierde* moves consciousness from its first rising, from the level of animal appetite satisfaction towards each next developed stage of consciousness. This path is described in Hegel's *Phenomenology of Spirit* (1807).

Appetite needs satisfaction and satisfying needs (*Bedürfnisbefriedigen* in German) is what individuals seek. Consciousness rises from mere animal appetite satisfaction,[21] to the stage where production and trade dominate. In the long run, the collective level reached is the economy as human beings have turned mere things (*Dinge*) into goods (*Güter*) and wares for trade (*Waare* [*sic*]). The open field to consumption at individual level rises at a par with self-consciousness (*Selbstbewußtsein*).[22] *Begierde* appears as the engine of economic activity, production and consumption. Even as mere consumption gets exhausted within its actualization, the spirit lead by *Furcht, Arbeit*, and *Bildung* leads to another stage of individual freedom (Hegel labels it the 'stoic mind' upon the model of Epictetes). Steuart is quite far from such considerations. Chamley does not discuss in detail that dialectics but tends to bring these notions close as illustrations of actual social relationships. Bearing caveats in mind, let us say that analysis in terms of social class within civil society is undue whereas some commentators (to begin with Hegel's own disciples!) did not refrain from it. Do notions Hegel found in Steuart apply here? Can individual desire tend to discipline itself brings stability?

> The need for food and clothing, the necessity of renouncing raw food and of making it fit to eat and destroying its natural immediacy, means that the human being's life is less comfortable than that of the animal – as indeed it ought to be, since man is a spiritual being. The understanding, which can grasp distinctions, brings multiplicity into these needs; and since taste and utility become criteria of judgement, the needs themselves are also affected by them. In the end, it is no longer need but opinion which has to be satisfied, and it is a distinctive feature of education that it resolves the concrete into its particulars.
>
> (Hegel 1821/2003: §190, 229)

In turn, the process of objective 'ethical life' ultimately pushes a zealous industry: 'When the activity of civil society is unrestricted, it is occupied internally with expanding its population and industry' (Hegel 1821/2003: §243, 266).

'Industry' firstly means activity, toil by the particular individual rather than the industrial machinery, but it finally encompasses the whole population as such. However, a most necessary input is still absent in Hegel's texts: that is *capital* (the word appears only twice in the 1821 *Elements* and with a general non-technical meaning of wealth). Steuart does not regard it either as Marx would, later on. Steuart discussed 'finance' in a society organized around a 'treasure', like the Cameralists did, whereas the notion of technical capital needs a more solid basis – which it finds in classical political economy.

Labor was already present in changing *Furcht* into *Bildung* in the 'master and slave' confrontation (Campagnolo 2009). But for *industry*, Steuart and Hegel clearly speak the same language – as Chamley stresses, to point to the zealous activities of producers (still mostly craftsmen; the move towards an 'Industrial revolution' was only incipient in German territories). But it is a sharp rise in products and in needs that feeds a loop that pushes the 'industry and ingenuity of fabricants who, each and every day, invent trough assiduous reflection the means to remedy or eliminate the defects [of already existing goods]' (Steuart 1767/1770: 23; our translation from the German version of Steuart text that Hegel used).

Once again, it is too simple to assimilate Steuart with loosely defined 'mercantilism'. This partly disregards detailed analysis of notions like appetite and industry (rather than capital and labour) and makes too general an argument. Now, was Hegel in his way 'filtering' Steuart's notions for speculative depiction of the progress of individual consciousness (*Phenomenology of Spirit*) or the collective (*Elements of the Philosophy of Right*)?

The 'System' probably incorporated these notions while he did not explicitly take them from Steuart's treatise. Steuart surely raised Hegel's awareness of 'civil society' *[bürgerliche Gesellschaft]*, but the story of agents having mutual needs and cooperating for their own sake and satisfaction through production and trade is a more general theme and one dear to the Scottish Enlightenment as a whole.

Besides Steuart, Adam Ferguson, for instance, used this notion, and Hegel might have known about it (like Marx) (Waszek 1988).

At the level of the 'objective spirit', where Hegel situates 'ethical life' (*Sittlichkeit*),[23] the stress by Steuart about the statesman is another key notion. It seems that it translates as the 'administration' (*Verwaltung*) forming *from within* economic life, through legal arrangements (commercial courts, for instance) and the 'police' (meaning public services and facilities). There is more to economic life than mere safekeeping of law and order and elements keen to Cameralists, mercantilists, or Steuart, while rather foreign to Smith and Ricardo appear part of the Hegelian scheme. This comes from the fact that Steuart's *Inquiry* leads from industry in the economic city life to the statesman.

Hegel calls that special character the 'Prince'. His importance among institutions provides an eminent role (Bourgeois 1979). Both Hegel and Steuart display various factors of economics related to political life, converging in stately or princely rules. In his philosophy of right, Hegel structures this into what he called a 'universal class' (civil servants of all kinds) that helps governing the multitude. Indeed, Steuart's statesman plays a role that is large enough to cover what Hegel considers the task fulfilled by a whole class, or rather Hegel needs a whole class to fulfill tasks that are considered as the statesman's role by Steuart. The character of the 'Prince' as a human being thus may come in Hegel just as the final decision maker when decisions are fruits of a larger body of counsellors acting in the name of universal interest within society. Such a Prince is devoid of arbitrariness because the final decision bears no self-interest. This is distinctive of Hegel's Prince with respect to the Cameralists' concern about *actual* princes. In the case of Steuart, some ambiguity remains but insofar as the statesman acts for his people, it is like in Hegel a keystone to hold together the whole structure of society (or 'ethical life' in Hegel's jargon). Maybe overdoing it, Chamley stresses that Hegel reached such understanding of the 'universal class' in reading Steuart's depiction, and he provides lengthy quotes in that perspective (Chamley 1963: *passim*).

In any case, Hegel was aware of Steuart's statesman as the dutiful agent who guarantees 'sustainable welfare' (I, 109). In German, the word *Wohlfahrt* is repeated and one notes that it is part of Hegel's view on institutions. It is less heralding a future 'welfare state' as it is recalling former Cameralistic concerns. Steuart stated that 'connecting all private interests is precisely what public welfare realizes – and only the Statesman may be judge thereof' (I, 6–7).

Primacy of that statesman in Steuart is thus paralleled in Hegel by the need for civil society to find a completeness it does not bear in itself. But the Hegelian state results from a dialectical process of suppressing/keeping the earlier stage (*Aufhebung*) where there is nothing like that in Steuart, for whom governments merely happen to exist in any case where societies grow. The Hegelian state must come in any case together with the system of needs, police and corporation, all 'reconciled':

> Indeed conditions of private property and bourgeois civil society are insuperable at their level – that is to say at the level of economic life. This fact in

> turn becomes conditional by the fact that they are both subordinate at another level, which is the level of political life in the rational State where the individual finds one's truly effective 'home to call one's own'. This is the truly real infinite and one cannot find in the undefined mechanisms of the economy.
> (Bourgeois 1979: 121; our translation)

The statesman is probably what Hegel and Steuart have most in common. This is where comparison of texts shows them closest, in line with Chamley's analysis. Moreover, Hegel never changed his view on this, from his early writings to the late philosophy of right. Economic growth has a dialectical basis and the objective spirit of 'ethical life' gets realized in institutions with a class of civil servants and a princely authority. The latter guarantees universal values (beware, national – this is a *Volksgeit*).[24] Now the body of law and finance literature (originated in the Cameralist literature in the German context) influenced Hegel not only already in the city of trade and fairs, but (as his correspondence shows) along the years. Steuart's statesman is another call for regulation from an institution, seen from a positive basis (Steuart) or a speculative mind (Hegel): These ideas go at a par.[25]

Cameralists on the one hand, classics on the other hand, point to paths taken by Hegel to understand economics at a theoretical level, besides his reading of Steuart. Where Hegel Steuart share common views, may those other sources display them as well? It is essential to search for the sources of Hegel's economic knowledge. Biographers listed these sources and among the 1606 volumes listed by Seebeck, one may point to the following: An English edition of the 1776 *Wealth of Nations* reprinted in Basel in 1791 (by the same publisher who reedited the English original text by Steuart, which competed with the German translation 20 years earlier), somehow faulty in various respects as already noted; a French translation of *The Principles of Political Oeconomy and Taxation* by Ricardo (first version published in Paris, 1819, hence without the chapter on machinery Ricardo added in the 1821 third edition – incidentally, the year Hegel published his *Elements of the Philosophy of Right*); the *Traité d'économie politique* by Jean-Baptiste Say (third edition in Paris, 1827); and a copy of the *Traité d'économie politique* by Destutt de Tracy (the leader of French so-called '*Idéologues*', volume published in Paris in 1823).

One point to stress as well is that one may have to consider hidden sources, as French historian of philosophy Jacques d'Hondt said in his *Hegel secret* (1968). Indeed Hegel had to face censorship in Prussia. He may have kept his views concealed. D. Losurdo (2001) and G. A. Magee (2001) take a similar stand, with variants in their analysis (Magee (2008) consequently modified his own work). A hermetic Hegelian tradition exists. Yet it remains unclear what to do with it: is it reasonable to discard what Hegel himself published to favour pieces where evidence may be missing, for the reason he would have applied self-censorship? Some suggestions, even based upon some evidence, cannot allow to discard more received traditions. Surely, pressure on scholars in Hegel's times should not be underestimated: Modern-style universities were built by a state as an instrument for national power and scholars otherwise constrained to private tutorship had no leverage. But to what extent can we know precisely?

There are also hints missing as to open sources: How do we know whether Hegel read the *De Aerario* by Besold or the *De Contributionibus* by Kaspar Klock, or the *Secreta Politica* by Obrecht? This is still a track for research – as Campagnolo (2010) hinted (Schefold 2010):

> In his presentation of the historical school, Campagnolo starts not from List but from the philosophers Fichte and Hegel, the latter having studied both classical economics and Cameralism in its developed form (also Steuart). . . . The heirs of the historical school in Germany were to develop the concept of economic style in order to characterize the co-evolution of social and economic forms on the one hand, mental dispositions – the spirit of the peoples – on the other hand. Kaspar Klock among the Cameralists went a long way in his *De Aerario*, written during the Thirty Years War, to carry out such a program. . . . If Campagnolo is right, the organicism of the historical school was due more to the common recollection of the cameralist ideal.
>
> (Schefold 2010: xxii–xxiii)

From the catalogue of Hegel's library, it is hard to derive to what extent Hegel had a clear knowledge of *ars mercatoria*. He was clearly more versed in *ars gubernandi*. This keen interest shows in constitutional matters from *Die Verfassung Deutschlands* (*The Constitution of Germany* 1800–1802) to 1817 comments on Baden-Württemberg and his 1830 essay on the English Bill of Reform, written in Berlin and partly censored (also self-censorship). Hegel would not appear as playing a part in the Cameralist tradition *per se*, yet he illustrated a pivotal moment when this tradition of 'regional' politics met new British political economy, when works by Steuart and Smith got imported in German territories.

What we see his works illustrate in this moment, like when considering Steuart's journey and readings in Tübingen is that we would be more at ease if we only had more material so as to build upon it. But, in this absence, in both cases, what we may plausibly come up with is that common notions did originate in a *Zeitgeist* that both writers rationalized in their own way, and that is probably a safer bet than to insist upon finding some direct influence of *ars mercatoria* on them.

Their training, especially for Hegel, was distinct from the body of works written by merchants or courtiers on policies (Schiera 1968) that only ultimately relate to what we call *economics*.[26]

While some traits of *Kameralismus* concur with Steuart's views, they can be seen as complements to Hegel's opinions. The *Kameral* category indeed existed as a label (for university chairs), authors in the field hardly consciously felt like 'one body', but perhaps for nationalistic pan-German traits. It is rather 19th-century German scholars who gathered predecessors under one and the same denomination.[27] In turn, Chamley was the more simplistic in calling Steuart a 'mercantilist' as his own results qualify this statement! And Chamley forgets to account for national ideals that played a role in economics like in politics.

Conversely, economists tended apparently to ignore the speculative philosophical framing whereas in reality their perspective was all embedded in it;

19th-century German historicists held on to a historical view that owed to Hegel's philosophy of history. And problems surge from there, hence some caveats we mentioned earlier.

Let us provide here only one example that is common to Steuart and Hegel: how distinction between medieval guilds (*Zünfte*) and the modern concept of corporations *(Korporationen)* is a relevant token of modernity. Earlier Cameralism still held on the former, while 19th-century economists debated the latter. This heritage significantly brought a major divergence that finds an explanation in Steuart's *Principles* as well as in Hegel's *Philosophy of Right*. The civil society evolves from a traditional system of craftsmanship (keeping traditions but blocking innovation and entrepreneurship) to the rise of modern corporations (together with unions, trade markets, etc.). Hegel's writings from Berlin (1830–1831) demonstrate that he favoured free competition and entrepreneurship (*Gewerbefreiheit*) (Campagnolo 2012), while safeguarding a notion of corporations adapted to it and rejecting ancient guilds. This is distinctive, since Smithian economics are centrally about welfare in the sense of both better primary need commodities (food, clothing, housing, etc.) and more ability to care for the vulnerable, provide public goods. In one word, Smith is vehemently anti-corporation and anti-guild, while Steuart is closer to a past from which Hegel detaches himself.

Both convergences and divergences count. The awareness of economic life in Hegel pervades economic theory on the notion of scarcity of resources; for instance, neither Steuart, nor Smith, nor Hegel resorts any longer to Providence as professed by the Physiocrats.[28] Now, Hegel was informed by his experience in the Alps and refuses to explain agriculture by the work of God, but this is still far from a theory of surplus extracted from land, or from a theory of *rent*. This holds in some way for all economists until Ricardo brought a supplement thought:

> Nothing is more common than to hear of the advantages which the land possesses over every other source of useful produce, on account of the surplus which it yields in the form of rent. Yet when land is most abundant, when most productive, and most fertile, it yields no rent; and it is only when its powers decay, and less is yielded in return for labor that a share of the original produce of the more fertile portions is set apart for rent. It is singular that this quality in the land, which should have been noticed as an imperfection, compared with the natural agents by which manufacturers are assisted, should have been pointed out at constituting its peculiar pre-eminence.
>
> (Ricardo 1821: 98)

This is just one example. Yet it shows well that where there seemed to be limits met in the analysis by Steuart or Smith, and naturally earlier Cameralist, mercantilist, and Physiocratic views, Hegel was pushed towards the political economy that emerged, not as philosophy but as a science of agents' interactions. Hegel recognized a new kind of knowledge in that incipient science and turned to Smith and Ricardo. His *marginalia* handwritten notes say 'Smith' in *Jenenser Realphilosophie*

(1805–1806/1932: 239 and *passim*) and add Ricardo and Say in his 1821 *Elements* as Seebeck's library catalogue shows. Hegel would no longer quote Steuart and rather refer to Smith, Ricardo, and Say, even where his understanding was still pervaded by his first reading of Steuart. Our judgment here is based upon the idea that parallels (as treated earlier) is a better support for how 'pervasive' Steuart's 'influence' was than Chamley's insights taken from merely putting excerpts side by side cunningly cut from texts. We argue here that the notion of influence has to be understood carefully, but not put aside – because it cannot be put aside altogether anyway. The issue remains to which extent a 'Hegelian system of political economy' exists as such. We shall now discuss this issue in some depth.

A 'Hegelian system of political economy'?

Chamley selected excerpts of interest based on his first assessment of the thesis that there surely exists a solid 'system of political economy' by Hegel. He assumed it rather than he found it as a result of his comparative study. But the main point is that one cannot derive a Hegelian economic system from the systematically speculative ground and, we shall argue, even less a 'Hegelian economic policy'. Hegel was neither Marx . . . nor Keynes.[29] Once this is proven against the commentator, converging views stop short of defining the positive orientation Chamley wished for. The Hegel-Steuart connection resembles more a rationalization of traditional German old-hat Cameralism mixed with Steuartian views, with an acute awareness of the movement of the incipient science of political economy, though.

> Political economy is the science which begins with the above viewpoints but must go on to explain mass relationships and mass movements in their qualitative and quantitative determinacy and complexity. – This is one of the sciences which have originated in the modem age as their element [*Boden*]. The development of science is of interest in showing how thought extracts from the endless multitude of details with which it is initially confronted the simple principles of the thing [*Sache*], the understanding which works within it and controls it (see Smith, Say, and Ricardo).
>
> (Hegel 1821/1991: §189, 227)

One may hesitate again upon the nature of the influence here. Still, even after Chamley did his comparative work, the insights he put forth remain insufficient to counter most Hegel scholars for whom there never was any economic theory *proprio dictu* in Hegel. Conversely, it is true that these scholars (for instance, bourgeois) could have dedicated more attention to economics as such, even where they rightly situate Hegel's institutionalism as a plea for 'institutions of liberty' (Kervégan 1998). In the speculative frame that encompasses the 'objective spirit', economics is one sphere of ethical life. To make a direct positive use, though, one has to 'deconstruct' the system, so to speak. Once piecemeal and/or outside their original frame, Hegelian economics can be put to use, yet within another frame: Marx gave an example of that in building his own version. It may even be best to do so, argues Rosenzweig:

> That that exists as some being understood as such in Hegel then fell into the History wherefrom it was born originally. Then History, once again, melted it into something that lives through a ceaseless unfolding process. Hegel's doctrine of natural right, taken as a whole, impacted the Hegelian school, but not real life. Conversely, life realized the unity of a thought that was split into many pieces, so that life can arrange these splitters into something entirely new.
>
> (Rosenzweig 1920: 379; our translation)

However, so-called 'German Idealism', especially in Hegelian form, never features a merely mechanistic device. One hears too often that mistaken opinion and dialectics cannot 'materialize' without putting speculation aside, with major loss as a consequence. The speculative moves a fully spiritual development of consciousness through the subjective, the objective, and the absolute spirit (*Geist*). It is impossible to reduce Hegel's views to positive creeds or, to use it as a materialistic stand, one must 'turn it upside down' as Marx intended to. But by acting so, one does not only lose the vantage point of the System *per se*, but deprives oneself of notions that justified *Vernunft* rationality, thus creating a gap that needs filling with another body of knowledge.

As pointed to earlier when discussing the dialectics of 'master and slave', Hegel depicted how a conscious spirit made to work produced the goods for consumption process for a master-self not his/her own. Labour is a key element in a process of *Bildung*. The necessity to choose between various accounts of key notions in economics thus surges from positive theories rather from their rational justification. Would Hegel take elements from notions in the *Wealth of Nations*? The Hegelian Prince remains closely associated with the Steuartian *Statesman* and far from a Smithian oriented image of the state (even more from the liberal famous Manchesterian 'night-watchman'). The role devolved for authority and free trade are fundamentally unified at the level of the rational process of civil society according to Hegel. But they differ in Steuart, Smith, and Ricardo. So Hegel found inspiration in them all but adopted his own perspective, while not building a unified economic view. To recall Chamley again, a striking convergence surges from the fact that the statesman (Steuart) would rather translate as the 'universal class of civil servants' than merely the 'Prince' because the range of tasks that are expected from 'the Prince' bears more concerns than any single character may handle.

> One may wonder what meaning to give to his character, the *Statesman*. Steuart clearly assessed it as a simplified view, without any direct relationship to an effectively existing constitutional regime. Yet that simplistic view looks strange, if not contradictory: in a book pervaded with such a sense of historical relativism, how can an abstract figure play the essential role?
>
> (Chamley 1963: 79, our translation)

In other terms, Hegel somehow heralded the sort of bureaucracy that later sociologists Werner Sombart and Max Weber would develop in considering advanced capitalism (*Hochkapitalismus*). Was it the case with Steuart? One may doubt it. In any case, both Steuart and Hegel came much before the time. Capitalism that Hegel knew was incipient (even in Frankfurt). Whereas Steuart probably influenced Hegel, *ars gubernandi* literature was probably a deeper source in Hegel's *Verfassung Deutschlands* and other texts on modernizing Baden-Württemberg. After his stay in Frankfurt, Hegel never quoted Steuart again.

One may pursue concerning the character of the statesman, which consists rather in articulating *ars gubernandi* to *ars mercatoria* in a 'Cameralist' perspective. A parallel source of inspiration seems more convincing again. Would both *artes* converge or develop in parallel? There is convergence in Steuart and Hegel as to institutionalist views – in that sense Chamley was right, at least besides the readings of Smith and Ricardo by Hegel. Hegel pits forth a princely figure, nourishes for Prussia some 'elective affinity', so to speak. That sets Hegel aside from his Scottish/British inspirers – or, like Marx said, in a 'German ideology'. This couple Hegelian Prince/Steuartian statesman is thus one key notion, but there are others.

In principle, within civil society, each and every individual is first and foremost guided by his/her own interest. Smith called it 'self-love' in *Wealth of Nations* after setting 'sympathy' as a functional device in his 1759 *Theory of Moral Sentiments*. Sympathy may be interpreted as operating as a function when guessing what another agent expects in return for some good or service, but the 1759 volume does not present things in that way, while, as is well-known, a famous quote in the *Wealth of Nations* describes how it is not from 'benevolence' that one may expect what one needs. This conundrum (how sympathy and self-love may relate) has probably been regarded as one of the most apparent paradoxes in economics and in Smith,[30] yet it was overcome from the start in the dialectical doctrine at the very essence of Hegel's 'system of needs' (*System der Bedürfnisse*). Hegel pointed out the irrelevance of 'well-meaning souls' ('*belles âmes*' in French). Effectiveness (*Wirklichkeit*) in the satisfaction of needs (*Bedürfnisbefriedigung*) is the key to human laws of exchange through production, trade and consumption of goods and services. In civil society, especially at the level of the satisfaction of needs, self-interest (or self-love, 'selfishness') is as unavoidable a methodological device as sympathy for (or understanding of) the partner obviously is. This is not a 'moralistic' viewpoint, it is a necessity, just like the notion of desire, appetite (*Begierde*) comes without moral judgment, and just as the work of dialectics in a philosophical approach of the phenomena of material life needs an engine, that helps derive views from individual tastes to collective interactions.

The growth of wealth on the one hand goes at a par with increasing poverty and misery, on the other hand, states Hegel ([1821/2013]: §195: 362). He stressed this since his *System der Sittlichkeit* (*System of ethical life*, 1800). He pointed to how unsatisfied desire creates a feeling of misery that duplicates in the mind the factual situation of poverty: A feeling of *misery* adds to sheer poverty. It resonates deep and turns mobs to resentment (*plebs* in Latin, *Pöbel* in German); the people (the proletariate in Marx) may form ideals and endorse humanitarian ideals while the

Pöbel restricted to mere survival seek any means for this purpose, losing dignity together with any means to live. Mobs differ from the people (*Volk*) as the underprivileged increasingly feel bad in society, while more wealth and plenty flows in.[31]

It is also true of economic life that boundless desire is the destiny (and the doom) of modern mankind (Hegel 1821/2013: §244, 404–405). There can thus exist an 'idea of luxury' that parallels the 'idea of misery' on the other end of the spectrum of wealth and that results from a dialectic of desire (Berry 1994). Entrepreneurship illustrates their notion both in Hegel and in the classical authors, while Steuart is not as expressive on that facet. It has to do with *freedom* to undertake and do business. As German historian of economics Bertram Schefold stresses: 'Hegel observes that the freedom of enterprise and state initiative combine in Germany' (Schefold 2010: xxii).

This is in accordance with Hegel's late writings in Berlin.[32] Hegel argues less from a moral stand (the *Moralität* section in the 1821 *Elements*) than upon the basis of the logical process within civil society. One finds close passages in Steuart's *Inquiry* as Chamley shows, but Hegel adds a systematized ethical life (*das sittliche Leben*) where entrepreneurial spirits play a role. Here one may debate whether Smith did borrow some views from Steuart: Chamley surely quotes his French translator:

> In his quite rightly famous volume *Wealth of Nations*, M. Smith himself combined in his first three books all that our author [*i.e.* Steuart] says on the very same topics, yet without giving them as much depth.
>
> (Chamley 1963: 79, n. 26; our translation)[33]

Does this explain traits that one could see Hegel sharing views with both Steuart and Smith? Hegel explains things at a general level of universality. He encounters classical political economists who sought 'laws' while arguably Steuart only defined 'situations' in context: The interest for laws about the rent, profit and wages, origins and how their levels are fixed directed Hegel towards Ricardo and later political economy. Steuartian views looked outdated in the 1820s, as alternative readings had swept the field of what aimed at being recognized a science at a par with natural sciences. Hegel acknowledged that claim:

> The sun and the planets also have their laws, but they are unaware of them. Barbarians are governed by drives, customs, and feelings, but they have no consciousness of these. When right is posited and known, all the contingencies of feeling and opinion and the forms of revenge, compassion, and selfishness fall away, so that right only then attains its true determinacy and is duly honoured.
>
> (Hegel 1821/1991: §211 Addition: 243)

Naturwissenschaften and *Geisteswissenschaften*: This is how Hegel regarded incipient political economy through an analogy with the system of planets.[34] In paralleling *Naturphilosophie* and economics, Hegel drew the latter towards some new approach of social sciences. There are even elements of an incipient epistemology, albeit it is safer to avoid extrapolating. Hegel sought a body of knowledge fitting his intention to get back to the life of the people. This fulfilled the promise he had made to himself in a letter to Schelling as early as 1800:

> In my scientific upbringing, which started with the subordinate needs of man, I was inevitably drawn to Science and the ideal of my youth inevitably had to become a kind of reflection and at the same time to mutate into a System. Indeed, I do wonder which way I will find to come back to interfere and connect with the concrete life of men.
>
> (letter to Schelling, November 2, 1800; Hegel 1969: I, 59; our translation)

Conclusion

In 1821, the fame of Smith had long outshined that of Steuart in Scotland and in Germany as well. Ricardo published the extended version of his *Principles of Political Economy and Taxation* (with the famous chapter on machinery) and Hegel's *Elements of the Philosophy of Right* was out. Hegel scholars probably rightly stress the influence of classical political economists was the most critical. But it appeared in Hegel's works that more attention was needed and Chamley called it upon Steuart by acknowledging Hegel's early readings. It is a pity that the commentary where Hegel displayed his budding interest in economic doctrine is missing.

Anyhow, Chamley rightly called for attention and assessed clearly Steuart's influence, even though he may have probably overdone it, starting from an excess of confidence. One may finally infer three stages in Hegel's economic matters:

- In Bern, Hegel formed in-depth interest for human material/economic life, beyond earlier studies in theology.
- In Frankfurt, Hegel read Steuart and received the initial push from mere interest to awareness of the need for a scientific basis for matters of economic life.
- In Jena and later on, in Berlin he explored the incipient science of classical political economy.

Thus, whereas it is true that Steuart had first raised Hegel's interest for a doctrine of political economy, Hegel had found later doctrines more palatable to a scientific approach. If Smith had copied some ideas by Steuart, this would still come as a title of glory to Steuart. And clearly Steuart influenced Hegel's incipient systematization of the 'objective spirit'.

Given the background of the times and its *Zeitgeist*, so to speak, the missing link between these authors in German context should be discussed more with keeping in mind the spirit inherited from the former body of literature called 'German Cameralism'. Both Steuart and Hegel extoled it in their own way, albeit it was later quite forgotten in view of the sweeping newer import of classical political economy. This may have been what Chamley sought, the cement that held together views otherwise formulated in parallel terms by Hegel and, before him and influencing him to some extent, by Steuart. A common relationship to the already existing tradition of older German Cameralism is where more specialists should indeed dig in.

Notes

1 Another question is how the Seminar (*Stift*) (where Hegel stayed with Hölderlin in the 1790s) related to the university. One may wonder Steuart's whereabouts and the atmosphere of those times – see Quentin Skinner (1993) and the latest German edition of Steuart's *Principles* (ed. B. Schefold 1993a).

2 In his *Observations on the Beautiful and Sublime* (*Beobachtungen über das Gefühl des Schönen und Erhabenen)*, Kant noted 'a mountain-range displays its snowclad summits above the clouds . . . we find therein a sort of pleasure mixed with terror. To be able to perceive in all its strength such an impressive view, one must have a sentiment of the sublime. . . . Whatever explicitly sublime there is in it will move one to a stir' (Kant 1764; our translation).

3 Those were then burgeoning activities among a newly wealthy leisure class, often British travellers with a strong appetite for the discovery of new landscapes beyond the traditional cultural 'Italy tour'.

4 Rousseau gave a mellow depiction of mid-mountain landscape in his epoch-making novel *La Nouvelle Héloïse*. Eighteenth century aesthetics depicted nature, like hero character Saint-Preux did, through the lens of artistic benevolence. This pervaded the 49 strophes of the poem by Haller (1732).

5 'The view of these massive rocky blocks forever deprived of life raised inside of me nothing, but the idea of their being so tedious, that it turned in the end into sheer boredom: "*so it is*"' (Hegel 1796; our translation).

6 The analysis of the circulation of goods (in monetary terms) is a major theme of Enlightenment economics (like in Cantillon, Mirabeau, and Quesnay), works apparently *not* known to Hegel.

7 One finds a similar story in *Collective Memory* by French sociologist Maurice Halbwachs (1950), who recalled economist François Simiand meeting a shepherd offering milk to travellers-by. The shepherd pretended *not* to know how much to ask for this, saying: 'Well, Sir, gi'me what it'd cost you down there in the city'. In reality, Hegel's cowherd and Simiand's shepherd know only too well that selling prices are never determined *in abstracto* (nor by an amount of incorporated labour to the good) but by what *buyers* are ready to pay for it. None is so isolated (from trade, even at such a petty scale) that they would not know this economic fact. Conversely, if the traveller is in such a need that he/she would pay much more, they would probably not object being paid *more*.

8 See the German title in references: The volume was published as a series of booklets first in Hamburg (1769–1770) then in Tübingen (1769–1772) listing: *Erstes Buch: Von der Vermehrung der Einwohner und dem Ackerbau* (1769); *Zweites Buch: Von der Handlung und Industrie* (1770); *Drittes Buch: Von Geld und Münze* (1770–1771); *Viertes Buch: Von Credit und Schulden* (1771–1772); and *Fünftes Buch: Von Anlagen und gehoriger Anwendung ihres Ertrags* (1772).

9 Hegel tutored the sons of wealthy wine trader Johann Noe Gogel, a kinship of the banker Gontard, in whose family Hölderlin also found employment.

10 About the city at the time of Goethe and when Hegel arrived there, see for instance (Voelker 1932).

11 Letters to Nanette Endel (February 9 or March 22, 1797), Hegel (1797–1831/1963: I, 52–53).

12 That notion is dated in the history of economic thought with Steuart scholars, like Skinner (and others like those gathered in the volume edited by Ramon Tortajada). In utilizing the 'mercantilist' label, one must remain aware that this commonplace view comes mostly from what classics did to discard their predecessors: Smith put forth the 'mercantilist' category in his *Wealth of Nations*, applying a strategy in that perspective.

13 In fact, Chamley tied up a third partner in his attempt, and that was John Maynard Keynes, and that was quite unfortunate. For the sake of this chapter, better to slide this aspect away. Chamley had an interest in defending Keynes as shows his study relating directly Steuart and Keynes (Chamley 1962), but this remained unconvincing: One may simply recall that it was proven Keynes never read Steuart (Tortajada 1999). In the volume centred on Hegel and Steuart (Chamley 1963), the addition of a Keynesian creed is very questionable. Here, we shall keep to discussing exclusively Hegel and Steuart, utilizing Chamley's valuable contribution in that regard only.

14 *Économie politique et philosophie chez Steuart et Hegel* was published in Paris – no English translation to our knowledge. Thus, in order to fully enjoy the volume, one has to master those three languages, which may be a hindrance. We would retort with Chamley however that if one is serious about studying Steuart and Hegel, this is indispensable. And Chamley was certainly free to write in his own language.

15 In his *Misère de la philosophie* (1847), Marx used the French translation. The time when English is the international idiom had not come yet, and German readers would tend to read works translated in their language or in French, which called for more international appeal. In his *Critique de l'économie politique* (1859), Marx mentioned 'the genial Englishman who was the first to study the system of the *bourgeois* economy as a whole: Sir James Steuart'. Marx used the Dublin edition of 1770 (rather than the London original edition of 1767). Later in the work (section on theories on money), Marx expressed his view on the first German translation: 'The honorable Büsch translated into the Hamburgian idiom the genial English prose of Steuart, and thus greatly caused to the original harm in each and every way that could be done'. We thank R. Tortajada for these indications.

16 About Hegel and David Hume, see notably (Berry 1982). Parallel to French Enlightenment, so-called 'Scottish Enlightenment' impacted Germany (Waszek 1988).

17 We mention here Klock or Obrecht (*De Aerario*), Justi and Sonnenfels (on law), Becher, Hörnigk, and Schröder, and the 'Imperial cameralists' from Austria. The body of literature (see Sommer 1920) that got denominated 'Cameralist' (from the word 'Court': *Hofkammer*) needs criteria for full identification (Humpert 1937).

18 We thank Christopher Berry for this remark. We have otherwise let aside this aspect from this chapter as we discussed more 'Romanticist' literary aspects (like Goethe's *Faust*) in our (Campagnolo 2010).

19 Noticeably, Chamley used little works by Hegel professional philosophers of his own times. One consequence is that he failed to use findings in the history of philosophy, as he himself recognized.

20 C.B. Macpherson (1962) thus titled his book dedicated to Hobbes and Locke. Macpherson later wrote on Hume. Although Hume was of notable influence on both Steuart and Smith, his case is far more complicated and independent from Hegel. We leave it aside.

21 'Appetite' may concretely mean eating and drinking, which the German language distinguishes for animals (*fressen)* and humans (*essen)* (one material difference is *cooking* food).

22 Hegel's dialectics show in the passage known as 'master and slave' (*Herr und Knecht*): The 'masterly consciousness' remains closed into one's subjective enjoyment and thus fails to overcome the 'I and I' stage (*Ich* = *Ich*). The servant mind (or 'Knecht', meaning rather service than slavery and allowing no direct translation at historical level) was first subjugated by fear of death (as it risks being murdered by the unsatisfied master). In turn it gets formed (*gebildet*) through its relationship to things as it elaborates them

through, to make goods for masterly consumption. It is *Bildung*. It is key to a future consciousness development, while the path of the master is a dead end.

23 *Sittlichkeit* consists in moments that appear throughout Hegel's works, although they vary from his *System of ethical life* (*System der Sittlichkeit* 1800) to his *Elements* of 1821 and the *Encyclopedia*.

24 In his youth, Hegel wrote *Die Verfassung Deutschlands* about governance in Baden-Württemberg. Close to his death, in his 1830 essay 'On the English Bill of Reform', Hegel favoured legislation concerned with economics within a national spiritual frame (*Volksgeist*). Values displayed by the universal class upon such national basis differ from Kantian cosmopolitanism. Hegel was denounced for a liking for Prussia.[unclear, please revise.]

25 To derive from there some support for 'welfare' policies, like Chamley, is too much to extrapolate.

26 Schiera (1968) shows how such views emerged from the necessity for princes to raise money to support newly gathered troops of soldiers, substituted for mercenaries with the Thirty Years War (1619–1648). In German provinces, the fear of 'universal' dominance by the French *Roi-Soleil* Louis XIV prompted authors: For example, Becher insisted on uniting 'all Germans' to face the French threat of a conquering 'universal monarchy' (Alsace in 1673) and economic domination. See Becher's *Machiavellus Gallicus seu Metempsychosis Machiavelli in Ludovico XIV Galliarum Rege* (1673). A polemist and an entrepreneur, Becher sought a German trade federation, including Austria, Bavaria, and Holland.

27 This parallels the fact that nowhere in Europe is one category unified under 'mercantilism' fully relevant. There was simply not one set of values, except for later observers who forged them retrospectively, either to indict them (like Smith polemicizing in the *Wealth of Nations*) or to promote them (e.g., like 'German precursors').

28 Physiocrats compared nature with a factory established by God where the 'Author of all things' was chief producer of all wealth. See Foucault's *The Order of Things* (Foucault 1966).

29 Chamley's bias shows there at its most: What he calls 'institutionalism' is a plea for 'Keynesianism'.

30 This twofold device comes as a consequence of solving the apparent paradox between the two notions that is known as the 'Adam Smith Problem' as formulated by Oncken in 1889 (English: *Economic Journal*: Oncken 1897).

31 In Marxian terms, this is the lumpen-proletariat rather than proletariat. It means a 'de-socialized' part of society, whose bitterness at not being recognized within society puts the latter at great risk.

32 See Hegel, *Berliner Schriften*, vol. XI of the *Gesammelte Werke* and (Campagnolo 2012).

33 The translator did not say that Smith was plagiarizing. Specialists of both Smith and Steuart debate the issue.

34 Hegel himself wrote on cosmology: His early essay *De Orbitis Planetarum* is usually regarded as unfortunate, but it bears witness to his genuine interest for natural science. One recalls Smith discussed cosmology.

Bibliography

Berry, C.J. (1982), *Hume, Hegel and Human Nature*, London: Springer.

———. (1994), *The Idea of Luxury: A Conceptual and Historical Investigation*, New York: Cambridge University Press.

Bourgeois, B. (1970), *Hegel à Francfort ou Judaïsme, Christianisme. Hégélianisme*, Paris: Vrin.

———. (1972), *L'article sur le droit naturel de Hegel*, Paris: Vrin.
———. (1979), Le prince hégélien, in B. Bourgeois, et al. (eds.), *Hegel et la Philosophie du droit*, Paris: PUF: 85–130.
Campagnolo, G. (2009), Hegel et l'économie politique: un nouveau concept de travail, in A. Alcouffe & C. Diebold (eds.), *Histoire de la pensée économique allemande*, Paris: Economica: 47–68.
———. (2010), *Criticisms of Classical Political Economy: Menger, Austrian Economics and the German Historical School*, London: Routledge.
———. (2012), Hegel und die Gewerbefreiheit der Modernen, in A. Arndt, M. Gerhard & J. Zovko (eds.), *Hegel-Jahrbuch 2012: Hegel und die Moderne*, Berlin: Akademie-Verlag: 140–148.
Chamley, P. (1962), Sir James Steuart, inspirateur de la *Théorie générale* de Lord Keynes?, *Revue d'économie politique* 72: 303–313.
———. (1963), *Économie politique et philosophie chez Steuart et Hegel*, Paris: Dalloz.
———. (1965), *Documents relatifs à Sir James Steuart*, Paris: Librairie Dalloz.
D'Hondt, J. (1968), *Hegel Secret*, Paris: PUF.
Ege, R. (1999), The New Interpretation of Steuart by Paul Chamley, in R. Tortajada (ed.), *The Economics of James Steuart*, London: Routledge: 84–101.
Foucault, M. (1966), *Les mots et les choses*, Paris: Gallimard.
Goethe, J.W. (1811–1833), *Aus meinem Leben. Dichtung und Wahrheit*, London: Kypros Press.
Halbwachs, M. (1950), *La mémoire collective*, Paris: Dunod.
Haller, A. von. (1732), *Die Alpen, Versuch Schweizerischer Gedichten*, Bern: Niclaus Emanuel Haller.
Hegel, G.W.F. (1796), *Ein Reisetagesbuch*, Appendix to Hegel's biography by Rosenkranz [1844].
———. (1797–1799), *Theologische Jugendschriften*, Tübingen: H. Nohl, 1907.
———. (1797–1831), *Briefe von und an Hegel*, Hamburg: Meiner, 1969.
———. (1802–1803/1805–1806), Erster und Zweiter Jenenser Realphilosophie, *Gesammelte Werke*, 19.
———. (1807), Die Phänomenologie des Geistes, in H. Glockner (ed.), *Hegels sämtliche Werke. Jubilaümsausgabe*, vol. 7, Stuttgart: Fromann Verlag, 1965.
———. (1821), *Grundlinien der Philosophie des Rechts*, Berlin: Nicolai.
———. (1821/2002), *Vorlesung über Naturphilosophie. Berlin 1821/1822*, Frankfurt/Main: Peter Lang Verlag.
———. (1973), *Vorlesungen über Rechtsphilosophie (1818–1831)*, Stuttgart-Bad-Canstatt: Friedrich Fromann.
Humpert, M. (1937), *Bibliographie der Cameralwissenschaften*, Köln: Kurt Schröder Verlag.
Ilting, K.-H. (1973), *Hegel, G. W. F. Vorlesungen über Rechtsphilosophie (1818–1831)*, Stuttgart-Bad-Canstatt: Friedrich Fromann.
Kant, I. (1764), *Beobachtungen über das Gefühl des Schönen und Erhabenen*, Königsberg: Jacob Kanter.
Kervégan, J.-F. (1998), *Les institutions de la liberté, Introduction to Principes de la philosophie du droit, the French translation of the Elements of Philosophy of Right*, Paris: Presses Universitaires de France: 5–49.
Losurdo, D. (2001), *L'Ipocondria dell'impolitico, la critica di Hegel ieri e oggi*, Lecce: Milella.

Macpherson, C.B. (1962), *The Political Theory of Possessive Individualism*, Oxford: Clarendon Press.
Magee, G.A. (2001/2008), *Hegel and the Hermetic Tradition*, Ithaca & London: Cornell University Press, rev. 2008.
Marx, K. (1857), *Grundrisse: Foundations of the Critique of Political Economy*, Harmondsworth: Penguin Books, 1973.
Meyer, D. (2009), Adam Müller et Othmar Spann: l'économie politique critique des sciences économiques, in A. Alcouffe & C. Diebold (eds.), *Histoire de la pensée économique allemande*, Paris, Economica: 69–90.
Oncken, A. (1897), The Consistency of Adam Smith, *The Economic Journal*, 7(27): 444–468.
Redman, D.A. & Starbatty, J. (1993), Die Figur des Staatsmanns bei Sir James Steuart im Lichte des kontinentalen Einflusses, in Schefold (1993a): 81–94.
Ricardo, D. (1821), *On the Principles of Political Economy and Taxation*, Harmondsworth: Penguin Books, 1971.
Rosenkranz, K. (1844), *G.W.F. Hegels Leben*, Berlin: Verlag von Duncker und Humblot.
Rosenzweig, F. (1920), *Hegel und der Staat*, Munich: Oldenburg Verlag.
Schefold, B. (1993a), *Steuart, James: An Inquiry into the Principles of Political Oeconomy*, Düsseldorf: Verlag Wirtschaft und Finanzen.
———. (1993b), Die Verbindung von Theorie, Geschichte und Politik bei James Steuart: Einleitung zur Neuausgabe von Steuarts, Political Oeconomy, in Schefold (1993a): 5–16.
———. (2010), Foreword, in Campagnolo (2010): xxi–xxiv.
Schiera, P. (1968), *Il Cameralismo e l'Assolutismo tedesco*, Milan: Giuffrè.
Seebeck, H. (1832), Verzeichniß der von dem Professor Herrn Dr. Hegel und dem Dr. Herrn Seebeck hinterlassenen Buecher-Sammlungen, Berlin: C.F. Müller.
Skinner, A. (1962), Sir James Steuart: Economics and Polities, *Scottish Journal of Political Economy*, 9: 17–37.
———. (1993), Sir James Steuart (1713–1780), in Schefold (1993a): 31–59.
Smith, A. (1776), *An Inquiry into the Causes and Nature of the Wealth of Nations*, German translation owned by Hegel: *Untersuchung über die Natur und Ursachen des Nationalrecihtums*, Leipzig: Breslau & Leipzig, 1794–1796.
Sommer, L. (1920), *Die oesterreichischen Kameralisten in dogmengeschichtlicher Darstellung*, Wien: Verlagsbuchhandlung Carl Konegen (Ernst Stülpnagel).
Steuart, J. (1767), *An Inquiry into the Principles of Political Oeconomy: Being an Essay on the Science of Domestic Policy in Free Nations*, London: Millar and Cadell. German editions: The translation that Hegel Possessed: A Series of Booklets First in Hamburg (1769–1770) Then in Tübingen (1769–1772) Listing *Sir James Stewart Baronets Untersuchung der Grundsätze von der Staats-Wirtschaft, als ein Versuch über die Wissenschaft von der Innerlichen Politik bei freien Nationen.*
———. (1993), *Neuausgabe von Steuarts 'Political Oeconomy' eine limitierte Ausgabe*, Düsseldorf: Verlag Wirtschaft und Finanzen.
Tortajada, R. (1999), *The Economics of James Steuart*, London: Routledge.
Voelker, H. (1932), *Die Stadt Goethes: Frankfurt-am-Main im achtzehnten Jahrhundert*, Frankfurt/Main: Blazek & Bergmann.
Waszek, N. (1988), *The Scottish Enlightenment and Hegel's Account of Civil Society*, Dordrecht: Kluwer.

15 Giovanni Tamassia and the early Italian reception of Steuart's *Principles of Political Economy*[1]

Cecilia Carnino

Steuart in Italy: The early reception

In the framework of the studies on the first circulation of the ideas of James Steuart, the Italian context has remained largely unexplored. On one hand, the penetration in Italy of Steuart's reflection has been the subject of much less attention than that of other 18th-century Scottish authors, in particular David Hume and Adam Smith.[2] On the other, while the more recent historiography has begun to pay some limited attention to the reception accorded to Steuart's work in Italy in the early decades of the 19th century,[3] the writing that first enabled the ideas he developed in the *Inquiry into the Principles of Political Economy* to be communicated in Italian has largely been ignored. This was the pamphlet entitled *Dello spirito di riforma considerato relativamente a un progetto di legge agraria*, which was written between the second half of 1799 and the first half of 1800 and then published in Milan. By summarizing and re-proposing Steuart's considerations on the crucial issues of redistribution of property and land, of luxury, and of the comparison between ancient and modern times, the pamphlet contributed decisively to the first penetration and circulation of the Scottish author's ideas in Italy.

The author of the work, which appeared shortly after the establishment of the second Cisalpine Republic, was Giovanni Tamassia. A leading force in the Municipality of Mantova that emerged in 1796 after the arrival of French forces in Italy, Tamassia was then nominated, in 1797, as a representative to the first Cisalpine Republic. Subsequently forced to flee Italy and take refuge in Marseilles during the short period of the first Habsburg Restoration in 1799, Tamassia returned to Italy in 1800 after Bonaparte's victory in Marengo, when he published the pamphlet to support his candidacy for the chair of public economics recently established at the University of Pavia.

Initially conceived as an occasional writing, aimed at obtaining the chair of public economics, *Dello spirito di riforma* was Tamassia's first attempt to grapple with economic issues. The result was a reflection with few original ideas. Indeed, when he sent the "small pamphlet" to the governing committee of the Cisalpine Republic in order to strengthen his candidacy for the chair of public economics, he openly admitted in a hand-written cover letter that the work was not at all innovative but merely offered a summary in Italian of the most advanced ideas in 'relation to the economic science', primarily those that came from Great Britain. He hoped in this way to bridge a gap in 'public education' which partly because of the 'political state of . . . the country' had not yet developed a 'new exposition of the aforementioned theories of use to its own citizens'.[4]

Nevertheless, the pamphlet ended up being entirely original in the context of the Italian economic culture of the period, precisely because it introduced Steuart for the first time as the main point of reference for economic analysis. In his cover letter Tamassia, after accusing the 'disciples of Quesnay' of having 'permeated [economic thought] with sophisms that are as much pleasant to the imagination as they are pernicious in practice', had declared his debt to 'the great writers of England', who had 'brought the most profound analysis to Economic Theories'.[5] In the pamphlet, Tamassia made more explicit his intellectual debt, by declaring that the 'profound Steuart' had been his most important guide in the reconnaissance of the 'modern system of political economics' (Tamassia 1799–1800: 18).

Even at the very end of the 18th century, Steuart represented a reference point that was most unusual in the Italian economic culture of the time. Published in 1767, his *Inquiry into the Principles of Political Economy* [hereafter *Principles*] had not only not been translated into Italian (and never would be), but – despite having been mentioned in 1767 in the periodical *Estratto della letteratura europea*[6] – up to that moment had never been the subject of specific attention by Italian authors.

Principles had a difficult circulation in Italy, in the context of a more general complex penetration in the peninsula of English language books in that period, and in fact Tamassia read *Principles* for the first time not in Italy but in France, during his months in exile in Marseilles. He therefore probably read the work in the French translation,[7] despite the fact that he had a very good command of English, as his later translations from English, for example of Benjamin Franklin's *The Way of Wealth*,[8] demonstrate. As he recalled years later in his work *Lezione di economia politica*, he had become friends

> with a young Tuscan man of the highest insight and knowledge, who was the first to suggest that I should read Steuart, whom I had not even heard mentioned since in Lombardy . . . there is not much news on matters of literature.
> (Tamassia 1807a: 4)

Nothing more is known of the 'young Tuscan' who led Tamassia to discover Steuart, but it is possible that he had read *Principles* in Tuscany where, from at least 1792, the first English edition was in circulation and included in the publisher Giuseppe Molini's catalogue of books.[9]

Tamassia was therefore the first Italian author to openly refer to *Principles* as a primary source for economic thought. It should however be noted that the patriot Matteo Angelo Galdi, from1799 a Cisalpine diplomatic envoy to the Batavian Republic, had referred to 'the Stewarts' in his pamphlet *Rapporti economici tra le nazioni libere* of 1798, along with 'the Humes, the Lockes, the Smiths, the Brotvnz, the Melons, the Dutotts, the Condillacs and the Montesquieus', as the 'peaceful philosophers' who in the 18th century had written about the *ancien regime*

(Galdi 1798: 215). While it has been assumed that he had in mind Dugald Stewart (Cantimori & De Felice 1964: 332), the frequent confusion between the two Scottish authors, which in Italy lasted at least until the early 19th century, means that he may in fact have been referring to the author of *Principles*. But be that as it may, the fact is Steuart remained largely unknown until the publication of *Dello spirito di riforma*, and even after the publication of the pamphlet and at least for the first decade of the 19th century, if he was known at all, he was seldom cited in Italy.

Among the few authors on whom the Scottish philosopher and economist exerted an influence was Adeodato Ressi, who held the post of professor of political economy in Pavia that Tamassia had coveted. Ressi's 1801 lectures were largely inspired by *Principles*, and not only did he quote passages from the Scottish author's work in them but he also seems to have taken the concepts of value, population and competition directly from it (Bianchini 1988: 72). Moreover, Ressi also cited *Principles* extensively in his subsequent work, *Dell'economia della specie umana*, published in four volumes between 1817 and 1820. In this writing, inspired by free trade principles yet distinguished by an anti-Smithian approach discernible principally in his criticism of the distinction between productive and unproductive work, Ressi called Steuart 'the celebrated writer . . . who brought the mercantile system to its highest level of perfection'.

Following the chapters dedicated to Quesnay and Smith's 'system', Chapter 4 of Book III was entirely focused on the analysis of 'Steward's system', which Ressi saw as having pioneered the 'regulatory or mercantile system':

> The celebrated Mr. James Stewart can also deservedly call himself the Author of a system, as G.B. Say would say, since he establishes a different principle to those of the others, on which he founds the entire outline of the public administration. . . . I call Steward the author of this system, even though some of his compatriots have already preceded him in some . . . ideas. I do not know of an author who could have left such a complete plan, from its first principles to its final consequence, as the aforementioned Steward, to whom the glory of a pioneer is rightfully due, has done.
>
> (Ressi 1817–1820: III, 45–46)

Also in 1801, another anti-Smithian writer, Carlo Bosellini of Modena, who between 1816 and 1817 published the work *Nuovo esame delle sorgenti della privata e pubblica ricchezza* and then wrote a series of articles on the history of economic doctrines for the *Giornale arcadico*, cited Steuart in his *Discorso sui principi in materia di finanze*. Invoking *Principles* in support of a moderately protectionist manufacturing policy, he quoted a passage from Book III on the benefits of large-scale factories in which favourable conditions could be created to incentivise 'emulation', 'multiply strength', and 'develop talent' (Bosellini 1801: 59).[10]

The attention attracted, even among Italian authors, by Jean-Baptiste Say's *Traité d'économie*, which frequently quoted *Principles*, doubtlessly contributed to a broader understanding and diffusion of Steuart's ideas in Italy. One might, for example, recall Luigi Valeriani Molinari, a former member of the Council of the

Cisalpine Republic to whom Napoleon had granted the chair in political economy at the University of Bologna in 1801. In *Del prezzo delle cose tutte mercatabili*, published in Bologna in 1806,[11] Valeriani referred to Steuart – whom he described as an 'observer no less than a great gatherer of commercial news, without whom by chance Smith would not have come, like Newton without Galileo' (1806: x) – in his reflection on money as a measure of value. Almost 20 years later, setting out from a highly critical analysis of Say's treatise that in fact brought a direct reaction from the French economist, Nicola Porcinari underlined the influence of Steuart's *Principles* on the development of Scottish economic thought and in particular on the ideas of Smith: 'If any author was able to offer Smith the materials for his work, it was in fact Steuart' (Porcinari 1824: 8).[12]

Tamassia, reader of Steuart

Thus while in the early decades of the 19th century Steuart's ideas started to become familiar to and cited even by Italian authors, especially those who were reading Say, the first occasion in which the ideas of the Scottish economist were circulated in Italy was without doubt owed to Tamassia, and in particular to the publication of his pamphlet, *Dello spirito di riforma.*

In the previously mentioned *Lezione di economia politica*, published a few years after *Dello spirito di riforma*, Tamassia declared that Steuart had triggered a veritable 'revolution' with his economic ideas (Tamassia 1807a: 4). Before reading *Principles*, there were two works that had prompted him to reflect on political economy: Montesquieu's *Esprit des lois* and Fliangieri's *Scienza della legislazione*. Montesquieu – 'too brisk in the discussion of his subjects' – had left him with little more than 'vague and superficial ideas' (*ibidem*, 42). From the *Scienza della legislazione*, in which Filangieri deemed the theory of equal distribution of wealth and land to be utopian and no longer applicable to modern societies,[13] Tamassia declared that he had drawn the belief that 'healthy politics' must always promote 'the subdivision of property as being extremely favourable to agriculture and the simplicity of customs' (Tamassia 1799–1800: 2). *Principles* had conversely led him to mature the idea that 'politics' stopped being such 'when its operations are not adapted to customs and habits' (*ibidem*, 4).[14] Apropos of this he quoted almost verbatim a passage from the preface to Book I of *Principles*: 'According to my way of treating this subject no *general* rule can be laid down in political matters: every thing *there* must be considered according to the circumstances and spirit of the nations to which they relate' (I, vii).

While Steuart had used these words to underline the need to bear in mind the specificity of national contexts when assessing the possibilities of particular economic policies, Tamassia instead applied them to the political-economic debate of the Italian revolutionary *Triennio*. His objective was to close the accounts with those who during the brief revolutionary phase had entertained the possibility of a model of political economy based on old republican ideals, that is to say on frugality, on agricultural activity, and on the redistribution of land ownership. Since the fall of the *ancien régime* called for a new way of thinking about economic issues in a way compatible with the new republican and democratic principles, to Tamassia's mind *Principles* represented a proposal for a modern republican economic model to set against the ancient one envisaged by Mably and by Rousseau.

In this perspective, Tamassia's pamphlet drew mainly from four chapters of *Principles*, namely Chapter 5 (*In what Manner, and according to what Principles, and political Causes, does Agriculture augment Population?*) of Book I and Chapters 14 (*Security, Ease and Happiness, no inseparable Concomitants of Trade and Industry*), 26 (*Of the Vibration of the Balance of Wealth between the Subjects of a modern State*), and 20 (*Of Luxury*) of Book II. These choices make clear how Tamassia's interest did not centre on Steuart's ideas on monetary and banking issues, nor on his theory of price or even on his protectionist propositions but rather on the schematic description of commercial society that he expounded. He focused exclusively on the model of 'political oeconomy of modern time', as opposed to the 'political oeconomy of the antients' (I, 167), that is, on a model of political economy based not only on agriculture but also on the development of trade, manufacturing, and industry.

Dello spirito di riforma began with an analysis of the different 'classes' that made up modern societies, namely the 'lazy consumers' (*consumatori oziosi*), who 'live on an already acquired income', the "manufacturers' (*manifatturieri*) who used 'their industry to modify the products of nature', and the 'cultivators' (*coltivatori*) who 'direct their labour on the cultivation of the earth to provide our general subsistence' (Tamassia 1799–1800: 5). This subdivision, the expression of a wholly economic vision of society, was taken directly from *Principles*, where Steuart had distinguished between 'idle consumers', 'farmers', and 'free hands' (I, 58–62).[15] Starting from this analysis of the productive classes, Tamassia discussed at length and in detail the consequences, entirely negative and again taken entirely from Steuart, of an equal distribution of land.

First of all, Tamassia argued that this socioeconomic system would prove to be ineffective, since it would end up reproducing, given the 'different attitude of the three classes' to the cultivation of land, the inequality that it 'aimed to eliminate', causing some to 'live with difficulty' and others 'to be provided sufficiently with the necessary sustenance' (Tamassia 1799–1800: 4). Furthermore, an equal division of property would hinder any population increase, in that it would remove an outlet for any eventual surplus workforce for the manufacturing sector (*ibidem*). In his opinion, the two other remedies explored – the 'destruction of excess population' and emigration – seemed much more 'barbarian' than the economic inequality which the agrarian law was designed to eliminate. While referring extensively in this work to *Principles*, in particular to Chapter 5 of Book I,[16] Tamassia greatly simplified Steuart's ideas: the Scottish author had in fact followed an in-depth and articulated line of analysis, indicating three possible solutions to population growth in a purely agricultural society: Charity, barter, and slavery.

A third argument touched more directly on the question of economic development. Without a large class of 'manufacturers', in other words a class of non-landowners, not only would the development of the manufacturing system remain a chimera, but agriculture would not rise beyond subsistence level. The main driver of agricultural development was the desire of landowners to obtain a surplus from land cultivation to spend on things unconnected to subsistence:

> if in the political economy of modern times the cultivator produces a surplus . . . it is because he has an interest in producing one that he can exchange with the industrious, who provides for his other needs: if he does not care to produce any surplus from his land, he cannot satisfy his tastes.
>
> (Tamassia 1799–1800: 36ss)[17]

This conviction was taken directly from *Principles*, where Steuart had observed how 'the laziest part of farmers, disgusted with a labour which produces a plenty superfluous to themselves, which they cannot dispose of for an equivalent, will give over working and return to their ancient simplicity' (I, 38). It should, however, be noted how the connection between the increase of agrarian production and the availability of convenience in a developed manufacturing system had already been pointed out, before Steuart, in the *Considerazioni sul commercio* by Pietro Verri, who Tamassia named as one of the Italian authors who had had the most impact on his economic ideas (Tamassia 1838: 48, 1807a: 12). The *Considerazioni* were published in the Milan-based journal *Il Caffè* in 1764, in the wake of a reflection carried out by Cantillon that linked together psychological analysis and economic reasoning and which was directly influenced by the physiocratic interest in the role of the spending of landowners in the economic process of wealth generation (Cantillon 1755: 76–85).

For his part, Verri – in the course of an analysis so similar to Steuart's that we ought to reflect more deeply on the possible influences between the two authors and which in any case is evidence of the spread of a common economic culture – saw the desire to satisfy growing needs through the acquisition of market goods as the most powerful incentive for landowners to invest in their estates in an effort to produce a 'surplus' (Verri 1764: I, f.3, 30–38).[18]

In this theoretical framework, which Tamassia made his own by rejecting the old frugal republican model, not only were hope and desires for a better life responsible for generating growth in the agricultural sector, but, more generally, the aspiration for happiness and wellbeing constituted the foundation of economic development by virtue of a determined effort to realize work-based desires, and was capable, precisely for that reason, of combining personal interest and public happiness. The development of a market economy would moreover enable the launch of a real process of wealth circulation, unachievable in a society stuck fast at the level of pure subsistence (Tamassia 1799–1800: 23). Once more Steuart's considerable influence emerges here, given that he had declared industry to be the privileged means through which to bring about greater economic equality among individuals:

> If therefore such variations in the balance of wealth depend on the difference of *genius* among men, what scheme can be laid down for preserving equality, better than that of an unlimited industry equivalent to an universal circulation

of all property, whereby dissipation may correct the effects of hoarding, and hoarding again correct those of dissipation? This is the most effectual remedy both against poverty and overgrown riches; because the rich and the poor are thereby perpetually made to change conditions.

(II, 40)

From *Principles* Tamassia also took the idea that ties between individuals, seen as the only true foundation of societies, derived in the final analysis from the need to satisfy 'reciprocal needs', that is, in the words of Steuart, those 'reciprocal wants' that 'promote industry' and in the exercise of which Tamassia saw, in open disagreement with Rousseau, the only 'true happiness' (Tamassia 1799–1800: 8–9). Looking at it this way it is not surprising to find that a large part of *Dello spirito di riforma* was dedicated to the subject of luxury, defined, in the course of a mature economic conceptualization and in the wake of Steuart, as 'the acquisition of superfluous things with the aim of consuming them' (*ibidem*, 26).[19]

By tackling the issue of luxury, Tamassia became involved in an already long-running and complex debate, which, however, he appeared to understand well when referring to the 'abuse of terms', in other words to the question of the difficulty of defining the notion of luxury that, beginning with Jean-François Melon's *Essai politique sur le commerce*, had become central to the discussion of the subject (Melon 1736: 113). In particular, Tamassia not only identified luxury as an instrument capable of ensuring economic growth and wealth redistribution – Italian authors like Ferdinando Galiani, Antonio Genovesi, Pietro Verri, Cesare Beccaria, and Gaetano Filangieri had, after all, done this before him – but in a process that revealed the central role accorded to the economic aspect of political emancipation, he also saw it as the guarantor of the political independence of individuals. Luxury, according to an interpretation already put forward by Beccaria in *Dei delitti e delle pene*, published in 1764, had in fact contributed to 'breaking the chains' of 'feudal slavery' and to giving birth to a society no longer based on political dependency but on economic relations (Tamassia 1799–1800: 28).

Although Tamassia echoed arguments and considerations put forward by Italian authors who had contributed to the debate on luxury before him, his entire analysis could be traced back to Chapters 20 (*Of Luxury*) and 21 (*Of Physical and Political Necessaries*) of the Book II of *Principles*,[20] which in turn had been heavily influenced by Hume's *Discourse of Luxury* (whose title was, significantly, changed to *Of refinement in the Arts* from the 1760 edition onwards). Furthermore, the debt that the Italian author owed to Steuart was something that he openly conceded: 'The analysis of luxury carried out up to now is almost literally copied from the research on the principles of economy by Steuart. And what could I have used that is more precise and eloquent?' (Tamassia 1799–1800: 32). Thus at the end of the 18th century Steuart's ideas had assumed a paradigmatic position in the long-running debate on luxury. In the wake of Steuart, Tamassia on the one hand distinguished between the benefits and damage that luxury could generate, and on the other contrasted the 'luxury of the ancients' to 'modern luxury' (*ibidem*). The former, based on 'robbery and conquest' was arbitrary and damaging, while the latter, being founded on the productive and creative abilities of mankind, held only positive implications for society.

On the economic level, luxury was a factor in the progress of international trade and in the development of manufacturing as well as providing an incentive to work, while on the political and social level it played a fundamental role both because it created new work opportunities and because it represented an important instrument for wealth redistribution. The growth of luxury goods was linked directly to the progress of society and also represented its clearest evidence (Ramos 2011).

So, while Tamassia's considerations on luxury were not original, as they followed faithfully Steuart's ideas, the large number of pages that the *Spirito di riforma* reserved to the subject and the attention that Tamassia opted to pay to it in the context of his short pamphlet demonstrate in the clearest possible terms which aspects of Steuart's wider analysis most caught the attention of the Italian author in the moment of his discovery of economics. Tamassia's long reflection on luxury is the best demonstration that what he took from Steuart was above all his belief in a type of trading economy founded on the development of commerce and international economic relations and characterized by a high level of interdependence between the productive sectors and individuals (in other words the productive classes). In this model, the appreciation, which Steuart in turn took from Hume, of the passions and of private wellbeing as the drivers of national prosperity was linked to a dynamic vision of the economy in which the production of goods and the greatest possible circulation of products were at the forefront of national wealth.

By adhering to this model of economic and social development, Tamassia was in line with the thinking of those authors who, during the revolutionary phase, dealt more directly with economic issues, such as Matteo Angelo Galdi, Giuseppe Compagnoni, Vincenzo Cuoco and Melchiorre Gioia. As a whole, these authors outlined, in consonance with the economic reflection that was taking shape in Directorial France, a dynamic and industrious society anchored on the basis of a strong valorization of the expansion of needs and desires (Carnino 2018).

In the new political, institutional and ideological context of the *Triennio*, Steuart's *Principles* appeared to propose an economic model compatible with republican values: one based on the development of commerce and on the pursuance of private interest, which in turn was the foundation of the public good, and on work, which became a new virtue on which to build society. Above all, the model also granted a key role to the institutions (despite the fact that institutions of the *ancien régime* to which Steuart referred were of course radically different to those that the Italian authors emerging from the experience of the revolutionary *Triennio* had in mind), which played a pivotal part in guaranteeing the development of the commercial society and the fulfilment of personal ambitions (Menudo 2018). By breaking the chains and hierarchies of *ancient régime* society the new republican institutions facilitated economic growth and public and private prosperity. At the same time, the economic development and wellbeing that they brought and which all social classes could potentially enjoy, legitimized the new political system, establishing its ability to secure public happiness, greater social justice, as well as individual interests.

In contrast to the suggestions of Steuart, the task of the institutions was therefore above all to eliminate the constraints and privileges that had characterized the society of the *ancien régime* and were by then seen as a brake on economic development and individual realization. In this context, for Tamassia the importance accorded to the role of the institutions was linked to the defence of the principle of economic liberty, which he saw as being intrinsically connected to the recently acquired political freedom. This therefore explains the Italian author's decision by and large to ignore the late mercantilist ideas contained in Steuart's *Principles*, which stated that politicians were responsible for taking direct control of the individual impulse towards personal profit.

Steuart and Smith: A liberal economic interpretation of *Principles*

In the *Dello spirito di riforma*, Tamassia had not felt the need to justify the coexistence of the adherence to economic freedom with the assumption of Steuart as a main reference for his economic analysis, but the perspective changed some years later. Tamassia's reading of Smith and his comparison of the two Scottish authors' ideas led him to explain his position more clearly.

The first traces of this comparison can be found in the already quoted *Lezione di economia politica*, published in 1802 and reprinted in 1807 following its publishing success. On the whole, the pamphlet was presented as a veritable compendium of what in Tamassia's opinion constituted the foremost theories of economic science, the knowledge of which he deemed necessary and sufficient for grasping the principles of political economy. While citing Italian, English, French, German, Swiss, and Spanish authors – from Smith to Hume, from Verri to Mengotti, from Galiani to Genovesi, from Forbonnais to Montesquieu, from Herrenschwand to Ustaríz, and from Condillac to Bielfeld – Tamassia once again accorded primacy to Steuart, whose 'great and illuminating' principles had demonstrated first and most clearly the need to adapt economic policies to the specificities of local realities (Tamassia 1807a: 4).

He revived Steuart's condemnation – already advanced in *Dello spirito di riforma* – of the classical republican model based on frugality and the contraction of consumption, even if by then the issue of agrarian law was given less emphasis in order to focus more on the drivers of economic growth. The crucial factor in economic development was identified once again in 'industry', in the sense of industriousness or diligent endeavour, which in turn lay at the root of social justice through a process of wealth circulation based on labour, which made possible the flow of the surplus from the rich to the poor (Tamassia 1807a: 5). The idea that the 'formation of surplus' was ensured only by the presence of large estates was also taken from Steuart. The lengthy 'Annotation I', in which Tamassia cited Arthur Young's *Travels* in support of his own theories, was dedicated to demonstrating the economic advantages of large landholdings, which could guarantee the 'large capital' required for agricultural development and which had been bolstered in Lombardy by the policy of selling domestic goods.[21]

In order of importance, after Steuart came Smith, who Tamassia discovered after the author of *Principles* and who he described as having developed a particularly complex economic analysis: 'perhaps some effort of mind will be necessary at first, since his [Smith's] principles are interlinked with each other in such a way that obscuring only one of them leads to a general obscurity' (Tamassia 1807a: 9). The main point of his attention was of course the *Inquiry into the Nature and Causes of the Wealth of Nations*, and he recommended Germain Garnier's French translation 'for the youth that cannot read the original English' and praised it as 'excellent in itself and enriched by interesting notes'.[22] In an attempt to summarize in just a few pages the *Wealth of Nations*, Tamassia concentrated on two of 'Smith's main theories' (*ibidem*, 9). These were the division of labour, defined as 'the main albeit little observed cause' of public and private wealth and the accumulation of capital (*ibidem*, 10).

Following an approach that looked at the economic role of all classes in society – that is, of all the productive classes – the capital to which Tamassia referred, complying with Smith, were the 'gradual' savings that came as much from the revenues of landowners and businessmen as from the work of 'the hard-working individual' (*ibidem*, 11). An essential condition for the reinvestment of this capital in the economic circuit was the unrestricted pursuit of individual interests, considered to be compatible with the public interest. The intervention of public power in economics had to be limited and could under no circumstances be allowed to challenge private interest without causing 'serious injury to annual production' – according to terminology taken directly from Smith but already used by Pietro Verri in his *Considerazioni sull'economia politica* – on which public wealth was founded.[23]

Tamassia was perfectly well aware of the contrast between Smith's free trade approach and Steuart's late-mercantilist economic approach and for this very reason he attempted to explain, and in some ways to justify, his decision to assume both Scottish authors as special reference points for his economic analysis. First, Tamassia underlined the strong affinity between the works of the two authors, pointing out, on the one hand, how Smith seemed to have taken some of his principles from Steuart and, on the other, the originality of the two authors:

> I should not hide that some of the fundamental principles of political economics noted by Smith seem to have been taken from Steuart. Also, observing the detail of these principles in the two authors that I propose, the originality shines through easily in the writings of the one and the other.
>
> (*ibidem*, 9)

But above all Tamassia tackled what he believed to be the crux of the confrontation between Steuart and Smith on the specific issue of economic freedom, thus focusing on an economic liberal reading of the author of *Principles*. In this perspective, he tried to demonstrate how the differences between Smith and Steuart in matters of free trade were 'only apparent':

> [Smith's] free trade . . . will seem, at first glance, in opposition with the teachings of Steuart; but do not tire to read and compare these two celebrated authors, and eventually you will realise that the disparity between their opinions is only apparent, and that the result of their profound meditations are almost similar.
>
> (*ibidem*: 13–14)

The *Annotazione III* placed at the end of his *Lezione di economia* was dedicated to this issue. Here Tamassia explicitly recognized for the first time how Steuart had been, 'like the majority of the Economic Writers of his time' in favour 'of the brilliant but futile idea of the *balance of trade*; and his arguments are sometimes affected by this predisposition'. At the same time, however, Tamassia showed how a deeper reading of *Principles* would demonstrate that Steuart's 'final maxim' was 'only a little dissimilar from that of Smith' (*ibidem*, 32).

This reading, made through his interpretative lens, deliberately downplayed the importance attributed by Steuart to protectionist policies in support of equilibrium in the balance of trade and the development of national manufacturing. According to Tamassia, the state interventionism invoked by Steuart was in fact confined to the theoretical, being seldom realized practically. Translating a long passage from Chapter 24 of Book II of *Principles* on public intervention in the balance of trade,[24] Tamassia strove to demonstrate how in Steuart's interpretation it was possible to intervene usefully in favour of a positive trade balance only when a government had a real understanding of 'the entire chain of consequences' that might result from this action. Since the complexity of the commercial exchange of modern societies ruled out this understanding, for Steuart any protectionist intervention had to be 'merely hypothetical' (*ibidem*, 34).

Tamassia would put forward the same liberalist reading of Steuart a few months later in another writing, titled *Delle scienze e della libertà relativamente al commercio* and published in 1802. In this work Steuart was cited, along with Smith, in support of the economic freedom of all productive sectors, conceived as a prerequisite for achieving the economic balance between supply and demand on which national prosperity relied. In the long final appendix Tamassia argued against the thesis, sustained by 'many writers of public Economics', that the prohibition on the importation of foreign goods was 'the primary cause of the prosperity of trade'.[25] Significantly, Steuart was not listed among the ranks of those who had upheld this principle, but was named as an author who had warned against adopting protectionist policies without first having a thorough understanding of the effects that these would have on the national economy as a whole. He was referring again to Chapter 24 of Book II of *Principles*, in particular to the 'chain of consequences' that it was necessary to draw up and assess before resorting to such policies. Steuart was once more placed alongside Smith. The latter had set out a few exceptions to the 'general rule of free trade', and Steuart had done nothing more than 'declaring in more general terms the same exceptions' (*ibidem*, 52).

According to Tamassia's interpretation, Steuart could therefore be counted among the authors in favour of economic freedom. The attention that the Scottish author had paid to different situations and economic conditions had led him to see a protectionist intervention might sometimes be appropriate, especially when aimed above all at safeguarding new born manufacturers and economic systems undergoing their first phase of development, but this did not invalidate a liberalist orientation on the more general level of economic principles. This interpretation was clearly conditioned by the economic convictions that Tamassia was developing, in part after his experience serving as a vice prefect in the Napoleonic administration, as emerges most clearly in the *Esame del problema se ed in quali circostanze convenga la proibizione delle merci straniere*, published in 1807 as an appendix to the work *Quadro economico dei cantoni di Asso e Bellano*. This work was meant as a partial and well-defined critique of the liberal ideas of Smith regarding the import of foreign manufactured goods, as they had been set out in Chapter 2 of Book IV of *Wealth of Nations* ('*Of Restraints upon the Importation from Foreign Countries of such Goods as can be Produced at Home*').[26]

While never calling into question the general principle of economic freedom and its fundamental importance to national prosperity, Tamassia was aware, due to his reading of Steuart, of the need to marry the liberalist principles of Smith to a focus on specific aspects of local situations in the Italian economy, which was characterized by a level of industrial and commercial development well below that of the British model that Smith had examined. This was the basis for his admission of the potential benefit of adopting certain limited protectionist measures in support of national industry. This therefore involved placing the overall interest of society above the immediate interest of individual producers and consumers and, from this point of view, the reflection quickly shifted from the more strictly economic level of analysis to that of political utility. It was in fact 'humanity' and 'politics' that ensured that private interests were subservient to the 'general advantage of society' (Tamassia 1807b: 74–75).

Nevertheless, despite all these considerations, the *Esame* did not in any way undermine Tamassia's liberal convictions, which he was careful to reaffirm in the 'Corollaries' that ended the work. In these, he again maintained how any protectionist measure had to be adopted only with the greatest possible caution, given the extreme difficulty 'for the administrator' to comprehend in advance all the effects that his interventions might have and thus, in the final analysis, also the difficulty in establishing the true advantage that such actions might bring to society. In general, the best solution was to trust 'personal interest', which was always preferable to a 'well understood code of prohibitions' (*ibidem*, 81).

It was precisely the conviction that the adoption of limited and temporary protectionist measures was, when these were seen as exceptional measures imposed by circumstance, compatible with an outlook that favoured economic liberalism as the principle on which to found public prosperity that gave substance and legitimacy to the liberalist interpretation of Steuart proposed by Tamassia. At the same time, through this interpretation, which of course greatly simplified and even distorted the Scotsman's analysis, Steuart was able to become a key author of reference in revolutionary and Napoleonic Italy, where the defence of economic freedom, in opposition to the limits and restrictions of the *ancien régime*, established itself as a cardinal principle of economic thought.

Closing remarks

Steuart's *Principles* circulated in Italy for the first time relatively late, through Tamassia's pamphlet *Dello spirito di riforma*, written between 1799 and 1800 and then published, in the aftermath of the fall of the *ancien régime*, during the Napoleonic period. In this complex political and ideological framework, *Principles* represented for Tamassia, above all, a model of economic development compatible with the new republican principles that was based on international commerce, the expansion of needs and desires, the economic relations between individuals, and especially on work. It was exactly these ideas of *Principles* that attracted Tamassia's attention and that consequently circulated in Italy at the very beginning of early the 19th century. His further deeper economic analysis and especially the reading of Smith led Tamassia to reflect more analytically on the economic ideas of Steuart and in particular on the theme of economic freedom. Precisely the need to demonstrate the compatibility of Steuart's ideas with the principle of economic freedom, which constituted a key element of the Italian revolutionary economic reflection, compelled Tamassia to provide an economic liberal reading of *Principles*, by attempting to demonstrate the tight connections between the economic ideas of Steuart and those of Smith in matters of free trade. Rather than being based on the grounds of a rigorous economic analysis, Tamassia's reading was a conscious and deliberate attempt to make Steuart's reflection compatible with an economic and, above all, political culture – forged during the revolutionary period – centred on the defence of freedom.

Furthermore, at the time in which Tamassia wrote the *Lezione di economia politica* and *Delle scienze e della libertà relativamente al commercio* this liberal reading of Steuart could still be presented and perceived as legitimate, although this would change in the course of only a few months with the publication in 1803 of Say's *Traité d'économie politique*. Only after Say did a reading of Steuart as a champion of protectionism directly opposed to Smith, who was represented as the defender of economic freedom, assert itself and become codified:

> On a dit que Smith avait de grandes obligations à Steuart . . . Je ne vois pas en quoi consistent ces obligations . . . Steuart a soutenu un système déjà embrassé par Colbert . . . et qui fait dépendre les richesses d'un pays, non du montant de ses productions, mais du montant de ses ventes à l'étranger. Smith a consacré une partie importante de son livre à confondre ce système.
>
> (Say 1803: xxii)[27]

The progressive definition of the paradigm of classical economics, by contributing to establishing a negative interpretation of mercantilist economic policies, significantly reduced the space for alternative readings of *Principles*, which was often invoked as an emblematic example of the 'mercantile system'.[28] The first penetration of Steuart in Italy had, however, taken place in a different background of economic culture, in which economic science appeared in some ways more fluid and less restricted to narrow analytical and interpretative categories. The primacy ascribed to the evaluation of local circumstances with respect to defining abstract economic law and paying heed to the practical dimension of political economy, which characterized Italian economic thought during the late 18th century and early 19th, had allowed Tamassia to perceive and present the model of political economy outlined in *Principles* as compatible with an invisible hand that had the ability to refashion the individual interests that undergird public prosperity.

Notes

1 This is an updated and extended version of an article published, under the title 'The first reception of James Steuart in Italy: Giovanni Tamassia and his liberal economic reading of the Principles of Political Economy,' *History of European Ideas*, 44/2 (2018): 182–193.
2 See, for example, Baldi (1983), Mazza (2005), Zanardi (2005), Vercillo (1963), Gioli (1972), and Parolini (1980).
3 On the circulation of the economic culture in Italy in the first half of the 19th century, see Augello and Guidi (2000) and Augello, Bianchini and Guidi (1996).
4 Giovanni Tamassia, Manuscript letter dated Brumal 6, year VIII, in Archivio di Stato di Milano, *Autografi*, 157 (Giovanni Tamassia).
5 Tamassia, Manuscript letter, cit.1
6 *Novelle letterarie*, "Estratto della letteratura europea", III, 1767, p. 208.
7 The *Recherche des principes de l'économie politique* (Imprimerie de Didot l'âiné, Paris, 1789–1790) was published during the years of the French Revolution on the initiative of Alexandre-Théophile Vandermonde, the first French professor of political economics, who would later make widespread use of Steuart's treatise in lectures delivered in 1795 at the École normale. On this French translation of Steuart's *Principles*, see Albertone (1999).
8 Benjamin Franklin, *La via della fortuna, del dottor Beniamino Franklin traduzione dall'inglese con aggiuntavi L'arte di leggere i libri con profitto del cavaliere Giovanni Tamassia* (Bergamo: Mazzoleni, 1830).
9 *Catalogo di lingua inglese dei libri vendibili presso Giuseppe Molini* (Florence: Molini, 1792), p. 20.
10 On Bosellini's economic ideas, see Bano (1982).
11 On Valeriani, see Pucci (1990).
12 In a missive sent to the Neapolitan man of letters and patriot Francesco Saverio Salfi in November 1825, Say responded to the criticisms put forward by Porcinari: 'Cet anonyme A. est bien maladroit de faire le procès à toute l'Europe qui a traduit mon Traité dans toutes les langues et qui y a trouvé la mieux distribuée et la plus complète exposition des principies de l'economie politique. Quiconque écrit sur les sciences et se cache, a la convinction qu'il a tort' (Biblioteca Nazionale di Napoli Vittorio Emanuele III, Nazionale, Lettere autografe d'illustri uomini a Francesco Saverio Salfi, Busta

XX 77, Fasc. 1, 4). For a more detailed discussion on the contrast between Say and Porcinari, see Di Battista (1983: 78–79) and, more recently, Guidi and Potier (2003: 179–181).

13 On the economic thinking of Filangieri, see Silvestrini (2006).

14 For a detailed analysis of Steuart's reflection on the issue of the redistribution of land, see Skinner (1962).

15 For a synthesis of the economic ideas that are presented in *Principles*, see Skinner (2006).

16 'Agriculture among a free people will augment population, only in proportion as the necessitous are put in situation to purchase subsistence with their labour' (I, 36).

17 On Steuart's reflection on the issue of population, see Gislain (1999).

18 On this aspect, see Carnino (2014).

19 Steuart defined luxury as: "the providing of superfluities, in favour of a consumption" (I, 405).

20 Steuart (II, Chap. XX e Chap XXI). For a detailed analysis of Steuart's ideas on luxury, see Ramos (2007: 161–188), Sen (1957: 46–49), Caboret (1999: 57–75), and Yang (1994: 93–103).

21 'Annotazione I', in Tamassia (1807a: 19–23); Arthur Young, *Travels during the Years 1787, 1788 and 1789, Undertaken More Particularly with a View of Afcertaining the Cultivation, Wealth, Resources, and National Prosperity, of the Kingdom of France: To Which Is Added, the Register of a Tour into Spain* (Dublin: M'Kenzie, and Rice, 1793).

22 Tamassia (1807a: 8); Adam Smith, *Recherches sur la nature et les causes de la richesse des nations, Traduction nouvelle, avec des notes et observations; par Germain Garnier, . . . avec le portrait de Smith*(Paris: Agasse, 1802).

23 Pietro Verri, *Meditazioni sulla economia politica* (Livorno: Stamperia dell'Enciclopedia, 1771).

24 'Nothing is more complex than the interests of trade, considered with respect to a whole nation. It is hardly possible for a people to have every branch of trade favourable for the increase of her wealth: consequently, a statesman who, upon the single inspection of one branch, would lay the importation of it under limitations, in proportion as he found the balance upon it unfavourable to the nation, might very possibly undo a flourishing commerce. He must first examine minutely every use to which the merchandize imported is put: if a part is re-exported with profit, this profit must be deducted from the balance of loss incurred by the consumption of the remainder. If it be consumed upon the account of other branches of industry, which are thereby advanced, the balance of loss may still be more than compensated. If it be a mean of supporting a correspondence with a neighbouring nation, otherwise advantageous, the loss resulting from it may be submitted to, in a certain degree. But if upon examining the whole chain of consequences, he find the nation's wealth not at all increased, nor her trade encouraged, in proportion to the damage at first incurred by the importation; I believe he may decide such a branch of trade to be hurtful; and therefore that it ought to be cut off, in the most prudent manner, according to the general rule' (II, 4–5).

25 Giovanni Tamassia, 'Appendice', in Tamassia (1807a: 42).

26 Smith (1776: Book IV, Chap. II).

27 Say (1803: XXII).

28 From this perspective, see for example Sismonde de Sismondi in his work *Nouveaux principes d'économie politique*: 'Le système mercantile se trouve développé dans divers ouvrages de Charles Davenant, 1699, 1700; dans Melon, *Essai politique sur le Commerce*, 1734; dans James Steuart, *Inquiry into the Principles of Political Oeconomy*, 4 vols. (Lond, 1763); et dans Anton. Genovesi, *Lezioni di Commercio, ossia d'Economia civile*, 1 vol. (Milano, 1768)' (Sismondi 1819: 30).

Bibliography

Albertone, M. (1999), The Difficult Reception of James Steuart at the End of the Eighteenth Century in France, in R. Tortajada (ed.), *The Economics of James Steuart*, London: Routledge: 41–56.

Augello, M.M., Bianchini, M. & Guidi, M.E.L. (1996), *Le riviste di economia in Italia, 1700–1900. Dai giornali scientifico-letterari ai periodici specialistici*, Milan: FrancoAngeli.

Augello, M.M. & Guidi, M.E.L. (2000), *Associazionismo economico e diffusione dell'economia politica nell'Italia dell'Ottocento. Dalle società economico-agrarie alle associazioni di economisti*, Milan: FrancoAngeli.

Baldi, M. (1983), *David Hume nel Settecento italiano: filosofia ed economia*, Firenze: La Nuova Italia.

Bano, D. (1982), Un economista pre-neoclassico: Carlo Bosellini, *Ricerche economiche*, 36: 75–95.

Beccaria, J.-F. (1764), *Dei delitti e delle pene*, Livorno: Coltellini.

Bianchini, M. (1988), Una difficile gestazione: il contrastato inserimento dell'economia politica nelle università dell'Italia nord-orientale (1769–1866), in M.M. Augello, M. Bianchini, G. Gioli & P. Roggi (eds.), *Le cattedre di economia politica in Italia. La diffusione di una disciplina 'sospetta' (1750–1900)*, Milan: FrancoAngeli.

Bosellini, C. (1801), *Discorso sui principi di giustizia in materia di finanze, o Nuova teoria delle imposte*, Milan: Tipografia milanese.

Caboret, D. (1999). The Market Economy and Social Classes in James Steuart and G. W. F. Hegel, in R. Tortajada (ed.), *The Economics of James Steuart*, London: Routledge: 57–75.

Cantillon, R. (1755), *Essai sur la nature du commerce en général*, London: Gyles.

Cantimori, D. & De Felice, R. (1964), *Giacobini italiani*, vol. 2, Bari: Laterza.

Carnino, C. (2014), *Lusso e benessere nell'Italia del Settecento*, Milan: FrancoAngeli.

———. (2018), Libertà e prosperità: l'economia politica dell'Italia rivoluzionaria (1796–1799), *La Révolution française*, 14: online journal.

Delfico, M. (1785), *Memoria sul tribunal della Grascia e sulle leggi economiche delle provincie confinanti del Regno*, Naples: Porcelli.

Di Battista, F. (1983), *L'emergenza ottocentesca dell'economia politica a Napoli*, Bari: Facoltà di Economia e Commercio.

Galdi, M.A. (1798), *Dei rapporti politico-economici fra le nazioni libere*, Milan: Pirotta e Maspero.

Gioli, G. (1972), Gli albori dello smithianesimo in Italia, *Rivista di Politica Economica*, 7: 3–48.

Gislain, J.J. (1999), James Steuart: Economy and Population, in R. Tortajada (ed.), *The Economics of James Steuart*, London: Routledge: 169–185.

Guidi, M.E.L. & Potier, J.-P. (2003), Fantasia italiana. La ricezione del pensiero economico di Jean Baptiste Say nell'età del Risorgimento, in P. Barucci (ed.), *Le frontiere dell'economia politica. Gli economisti stranieri in Italia*, Florence: Polistampa: 179–181.

Hume, D. (1752), *Political Discourses, Discourse II of Luxury*, Edinburgh: Fleming.

Mazza, E. (2005), *Translations of Hume's Works in Italy*, in P. Jones (ed.), *The Reception of David Hume in Europe*, London and New York: Thoemmes Continuum: 182–194.

Melon, J.-F. (1736), *Essai politique sur le commerce. Nouvelle Edition augmentée de sept Chapitres*, s.l.: s.e.

Mengotti, F. (1792), *Il Colbertsimo. Dissertazione coronata dalla reale società economica fiorentina, edizione seconda*, Venezia: Bettinelli.

Menudo, J.M. (2018), Sir James Steuart on the Origins of Commercial Nations, *Journal of the History of Economic Thought*, 40(4): 561–578.

Parolini, M.L. (1980), La risonanza del pensiero smithiano in Italia tra il 1776 e il 1850, in G. Vivenza, P. Lanaro Sartori & M.L. Parolini (eds.), *Aspetti della formazione culturale di Adam Smith: la prima diffusione del suo pensiero nella dottrinaitaliana*, Verona: Istituto di Storia economica e sociale: 143–234.

Porcinari, N. (1824), *Riflessioni sul trattato di economia politica del sig Say*, Naples: Porcelli.

Pucci, L. (1990), *Luigi Valeriani Molinari (1758–1828). Un economista tra rivoluzione e restaurazione*, Florence: Arnaud.

Ramos, A. (2007), *Economy, Empire, and Identity: Rethinking the Origins of Political Economy in Sir James Steuart's Principles of Political Economy*, Indiana: University of Notre Dame.

———. (2011), Luxury, Crisis, & Consumption: Sir James Steuart, Mirabeau, and the Eighteenth-Century Luxury Debate, *History of Economics Review*, 53(1): 55–72.

Ressi, A. (1817–1820), *Dell'economia della specie umana*, vol. 3, Pavia: Bizzoni.

Say, J.-B. (1803), *Traité d'économie politique, ou simple exposition de la manière dont se forment, se distribuent, et se composent les richesses*, vol. 1, Paris: Economica, 2006.

Sen, S.R. (1957), *The Economics of Sir James Steuart*, London: Bell & Sons.

Silvestrini, M.T. (2006), Free Trade, Feudal Remnants and International Equilibrium in Gaetano Filangieri's Science of Legislation, *History of European Ideas*, 32: 502–524.

Sismondi, J.-Ch.-L- (1819), *Nouveaux principes d'économie politique, ou de la richesse dans ses rapports avec la population*, Paris: n.p.

Skinner, A. (1962), Sir James Steuart: Economics and Politics, *Scottish Journal of Political Economy*, 9: 17–37.

———. (2006), Sir James Steuart's Principles of Political Economy, in A. Dow & S. Dow (eds.), *A History of Scottish Economic Thought*, London: Routledge: 71–101.

Smith, A. (1776), *An Inquiry into the Nature and Causes of the Wealth of Nations*, London: Strahan & Cadell.

Tamassia, G. (1799–1800), *Dello spirito di riforma considerato relativamente al progetto di una legge agraria. Del cittadino Tamassia*, Milan: Stamperia di S. Zeno.

———. (1802), *Delle scienze e della libertà relativamente al commercio*, Milan: Stamperia del Genio tipografico.

———. (1807a), *Lezione di economia politica*, Bresia: Bettoni.

———. (1807b), *Quadro economico dei cantoni di Bellano ed Asso; distretto IV, dipartimento del Lario*, Como: Ostinelli.

———. (1838), *Reminiscenze o brano della sua vita scritta da lui medesimo*, Lodi: Orcesi.

Valeriani, L. (1806), *Del prezzo delle cose tutte mercatabili trattato legale-economico ove incidentemente si additano i veri principj della moneta*, Bologna: Tipografia di Ulisse Ramponi a San Damiano.

Vercillo, O. (1963), Della conoscenza di Adamo Smith in Italia nel secolo XVIII, *Economia e storia*, 3: 413–424.

Verri, P. (1764), Elementi del commercio, in G. Francioni & S. Romagnoli (eds.), *'Il Caffè', 1764–1766*, Turin: Bollati Boringhieri, 1993.

Yang, H.-S. (1994), *The Political Economy of Trade and Growth: An Analytical Interpretation of Sir James Steuart's 'Inquiry'*, Aldershot: Edward Elgar.

Zanardi, P. (2005), Italian Responses to David Hume, in P. Jones (ed.), *The Reception of David Hume in Europe*, London: Thoemmes Continuum: 161–181.

Index

Note: Page numbers in *italic* indicate a figure and page numbers in **bold** indicate a table on the corresponding page.

Printed in the United States
by Baker & Taylor Publisher Services